THE TRAFFIC OFFICER'S COMPANION

13th Edition

Gordon Wilson

BA (Law), MSc

Further titles available:

- Part I Promotion Crammer for Sergeants and Inspectors ● Action Stations - a guide to Part II of the Promotion Examination ● Beat Officer's Companion
- Scottish Beat Officer's Companion
- Drug Officer's Companion ● Financial Investigator's Companion
- Summonses and Charges
- Street Survival Skills ● Practical Police Management

To order or for further details phone +44 (0) 20 8700 3700 or fax +44 (0) 20 8763 1006

By the same author:
The Beat Officer's Companion

No part of this publication may be reproduced
or transmitted in any form or by any means, or
stored in any retrieval system of any nature, without prior
written permission, except for permitted fair dealing under
the Copyright, Designs and Patents Act 1988, or in accordance
with the terms of a licence issued by the Copyright Licensing Agency
in respect of photocopying and/or reprographic reproduction.
Application for permission for other use of copyright material
including permission to reproduce extracts in other published works
shall be made to the publishers. Full acknowledgement of
author, publisher and source must be given.

Crown copyright material is reproduced with the
permission of the controller of HMSO and the
Queen's Printer for Scotland

© Gordon Wilson 2003

7th edition 1992
8th edition 1993
9th edition 1995
10th edition 1997
11th edition 1999
12th edition 2002
13th edition 2003

ISBN 07106 26479

Jane's Information Group
Sentinel House
163 Brighton Road
Coulsdon
Surrey CR5 2YH

Printed and bound in Great Britain by
Biddles Ltd, www.biddles.co.uk

PREFACE

The present-day police officer engaged in the enforcement of traffic law is faced with the onerous task of interpreting, committing to memory and, whenever the situation demands, instantaneously recalling and making decisions upon, an immense field of technical legislation. This manual attempts to assist in handling the problems encountered, by presenting the more practical aspects of traffic policing in a fashion which facilitates speedy reference and easy interpretation.

In recent years a myriad of text books have been published, many of which contain a comprehensive coverage of traffic legislation. Their authors are to be congratulated in their presentation of a subject which is renowned for its complexity and obscurity. But in the majority of cases such works, whilst ideally suited to the legal practitioner engaged in the wider aspects of the law, are not in keeping with the more urgent demands of the operational police officer dealing with incidents.

The problems experienced in compiling this guidebook have surrounded the need to balance the selection of material thought to be a possible source of assistance, with an easily read and understood format whilst, at the same time, maintaining a system which would facilitate speedy reference. With this in mind material has been presented in almost every case in a diagrammatic or pictorial manner.

Because the book is intended to serve merely as a guide to the operational police officer, the relevant legislation has been subjected to a practical interpretation. It should not, therefore be regarded as a definitive work of reference and specific technical details may require further research.

Gordon Wilson
Former Superintendent
Warwickshire Constabulary

CONTENTS

Part 1: CONSTRUCTION AND USE — 1

VEHICLE DEFINITIONS	2 - 5
MAXIMUM LENGTH	6 - 9
OVERHANG	10
TURNING CIRCLES	11
MINIMUM GROUND CLEARANCE	12
MAXIMUM WIDTH	13
CALCULATION OF WIDTH	14
MAXIMUM HEIGHT - BUSES	15
WEIGHT	16 - 32
TRAVELLING HEIGHT	33
HIGH-LEVEL EQUIPMENT	34 - 35
TRAILERS	36 - 41
DANGEROUS VEHICLES	42
SILENCERS	43
EMISSIONS OF SMOKE ETC	44 - 45
TYRES	46 - 51
WARNING INSTRUMENTS	52
SPEEDOMETER	53
SEAT BELTS	54 - 63
MIRRORS	64 - 65
VISION, WINDOWS, TRANSMISSION OF LIGHT	66
GLASS, WINDSCREEN WIPERS AND WASHERS	66
SMOKE	67
SPECIAL TYPES VEHICLES	68 - 87
SIDEGUARDS	88
REARGUARDS	89
SPRAY SUPPRESSION DEVICES	90
MISCELLANEOUS	91 - 93

Part 2: DOCUMENTATION — 95

HGV DOCUMENTATION	96
DRIVING LICENCES	97 - 120
DRIVING WHILST DISQUALIFIED	121
INSURANCE	122

vi *The Traffic Officer's Companion*

OPERATORS' LICENCES	123- 126
EXCISE LICENCES	127 - 131
REGISTRATION MARKS	132 - 137
PLATING AND TESTING OF GOODS VEHICLES	138 - 143
MOTORCYCLE PLATES	144
TRADE LICENCES	145 - 146
PUBLIC SERVICE VEHICLES	147 - 150
MINIBUSES	151 - 154
HACKNEY CARRIAGES	155
BUSES CARRYING CHILDREN	156
INTERNATIONAL OPERATIONS	157 - 158

Part 3: LIGHTING AND MARKING 159

OBLIGATORY LAMPS ETC.	160 - 165
GENERAL EXEMPTIONS	166 - 167
USE OF LAMPS	168 - 169
MOVEMENT OF LAMPS	170
COLOUR OF LIGHTS	171
HEADLAMPS	172 - 173
FRONT POSITION LAMPS	174 - 175
REAR POSITION LAMPS	176 - 177
REAR REFLECTORS	178 - 179
FRONT REFLECTORS	180
SIDE REFLECTORS	181
DIRECTION INDICATORS	182 - 183
STOP LAMPS	184 - 185
REAR FOG LAMPS	186 - 187
FRONT FOG LAMPS	188
REVERSING LIGHTS	189
HAZARD WARNING	190
REAR REGISTRATION PLATE LAMP	190
WARNING BEACONS	191
SIDE MARKER LAMPS	192 - 193
END-OUTLINE MARKER LAMPS	194
REAR REFLECTIVE MARKERS	195 - 198
LAMPS ON PROJECTING LOADS	199
PROJECTION MARKERS	200
TRAILER PLATES	201

Contents **vii**

Part 4: DRIVERS' HOURS AND RECORDS 203

DRIVERS' HOURS AND RECORDS (GENERAL)	204 - 207
VEHICLE CATEGORIES	208 - 211
HOURS	212 - 215
DEFINITIONS	216
RECORDS	217 - 219
TACHOGRAPHS	220 - 230

PART 5: MISCELLANEOUS 233

TESTING ON ROADS	234 - 235
TESTING ON PREMISES	236
REMOVAL OF VEHICLES	237
MOTOR SALVAGE OPERATORS	238
TAKING CONVEYANCE WITHOUT AUTHORITY	239
VEHICLE INTERFERENCE	240
DRINK/DRIVING	241 - 245
SPEED LIMITS	246 - 249
SPEED LIMITERS	250
DANGEROUS SUBSTANCES	251 - 268
ANIMALS IN TRANSIT	269 - 276
REPORTING OF ACCIDENTS	277
DUTY TO GIVE INFORMATION AS TO DRIVER	278
POWERS OF ARREST	279 - 283
ROAD CHECKS	284
STOP AND SEARCH	285
POWER TO STOP VEHICLES	286
SEIZURE OF VEHICLES	287
TAXI TOUTS	288
BUILDERS' SKIPS	289
NOTICE OF INTENDED PROSECUTION	290
CRASH HELMETS	291
EYE PROTECTORS	292
MOTORWAYS	293
EYESIGHT	294
PHYSICAL HEALTH	294
STOPPING DISTANCES	294
DRIVING INSTRUCTION	295
PEDESTRIAN CROSSINGS	296
MISCELLANEOUS DRIVING OFFENCES	297
PARKING	298

PART 6: SCOTTISH TRAFFIC OFFICERS 299

INTRODUCTION	300
DEFINITION (ROAD)	301
BUILDER'S SKIPS	302 - 303
OBSTRUCTION OF ROADS	304
PLACING BRIDGES	305
MUD ON ROAD	306
DAMAGE TO ROADS	307
ROPES ETC IN ROAD	308
AIDING AND ABETTING	309
TAKING VEHICLES WITHOUT AUTHORITY	310
USE OF TELEPHONES	311
POWER OF ARREST	312
PEDAL CYCLES	313 - 314

CONVERSION TABLES 315-316

INDEX 317-320

PART 1

CONSTRUCTION AND USE

In Part 1 we will start with relevant vehicle definitions, and then go on to consider some of the more complex issues of Construction and Use (C&U) Regulations in summarised form, aided by a series of diagrams

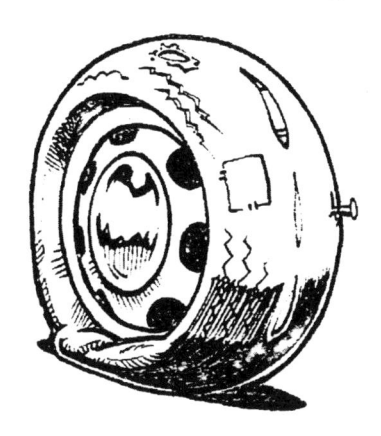

VEHICLE DEFINITIONS

Before we go on to consider the main contents of this book, we should consider some of the more important vehicle definitions you are likely to encounter.

MOTOR VEHICLE
Mechanically propelled vehicle intended or adapted for use on the roads.

REG 3 ROAD VEHICLES (CONSTRUCTION AND USE) REGULATIONS 1986

NOTE

The term **'mechanically propelled'** includes all known means of propulsion, eg petrol, diesel, gas, electricity. The test for whether a mechanically propelled vehicle is a motor vehicle is simply that of establishing if the vehicle in question is intended or adapted for use on a road. If the vehicle meets that criteria it is a motor vehicle, if it does not it is a mechanically propelled vehicle.

The Road Traffic Act 1991 made amendments to the Road Traffic Act 1988 which resulted in many (but not all) offences which related to motor vehicles being extended to the wider term of mechanically propelled vehicle.

MOTOR CAR
Under the C&U Regulations a **'motor car'** is a mechanically propelled vehicle, not being a motor tractor, motor cycle or invalid carriage, constructed and adapted for load or passengers, unladen weight (UW) not exceeding:
- if not more than seven passengers and effects, 3,050kg;
- if for goods or burden, 3,050kg; and
- in any other case, 2,450kg.

REG 3 ROAD VEHICLES (CONSTRUCTION AND USE) REGULATIONS 1986

However, under the RTA 1988 a **'motor car'** is a mechanically propelled vehicle, not being a motor cycle or invalid carriage, which is constructed itself to carry a load or passengers and of which the UW:
- does not exceed 3,050kg if constructed solely for the carriage of not more than seven passengers and their effects and is fitted with pneumatic tyres;
- does not exceed 3,050kg (3,500kg if gas propelled) if constructed or adapted for the conveyance of goods or burden of any description;
- does not exceed 2,540kg in cases falling within neither of the above descriptions.

SECTION 185 ROAD TRAFFIC ACT 1988

Part 1: Construction and use **3**

You will have noted that there is little difference between the two definitions. However, you must apply the C&U definition to vehicles coming within the scope of those Regulations and the RTA definition to vehicles coming within the scope of that legislation.

Matters are further complicated by the insertion of a third definition by S 141A of the RTA 1988 for the purposes of Part V of the Act (Driving Instruction):
'a motor vehicle (other than an invalid carriage or motor cycle)
(a) not constructed or adapted to carry more than 9 persons inclusive of the driver, and
(b) which has a maximum gross weight not exceeding 3.5 tonnes' (S.I. 1996/1974).

HEAVY MOTOR CAR

Under the C&U Regulations a heavy motor car is a mechanically propelled vehicle, not being a locomotive, motor tractor or motor car, which is constructed itself to carry a load or passengers, UW exceeds 2,540kg,
REG 3 ROAD VEHICLES (CONSTRUCTION AND USE) REGULATIONS 1986

Under the RTA 1988 it is a mechanically propelled vehicle, not being a motor car, which is constructed itself to carry a load or passengers and the UW exceeds 2,540kg.
SECTION 185 ROAD TRAFFIC ACT 1988

MOTOR TRACTOR

Mechanically propelled vehicle not constructed itself to carry a load other than equipment for propulsion, loose tools and loose equipment, UW not exceeding 7,370kg.
SECTION 185 ROAD TRAFFIC ACT 1988

LIGHT LOCOMOTIVE

Mechanically propelled vehicle not itself constructed to carry load other than equipment for propulsion, loose tools and loose equipment, UW exceeding 7,320kg but not exceeding 11,690kg.
SECTION 185(1) ROAD TRAFFIC ACT 1988

HEAVY LOCOMOTIVE

Mechanically propelled vehicle not itself constructed to carry load other than equipment for propulsion, loose tools and loose equipment, UW exceeding 11,690kg.
SECTION 185(1) ROAD TRAFFIC ACT 1988

GOODS VEHICLE

Motor vehicle or trailer constructed or adapted for use for carriage or haulage of goods or burden of any description.
REG 3 ROAD VEHICLES (CONSTRUCTION AND USE) REGULATIONS 1986

(See later for large and medium-sized goods vehicle.)

ARTICULATED VEHICLE

Under the C&U Regulations 1986, an articulated vehicle is a heavy motor car, or motor car not being an articulated bus, with trailer so attached that part of the trailer is superimposed upon the drawing vehicle and not less than 20 per cent of weight of load is borne by drawing vehicle.

REG 3 ROAD VEHICLES (CONSTRUCTION AND USE) REGULATIONS 1986

Under the RTA 1988 an articulated vehicle is:
a) a vehicle so constructed that it can be divided into two parts
   - both of which are vehicles, and one of which is a motor vehicle
   - and shall (when not so divided) be treated as that motor vehicle with the part attached as a trailer; or
b) a passenger vehicle (ie a vehicle constructed or adapted for use solely or principally for carriage of passengers) so constructed that it can be divided into two parts
   - both of which are vehicles and one of which is a motor vehicle
   - but cannot be so divided without the use of facilities normally available only at a workshop
   - and passengers carried by it, when not so divided can at all times pass from either part to the other, and
   - it shall, when not so divided, be treated as a single motor vehicle.

SECTION 187 ROAD TRAFFIC ACT 1988

DUAL PURPOSE VEHICLE

A vehicle constructed and adapted for both the carriage of passengers and goods UW not exceeding 2,040 kg and
a) is so constructed or adapted that the driving power of the engine is, or by appropriate use of the controls can be, transmitted to all wheels of the vehicle, or
b) it is constructed so that:
   - it has a rigid roof, with or without a sliding roof panel,
   - the area of the vehicle to the rear of the driver's seat must have at least one row of properly upholstered transverse seats (fixed or folding) capable of carrying at least two persons,
   - the distance between the steering wheel and the backrest of the rear most seats must not be less than one third of the distance between the steering wheel and the rearmost part of the floor, and
   - the windows to rear of drivers seat must have an area of not less than 1,850sq cms on either side and not less than 770sq cms at the rear.

REG 3 ROAD VEHICLES (CONSTRUCTION AND USE) REGULATIONS 1986

MEDIUM-SIZED GOODS VEHICLE

A motor vehicle which is constructed or adapted to carry or to haul goods and is not adapted to carry more than nine persons inclusive of the driver and the permissible maximum weight of which exceeds 3.5 but not 7.5 tonnes.

SECTION 108(1) ROAD TRAFFIC ACT 1988

Part 1: Construction and use **5**

SMALL VEHICLE

NOTE: The terms 'small goods' and 'small passenger vehicles' have now been replaced by the new term 'small vehicle'.

A small vehicle is a motor vehicle, other than an invalid carriage, moped or motor bicycle which:
a) is not constructed to carry more than nine passengers inclusive of the driver; and
b) has a maximum gross weight not exceeding 3.5 tonnes; and includes a combination of such motor vehicle and trailer.

INVALID CARRIAGE

A mechanically propelled vehicle, the weight of which unladen does not exceed 254kg and which is specially designed and constructed – not merely adapted – for use of a person suffering from some physical defect or disability and is used solely by such a person.

REG 3 ROAD VEHICLES (CONSTRUCTION AND USE) REGULATIONS 1986
AND SECTION 185(1) ROAD TRAFFIC ACT 1988

LARGE GOODS VEHICLE

A motor vehicle (not being a medium-sized goods vehicle) which is constructed or adapted to carry or to haul goods and the maximum permissible weight of which exceeds 7.5 tonnes.

SECTION 121 ROAD TRAFFIC ACT 1988

MOTOR CYCLE

Mechanically propelled vehicle, not being an invalid carriage, with less than four wheels and the weight unladen does not exceed 410kg.

REG 3(1) ROAD VEHICLES (CONSTRUCTION AND USE) REGULATIONS 1986
AND SECTION 185(1) ROAD TRAFFIC ACT 1988

MOPED

first used on or after 1.8.77

This is a motor cycle, not being a mowing machine or a pedestrian controlled vehicle, which has a maximum design speed which does not exceed 30mph, a kerbside weight which does not exceed 250kg and, if propelled by an internal combustion engine, an engine which does not exceed 50cc. Alternatively;

first used before 1.8.77

A motor cycle which has an engine with a cylinder capacity not exceeding 50cc and is equipped with pedals by means of which the cycle is capable of being propelled.

REG 3 MOTOR VEHICLES (DRIVING LICENCES) REGULATIONS 1987

PASSENGER CARRYING VEHICLE

(a) **large passenger carrying vehicle**, that is to say, a vehicle used for carrying passengers which is contructed or adapted to carry more than 16 passengers, or

(b) **a small passenger carrying vehicle**, that is to say, a vehicle used for carrying passengers for hire or reward which is constructed or adapted to carry more than 8 but not more than 16 passengers, and includes a combination of such a motor vehicle and a trailer.

SECTION 121 ROAD TRAFFIC ACT 1988

MAXIMUM LENGTH

REG 7 ROAD VEHICLE (CONSTRUCTION AND USE) REGULATIONS 1986
If the maximum is exceeded refer to 'special types' (see later)

Vehicle combinations

(1) Motor vehicle (not mentioned in (2) below) drawing one trailer which is not a semi-trailer – **18.75m.**

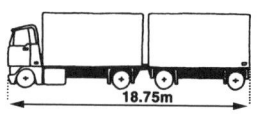

(IF SHOWMAN'S VEHICLE AND LIVING ACCOMMODATION TRAILER – 22M)

(2) Until 31.12.2006, motor vehicle manufactured before 1.6.98 drawing one trailer where
   (a) distance from foremost point of loading area behind the drivers cab to rear of trailer (marked 'A' below) less distance between rear of motor vehicle and the front of the trailer ('B') exceeds 15.65m, and
   (b) distance (A) does not exceed 16.4m, and the trailer is not a semi-trailer –
   18m.

> Notes (1) The thickness of any wall at the forward end of the loading area shall be regarded as part of the loading area
> (2) any towing attachment in area 'B' shall be disregarded.

(3) Articulated bus – **18.75m**
    Bus drawing a trailer - **18.75m**

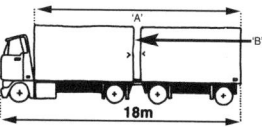

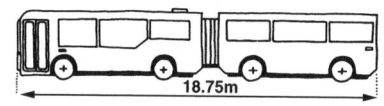

(4) Articulated vehicle, where:
   (a) distance from king pin to rear of semi-trailer (A) does not exceed –
      (i) 12.5 m in the case of a car transporter, or
      (ii) 12m in any other case; and
   (b) distance between king pin to front of trailer (B) does not exceed –
      (i) 4.19m in the case of a car transporter or
      (ii) 2.04m in any other case,
      and is not a low loader – **16.5m.**

> Notes Where there is more than 1 kingpin, where the vehicle was manufactured after 1.1.99, the measurement is taken from the foremost kingpin, otherwise the rearmost is used.

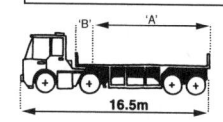

(5) Articulated vehicle where the semi-trailer does not meet the above requirements and is not a low loader – **15.5m.**

(6) Articulated vehicle where semi-trailer

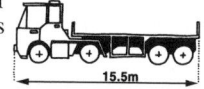

Part 1: Construction and use **7**

MOTOR VEHICLES

(7) A wheeled motor vehicle other than a bus – **12m**.

(IF TRACK-LAYING 9.2M)

(8) A bus with 2 axles - **13.5m.**
(9) A bus with more than 2 axles - **15m**

Trailers (See also notes on following page)

(10) Agricultural trailed appliance manufactured on or after 1.12.1985 – **15m**.
(11) Semi-trailer manufactured on or after 1.5.1983 which does not meet the requirements mentioned in item (4) above and is not a low loader – **12.2m**.

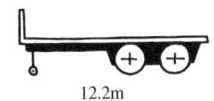

(12) Composite trailer (combination of converter dolly and trailer) drawn by
 (a) a goods vehicle over 3,500Kg maximum gross weight or
 (b) an agricultural motor vehicle – **14.04m**.

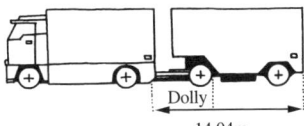

(13) Trailer (not being a semi-trailer or composite trailer) with at least 4 wheels, which is
 (a) drawn by a goods vehicle over 3,500Kg gross vehicle weight or
 (b) an agricultural trailer – **12m**.

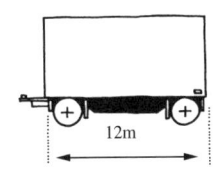

(14) Any other trailer not being an agricultural trailed appliance or semi-trailer – **7m**.

8 The Traffic Officer's Companion

Notes:
(1) Items 1, 2, 4, 5, & 6 do not apply to indivisible load trailers, to broken down vehicles being towed, nor to an articulated vehicle with low loader semi-trailer manufactured before 1.4.91.

(2) Items 10 to 14 do not apply to indivisible load trailers, to broken down vehicles being towed, nor to a trailer being drying or mixing plant for tarmacadam, etc. used for road construction, or a road planing machine so used.
(3) Item 11 does not apply to a semi-trailer which is a car transporter, or normally used for international journeys.

(4) Where a motor vehicle is drawing –
   (a) 2 trailers, only 1 may exceed 7m
   (b) 3 trailers, none may exceed 7m
   Note: A broken down articulated vehicle being towed is regarded as being only 1 trailer.

(5) Where a motor vehicle is drawing –
   (a) 2 or more trailers, or
   (b) 1 trailer for indivisible loads of exceptional length, then
   (i) overall length of motor vehicle not to exceed 9.2m, and
   (ii) overall length of combination not to exceed 25.9m unless 2 days notice is given to the police and at least 1 attendant is carried.
(6) A motor vehicle drawing a trailer which is not a semi-trailer must not exceed the requirements mentioned in item 2.
(7) A trailer over 18.65m may only be used if 2 days notice is given to the police and an attendant is carried.

Part 1: Construction and use

CALCULATION OF LENGTH

ROAD VEHICLES (CONSTRUCTION AND USE) REGULATIONS 1986.
REGS 7 & 81

The overall length of a combination of vehicles is calculated in accordance with the following:

(1) Where there are 1 or more trailers being drawn, the combination includes any other motor vehicle which is assisting in the propulsion of the trailer(s).
(2) Measurement of the foremost and rearmost points of the combination are taken in the same vertical plane:

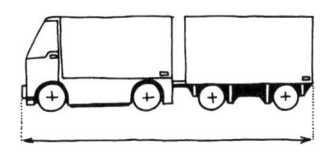

(3) References to the front of the vehicle, rear of the vehicle and king-pin means the transverse plane passing through each:

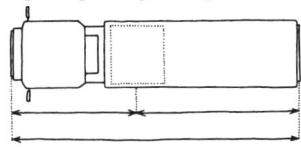

(4) References to the front and rear of the vehicle includes all parts of the vehicle, any receptacle which is a permanent fitting and strong enough for repeated use, and any fitting on or attached to the vehicle but excluding:
   (a) driving mirror
   (b) expanding or extending turntable fire escape
   (c) snow plough
   (d) customs clearance seals
   (e) tailboard let down when vehicle is stationary for loading/unloading
   (f) tailboard let down to accomodate long loads
   (g) fittings etc, on vehicles or receptacles to enable it/them to be transferred to or from a road vehicle to or from a railway vehicle
   (h) bridging plate on trailer to allow vehicles to be moved between that trailer and the attached drawing motor vehicle
   (i) sheeting or other flexible means for covering or securing a load
   (j) empty receptacle forming a load
   (k) receptacle containing indivisible load of exceptional length
   (l) receptacle manufactured before 30.10.85 not being a maritime container
   (m) special appliance (crane, etc) which is a permanently fitted fixture
   (n) rearward projecting buffer
   (o) in the case of a semi-trailer, any part designed to attach it to another vehicle (but not the drawbar, etc, of an agricultural trailed appliance)

10 The Traffic Officer's Companion

OVERHANG

REGS 3(1) AND 11(1) ROAD VEHICLES (CONSTRUCTION AND USE) REGS 1986

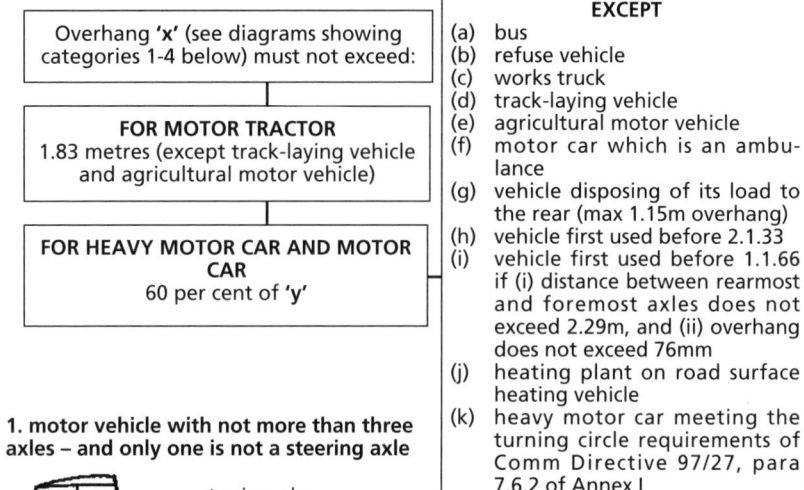

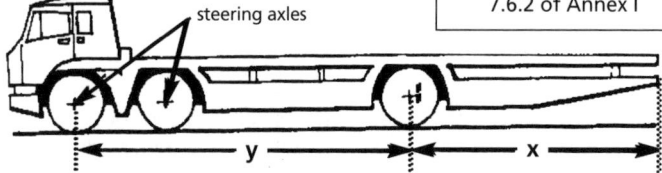

Overhang **'x'** (see diagrams showing categories 1-4 below) must not exceed:

FOR MOTOR TRACTOR
1.83 metres (except track-laying vehicle and agricultural motor vehicle)

FOR HEAVY MOTOR CAR AND MOTOR CAR
60 per cent of **'y'**

EXCEPT
(a) bus
(b) refuse vehicle
(c) works truck
(d) track-laying vehicle
(e) agricultural motor vehicle
(f) motor car which is an ambulance
(g) vehicle disposing of its load to the rear (max 1.15m overhang)
(h) vehicle first used before 2.1.33
(i) vehicle first used before 1.1.66 if (i) distance between rearmost and foremost axles does not exceed 2.29m, and (ii) overhang does not exceed 76mm
(j) heating plant on road surface heating vehicle
(k) heavy motor car meeting the turning circle requirements of Comm Directive 97/27, para 7.6.2 of Annex I

1. motor vehicle with not more than three axles – and only one is not a steering axle

2. motor vehicle with three axles if only front one steers, and
3. motor vehicle with four axles if only front two steer:

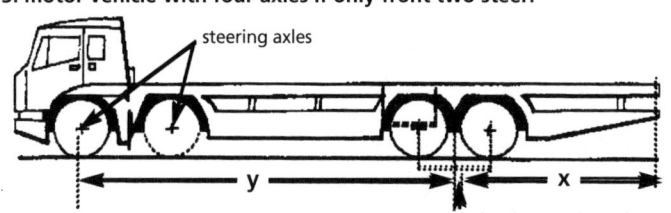

4. any other case

110 mm behind centre line of two rearmost axles

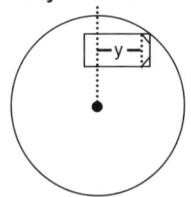

'y'= the distance between the centre of the foremost wheel and a point along the length of the vehicle from which a line drawn at right angles would pass through the centre of the minimum turning circle of the vehicle.

Part 1: Construction and use **11**

TURNING CIRCLES
ROAD VEHICLES (CONSTRUCTION AND USE) REGULATIONS 1986

Subject to the provisions mentioned below, buses, articulated vehicles and heavy motor cars must be able to turn on either lock, both with and without all its wheels in contact with the ground, so that no part of the vehicle projects outside the area between concentric circles with radii of 12.5m and 5.3m. If manufactured before 1.6.98, the reference to 'with and without all wheels on the ground' does not apply.

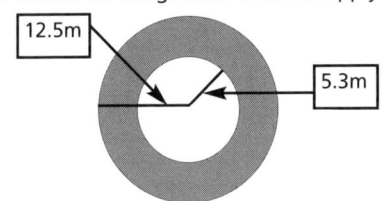

(1) **Buses. (Reg.13)** Only applies to buses first used on or after 1.4.82.
(2) **Articulated vehicles other than car transporters. (Reg.13A)** Does not apply to:
   a) semi-trailer manufactured before 1.4.90 and has not been lengthened since then;
   b) car transporter;
   c) low loader;
   d) semi-trailer constructed for indivisible long loads;
   e) vehicle with overall length not over 15.5m and either the drawing vehicle or trailer was first used before 1.6.98;
   f) vehicle when axle is raised to add traction; or
   g) projections set out in paras. (a) to (m) in definition of 'overall width' (see later) or in paras. (4)(a) to (o) in 'Calculation of Length' page (see earlier)
(3) **Articulated vehicles incorporating a car transporter. (Reg.13B)** Applies to vehicles with overall length over 15.5m. Regs. do not apply to:
   a) semi-trailer manufactured before 1.4.90 and has not been lengthened since then;
   b) low loader;
   c) stepframe low loader; or
   d) projections set out in paras. (a) to (m) in definition of 'overall width' (see later) or in paras. (4)(a) to (o) in 'Calculation of Length' (see earlier).

(4) **Heavy motor car. (Reg.13C)** Manufactured after 31.5.98. Includes when drawing a trailer which is not a semi-trailer. Does not apply to vehicles included in one of the above categories; to a vehicle with 4 or more axles where distance between front and rear axles exceeds 6.4m; to vehicles constructed for indivisible long loads; or to projections set out in paras. (a) to (m) in definition of 'overall width' (see later) or in paras. (4)(a) to (o) in 'Calculation of Length'(see earlier).

12 The Traffic Officer's Companion

MINIMUM GROUND CLEARANCE

ROAD VEHICLES (CONSTRUCTION AND USE) REGULATIONS 1986.
REG 12.

A wheeled trailer which is a goods vehicle manufactured on or after 1.4.84.

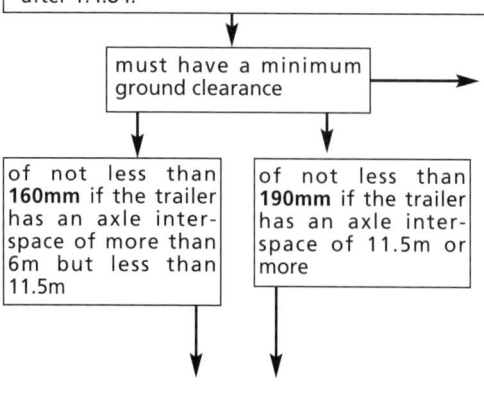

must have a minimum ground clearance

of not less than **160mm** if the trailer has an axle interspace of more than 6m but less than 11.5m

of not less than **190mm** if the trailer has an axle interspace of 11.5m or more

'ground clearance' means the shortest distance between the ground and the lowest part of the trailer. This is measured within the area formed by the overall width and the middle 70% of the axle interspace, but excludes suspension, steering or braking system attached to any axle, any wheel or any air skirt. Suitable tyres, correctly inflated must be fitted and the vehicle must be reasonably horizontal on reasonably flat ground.

"Axle interspace" means:
(a) **Semi-trailer**, the distance between the point of support of the semi-trailer at its forward end and the centre of the rear axle (or if more than 1 rear axle, the point half way between the centres of the foremost and rearmost axles.)
(b) **Any other trailer**, the distance between the centre of the front axle (or if more than one, the point halfway between the foremost and rearmost axles) and the centre of the rear axle (or if more than one, the point halfway between the centre of the foremost and rearmost axles).

SEMI-TRAILER

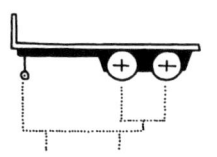

measurement taken in middle 70%

ANY OTHER TRAILER

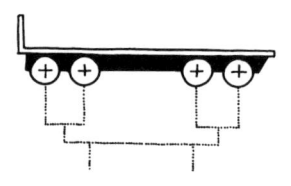

measurement taken in middle 70%

Exemptions
The requirement does not apply to a trailer –
(a) fitted with adjustable suspension to lower the trailer to clear bridges etc, while being operated, (but must not touch the ground), or
(b) while being loaded or unloaded.

Part 1: Construction and use **13**

MAXIMUM WIDTH

REG 8 (CONSTRUCTION AND USE) REGULATIONS 1986

If the maximum is exceeded, refer to 'Special Types' (see later).

Locomotive	2.75 m
Refrigerated vehicle A vehicle specially designed for the carriage of goods at low temperatures and the thickness of each side-wall including insulation is at least 45mm	2.6 m
Any other motor vehicle	2.55 m
Trailer drawn by a motor vehicle (having max gross weight exceeding 3,500 kg) **Agricultural trailer** **Agricultural trailed appliance,** **or an off-set combination of an agricultural motor vehicle drawing a wheeled trailer**	2.55 m
Any other trailer drawn by a vehicle other than a motor cycle	2.3 m
Trailer drawn by motor cycle	1.5 m

14 The Traffic Officer's Companion

CALCULATION OF WIDTH
ROAD VEHICLES (CONSTRUCTION AND USE) REGULATIONS 1986

'Lateral projection' (Reg.81) means that part of the load which extends beyond a side of the vehicle. The width of any lateral projection is to be measured between longitudinal planes passing through the extreme projecting point on that side and that part of the projection furthest from that point:

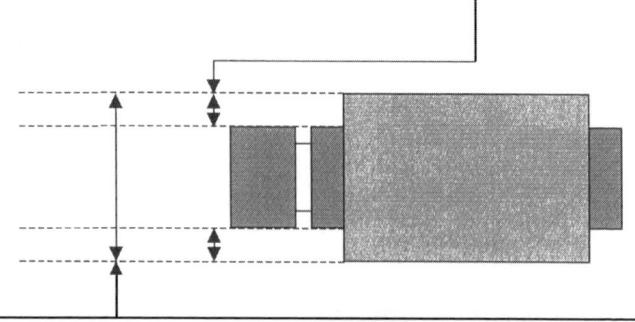

'Overall width' (Reg.3) means the distance between longitudinal planes passing through the extreme lateral projecting points of the vehicle including all parts of the vehicle, any permanent receptacle which is strong enough for repeated use, and any fitting on, or attached to, the vehicle except-
  a) Driving mirror;
  b) Snow plough fixed to the front;
  c) Distortion of the tyre caused by the weight of the vehicle;
  d) Customs seals;
  e) Lamp or reflector fitted in accordance with the Lighting Regulations;
  f) Sideboard let down while vehicle is stationary, for loading or unloading;
  g) Any fitting or receptacle which does not increase the carrying capacity of the vehicle, but which allows it to be transferred to or from a railway vehicle; is secured to a railway vehicle by a locking device; and carried on a railway vehicle by the use of stanchions;
  h) Sheeting or other flexible means of covering or securing the load;
  i) Receptacle with external width not over 2.5m;
  j) Empty receptacle which itself forms a load;
  k) A receptacle which contains an indivisible wide load;
  l) A receptacle manufactured before 30.10.85, not being a maritime container;
  m) A permanent crane, special appliance or apparatus, which does not increase the carrying capacity of the vehicle;
  n) Apparatus fitted to a bus to guide it by wheels bearing outwards provided it does not project more than 75mm beyond the side of the bus.

Part 1: Construction and use **15**

MAXIMUM HEIGHT – BUSES

REG.9 ROAD VEHICLES (CONSTRUCTION AND USE) REGULATIONS 1986

DEFINITION
A bus is a motor vehicle constructed or adapted to carry more than eight seated passengers in addition to the driver.

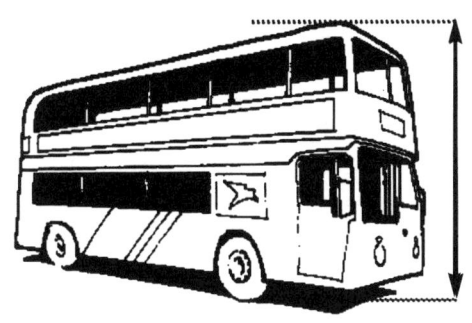

The overall height of a bus shall not exceed **4.57 metres**

NOTE: See later this section for overall travelling heights

16 The Traffic Officer's Companion

WEIGHT

Regulations prohibiting excess axle weight are designed primarily to prevent damage to the road surfaces and foundations, while those relating to excess overall weight are aimed at ensuring the design limits are not exceeded and that the vehicle can stop within the distance for which its brakes were designed. There are therefore separate offences of:

excess axle weight and
excess overall weight.

All locomotives, motor tractors, and heavy motor cars must have the unladen weight (UW) marked on the near side of the vehicle.

Vehicles should be equipped with a

Manufacturer's plate and a
Ministry plate *

containing details of the maximum axle, gross and train weights.

Offences may be committed if the maximum permitted weight contained in C&U Regulations 1986, the manufacturer's plate or the Ministry plate are exceeded. *The following chart may be a guide to procedure:*

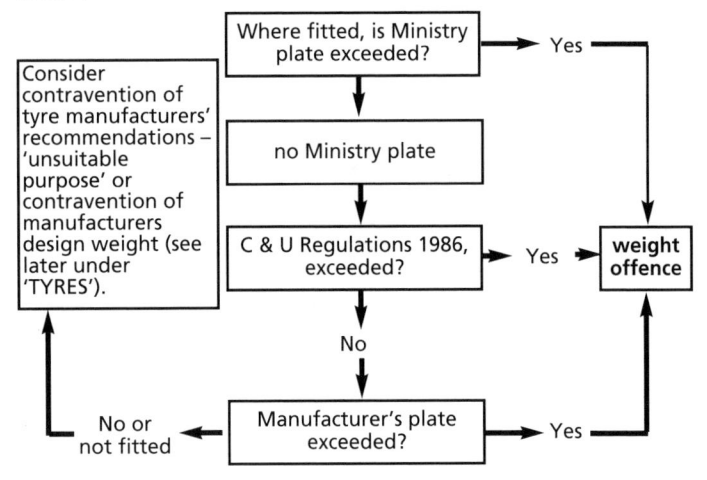

```
                    ┌──────────────────────┐
                    │ Where fitted, is     │
                    │ Ministry plate       │──► Yes ──┐
                    │ exceeded?            │          │
                    └──────────┬───────────┘          │
┌─────────────────┐            ▼                      │
│ Consider        │  ┌──────────────────────┐         │
│ contravention of│  │   no Ministry plate  │         │
│ tyre            │  └──────────┬───────────┘         │
│ manufacturers'  │             ▼                     ▼
│ recommendations─│  ┌──────────────────────┐    ┌─────────┐
│ 'unsuitable     │  │  C & U Regulations   │──► │ weight  │
│ purpose' or     │  │  1986, exceeded?     │ Yes│ offence │
│ contravention of│  └──────────┬───────────┘    └─────────┘
│ manufacturers   │             │ No                  ▲
│ design weight   │             ▼                     │
│ (see later      │  ┌──────────────────────┐         │
│ under 'TYRES'). │◄─│  Manufacturer's      │──► Yes ─┘
└─────────────────┘  │  plate exceeded?     │
         No or       └──────────────────────┘
         not fitted
```

NOTE: *For further details see Plating of goods vehicles, in Part 2.

Part 1: Construction and use **17**

POWER TO WEIGH VEHICLES
ROAD TRAFFIC ACT 1988

Failure to comply or obstructing the exercise of functions is an offence
(S 78(3))

On production of his authority **a constable authorised by the chief constable** may require a person in charge of a motor vehicle to
1. proceed to a weighbridge (or other machine for weighing vehicles)
2. allow the vehicle or trailer to be weighed, either laden or unladen and the weight transmitted to the road by any part of the vehicle or trailer in contact with the road to be tested.

S 78(1)

↓

NOTE: An authorised officer has no power to require the person in charge of a motor vehicle to unload the vehicle or trailer or to cause or allow it to be unloaded in order to have it weighed unladen.   S 78(4)

↓

Where a goods vehicle or a motor vehicle adapted to carry more than eight passengers has been weighed under the provision of S 78, and it appears to the authorised officer that the weights imposed by the C&U Regulations 1986 have been exceeded – or would be exceeded were it used on a road – he may give notice* in writing to the person in charge of the vehicle prohibiting it being driven on a road until
(a) the weight is reduced to the limit, and
(b) the person in charge has been notified in writing that it is allowed to proceed.   S 70(2)

* This notice may be withheld until the vehicle has been weighed to satisfy the constable that the weight has been sufficiently reduced.

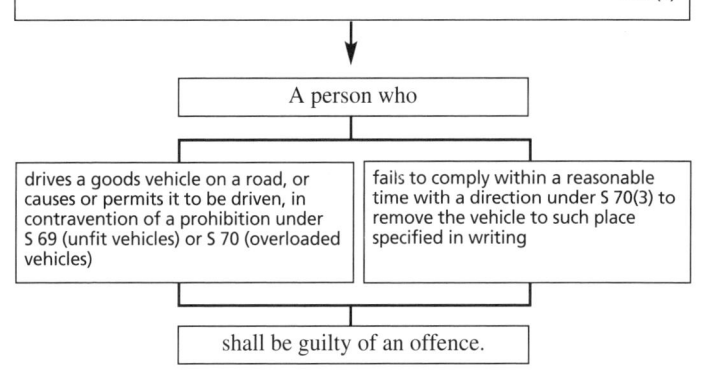

S 70(4)

↓

A person who

| drives a goods vehicle on a road, or causes or permits it to be driven, in contravention of a prohibition under S 69 (unfit vehicles) or S 70 (overloaded vehicles) | fails to comply within a reasonable time with a direction under S 70(3) to remove the vehicle to such place specified in writing |

shall be guilty of an offence.

S 71(1) (AS SUBSTITUTED BY S 14 RTA 1991)

MAXIMUM OVERALL WEIGHT
ROAD VEHICLES (CONSTRUCTION AND USE) REGULATIONS 1986

If the maximum is exceeded, refer to 'Special Types' (see later).

Most of the maximum weight for combinations, vehicles and axles are contained in regulations 75 to 79. However, under certain circumstances the maximum weight may be exceeded, as authorised by the Road Vehicles (Authorised Weight) Regulations 1998 (see later under Additional Authorised Weights).

LOCOMOTIVE REG 75

If fitted with suitable tyres & springs:

with less than 6 wheels	22,360kg
with 6 wheels	26,420kg
more than 6 wheels	30,490kg

Not conforming as above   20,830kg

Total weight of all trailers laden or unladen, drawn by a locomotive   44,000kg

BUS REGS 75 & 78

The maximum permitted laden weight is the same as a heavy motor car or motor car but the weight is calculated when the vehicle is complete and fully equipped for service with:

roof luggage space – uniformly distributed load at 75kg per square metre

63.5kg per person who could legally be carried (65kg if bus first used after 1.4.88)

100kg per cubic metre of luggage space or 10kg per person who could legally be carried whichever is less

full supply of water, oil and fuel

Part 1: Construction and use **19**

MAXIMUM OVERALL WEIGHT cont
ROAD VEHICLES (CONSTRUCTION AND USE) REGULATIONS 1986

If the maximum is exceeded, refer to 'Special Types' (see later).

VEHICLE WITH TRAILER (REG 76)

The **total laden weight** of a trailer together with that of any motor tractor, heavy motor car or motor car drawing such trailer

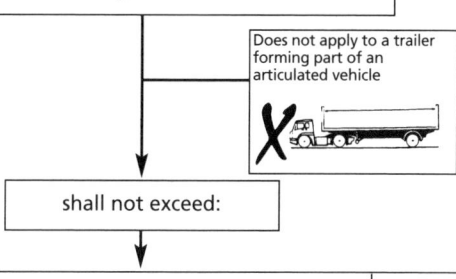

Does not apply to a trailer forming part of an articulated vehicle

shall not exceed:

if trailer and vehicle both have wheels and: combination has total of 4 axles; and drawing vehicle first used on or after 1.4.73 and has relevant brakes	35,000kg
as above but with total of 5 or more axles	38,000kg
if trailer and vehicle are not mentioned above and both have wheels – and brakes as below a) power assisted brakes b) brakes can be operated by driver of drawing vehicle c) brakes will not become ineffective when engine is switched off d) drawing vehicle has warning device, visible to driver, to indicate impending failure of braking system	32,520kg
a wheeled trailer manufactured on or after 27.2.77 and fitted with automatic brakes, drawn by a vehicle first used on or after 1.4.73 and has relevant brakes	29,500kg
if trailer and vehicle are not mentioned above and both have wheels	24,390kg
if trailer or vehicle is track laying	22,360kg

MAXIMUM OVERALL WEIGHT cont

RIGID VEHICLES (REG 75)

The sum of the weights transmitted to the road surface by all the wheels of a heavy motor car, motor car or trailer, in each case not forming part of an articulated vehicle,

and which:
a) complies with the relevant braking requirements;
b) every driving axle other than a steering axle has twin tyres; and
c) either every driving axle has road-friendly* suspension or does not exceed 9,500kg;

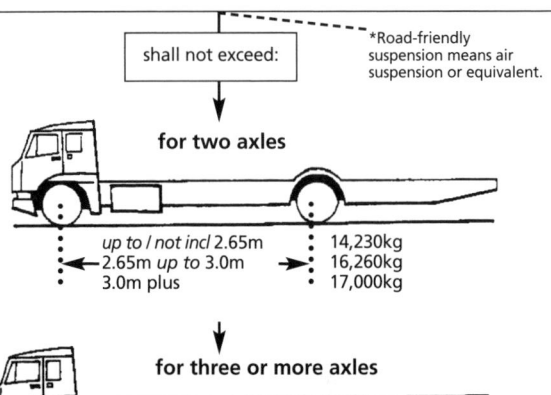

shall not exceed:

*Road-friendly suspension means air suspension or equivalent.

for two axles

up to / not incl 2.65m	14,230kg
2.65m up to 3.0m	16,260kg
3.0m plus	17,000kg

for three or more axles

Distance between foremost and rearmost axles (m)

Distance between foremost and rearmost axles (m)	Maximum axle weight	Maximum permitted laden weight
up to but not incl 3.0m	10,170kg	16,260kg
3.0m up to 3.2m	10,170kg	18,290kg
3.2m up to 3.9m	10,170kg	20,330kg
3.9m up to 4.9m	10,170kg	22,360kg
4.9m up to 5.2m	10,170kg	25,000kg
5.2m plus	10,170kg	26,000kg

for four or more axles

Distance between foremost and rearmost axles (m)

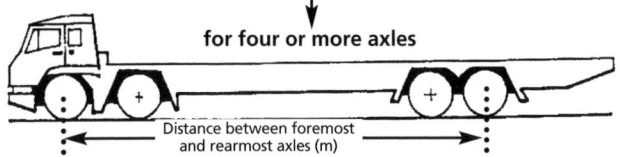

Distance between foremost and rearmost axles (m)	Maximum permitted laden weight
5.2m up to / not incl 6.4 m	distance (m) x 5,000 rounded up to next 10kg
6.4 m plus	32,000 kg

Part 1: Construction and use **21**

MAXIMUM OVERALL WEIGHT cont
ROAD VEHICLES (CONSTRUCTION AND USE) REGULATIONS 1986

If the maximum is exceeded, refer to 'Special Types' (see later).

RIGID VEHICLES cont (REG 75)

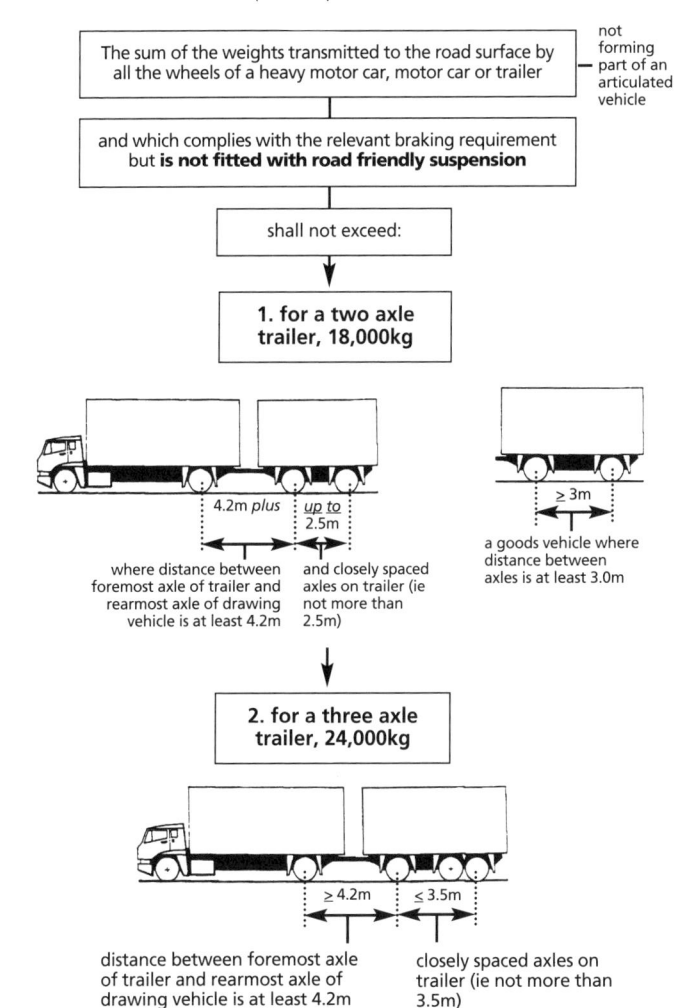

The sum of the weights transmitted to the road surface by all the wheels of a heavy motor car, motor car or trailer — not forming part of an articulated vehicle

and which complies with the relevant braking requirement but **is not fitted with road friendly suspension**

shall not exceed:

1. for a two axle trailer, 18,000kg

4.2m *plus* <u>up to</u> 2.5m

where distance between foremost axle of trailer and rearmost axle of drawing vehicle is at least 4.2m

and closely spaced axles on trailer (ie not more than 2.5m)

≥ 3m

a goods vehicle where distance between axles is at least 3.0m

2. for a three axle trailer, 24,000kg

≥ 4.2m   ≤ 3.5m

distance between foremost axle of trailer and rearmost axle of drawing vehicle is at least 4.2m

closely spaced axles on trailer (ie not more than 3.5m)

continued on following page

MAXIMUM OVERALL WEIGHT cont
ROAD VEHICLES (CONSTRUCTION AND USE) REGULATIONS 1986,

If the maximum is exceeded, refer to 'Special Types' (see later).

RIGID VEHICLES cont (REG 75)

continued from previous page

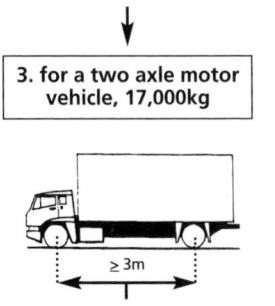

> **3. for a two axle motor vehicle, 17,000kg**

≥ 3m

a goods vehicle where distance between axles is at least 3.0m

If the vehicle is not within the description of the above three categories, max weight is as follows:

No of axles	Distance between foremost and rearmost axles	Max laden weight
2	*up to/not incl* 2.65m	14,230kg
2	2.65m *plus*	16,260kg
3 or more	*up to* 3.0m	16,260kg
3 or more	3.0m *up to* 3.2m	18,290kg
3 or more	3.2m *up to* 3.9m	20,330kg
3 or more	3.9m *up to* 4.9m	22,360kg
3	4.9m *plus*	25,000kg
4 or more	4.9m *up to* 5.6m	25,000kg
4 or more	5.6m *up to* 5.9m	26,420kg
4 or more	5.9m *up to* 6.3m	28,450kg
4 or more	6.3m *plus*	30,000kg

Part 1: Construction and use **23**

MAXIMUM OVERALL WEIGHT cont
REGS 75 & 77 & SCHED 11 ROAD VEHICLES (C&U) REGS 1986

If the maximum is exceeded, please refer to 'Special Types' (see later).
GVW=Gross Vehicle Weight, GCW=Gross Combined Weight

ARTICULATED

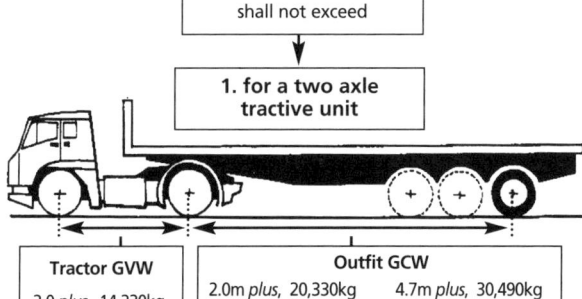

The sum of the weights transmitted to the road surface by all the wheels of a heavy motor car or motor car forming part of an articulated vehicle

shall not exceed

1. for a two axle tractive unit

Tractor GVW

2.0 *plus*, 14,230kg
2.4 *plus*, 16,260kg
2.7 *plus*, 17,000kg

Outfit GCW

2.0m *plus*, 20,330kg	4.7m *plus*, 30,490kg
2.2m *plus*, 22,360kg	5.0m *plus*, 31,500kg
2.6m *plus*, 23,370kg	5.3m *plus*, 32,520kg
2.9m *plus*, 24,390kg	5.5m *plus*, 33,000kg
3.2m *plus*, 25,410kg	5.8m *plus*, 34,000kg
3.5m *plus*, 26,420kg	6.2m *plus*, 35,000kg
3.8m *plus*, 27,440kg	6.5m *plus*, 36,000kg
4.1m *plus*, 28,450kg	6.7m *plus*, 37,000kg
4.4m *plus*, 29,470kg	6.9m *plus*, 38,000kg

2. for a three or more-axled tractive unit

Tractor GVW

3.0m *plus*, 20,330kg
3.8m *plus*, 22,360kg
4.0m *plus*, 22,500kg
4.3m *plus*, 24,390kg
4.9m *plus*, 24,390kg

Max intermed. axle weight*

8,390kg
8,640kg
10,500kg
9,150kg
10,500kg

Outfit GCW

2.0m *plus*, 20,330kg	4.7m *plus*, 30,490kg
2.2m *plus*, 22,360kg	5.0m *plus*, 31,500kg
2.6m *plus*, 23,370kg	5.3m *plus*, 32,520kg
2.9m *plus*, 24,390kg	5.4m *plus*, 33,000kg
3.2m *plus*, 25,410kg	5.6m *plus*, 34,000kg
3.5m *plus*, 26,420kg	5.8m *plus*, 35,000kg
3.8m *plus*, 27,440kg	6.0m *plus*, 36,000kg
4.1m *plus*, 28,450kg	6.2m *plus*, 37,000kg
4.4m *plus*, 29,470kg	6.3m *plus*, 38,000kg

* Maximum intermediate axle weight, as shown in column 2 of the DTP plate, or, where the vehicle has not been fitted with a DTP plate, on the manufacturer's plate.

continued on following page

MAXIMUM OVERALL WEIGHT cont

ARTICULATED cont

HOWEVER

Articulated vehicles with relevant braking requirements must comply with whichever is the lower of those weights listed on the previous page, or those below:

Motor vehicle first used on or after 1.4.73 and semi trailer having total of 5 or more axles:	38,000kg
Motor vehicle with 2 axles first used on or after 1.4.73 and semi trailer with 2 axles used on international transport:	35,000kg
Motor vehicle with 2 axles first used on or after 1.4.73 with driving axles having twin tyres and friendly suspension, and semi trailer with 2 axles:	35,000kg
Motor vehicle and semi trailer not listed above, with 4 or more axles:	32,520kg
Motor vehicle with 2 or more axles first used on or after 1.4.73 with twin tyres and friendly suspension on driving axles, and semi trailer with 1 axle:	26,000kg
Motor vehicle with 2 axles and semi trailer with 1 axle, not described above:	25,000kg

Articulated vehicles not complying with the relevant braking requirements are permitted the following maximum laden weight:

less than 4 wheels	20,330kg
4 wheels or more	24,390kg

REG 77

ARTICULATED VEHICLE MATCHING

- Tractive units and semi-trailers are plated separately.
- When loading articulated outfits the plated weights of both the tractive unit and the trailer must be taken into consideration.
- Difficulties may arise where various trailers covering a range of plated weights are used with a tractive unit.
- The same problem arises in relation to excise duty rating where incorrect matching may result in excise offences being committed.

Examples:
Tractive unit plated for operation at 32 tons gross weight when used with a long tandem-axle semi-trailer

For the same tractive unit linked with a short single-axle trailer, a lower weight must be observed, limited by the shorter trailer's gross plated weight.

Part 1: Construction and use 25
MAXIMUM OVERALL WEIGHT cont

ROAD VEHICLES (CONSTRUCTION AND USE)
REGULATIONS 1986. REGS 15, 16, 75 & 87)

TRAILERS

Qualification		Max Weight (Kg)
Does the trailer have brakes? ↓ Yes	→ No →	1) laden weight not to exceed max gross weight 2) kerbside weight of drawing vehicle must be at least twice weight of trailer plus load. 3) 750
Manufactured on or after 27.2.77 having overrun brakes except (agricultural trailer) ↓ No	→ Yes →	3,500
Manufactured before 27.2.7 having overrun brakes ↓ No	→ Yes →	3,560
Track laying ↓ No	→ Yes →	12,210
Balanced agricultural ↓ No	→ Yes →	See previous pages, but subject to max of 18,290
Unbalanced agricultural ↓ No	→ Yes →	18,290
Drawn by motor tractor, heavy motor car or motor car, and having pressure brakes (but not semi-trailer) ↓ No	→ Yes →	See previous pages, depends upon number and spacing of axles.
Less than 6 wheels or agricultural trailed appliance	→ Yes →	14,230

COMBINED TRANSPORT OPERATIONS

REGULATIONS 76 (1A), 77 (2A) AND SCHED. 11A ROAD VEHICLES
(CONSTRUCTION & USE) REGS 1986

The maximum overall weight for vehicles and trailers, and for articulated vehicles, laid down in regulations 76 and 77 do not apply in the case of **COMBINED TRANSPORT OPERATIONS**

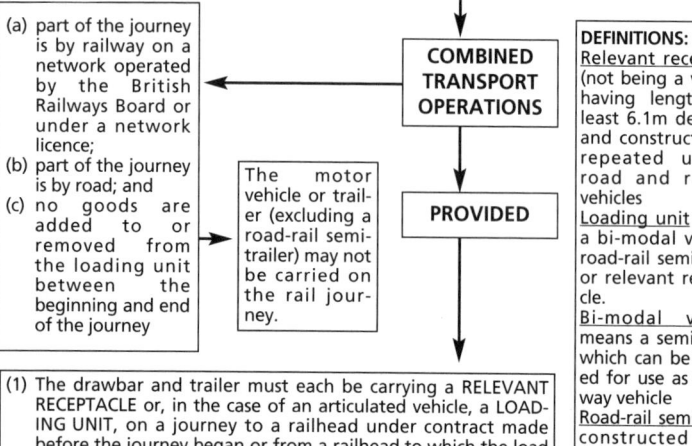

(a) part of the journey is by railway on a network operated by the British Railways Board or under a network licence;
(b) part of the journey is by road; and
(c) no goods are added to or removed from the loading unit between the beginning and end of the journey

The motor vehicle or trailer (excluding a road-rail semi-trailer) may not be carried on the rail journey.

PROVIDED

(1) The drawbar and trailer must each be carrying a RELEVANT RECEPTACLE or, in the case of an articulated vehicle, a LOADING UNIT, on a journey to a railhead under contract made before the journey began or from a railhead to which the load has been transported by railway.
(2) A document must be carried in the cab of the vehicle specifying (a) if going to a railhead, the railhead and the date the contract was made and the parties thereto; and (b) if from a railhead, the railhead and the time and date the load was collected.
(3) The motor vehicle must comply with the relevant braking requirements.
(4) Every driving axle not being a steering axle must have twin tyres.
(5) Either every driving axle has road friendly suspension or no axle exceeds 8,500kg.
(6) The motor vehicle and trailer (or articulated vehicle) must have at least 6 axles.

DEFINITIONS:
Relevant receptacle (not being a vehicle) having length of at least 6.1m designed and constructed for repeated use on road and railway vehicles
Loading unit means a bi-modal vehicle, road-rail semi-trailer or relevant receptacle.
Bi-modal vehicle means a semi-trailer which can be adapted for use as a railway vehicle
Road-rail semi-trailer constructed or adapted so as to be capable of use both on roads and railway.
Road Friendly suspension means air suspension or equivalent.

DRAWBAR COMBINATIONS must not exceed 44,000kg.

ARTICULATED VEHICLES
The motor vehicle must have at least 3 axles. The laden weight must not exceed the number of kg. which result from multiplying the distance in metres between the kingpin and the centre of the rearmost axle of the semi-trailer by 5500 rounded up to the nearest 10kg. (Max 44 tonnes).

Part 1: Construction and use 27

MAXIMUM GROSS AXLE WEIGHT

REG 78 ROAD VEHICLES (CONSTRUCTION AND USE) REGULATIONS 1986

If the maximum is exceeded, refer to 'Special Types' (see later).

For wheeled heavy motor cars, motor cars and trailers, complying with relevant braking requirements, max gross axle weights are as follows:

One wheeled axles REG 78	No other wheel in the same line transversely and single tyred not less than 300mm wide *or* double tyred not less than 300mm apart	**5,090kg**
	otherwise	**4,600kg**
More than 2 wheels in line transversely REG 78	• Manufactured before 1.5.83 where the wheels are on one axle of a group of closely spaced axles (see later for definition)	**10,170kg**
	• Manufactured on or after 1.5.83	**10,170kg**
	• Any other case	**11,180kg**
Two wheels in line transversely single tyred not less than 300mm wide or double tyred not less than 300mm apart	If wheels are on the sole driving axle	**10,500kg**
	Not as above	**10,170kg**
	not tyred as above	**9,200kg**

For wheeled heavy motor cars, motor cars and trailers not falling within the above

More than 2 wheels transmitting weight to a strip of road between 2 parallel lines at right angles to the longitudinal axis of the vehicle

up to 1.02m	**11,180kg**
1.02m *up to* 1.22m	**16,260kg**
1.22m *up to* 2.13m	**18,300kg**

Two wheels in line transversely	**9,200kg**
One wheel, where no other wheel is in the same line transversely	**4,600kg**

For wheeled locomotives

Two wheels in line transversely (except road roller, or vehicle with not more than 4 wheels first used before 1.6.55)	**11,180kg**
Any two wheels of vehicle having not more than 4 wheels first used before 1.6.55 (not being a road roller or agricultural motor vehicle driven at more than 20mph)	**three quarters of total weight of locomotive**

28 The Traffic Officer's Companion

MAX GROSS AXLE WEIGHT cont

REG 79 and SCHED 11 ROAD VEHICLES (CONSTRUCTION AND USE) REGS 1986

This Regulation applies to:

(a) a wheeled motor vehicle which complies with the relevant braking requirements; (b) a wheeled trailer drawn by such a vehicle; and (c) an agricultural motor vehicle, trailer or appliance, as follows

Two closely spaced axles *

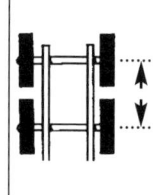

Motor vehicle
- *up to* 1.3m **16,000kg**
- 1.3m *plus* **18,000kg**
- 1.3m *plus* and (a) driving axles other than steering axles has twin tyres and (b) either every axle has road friendly suspension or neither has an axle weight over 9,500kg **19,000kg**

Trailer
- *up to* 1.3m **16,000kg**
- 1.3m *up to* 1.5m **18,000kg**
- Both axles driven from drawing vehicle and fitted with twin tyres; and either have road friendly suspension or neither has axle weight over 9,500kg **19,000kg**
- 1.5 *up to* 1.8m **19,320kg**
- 1.8m *plus* **20,000kg**

Three closely spaced axles *

Distance between any 2

- *up to* 1.3m **21,000kg**
- 1.3m *plus* and at least one axle does not have air suspension **22,500kg**
- 1.3m plus and all three axles have air suspension **24,000kg**

Four or more closely spaced axles *

24,000kg

* 'Closely spaced axles' means
(a) 2 axles not falling within (b) or (c) below, spaced not more than 2.5m apart;
(b) 3 axles not falling within (c) below, the outermost placed not more than 3.25m apart; or
(c) 4 or more axles, the outermost placed not more than 4.6m apart.

Exemptions

(a) vehicles first used before 1.6.73 (provided it complies with the requirements of Reg 78 relating to vehicles not complying with braking requirements);
(b) plating certificate issued immediately before 1.1.93 (provided no axle weight exceeds the weight on the certificate) as being the weight not to be exceeded in Great Britain for that axle.

Part 1: Construction and use **29**

NOTIONAL GROSS WEIGHT

GOODS VEHICLES (ASCERTAINMENT OF MAXIMUM GROSS WEIGHTS) REGULATIONS 1976

A notional gross weight can be obtained from an unladen weight by multiplying the unladen weight by the following prescribed factor:

This can be used where the appropriate gross weight or train weight is not marked on the vehicle in accordance with C&U Regulations, 1986.

Class of Vehicle — Multiplier

Motor Vehicles

Class of Vehicle	Multiplier
Dual Purpose Vehicle	1.5
Break-down Vehicle	2
Works Trucks	2
Electrically Propelled	2
Salt/grit Spreader	2
Hauling Lifeboats	2
Living Vans	1.5
Vehicle with permanently affixed equipment for medical, dental, veterinary, health, display or clerical purposes	1.5
3 wheeled street cleaners	2
Steam-propelled vehicles	2
Aircraft Servicing vehicles	2
Permanently attached equipment and not mentioned above	1
Heavy motor cars and motor cars first used before 1.1.68 and not mentioned above	2
Locomotives and motor tractors first used before 1.4.73	2
Any motor vehicle not mentioned above	4

Class of Vehicle — Multiplier

Trailers

Class of Vehicle	Multiplier
Engineering plant	1
Asphalt or tarmac producers	1
Agricultural trailer	1
Works trailers	1
Living vans	1.5
Any not mentioned above	3

Articulated

Class of Vehicle	Multiplier
Goods combinations with trailer of a type listed above	1.5
Any other	2.5

ADDITIONAL AUTHORISED WEIGHTS
ROAD VEHICLES (AUTHORISED WEIGHT) REGS 1998
(AS AMENDED BY S.I. 2000/3224)

The maximum weights authorised by construction and Use regulations are increased by these regulations provided certain conditions are complied with.

The regulations apply to the following types of vehicle:

Category	Type
M2	Passenger vehicle with more than 8 seats in addition to the drivers' with max mass not over 5 tonnes.
M3	Passenger vehicles with more than 8 seats in addition to the drivers' and with max mass over 5 tonnes
N2	Goods vehicles with max mass over 3.5 tonnes but not over 12 tonnes
N3	Goods vehicles having max mass over 12 tonnes
O3	Trailers with max mass over 3 tonnes but not over 12 tonnes
O4	Trailers with max mass over 12 tonnes

The regulations do not apply to "Combined Transport Operations" (see earlier).

The new authorised weights are determined according to
(a) vehicle (b) combinations (c) number of axles
but in each case there is a weight not to be exceeded in any circumstances and a weight determined by axle spacing. Where the weight by axle spacing is greater than that according to vehicle combination or number of axles, the latter will restrict the maximum weight.

VEHICLES

Weight not to be exceeded in any circumstances:

Type of vehicle	Number of axles	max weight (kg)
Rigid motor vehicle	2	18,000
Rigid motor vehicle satisfying below conditions	3	26,000
	4 or more	32,000
Rigid motor vehicle not satisfying below conditions	3	25,000
	4 or more	30,000
Tractor unit	2	18,000
Tractor unit satisfying below conditions	3 or more	26,000
Tractor unit not satisfying below conditions	3 or more	25,000
Trailer not being a semi-trailer or centre-axle trailer	2	18,000
	3 or more	24,000
Articulated bus	Any number	28,000

Conditions:
either (a) the driving axle if not a steering axle, is fitted with twin tyres and road friendly suspension, or
(b) each driving axle is fitted with twin tyres, and the maximum weight for each axle does not exceed 9,500kg.

Weight by reference to axle spacing

Multiply the distance in metres between the foremost and rearmost axles by the factor specified below to give the maximum weight in Kg. (rounded up to nearest 10Kg if above weight would not be exceeded).

Type of vehicle	Number of axles	Factor
Rigid motor vehicle	2	6,000
	3	5,500
	4 or more	5,000
Tractor unit	2	6,000
	3 or more	6,000
Trailer not being semi-trailer or centre-axle trailer	2	6,000
	3 or more	5,000
Articulated bus	Any number	5,000

VEHICLE COMBINATIONS

Weight not to be exceeded in any circumstances

Combination	Conditions	No. of Axles	Max Weight (kg)
Articulated vehicle	None	3	26,000
"	(a) 2 axle tractor unit and 2 axle trailer, (b) tractor unit not over 18,000kg, (c) sum of semi-trailer axles not over 20,000kg, and (d) driving axle has twin tyres and road friendly suspension	4	38,000
"	Not complying with above	4	36,000
"	None	5 or more	40,000
"	(a) no driving axle over 10,500kg (b) either (i) all driving axles have twin tyres and road friendly suspension, or (ii) all driving axles not being steering axles have twin tyres and not over 8,500kg (c) all trailer axles have road friendly suspension and, (d) each vehicle in combination has at least 3 axles	6 or more	41,000
"	In addition to (a) and (d) above, the vehicle is fitted with a low pollution engine.	6 or more	44,000
Rigid vehicle towing a trailer	Distance between rear axle of motor vehicle and front axle of trailer not less than 3m.	3	26,000
"	"	4	36,000
"	"	5 or more	40,000
"	Not complying with previous condition	3	22,000
"	"	4	30,000
"	"	5 or more	34,000
"	Complying with conditions applicable to articulated vehicles with 6 or more axles	6 or more	41,000
"	Complying with the above conditions and the vehicle is fitted with a low pollution engine	6 or more	44,000

Weight by reference to axle spacing

This only applies to articulated vehicles with 3 or more axles. The maximum weight (in Kg) is ascertained by multiplying the distance in metres between the kingpin and the centre of the rearmost axle of the semi-trailer by a factor of 5,500. The answer may be rounded up to the nearest 10kg provided this is less than the above weights.

MAXIMUM AXLE WEIGHTS

Weight not to be exceeded in any circumstances

Description of axle	max weight (kg)
Single driving axle	11,500
Single non-driving axle	10,000
Driving tandem axle meeting either of the below conditions	19,000
Driving tandem axle not meeting either of the below conditions	18,000
Non-driving tandem axle	20,000
Triaxle	24,000

Conditions

Either (a) driving axle has twin tyres and road friendly suspension, or
(b) each driving axle has twin tyres and no axle is over 9,500kg.

Weight by reference to axle spacing

Description of axle	Dimension	Length (m)	Max weight (kg)
Driving tandem axle	Distance between the two axles	Less than 1	11,500
"		Not less than 1 but less than 1.3	16,000
Non-driving "		Less than 1	11,000
"		Not less than 1 but less than 1.3	16,000
"		Not less than 1.3 but less than 1.8	18,000
Triaxle	Distance between any 2 adjacent axles	1.3 or less	21,000

RETRACTABLE AND LOADABLE AXLES

A vehicle first used on or after 1.1.2002 which is fitted with one or more retractable or loadable axles may have maximum authorised axle weight in accordance with the above tables under all driving conditions if the retractable or loadable axle is automatically lowered to the ground when the front axle (or nearest if in a group) is laden to that maximum authorised weight. However this will not apply (subject to further conditions) if the vehicle is in slippery road conditions and it is necessary to raise the axle in order increase the traction of the remaining tyres.

DEFINITIONS

"centre axle trailer" – having only a single axle or single group of axles positioned at or near to the centre of gravity so that the load transmitted to the drawing vehicle does not exceed 10% or 1,000kg whichever is the less.

"loadable axle" - the load on which can be varied without the axle being raised by an axle-lift device.

"retractable axle" - raised or lowered by an axle-lift device.

"road friendly suspension" – at least 75% of the spring effect is produced by air or other compressible fluid under pressure, or suspension recognised as being equivalent within the community.

"steering axle" – positively steered by the actions of the driver

"tandem axle" – 2 axles not more than 2.5m apart sharing the load

"triaxle" – (a) 3 axles where none is more than 3.25m apart from any other, or (b) more than 3 axles where none is more than 4.6m from any other. The load is shared by them all.

Part 1: Construction and use **33**

TRAVELLING HEIGHT – CAB NOTICES

ROAD VEHICLES (CONSTRUCTION AND USE) REGS 1986 REG 10
(for interpretation of terms see definitions page)

A motor vehicle with an overall travelling height over 3 metres must display a notice in the cab indicating the vehicle height.

Requirements of the notice:
(a) height expressed in feet and inches or both feet and inches and in metres;
(b) if in feet and inches, numbers to be at least 40mm tall;
(c) the height expressed is the overall travelling height (or, if a vehicle to which the next regulation applies (warning device required), the 'overall travelling height' or 'predetermined height', whichever is the greater);
(d) if not a 'relevant vehicle' the height expressed must not exceed the 'overall travelling height' by more than 150mm.
(e) if a 'relevant vehicle' the height expressed must not exceed the 'overall travelling height' by more than 1m;
(f) if the height is expressed in both feet and inches and metres they must not differ by more than 50mm.
(g) no other letters or numbers which could be understood as an indication of height may be displayed in the notice.

Exemptions:
(a) Highly unlikely driver would encounter a bridge, etc, which was not at least 1 metre higher than the 'overall travelling height', (or, if applicable, the 'maximum travelling height' for vehicles needing a warning device);
(b) Driver has documentation giving information regarding a risk-free route and the driver is following the route or an unforeseen diversion;
(c) Driver has bridge height information for a particular route indicating structures under which the vehicle will/will not pass;
(d) Vehicles not over 4m 'overall travelling height', registered in an EEA state being used in international traffic.

HIGH LEVEL EQUIPMENT – WARNING DEVICE

ROAD VEHICLES (CONSTRUCTION AND USE) REGULATIONS 1986. REGS 10A AND 10B

(For interpretation of terms see definitions page)

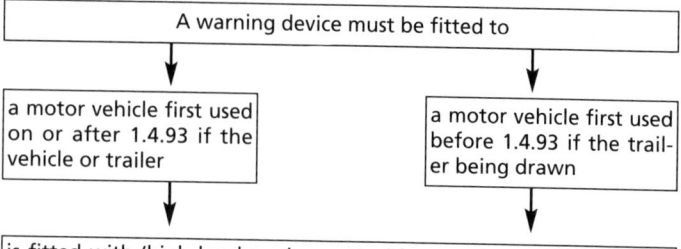

```
┌─────────────────────────────────────────────────┐
│        A warning device must be fitted to       │
└─────────────────────────────────────────────────┘
           │                          │
           ▼                          ▼
┌─────────────────────┐    ┌─────────────────────┐
│a motor vehicle first│    │a motor vehicle first│
│used on or after     │    │used before 1.4.93 if│
│1.4.93 if the vehicle│    │the trailer being    │
│or trailer           │    │drawn                │
└─────────────────────┘    └─────────────────────┘
           │                          │
           ▼                          ▼
┌─────────────────────────────────────────────────┐
│is fitted with 'high level equipment' with a     │
│maximum height over 3 metres                     │
└─────────────────────────────────────────────────┘
```

Requirements of the warning device:

Constructed, maintained, adjusted and connected so that it gives a visible warning to the driver if, whilst the vehicle is being driven, the height of the 'high level equipment' exceeds a 'predetermined height'. The 'predetermined height' shall not exceed the 'overall travelling height' by more than 1m.

Exemptions:

(a) Unlikely driver would encounter a bridge, etc. which was not at least 1 metre higher than the 'maximum travelling height';
(b) 'Overall travelling height' of not more than 4 metres and registered in an EEA state being used on international traffic;
(c) agricultural motor vehicle;
(d) industrial tractor;
(e) works truck;
(f) naval, military or air force vehicle;
(g) fire brigade vehicle;
(h) vehicle constructed and normally used for carrying at least 2 other vehicles;
(i) motor vehicle drawing a car transporter;
(j) motor vehicle where 'maximum travelling height' does not exceed its 'overall travelling height'.

Part 1: Construction and use **35**

CAB NOTICES AND WARNING DEVICES – DEFINITIONS
ROAD VEHICLES (CONSTRUCTION AND USE) REGULATIONS 1986. REG 10C

High Level Equipment is equipment so fitted that –
(a) it can be raised by means of a power operated device, and
(b) the raising or lowering is capable of altering the overall travelling height when the vehicle and every trailer is unladen.

In relation to a tipper which is (a) a motor vehicle first used before 1.4.98, or (b) a trailer manufactured before that date, "high level equipment" does not include the relevant part of the tipper.

Where (a) the equipment is so designed and constructed that it can be fixed in a stowed position by a locking device and it is not possible for a person in the cab to interfere with the locking device; and (b) the equipment is fixed in that position by the locking device, the equipment shall not be regarded as "high level equipment".

Maximum Height in relation to high level equipment means the height of the highest point of that equipment when it is raised as far as possible and the vehicle is unladen.

Maximum Travelling Height means (i) if the overall travelling height could be increased by raising the high level equipment, the highest level to which it could be raised, or (ii) in any other case, the overall travelling height.

Overall Travelling Height means the overall height for the time being of the vehicle (or combination of vehicles), its equipment and load.

Tipper means a vehicle which can be unloaded by part of the vehicle (the relevant part) being tipped sideways or rearwards.

TRAILERS

REG 83 ROAD VEHICLES (CONSTRUCTION AND USE) REGULATIONS 1986

Description of vehicle	Max no of trailers
Motor tractor See definition at front of book– basically a motor vehicle for hauling trailers with wide load etc — If both tractor and trailer are unladen	1
	2
Locomotive	3
Motor car or heavy motor car (not being a straddle carrier, articulated bus or a bus) (for buses see following page)	1
If one of the trailers being drawn is a towing implement (ie a 'dolly') and the other is an articulated type semi trailer secured to and resting on, or suspended from, the dolly *The following diagram shows a conventional 6-wheel rigid vehicle drawing a dolly mounted semi-trailer.*	2
Agricultural motor vehicle This is a motor vehicle constructed and adapted for use off roads for agricultural, horticultural or forestry and which is primarily used for one or more of those purposes – not being a dual purpose vehicle 1. With non-agricultural trailers or appliances	As for locomotive motor tractor or heavy motor car above
2. With agricultural trailers or trailed appliances An agricultural trailer is a trailer constructed or adapted for the purpose of agriculture, horticulture or forestry and only used for one or more of those purposes An agricultural trailed appliance is a trailer which is an implement constructed or adapted for the use off roads for the above purposes	**2** unladen agricultural trailers; or **1** agricultural trailer and **1** agricultural trailed appliance; or **2** agricultural trailed appliances

Part 1: Construction and use **37**

TRAILERS cont

ROAD VEHICLES (CONSTRUCTION AND USE) REGULATIONS 1986

ARTICULATED TRACTIVE UNIT
DRAWING TWO SEMI-TRAILERS   REG 83

> An articulated tractive unit drawing two semi-trailers (a double bottom) will be permitted by the DTP subject to special ministerial permission

> subject to a 30mph limit (40mph on motorways) and prescribed routes.

> Must comply with C&U Regs 1986 but carry additional lights and mirrors. No maximum weights and lengths are specified.

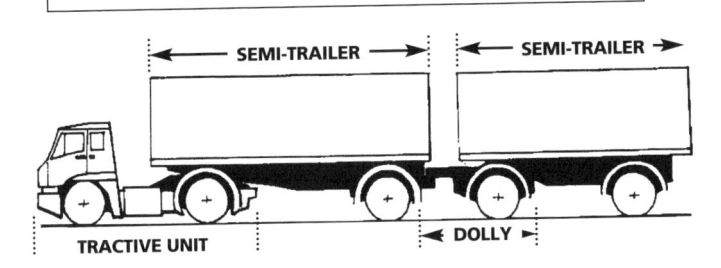

NOTES

- *'Trailer' does not include a water carrying vehicle drawn for the purpose of a steam powered drawing vehicle.*

- *A broken down unladen articulated vehicle being towed will be counted as only one trailer.*

MOTOR VEHICLE DRAWING A TRAILER BY ROPE OR CHAIN

REG 86

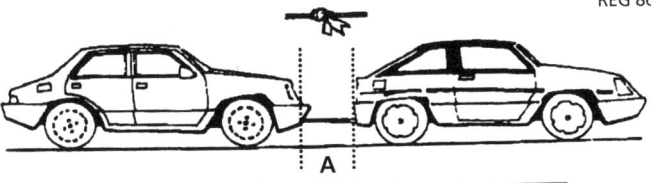

> 'A' must not exceed 4.5m. If it exceeds 1.5m the rope or chain must be made clearly visible

TRAILERS cont

ROAD VEHICLES (CONSTRUCTION AND USE) REGULATIONS 1986

MOTOR CYCLES REG 84

> A person using, or causing or permitting **ANY MOTOR CYCLE** to be used, on a road, may not:

1. draw more than one trailer;
2. draw a trailer carrying a passenger (unless broken down);
3. draw a trailer with UW over 254kg.

A **TWO-WHEELED MOTOR CYCLE**, (not with a sidecar)

and engine cc not over 125cc shall not

draw a trailer except a broken-down motor cycle being ridden.

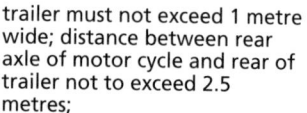

with engine capacity over 125cc may draw a trailer subject to the following

trailer must not exceed 1 metre wide; distance between rear axle of motor cycle and rear of trailer not to exceed 2.5 metres;
- motor cycle to be marked with kerbside weight (unless broken down);
- trailer to be marked with unladen weight (unless broken down);
- laden weight of trailer not to exceed 150kg or two-thirds kerbside weight of motor cycle, whichever the less (unless broken down).

TRAILERS cont
ROAD VEHICLES (CONSTRUCTION AND USE) REGULATIONS 1986

Leaving trailers at rest (Reg. 89)
It is an offence to cause or permit a trailer to stand on a road when detached from the drawing vehicle unless at least one of its wheels (or if track-laying, its tracks) is prevented from revolving by the setting of a parking brake or the use of a chain, chock or other efficient device.

Maximum weight of unbraked trailers (Reg. 87)

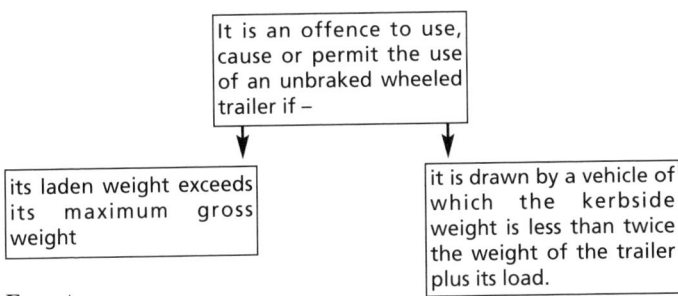

It is an offence to use, cause or permit the use of an unbraked wheeled trailer if –

- its laden weight exceeds its maximum gross weight
- it is drawn by a vehicle of which the kerbside weight is less than twice the weight of the trailer plus its load.

Except
(a) street cleansing trailer not carrying a load
(b) agricultural trailer manufactured before 1.7.47 drawn by motor tractor or agricultural motor vehicle at not more than 10mph, with unladen weight not over 4,070kg, and being the only trailer drawn
(c) trailer drawn by a motor cycle in accordance with Reg 84.
(d) agricultural trailed appliance
(e) agricultural trailed appliance conveyor
(f) broken down vehicle
(g) gritting trailer with max gross weight not over 2,000kg

40 The Traffic Officer's Companion

TRAILERS cont

ROAD VEHICLES (CONSTRUCTION AND USE) REGULATIONS 1986

PASSENGERS IN TRAILERS (REG 90)

no person shall use, cause or permit to be used on a road

↓

any trailer for the carriage of passengers for hire or reward

except a wheeled trailer which is, or is carrying, a broken down motor vehicle if
(a) not exceeding 30mph; and
(b) if the trailer is, or is carrying, a broken down bus, it is attached by a rigid draw bar. (Reg 90(1))

a wheeled trailer in which any person is carried and which is a living van having either –
(a) less than 4 wheels; or
(b) 4 wheels consisting of two close-coupled* wheels on each side

* 'close coupled' means wheels on the same side having their centres not more than 1m apart.

except if being tested by its manufacturer, repairer, distributor or dealer in trailers. (Reg 90(2))

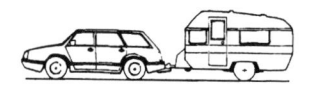

REG 90

A BUS

A bus – not being an articulated bus or mini-bus – may draw:

a broken-down bus – where no person other than the driver is carried on either vehicle – or

one trailer.

REG 83
BUT REFER TO REG 7 FOR MAXIMUM LENGTH

TRAILERS cont

SECONDARY COUPLING (REG 86A)

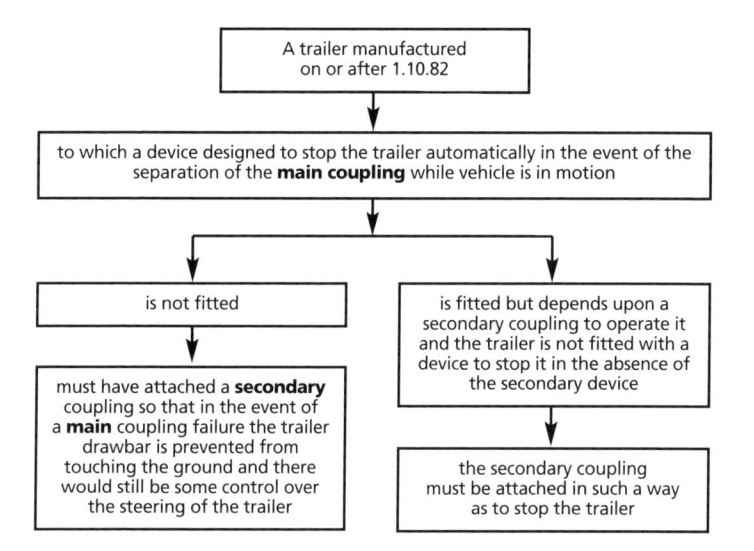

```
A trailer manufactured
on or after 1.10.82
        │
        ▼
to which a device designed to stop the trailer automatically in the event of the
separation of the main coupling while vehicle is in motion
```

┌─── is not fitted

must have attached a **secondary** coupling so that in the event of a **main** coupling failure the trailer drawbar is prevented from touching the ground and there would still be some control over the steering of the trailer

└─── is fitted but depends upon a secondary coupling to operate it and the trailer is not fitted with a device to stop it in the absence of the secondary device

the secondary coupling must be attached in such a way as to stop the trailer

Except:
Agricultural trailer or appliance not exceeding 20mph. Vehicle with max speed not over 25km/h. Works trailer. Public works vehicle. Trailer designed, constructed or adapted to be drawn by a locomotive, motor tractor, vehicle with max speed not exceeding 25km/h, works truck or public works vehicle. Street cleansing trailer. Max total design axle weight not over 750kg. Motor cycle trailer. Broken down vehicle. Gritting trailer with max gross weight not over 2,000kg.

THESE EXCEPTIONS TO REG 86A ARE CONTAINED WITHIN REG 15 C&U REGS 1986

SIDECARS (REGS 92 & 93)

The sidecar wheel must not be wholly outside this space.

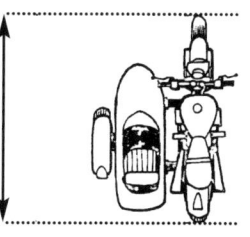

It is an offence to use, cause or permit to be used a 2-wheeled motor cycle registered on or after 1.8.81 (other than one brought temporarily into Great Britain by a person resident abroad) if the sidecar is attached to the right (or offside) of the motor cycle.

42 The Traffic Officer's Companion

DANGEROUS VEHICLES

REG 100 ROAD VEHICLES (CONSTRUCTION AND USE) REGULATIONS 1986
SECTION 40A ROAD TRAFFIC ACT 1988

A motor vehicle, every trailer drawn thereby and all parts and accessories shall at all times be such

that no danger is caused or is likely to be caused to any person

in or on the vehicle or trailer, or on a road, by reason of:

condition or unsuitable purpose

number of passengers
(may not apply to vehicles subject to PSV (Carrying Capacity) Regs 1984)

manner passengers carried

weight, distribution, packing and adjustment of load

The load shall be so secured by physical restraint and be in such a position that

neither danger nor nuisance is likely to be caused to any person or property

by reason of the load moving or being blown or falling from the vehicle.

Part 1: Construction and use **43**

SILENCERS

ROAD VEHICLES (CONSTRUCTION AND USE) REGULATIONS 1986

MOTOR CYCLE SILENCER AND EXHAUST SYSTEM REGS 1995

Every vehicle propelled by an internal combustion engine shall be fitted with an **exhaust system including a silencer** suitable and sufficient for reducing, as far as may be reasonable, the noise caused by the escape of the exhaust gases from the engine.

No person shall use, cause or permit to be used, a vehicle on a road if exhaust gases from the engine escape into the atmosphere without first passing through the silencer, etc.

The silencer etc shall at all times when the vehicle is used on a road be maintained in good and efficient working order and shall not, after the date of manufacture, have been altered in any way which makes the noise of escaping gases greater.
REG 54 C&U REGS 1986

Motor cycle and moped silencers must now meet requirements of specified EC Directives with a distinction being made between those first used before 1.2.96 and those first used after that date.

A silencer marked 'not for road use' may not be used on a road by such a vehicle.
REG 57A C&U REGS 1986

Using a motor cycle or moped on a road if it does not meet noise limit requirements and it is not in good or efficient working order or has been altered and the noise is therefore greater is an offence
REG 57B C&U REGS 1986

Supply of motor cycle silencers: In the course of a business, no person may supply or offer or agree to supply or expose or have in his possession for the purpose of supplying, an exhaust system, silencer or component for such a system unless it is clearly and indelibly marked with the relevant British Standard Specification or EEC Directive. The above does not apply if the silencer or exhaust system is clearly and indelibly marked 'NOT FOR ROAD USE' or 'PRE-1985 MC ONLY'

S1 MOTOR CYCLE NOISE ACT 1987
AND REGS 3, 4 & 5 MOTOR CYCLE SILENCER AND EXHAUST SYSTEM REGS 1995

As to sound levels generally, see Reg 55, C&U Regulations 1986

No motor vehicle shall be used on a road in a manner which causes any excessive noise which could have been avoided by reasonable care by the driver.
REG 97 C&U REGS 1986

EMISSIONS OF SMOKE ETC.
REGS. 61 & 61A ROAD VEHICLES (CONSTRUCTION AND USE) REGULATIONS 1986

1) All Vehicles

Emission of Smoke or Vapour
Unless complying with a relevant instrument (Community Directive, ECE Regulation, or the table below), every vehicle shall be constructed and maintained so as not to emit any avoidable smoke or visible vapour.

Emission of Ashes, Cinders, etc
Every motor vehicle using solid fuel shall be fitted with a tray or shield to prevent ashes or cinders from falling onto the road; and an appliance to prevent any emission of sparks or grit.

Emissions likely to cause Damage or Injury
No person may use, cause or permit the use of a motor vehicle from which any smoke, visible vapour, grit, sparks, ashes, cinders or oily substance is emitted if it causes, or may cause, damage to any property or injury or danger to any person who is, or may be, on the road.

Carbon Monoxide and Hydrocarbon
(1) No person may use, cause or permit the use of a 4-stroke spark ignition engine vehicle first used on or after 1.8.75 if
1. when idling, the carbon monoxide content of the exhaust exceeds 4.5% (if first used before 1.8.86) or 3.5% (if first used on or after that date);
2. when running without load at 2000 rpm the hydrocarbon content of the exhaust exceeds 0.12%.

This requirement does not apply (a) to vehicles which, when manufactured, could not comply, (b) to vehicles to which the following provision applies, or (c) to vehicles contained in the 'exemptions' box below.

(2) No person may use, cause or permit the use of –
1. a passenger car first used on or after 1.8.92 and before 1.8.95, and is mentioned in the emissions publication (a DETR document);
2. a vehicle which is not a passenger car, is first used on or after 1.8.94, and is mentioned in the emissions publication; or
3. a passenger car first used on or after 1.8.95,

if, **when the engine is idling,** the carbon monoxide content of the exhaust exceeds the level mentioned in the emissions publication or, if the vehicle is not mentioned in the publication, 0.5%, or if, **when the engine is at fast idle**, (a) carbon monoxide exceeds the amount mentioned in the publication, or, if the vehicle is not mentioned in the publication, 0.3%; (b) the hydrocarbon content exceeds 0.02%; or (c) the lambda value (ratio of air to petrol vapour) is outside limits.

This requirement does not apply to vehicles which, when manufactured, could not comply, nor to vehicles contained in the 'exemptions' box below.

Exemptions
(a) vehicle being taken for repairs, (b) vehicle constructed by a person not in the vehicle manufacturing business and first used before 1.7.98, (c) a vehicle with: less than 4 wheels; max. gross weight less than 400kg; max. speed less than 25 km/hr; or an agricultural motor vehicle, (d) goods vehicle with max. gross weight over 3,500kg, (e) engineering plant, industrial tractor or works truck, (e) vehicle with rotary piston engine first used before 1.8.87.

Part 1: Construction and use **45**

EMISSIONS OF SMOKE ETC. cont
REGS. 61 & 61A ROAD VEHICLES (CONSTRUCTION AND USE) REGULATIONS 1988

No person shall use, cause or permit the use of a compression ignition vehicle if the coefficient of absorption of the exhaust emissions exceeds-
1. if turbo-charged, 3.0 per metre, or
2. if not, 2.5 per metre.

This requirement does not apply to (a) vehicles which, when manufactured, could not comply, (b) vehicle going for repairs, (c) a vehicle with: less than 4 wheels; max. gross weight less than 400kg; max. speed less than 25 km/hr; or an agricultural motor vehicle, (d) engineering plant, industrial tractor or works truck, or (e) vehicles subject to the testing regs. in class III, IV, V or VII.

2) Vehicles used before 1.1.2001

Every wheeled vehicle shall be constructed so as to comply with the following:

Item	Class of Vehicle	Requirements	Exemptions
1	Vehicles with compression ignition engine fitted with a device to facilitate starting by supplying excess fuel.	The device must not be operable by a person inside the vehicle	(a) Works truck (b) Vehicle with device designed so that (i) its use after the engine has started cannot cause the engine to be supplied with excess fuel, or (ii) it does not cause any increase in the smoke or visible vapour emitted
2	Vehicles first used on or after 1.4.73 with compression ignition engine	Must have a type test certificate in accordance with BS AU 141a; 1971	(a) vehicle manufactured before 1.4.73 with a Perkins 6.354 engine, (b) vehicle with not more than 2 cylinders, being an agricultural vehicle (first used before 1.6.86), an industrial tractor, a works truck or engineering plant.
3	Vehicles first used on or after 1.1.72 with a spark ignition engine other than a 2-stroke engine	Must have a means to ensure that when the engine is running, any vapours or gases in the crank case or other part of the engine are prevented from passing into the atmosphere except through the combustion chamber	Two-wheeled motor cycle with or without a sidecar attached. A vehicle to which any item in Table 2 in the Regulations applies (which requires compliance with Community Directives or ECE Regulations).

Readers are referred to a further table in Reg. 61 containing details of the various Community Directives and ECE Regulations with which vehicles must comply.

3) Vehicles first used on or after 1.1.2001

Reg. 61A contains details of Directives and ECE Regs. which impose further requirements for certain motor vehicles first used on or after 1.1.01.

TYRES

REGS 26 AND 27 ROAD VEHICLES (CONSTRUCTION AND USE) REGULATIONS 1986

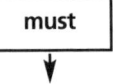

must

BE SUITABLE having regard to the use to which the vehicle or trailer is being put or to the types of tyres fitted to its other wheels.

BE INFLATED so as to be fit for use to which vehicle is being put

Have no portion of the **PLY OR CORD EXPOSED**

have **NO LUMP, BULGE OR TEAR** caused by separation or partial failure of its structure.

HAVE THE BASE OF ANY GROOVE which showed in the original tread pattern **CLEARLY VISIBLE**

does not apply to:
1. a 3-wheeled motor cycle UW not over 102kg and incapable of more than 12mph on level; or
2. a pedestrian-controlled works truck

NOT BE A 'TEMPORARY USE SPARE TYRE' (for use only if normal tyre fails and used at lower speed

unless either:
1. a passenger vehicle first used before 1.4.87, or
2. complying with ECE Reg 64 or Community Directive 92/93

(REG 24(3))

Part 1: Construction and use **47**

TYRES cont
REGS 26 AND 27 ROAD VEHICLES (CONSTRUCTION AND USE) REGULATIONS 1986

must

FOR TWO AXLE-VEHICLES – not have:
1. diagonal ply or bias-belted on rear with radial ply on front;
2. diagonal ply on rear and bias belted on front

NOT BE RECUT TYRES if:
1. ply or cord has been cut or exposed, or
2. wholly or partially different pattern to manufacturer's recut tread pattern

HAVE NO CUT in excess of 25mm or 10 per cent of width, whichever is greater, measured in any direction on outside of tyre, deep enough to reach the ply or cord

HAVE EITHER:
1. depth of groove of tread pattern at least 1mm throughout continuous band of at least three quarters of breadth round entire circumference, or
2. where original tread did not extend beyond three quarters of breadth, whole of original tread to have depth of at least 1mm

does not apply to
1. 3-wheeled motor cycle UW not exceeding 102 kg and incapable of more than 12mph on level:
2. pedestrian controlled works truck; or
3. motor cycle not over 50cc

in the case of
1. passenger vehicles for not more than eight passengers in addition to the driver (other than motor cycles)
2. goods vehicles under 3,500kg,
3. and light trailers,
for 1mm read 1.6mm in the central three quarters of breath and round the entire outer circumference of the tyre.

continued on following page

48 The Traffic Officer's Companion

TYRES cont

REGS 26 AND 27 ROAD VEHICLES (CONSTRUCTION AND USE) REGULATIONS 1986

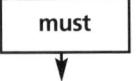

must

continued from previous page

BE MAINTAINED in such condition as to be fit for the use to which they are being put and free from any defect which might cause damage to the road surface or danger to persons in or on the vehicle or using the road

NOT HAVE DIFFERENT TYPES OF STRUCTURE where fitted to the same axle

FOR VEHICLES WITH MORE THAN 1 STEERABLE AXLE – not have different type of structure on different steerable axles; or

FOR VEHICLES WITH MORE THAN 1 DRIVEN AXLE NOT BEING STEERABLE AXLES – not have different type of structure on different non-steerable axles.

Part 1: Construction and use **49**

SUPPLY OF TYRES
MOTOR VEHICLE TYRES (SAFETY) REGULATIONS 1994

No person shall supply a tyre designed to be fitted to a	It is an offence to supply a tyre bearing a false mark for a

passenger car, light trailer, moped (not low performance), motor cycle, motor tricycle, three-wheel moped, or quadricycle	passenger car, commercial vehicle or trailer	moped, motor cycle, motor tricycle, three-wheel moped, or quadricycle on or after 1.1.04

or commercial vehicle

which is a **NEW TYRE**	which is a **PART-WORN TYRE**		which is a **RETREADED TYRE** (not part-worn)
unless it is marked to indicate that it complies with ECE Regulations or EC Directives as a new tyre	Unless it does not have- a) a cut in excess of 25mm or 10% of the width (whichever is the greater) deep enough to reach the ply or cord; b) any lump, bulge or tear caused by seaparion or failure of its structure; c) ply or cord exposed; d) penetration damage which has not been repaired; e) tread less than 2mm It must bear the word "PART-WORN"	unless it is not marked as a new tyre; it is marked as a retreaded tyre in accordance with B.S., ECE Regs. or EC Directives; and, after 1.1.04, has ECE type approval.	unless either- (a) it is not marked as a new tyre and ECE type approval has been granted; or (b) the following are met- (i) not marked as a new tyre; (ii) carcass not more than 7 yrs. old and conforms to ECE Regs. or Directives; (iii) not previously retreaded; (iv) marked with original manufacturer's details; (v) complies with ECE dimension & performance requirements; (vi) bears word "RETREAD"; (vii) has 'e' mark; (viii) if repaired, has been done properly; and (ix) must not show higher speed rating or load index than original carcass.

If it has not been retreaded it must bear the original speed category symbol and load capacity index

If it has been retreaded it must bear the appropriate B.S. or ECE approval mark, or be marked (by code or otherwise) with the original manufacturer's name and tyre model, and the word "RETREAD". If it bears the mark "BS AU 144e" it must show the original speed category and load index.

EXEMPTIONS

New or retreaded (including part-worn retreaded) Bias belted or diagonal ply for pre-1.1.49 vehicle or trailer; 'competition' tyres; 'off-road' tyres; tyres for test or trial; tyres for other than retail sale; and tyre sizes 185R16, 125R400, 135R400, 145R400, 155R400, 165R400, 175R400 or 185R400	**Part-worn** Where complete vehicle is supplied. If (a) for vehicle manufactured before 1.1.33; (b) limited run-flat tyre; or for agricultural use, need not bear approval marks etc.

TYRES – SIDEWALL SYMBOLS

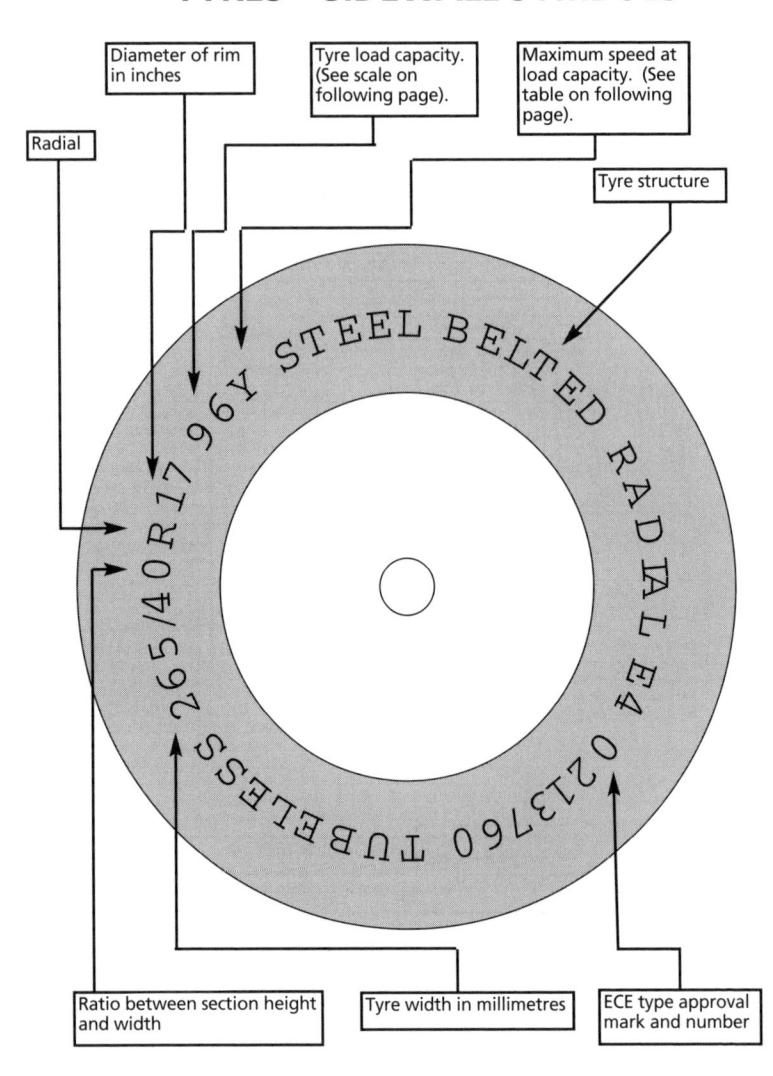

Tyre sidewall markings: **265/40R17 96Y STEEL BELTED RADIAL E4 0213760 TUBELESS**

- **Radial**: R
- **Diameter of rim in inches**: 17
- **Tyre load capacity** (See scale on following page): 96
- **Maximum speed at load capacity** (See table on following page): Y
- **Tyre structure**: STEEL BELTED RADIAL
- **Ratio between section height and width**: 40
- **Tyre width in millimetres**: 265
- **ECE type approval mark and number**: E4 0213760

TYRES – LOAD AND SPEED LIMITATIONS

CAR, VAN AND TRUCK LOAD CAPACITY PER WHEEL IN Kg.										
INDEX	LOAD	INDEX	LOAD	INDEX	LOAD	INDEX	LOAD	INDEX	LOAD
60	250	88	560	116	1250	144	2800	172	6300
61	257	89	580	117	1285	145	2900	173	6500
62	265	90	600	118	1320	146	3000	174	6700
63	272	91	615	119	1360	147	3075	175	6900
64	280	92	630	120	1400	148	3150	176	7100
65	290	93	650	121	1450	149	3250	177	7300
66	300	94	670	122	1500	150	3350	178	7500
67	307	95	690	123	1550	151	3450	179	7750
68	315	96	710	124	1600	152	3550	180	8000
69	325	97	730	125	1650	153	3650	181	8250
70	335	98	750	126	1700	154	3750	182	8500
71	345	99	775	127	1750	155	3875	183	8750
72	355	100	800	128	1800	156	4000	184	9000
73	365	101	825	129	1850	157	4125	185	9250
74	375	102	850	130	1900	158	4250	186	9500
75	387	103	875	131	1950	159	4375	187	9750
76	400	104	900	132	2000	160	4500	188	10000
77	412	105	925	133	2060	161	4625	189	10300
78	425	106	950	134	2120	162	4750	190	10600
79	437	107	975	135	2180	163	4875	191	10900
80	450	108	1000	136	2240	164	5000	192	11200
81	462	109	1030	137	2300	165	5150	193	11500
82	475	110	1060	138	2360	166	5300	194	11800
83	487	111	1090	139	2430	167	5450	195	12150
84	500	112	1120	140	2500	168	5600	196	12500
85	515	113	1150	141	2575	169	5800	197	12850
86	530	114	1180	142	2650	170	6000	198	13200
87	545	115	1215	143	2725	171	6150	199	13600

MAXIMUM SUSTAINABLE SPEED FOR THE TYRE AT THE LOAD CAPACITY GIVEN (NORMAL USE)		
SYMBOL	SPEED (KPH)	SPEED (MPH)
CAR		
S	180	111.8
T	190	118.1
U	200	124.3
H	210	130.5
V	240	149.1
W	270	167.8
Y	300	186.4
VR*	210+	130+
ZR*	240+	150+
WINTER/REINFORCED		
Q	160	99.4
R	170	105.6
VAN		
N	140	87
P	150	93.2
TRUCK		
J	100	62.1
K	110	68.4
L	120	74.6
M	130	80.8
* Old designation		

WARNING INSTRUMENTS

REGS 37 AND 99 ROAD VEHICLES (CONSTRUCTION AND USE) REGULATIONS 1986
(AS AMENDED BY S.I. 2000/1971)

Every motor vehicle
(having a maximum speed of more than 20mph)

does not apply to agricultural motor vehicle unless driven at more than 20mph

shall be fitted with a horn
(not being a reversing alarm or two-tone horn)

eg instrument – not being bell, gong, or siren – capable of giving audible and sufficient warning of approach or position of vehicle to which it is fitted

The sound emitted by any horn

other than a reversing alarm boarding aid alarm or two-tone horn

fitted to a wheeled vehicle
(first used on or after 1.8.73)

shall be continuous, uniform, and not strident.

NOTE: *A reversing alarm or boarding aid alarm fitted to a wheeled vehicle shall not be strident.*

No motor vehicle shall be fitted with a gong, bell, siren or two-tone horn → unless an emergency vehicle

Except: A bell, gong or siren may be fitted to prevent theft or to a bus to summon help for driver/conductor/inspector

Every bell, gong or siren fitted to prevent theft – and every device using a vehicle's horn (for vehicles first used on or after 1.10.82) – shall not sound for a continuous period of more than five minutes.

Warning devices may not be sounded
when stationary

unless a reversing alarm, but these may only be used on goods vehicles not less than 2,000kg max gross weight, buses, engineering plant, refuse vehicle, or works truck

or on a restricted road between 11.30pm and 7am

If carrying goods for sale

An instrument other than a two tone horn may be used to advertise perishable goods, for human consumption, between 12 noon and 7pm

But must not give reasonable cause for annoyance to persons in the vicinity.

S 62(3) CONTROL OF POLLUTION ACT 1974

Part 1: Construction and use **53**

SPEEDOMETER

REGS. 35 AND 36 ROAD VEHICLES (CONSTRUCTION AND USE) REGULATIONS 1986

> **A speedometer must be fitted to all vehicles,** with the following exceptions

- maximum speed not exceeding 25mph
- unlawful to drive at more than 25mph
- agricultural vehicle not driven at more than 20mph
- motor cycle first used before 1.4.84 not exceeding 100cc
- invalid carriage first used before 1.4.84
- works truck first used before 1.4.84
- vehicle first used before 1.10.37
- vehicle fitted with approved recording equipment indicating the speed.

> A speedometer must be fitted in such a position that the driver can see speed of vehicle

> and if vehicle first used on or after 1.4.84, must be capable of indicating speed in mph and kph

> **Must be maintained in good working order**
> and must be kept free from any obstruction
> which may prevent it being read but:
>
> **defence:**
> - if defect occurred during journey on which contravention detected
> - if steps have already been taken to have defect remedied with reasonable expedition.

54 The Traffic Officer's Companion

SEAT BELT ANCHORAGE POINTS
ROAD VEHICLES (CONSTRUCTION AND USE) REGULATIONS 1986

Anchorage points must be fitted in accordance with the table on the following page.

This regulation applies to a vehicle which is not an excepted vehicle and which is:
- bus first used on or after 1.4.82
- wheeled motor car first used on or after 1.1.65
- 3-wheeled motor cycle with unladen weight over 255 kg first used on or after 1.9.70
- heavy motor car first used on or after 1.10.88

Excepted vehicles are:
- goods vehicle (other than a dual purpose vehicle) –
    1. first used before 1.4.67,
    2. first used on or after 1.4.80 and before 1.10.88 having a gross maximum weight over 3500 kg. or
    3. first used before 1.4.80 or, if manufactured before 1.10.79, first used before 1.4.82 and, in either case, with unladen weight over 1525 kg;
- agricultural motor vehicle;
- motor tractor;
- works truck;
- electrically propelled goods vehicle first used before 1.10.88;
- pedestrian controlled vehicle;
- vehicle which has been used outside G.B., being driven from its place of arrival in G.B. to the owner's or driver's home, or to a place to be fitted with anchorage points and seat belts;
- vehicle having maximum speed not over 16 mph;
- motor cycle with seat for sitting astride, and which is constructed or assembled by a person not ordinarily engaged in the trade of manufacturing such vehicles;
- locomotive.

Definitions
1. **Exposed forward-facing seat** means:
    1. a forward-facing front seat (including any crew seat) and the driver's seat; and
    2. any other forward-facing seat which is not immediately behind and on the same horizontal plane as a forward-facing high-backed seat.
2. **Non-protected seat** – not a front seat and the screen zones within the protected area have a combined surface of less than 800 sq.cm.
3. **Urban bus** – a bus designed for urban use with standing passengers.
4. **Community Directives or ECE Regulations** (in item 2 of the table overleaf) means
    - Community Directive 76/115, 81/575, 82/318, 90/629 or 96/38, or
    - ECE Regulation 14, 14.04 or 14.05

    whether or not those instruments apply to the vehicle
5. **Specified passenger seat** means the forward-facing front seat alongside the driver or, if there is more than 1 such seat, the 1 furthest away. If there are no seats as above, the foremost forward-facing front passenger seat furthest from the driver (unless there is a fixed partition in front of it).

Part 1: Construction and use 55

SEAT BELT ANCHORAGE POINTS
ROAD VEHICLES (CONSTRUCTION AND USE) REGULATIONS 1986, REG.46

Item	Description of Vehicle	Seats for which anchorage points must be fitted (mandatory)	Installation Requirement
1	Any vehicle first used before 1.4.82	Driver's seat and specified passenger seat (if any)	Designed to hold seat belts securely in position
2	Minibus constructed or adapted to carry not more than 12 in addition to driver, motor ambulance or motor caravan, in any case first used on or after 1.4.82 but before 1.10.88	As item 1	In accordance with Community Directives or ECE Regulations
3	Minibus (not falling within items 7 or 8) with gross weight not over 3500kg, motor ambulance or motor caravan, in any case first used on or after 1.10.88	Driver's seat and each forward-facing front seat	As item 2
4	Goods vehicle first used on or after 1.10.88 but before 1.10.01 with gross weight over 3500kg	As item 3	2 or 3 anchorage points to hold seat belts securely.
5	Goods vehicle first used on or after 1.10.01 with gross weight over 3500kg	All forward-facing front seats	In accordance with Community Directive 96/38 or ECE Reg. 14.04 or 14.05
6	Coach first used on or after 1.10.88 but before 1.10.01	All exposed forward-facing seats	As item 2 or, if fitted before 1.10.01 and forming part of a seat, must not become detached from the seat when horizontal force is applied
7	Bus (other than urban bus) with gross weight over 3500kg and first used on or after 1.10.01	Every forward-facing and rearward-facing seat	As item 5
8	As item 7 but with weight not exceeding 3500kg	As item 7	As item 5
9	Passenger or dual purpose vehicle (other than a bus) first used on or after 1.4.82 and not falling within items 2 to 8	Every forward-facing seat constructed or adapted for not more than 1 adult	As item 2
10	Vehicle (other than a bus) first used on or after 1.4.82 and not falling within items 2 to 9	Every forward-facing front seat and every non-protected seat	As item 2

Where a vehicle to which this regulation applies is fitted with non-mandatory anchorage points, those points must comply with the requirements applicable to mandatory anchorage points, unless they are –
- anchorage points fitted to a mini bus before 1.4.86, or
- anchorage points fitted to any other vehicle before 1.10.88

SEAT BELTS - FITTING
ROAD VEHICLES (CONSTRUCTION AND USE) REGULATIONS 1986, REG.47

This regulation applies to every vehicle to which Reg.46 applies (see previous pages for application and definitions).

Seat belts must be provided in accordance with the following table:

Vehicle (reference to an item means an item in the table on the previous page)	Requirement
First used before 1.4.81	1. Adult body restraining seat belt for the driver's seat; and 2. Body restraining seat belt for specified passenger seat (if any)
First used on or after 1.4.81	3-point belts for the driver's seat and the specified passenger seat (if any).

Item 9 or 10 first used on or after 1.4.87	In addition to the item above,
	1. For any forward-facing front seat alongside the driver's seat, not being a specified passenger seat, a 3-point belt, lap belt or disabled person's belt;
	2. If a passenger or dual purpose vehicle having not more than 2 forward-facing seats behind the driver's seat must have either –
	  (A) an inertia reel belt for at least 1 of those seats, or
	  (B) a 3-point belt, a lap belt, a disabled person's belt or a child restraint for each seat;
	3. If a passenger or dual purpose vehicle having more than 2 forward-facing seats behind the driver's seat, must have either –
	  (A) an inertia reel belt for 1 of those 2 seats being an out board seat and a 3-point belt, a lap belt, a disabled person's belt or a child restraint for at least one other of those seats;
	  (B) a 3-point belt for 1 of those seats and either a child restraint or a disabled person's belt for at least one other of those seats; or
	  (C) a 3-point belt, a lap belt, a disabled persons belt or a child restraint for each of those seats.

Item 3	1. For the driver's seat and the specified passenger seat (if any) a 3-point belt; and 2. For any forward-facing front seat which is not a specified passenger seat, a 3-point belt or a lap belt.
Item 6	3-point belts, lap belts, or disabled person's belts.
Item 5	1. For the driver's seat, a 3-point belt or a lap belt; and 2. For every other forward-facing front seat, a 3-point belt, a lap belt, or a disabled person's belt.
Item 7	For every forward-facing and rearward-facing seat, an inertia ree belt; a retractable lap belt; a disabled person's belt, or a child restraint
Item 8	For every forward-facing seat, an inertia reel belt, a disabled person's belt, or a child restraint; For every rearward-facing seat, an inertia reel belt, a retractable lap belt, a disabled person's belt, or a child restraint.

Part 1: Construction and use 57

SEAT BELTS - FITTING cont
ROAD VEHICLES (CONSTRUCTION AND USE) REGULATIONS 1986, REG. 47

Exemptions
The requirement to fit seat belts in accordance with this regulation do not apply
- to a vehicle while it is being used under a trade licence;
- to a vehicle to which Type Approval Regs. do not apply and the vehicle is being delivered from the manufacturer, distributor or dealer to a distributor, dealer, purchaser or hirer.
- to a seat in relation to which there is a seat belt
    - (i) bearing the mark BS AU 183: 1983 and 'kite' mark,
    - (ii) which comprises a lap belt and shoulder straps bearing the mark BS 3254: 1960 or BS 3254; Part 1: 1988 and 'kite' mark or approval mark,
    - (iii) the standard of which corresponds with BS AU 183:1983, or
    - (iv) which is an adult belt comprising a lap belt and shoulder straps and which satisfies the standard referred to in (ii) above
- in relation to the driver's seat or the specified passenger's seat (if any) specially designed, constructed or adapted for a person suffering from a defect or disability
- to a vehicle to which item 4 of the table under 'Anchorage Points' applies.
- to a vehicle constructed or adapted for the transport of prisoners, in relation to seats for persons other than the driver and any front seat passenger provided those seats have anchorage points.

Padding
Where a lap belt is fitted to a forward-facing front seat of a minibus, motor ambulance or motor caravan, or to an exposed forward-facing seat of a coach (other than the driver's seat) either
1. at least 50mm padding shall be provided for any bar and any screen or partition which would be likely to be struck by the head of a passenger wearing the lap belt in the event of an accident, or
2. the requirements of Annex 4 of ECE Reg. 21 shall be met in respect of any such bar, screen or partition

but padding will not be required by (1) above on any surface more than 1m from the backrest or more than 150mm to either side or on any instrument panel of a minibus.

Securing to anchorage points
Seat belts must be secured to the anchorage points or, in the case of a child restraint, to specially provided anchorage points or, in the case of a disabled person's belt first fitted before 1.10.01, secured to the vehicle or to the seat being occupied.

BS Mark
Every seat belt except
1. a disabled person's seat belt
2. a seat belt bearing such marks as are mentioned above
3. an adult seat belt or a child restraint that satisfies the requirements of a standard corresponding to the appropriate British Standard (recognised as such by any EEA State)

shall be legibly and permanently marked either with a BS mark or with an EC Component Type-Approval Mark.

58 The Traffic Officer's Companion

SEAT BELTS AND ANCHORAGE POINTS – MAINTENANCE
ROAD VEHICLES (CONSTRUCTION AND USE) REGULATIONS 1986, REG. 48

This regulation applies to all seat belts and anchorage points which are required to be provided by Regs 46 and 47 of these regulations.

Use of anchorage points
Anchorage points for seat belts must only be used for anchorages for the seat belts for which they are intended to be used or are capable of being used.

Integral seat belts
Where a seat incorporates integral belt anchorages, the term 'anchorages' includes the system by which the seat assembly itself is secured to the vehicle structure.

The following maintenance requirements will not apply if the requirement ceased to be complied with after the start of that journey and steps have been taken for such compliance to be restored with all reasonable expedition.

Vehicle structure
All load-bearing members of the vehicle structure or panelling within 30 cms of each anchorage point shall be maintained in a sound condition and free from serious corrosion, distortion or fracture.

Adjusting device
The adjusting device and any retracting mechanism of the seat belt shall be so maintained that the belt may be readily adjusted to the body of the wearer, according to its design.

General defects
The seat belt, anchorages, fastenings and adjusting device shall be maintained free from any obvious defect which would be likely to adversely affect its performance.

Buckles, etc.
The buckle or other fastening of the seat belt shall be
- so maintained that it can be readily fastened or unfastened
- kept free from any temporary or permanent obstruction, and
- readily accessible to a person sitting in the seat (except in the case of a disabled person's seat belt)

Seat belt material
The webbing or other material which forms the seat belt shall be maintained free from cuts or other visible faults which would be likely to adversely affect its performance.

Securing to anchorages
The ends of every seat belt, other than a disabled person's seat belt, shall be securely fastened to the anchorage points.

Disabled person's seat belt
The ends of such belts when in use shall be securely fastened either to the structure of the vehicle or to the occupied seat so that the body would be restrained in the event of an accident.

Part 1: Construction and use **59**

SEAT BELTS – MINIBUSES AND COACHES REG 48A

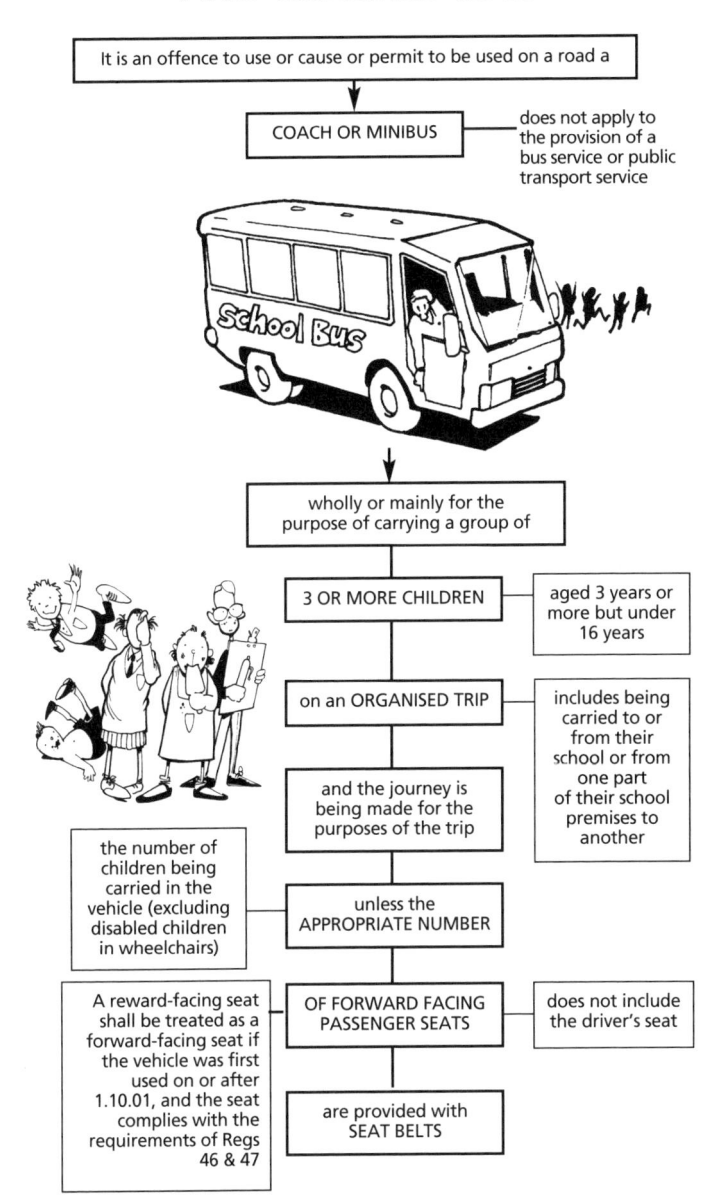

It is an offence to use or cause or permit to be used on a road a

↓

COACH OR MINIBUS — does not apply to the provision of a bus service or public transport service

↓

wholly or mainly for the purpose of carrying a group of

↓

3 OR MORE CHILDREN — aged 3 years or more but under 16 years

↓

on an **ORGANISED TRIP** — includes being carried to or from their school or from one part of their school premises to another

↓

and the journey is being made for the purposes of the trip

↓

the number of children being carried in the vehicle (excluding disabled children in wheelchairs) — unless the **APPROPRIATE NUMBER**

↓

A reward-facing seat shall be treated as a forward-facing seat if the vehicle was first used on or after 1.10.01, and the seat complies with the requirements of Regs 46 & 47 — **OF FORWARD FACING PASSENGER SEATS** — does not include the driver's seat

↓

are provided with **SEAT BELTS**

SEAT BELTS – WEARING BY ADULTS

MOTOR VEHICLES (WEARING OF SEAT BELTS) REGULATIONS 1993

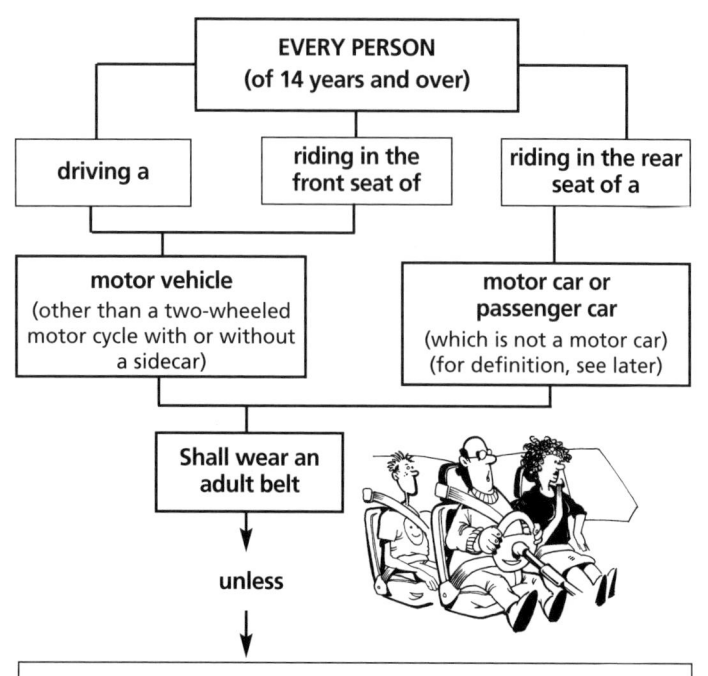

EVERY PERSON (of 14 years and over)

- **driving a**
- **riding in the front seat of**
- **riding in the rear seat of a**

motor vehicle (other than a two-wheeled motor cycle with or without a sidecar)

motor car or passenger car (which is not a motor car) (for definition, see later)

Shall wear an adult belt

unless

- delivering/collecting mail or goods on local rounds in vehicle constructed/adapted for that purpose
- driving examiner
- fire or police purposes or carrying person in custody
- holding a medical certificate
- no adult belt available
- private hire driver carrying passengers for hire
- procession commonly or customarily held, or notified under Public Order Act *(not applicable in Scotland)*
- procession organised by the Crown
- reversing (includes qualified driver supervising a learner)
- taxi driver while taxi being used as such
- trade licence while vehicle fault being investigated or remedied
- wearing of disabled person's belt by disabled person.

Part 1: Construction and use **61**

SEAT BELTS – WEARING BY CHILDREN IN FRONT SEATS

MOTOR VEHICLES (WEARING OF SEAT BELTS BY CHILDREN IN FRONT SEATS) REGULATIONS 1993, AND SECTION 15 ROAD TRAFFIC ACT 1988

A person must not without reasonable excuse

↓

drive on a road

a motor vehicle

↓

in the front of which is a child under 14 years

↓

unless the child is wearing a child restraint

except

- A child of three years or more where a child restraint is not available in the front or rear and the child is wearing an adult belt.
- Child holding a medical certificate.
- Child under 1 year in a carry cot restrained by the straps.
- Disabled child wearing disabled person's belt.
- Vehicle first used before 1.1.65 if there is no rear seat and no seat other then the driver's is provided with an appropriate belt.
- Vehicle providing a local service and is not a motor car or passenger car *(see previous page)*.

SEAT BELTS – WEARING BY CHILDREN IN REAR SEATS

MOTOR VEHICLES (WEARING OF SEAT BELTS) REGS 1993, AND S 15 RTA 1988

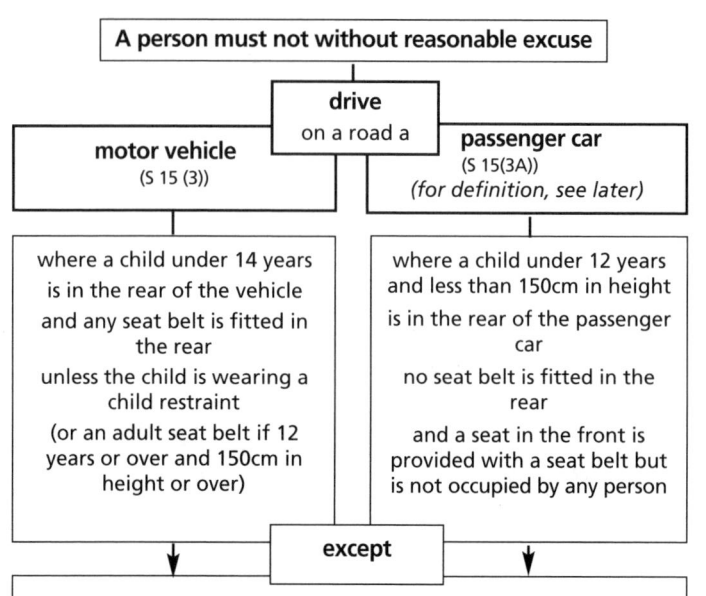

A person must not without reasonable excuse **drive** on a road a **motor vehicle** (S 15 (3)) or **passenger car** (S 15(3A)) *(for definition, see later)*

motor vehicle (S 15(3)): where a child under 14 years is in the rear of the vehicle and any seat belt is fitted in the rear unless the child is wearing a child restraint (or an adult seat belt if 12 years or over and 150cm in height or over)

passenger car (S 15(3A)): where a child under 12 years and less than 150cm in height is in the rear of the passenger car no seat belt is fitted in the rear and a seat in the front is provided with a seat belt but is not occupied by any person

except

- a child under 1 year in a carry cot restrained by the straps
- a child of 3 years or more for whom a child restraint is not available in the front or rear and who is wearing an adult belt
- disabled child wearing disabled person's belt
- holder of a medical certificate
- licensed taxis and licensed hire cars in which (in each case) the rear seats are separated from the driver, eg fixed partitions
- vehicles which are neither motor cars nor passenger cars

exceptions only applicable to S 15(3)

- a child under 12 years and less than 150cm in height if no appropriate seat belt is available in a passenger car in the front or rear (or in a vehicle other than a passenger car if no appropriate belt is available in the rear)
- a child 12 years or over and 150cm in height or over in any vehicle if no appropriate belt is available in the rear

exception only available to S 15(3A)

- a child for whom no appropriate belt is available in the front

SEAT BELTS – DEFINITIONS

PASSENGER CAR
A passenger car is a motor vehicle which:
- is constructed or adapted for the carriage of passengers and is not a goods vehicle;
- has no more than 8 seats in addition to the driver's;
- has 4 or more wheels;
- has a maximum design speed exceeding 25 km per hour; and
- has a maximum laden weight not exceeding 3.5 tonnes.

SECTION 15 ROAD TRAFFIC ACT 1988

AVAILABLE
A seat belt will be regarded as being available unless:
- another person is wearing the relevant belt;
- a child is occupying the relevant seat and wearing a child restraint which is an appropriate child restraint for that child;
- another person, being a person holding a medical certificate, is occupying the relevant seat;
- a disabled person (not being the person in question) is occupying the relevant seat and wearing a disabled person's belt;
- by reason of his disability, it would not be practicable for the person in question to wear the relevant belt;
- the person in question is prevented from occupying the relevant seat by the presence of a carry cot which is restrained by straps and in which there is a child aged under 1 year, unless the carry cot could reasonably have been carried and restrained in another part of the vehicle;
- the person in question is prevented from occupying the relevant seat by the presence of child restraint which could not readily be removed without the aid of tools; or
- the relevant seat is specially designed so that –
  (i) its configuration can be adjusted in order to increase the space in the vehicle available for goods or personal effects, and
  (ii) when it is so adjusted the seat cannot be used as such, and the configuration is adjusted in the manner described in sub-paragraph (i) and it would not be reasonably practicable for the goods and personal effects being carried in the vehicle to be so carried were configuration not so adjusted.

SCHED 2 MOTOR VEHICLES (WEARING OF SEAT BELTS) REGULATIONS 1993

MIRRORS

REG 33 ROAD VEHICLES (CONSTRUCTION AND USE) REGULATIONS 1986

	Type of vehicle	Requirement
1	Motor vehicle drawing a trailer and a person carried thereon has an uninterrupted view to the rear, and can communicate with the driver regarding the signals of other vehicles Works truck Track-laying agricultural vehicle } If driver has a view to the rear Wheeled agricultural vehicle first used before 1.6.78 Pedestrian-controlled vehicle Chassis driven to receive body Agricultural motor vehicle within unladen weight exceeding 7,370kg and is either track-laying or is wheeled and first used before 1.6.78	No requirement
2	Motor vehicle not mentioned in item 1 which is – i. a wheeled locomotive or motor tractor first used on or after 1.6.78 ii. agricultural motor vehicle not being track-laying UW not exceeding 7,370kg (see item 8) or a wheeled agricultural vehicle first used after 1.6.86 which is driven in excess of 20mph (see item 6)	At least one mirror fitted externally on the offside
3	Wheeled motor vehicle not mentioned in item 1 first used on or after 1.4.83 which is – (A) a bus; or (B) a goods vehicle with max gross weight exceeding 3,500kg (not being an agricultural vehicle or one which is driven at more than 20mph) other than a vehicle in item 4	(a) One mirror externally on offside; and (b) one mirror internally, unless not providing rear view; and (c) one mirror externally on nearside unless adequate internal one is fitted
4	Goods vehicle not being an agricultural vehicle with max gross weight exceeding 12,000kg first used on or after 1.10.88	One left and one right main mirror, one wide angle mirror and one close-proximity mirror
5	2-wheeled motor cycle with or without sidecar	No requirement
6	Wheeled motor vehicle not in items 1 - 5 first used on or after 1.6.78 (or if Ford Transit, 10.7.78)	(a) One mirror externally on offside; and (b) one mirror internally, unless not providing rear view; (c) and one externally on nearside unless adequate internal one is fitted
7	Wheeled motor vehicle not in items 1 - 5 first used before 1.6.78 (if ford transit 10.7.78) and track laying not being agricultural first used on or after 1.1.58 which is in either case – i. a bus; ii. DPV; or iii. goods vehicle	One mirror externally on offside and one either internally, or externally on nearside
8	Motor vehicle, wheeled or track-laying not in items 1 - 7 above	One internally or externally

MIRRORS – FITTING AND USE

REG 33 ROAD VEHICLES (CONSTRUCTION AND USE) REGULATIONS 1986

Requirement	Type of vehicle
Each exterior mirror shall, if the vehicle has a maximum permissible weight exceeding 3500kg, be a class 11 mirror and shall in any other case be a class 11 or 111 mirror	Vehicle in item 2 or 6 on preceding page
The edges of any internal mirror shall be surrounded by some material such as will render it unlikely that severe cuts would be caused if the mirror or material were struck by an occupant of the vehicle	Wheeled motor vehicle in item **1, 2, 7 or 8** *(on preceding page)* and first used on or after 1.4.69
Each mirror to be fixed so that it remains steady under normal driving conditions; Each exterior mirror on a vehicle fitted with windows to be visible to the driver through a side window or part of the windscreen swept by the wiper. If bottom edge of a mirror is less than 2m above the road surface when the vehicle is laden the mirror shall not project more than 20cm from the side of the vehicle (or trailer, when drawn, if wider). Interior mirrors must be capable of being adjusted from driving position. Unless the mirror is of a type which automatically adjusts itself when knocked out of alignment, each exterior mirror shall be capable or being adjusted by the driver from the driving position (but may be of a type which can be locked in position from outside the vehicle)	Wheeled vehicle in item 1 if first used on or after 1.6.78; Vehicle in item 5 if first used on or after 1.10.78; Vehicle in item 6 *(see previous page)*

Instead of complying with these requirements, vehicles may comply with the corresponding EC Directive	'Mirror' means a mirror to assist the driver of a vehicle to become aware of traffic: (a) internal – to the rear; and (b) external – rearwards on that side

VISION

View to the front (REG. 30)

Every motor vehicle shall be designed and constructed so that the driver can at all times have a full view of the road and traffic ahead of the vehicle.

All glass or other transparent material shall be maintained in such condition that it does not obscure the vision of the driver while the vehicle is being driven on a road.

Transmission of light

Windows and windscreens which are required to be fitted must be capable of transmitting light not less than-

motor vehicles first used before 1.4.85, 70% for all windows,

motor vehicles first used on or after 1.4.85 and trailers, 75% for windscreens and 70% for all other windows.

Windscreen Wipers and Washers (REG 34)

Every vehicle fitted with a windscreen shall, unless the driver can see to the front without looking through the windscreen, be fitted with one or more efficient **automatic windscreen wipers** capable of clearing the screen so the driver can see the road in front on both sides of the vehicle and the front.

Every wheeled vehicle required to be fitted as above, must also have a windscreen washer capable of clearing mud etc (except agricultural vehicles first used on or after 1.6.86 driven at not more than 20mph; track laying vehicles; vehicles with max speed not over 20mph; or local transport service vehicles).

Glass (REG 32)

Caravans first used on or after 1.9.78 and wheeled motor vehicles and trailers first used on or after 1.6.78 shall have windows as follows:

WINDOWS	REQUIREMENT
Windscreens and other windows wholly or partly on either side of the driver's seat.	Glass complying with British Standard Specification or ECE Regulations and bearing the relevant marking.
All other windows, windscreens of motor cycles, temporary replacements for windscreens or windows wholly or partly in front of or on either side of the driver's seat.	Materials other than glass which is so constructed or treated that if fractured it does not fly into fragments likely to cause severe cuts.
Screen or door in interior of a bus first used on or after 1.4.88.	Either of the above.
Police or security vehicles, engineering plant, etc; upper deck of buses; roof windows.	Either of the above or safety glass.

SMOKE

REG 61 ROAD VEHICLES (CONSTRUCTION AND USE) REGULATIONS 1986

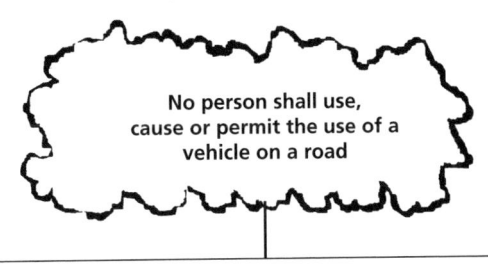

No person shall use, cause or permit the use of a vehicle on a road

---

if the engine is not so maintained that **vapours or gases** in the engine crank case or in other parts of the engine are prevented from **escaping into the atmosphere** otherwise than through the combustion chamber

---

if the fuel injection equipment, the engine speed governor or any other parts of the engine have in any way been **altered or adjusted** so as to **increase the emission of smoke**

---

from which any **smoke**, visible vapour, grit, sparks, ashes, cinders or oily substance is **emitted** if it causes or is likely to cause:

1. Damage to any property; or
2. Injury to any person who is, or may be reasonably expected to be on the road

---

if a device has been fitted which is designed to facilitate starting by causing the engine to be supplied with excess fuel, and the device is used while the vehicle is in motion – in addition, the device must not be operable by a person inside the vehicle.

In addition to the above generalisations, the reader is advised to consult the specific regulations in view of complexities recently introduced regarding types of vehicles involved, exemptions, dates of manufacture/first use, alternative compliance with EC provisions, and separate rules introduced for vehicles first used after 1.1.2001

SPECIAL TYPES VEHICLES

MOTOR VEHICLES (AUTHORISATION OF SPECIAL TYPES) GENERAL ORDER 1979

Special Types Orders may give exemption for certain vehicles as to compliance with C&U Regulations provided certain conditions are fulfilled.

The specific regulations from which exemption is given, together with the conditions to be met, are referred to in the following sections:

VEHICLE TYPE	SECTION
Naval, military, air force and aviation vehicles	A
Grass cutting machines and hedge trimmers	B
Track laying vehicles	C
Pedestrian controlled road maintenance vehicles	D
Vehicles used for experiments or trials	E
Straddle carriers	F
Wide agricultural vehicles	G
Agricultural vehicles with front or rear projections	H
Vehicles for moving excavated material	J
Vehicles for carrying or drawing abnormal indivisible loads	K
Other vehicles carrying loads exceeding 4.3 metres in width	L
Engineering plant	M
Vehicles propelled by natural gas	N
Vehicles constructed for use outside the UK or new or improved vehicles or equipment for test or trial	P

Part 1: Construction and use **69**

SPECIAL TYPES VEHICLES

NAVAL, MILITARY, AIR FORCE AND AVIATION VEHICLES (ART 6)

(A)

Type of vehicle	Exemption	Vehicle belonging to or under the control of
• Combat vehicles or trailers constructed for training in connection with combat. • Constructed for use in connection with instruments of war. • Motor vehicles or trailers constructed for carriage of tanks.	All C&U Regulations	Secretary of State for Defence or Industry, or any contractor or sub contractor making such vehicles for Secretary of State.
Motor vehicles or trailers for search lights and associated equipment.	Springs.	
Motor vehicles or trailers constructed for carriage of aircraft or aircraft parts.	Length, width of heavy motor car, overhang, width of trailer, lateral projection.	
Heavy motor cars and trailers constructed for use, and used only for flying operations, where additional width is necessary for equipment.	Width of heavy motor car and trailer.	
Motor tractors, heavy motor cars and trailers constructed before 1.1.49.	Width, overhang, trailer brakes.	Secretary of State for Defence or Industry.
Aircraft drawn by motor vehicles.	Springs, length, width and trailer brakes.	Secretary of State for Defence.
Motor vehicles and trailers used for generating equipment for military purposes.	Width, length, weight.	Minister of Transport.

70 The Traffic Officer's Companion

SPECIAL TYPES VEHICLES

(B)

GRASS CUTTING MACHINES AND HEDGE TRIMMERS (ARTS 7 & 9)

Motor vehicles constructed or adapted for use as grass cutters or hedge trimmers (not pedestrian controlled)

↓

need not comply with Reg 8 of the C&U Regs (Maximum Width) provided:

↓

- all other relevant C&U requirements are complied with
- overall width of vehicle, together with any equipment mounted on it, except when actually operating, shall not exceed 2.55 metres
- except when actually operating, all blades fitted or mounted shall be effectively guarded so that no danger is caused or likely to be caused to any person.

Trailers constructed or adapted for use as grass cutters or hedge trimmers

↓

need not comply with any C&U Regs applicable to trailers other than Reg 27 (Tyres) provided:

↓

weight	its UW must not exceed 1,020kg if drawn by a locomotive, motor tractor or heavy motor car, or 815kg in any other case;
width	• overall width of the drawing vehicle is not to exceed 2.6 metres, • overall width of the trailer, except when actually cutting grass, is not to exceed 2.6 metres, • overall width of the combination when being towed must not take up more than 2.6 metres of the road;
use	all cutting blades to be guarded so as not to be likely to cause danger, except when cutting grass etc;
speed	restricted to maximum speed of 20mph.

Part 1: Construction and use **71**

SPECIAL TYPES VEHICLES

TRACK LAYING VEHICLES (ART 5)

C

Track laying vehicles need not comply with C&U Regulations provided:

- used only for demonstration or to proceed to a railway station or port for shipment;
- consent in writing is obtained from every Highway Authority (or person responsible for the maintenance or repair) of any road on which it is proposed the vehicle shall be used;
- do not carry goods or burden for hire or reward;
- the drawing or launching of lifeboats is restricted to those owned by the RNLI.

PEDESTRIAN CONTROLLED ROAD MAINTENANCE VEHICLES (ART 10)

D

Pedestrian controlled road maintenance vehicles need not comply with the following C&U Regs:

- compensating arrangement for variation in wheel load REG 23
- parking brake REG 16
- brakes on motor tractors REG 16
- brakes on motor cycles REG 16

provided:

(a) all other C&U Regulations are complied with;
(b) weight of vehicle is not to exceed 410kg;
(c) must be capable of being brought to a standstill and held stationary, by brakes or otherwise.

72 The Traffic Officer's Companion

SPECIAL TYPES VEHICLES

VEHICLES USED FOR EXPERIMENTS OR TRIALS (ART 11)

E

If trials conducted under S 283
Highways Act 1980

↓

need not comply with any
of the C&U Regulations

STRADDLE CARRIERS (ART 12)

F

Straddled carriers are defined in C&Use Regulations as:

'a motor vehicle constructed to straddle and lift its load for purpose of transportation'.

They need not comply with the
following C&U Regulations:

↓

- springs.....................................REG 22
- direct mechanical brake ....REG 16
- vehicle plate ....REG 66
- power to weight ratio ....REG 45
- width of heavy motor car (2.5 m)..........REG 8
- overhang ....REG 11
- braking efficiencies ....REGS 16, 18
- maintenance of braking efficiencies ...REG 18

Provisions to be complied with:

↓

All other C&U requirements must be complied with.	
use	May only be used for demonstration, delivery following sale or for repairs. When so used, not to carry a load other than necessary gear and equipment.
speed	Speed restricted to 12mph.
width	Overall width not to exceed 2.9 metres.
length	Overall length of vehicle together with any load, if any, shall not exceed 9.2 metres, except with consent of Chief Officer of Police for each area in which it is proposed to be used. (Two days' notice to be given of vehicle, overall length, load carried and route proposed.)

Part 1: Construction and use **73**

SPECIAL TYPES VEHICLES

WIDE AGRICULTURAL VEHICLES (ARTS 13 & 13A) **G**

Wide agricultural vehicles, including:

- agricultural motor vehicles;
- agricultural trailers designed to perform functions other than carrying goods and, for the purpose of which, need to be over 2.55 metres wide;
- agricultural trailed appliances; and
- agricultural motor vehicles towing off-set agricultural trailer or trailed appliance which together exceed 2.55 metres wide – if width cannot be reduced without undue expense or risk of damage:

may be use on a road if the following conditions are complied with:

speed	if width exceeds 3.5 metres, maximum speed is 12mph. If width exceeds 2.55 metres maximum speed is 20mph.
notification	24 hours' notice must be given to the chief officer of police if width exceeds 3 metres and either: 1. the journey will be on a road where speed limit is 40mph or less, or 2. the distance to be covered will exceed 5 miles.
trailers	if motor vehicle (or combination of vehicle and trailer/appliance) exceeds 3 metres wide, no trailer (or other trailer) may be drawn except: 1. 2-wheeled trailer carrying equipment used on drawing vehicle; 2. agricultural trailed appliance; 3. harvester used with the drawing vehicle.
warning of danger	if width exceeds 3.5 metres a person other than the driver must warn people of any danger. The extremities of the vehicle shall be clearly visible to other road users in daylight and must be adequately lit in reduced visibility or darkness.
maximum width	in any case the width must not exceed 4.3 metres.

74 The Traffic Officer's Companion

SPECIAL TYPES VEHICLES (H)

AGRICULTURAL VEHICLES WITH FRONT OR REAR PROJECTIONS
(ART 13C)

This category, which includes:

- agricultural motor vehicles;
- agricultural trailers/trailed appliances with an agricultural implement rigidly mounted thereon (need not be permanent)

may be used on roads provided:

projection	condition to be complied with
1 metre	end of projection must be clearly visible to other road users. during the hours of darkness or reduced visibility, the lighting regulations must be complied with.
2 metres	projection markers provided *(see Part 3 later)*.
4 metres	projection markers provided *(see Part 3 later)*. notification to police as above.
6 metres	projection markers provided *(see Part 3 later)*. notification to police as above. person to warn of danger as above.

Part 1: Construction and use **75**

SPECIAL TYPES VEHICLES (J)
VEHICLES FOR MOVING EXCAVATED MATERIAL (ART 15)

This category, which includes:

heavy motor cars; trailers; or articulated vehicles specially designed and constructed for use on private premises for moving excavated material and fitted with tipping body, moving platform or other similar device;

are exempt from C&U Regs listed on the following page provided:

use	Only used going to and from private premises, or to and from a port, and shall not carry a load other than necessary gear and equipment.
trailer	1. If a heavy motor car not forming part of an articulated vehicle, shall not draw a trailer. 2. Where a trailer is drawn by motor vehicle, no other trailer may be drawn.

width	1. If width exceeds 5 metres, then:
	   a. journey must be in accordance with a written notice of the minister or the directions of the chief officer of police; and
	   b. notice of minister or police must be carried on the vehicle.
	2. if width exceeds 3.5 metres at least one attendant is required to tend the vehicle, load and give warning of danger. If three or more vehicles are travelling in convoy, only the first and last need an attendant.
	3. if width exceeds 2.9 metres, two days' notice is required by chief of police regarding particulars of vehicle, overall width, and time, date and route.

brakes	In the case of a trailer (whether articulated or not), provided an efficient brake or device to hold it stationary is fitted, the braking requirements of regulation 75 need not be complied with.
length	The overall length of a trailer shall not exceed 8.54 metres, and that of an articulated vehicle shall not exceed 13.4 metres.
speed	speed is restricted to 12mph other than on a motorway.
tyres	must have pneumatic tyres.
weight	If any weight regulation is contravened, two days' notice must be given to Highways Authority together with an indemnity. If a heavy motor car not forming part of articulated vehicle, or if an articulated vehicle, max weight transmitted by any 2 wheels in line transversely shall not exceed 22,860kg, and sum of weight transmitted by all wheels shall not exceed 50,800kg.

SPECIAL TYPES VEHICLES

VEHICLES FOR MOVING EXCAVATED MATERIAL – REGULATIONS FROM WHICH EXEMPT (ART 15)

J *(cont)*

> **A heavy motor car not forming part of articulated vehicle**
> is exempt from the following Regulations:

- braking efficiencies ....Regs 16,18
- laden weight...Regs 75, 76
- maintenance of brakes ....Reg 18 (except (1)(a))
- mechanical brake..Reg 16
- power to weight ratio..Reg 45
- springs..Reg 22
- vehicle plate ....Reg 66
- wheel ....Regs 93
- width (2.5 metres)..Reg 8
- wings ....Reg 63

> **A trailer not forming part of articulated vehicle**
> is exempt from the following Regulations:

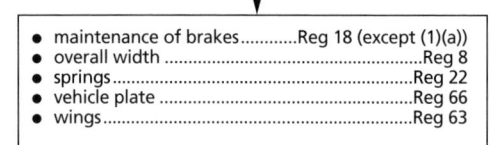

- maintenance of brakes............Reg 18 (except (1)(a))
- overall width ....Reg 8
- springs..Reg 22
- vehicle plate ....Reg 66
- wings ....Reg 63

> **An articulated vehicle**
> is exempt from the following Regulations:

- overall length ....Reg 7
- springs..Reg 22
- mechanical brake..Reg 16
- vehicle plate ....Reg 66
- power to weight ratio..Reg 45
- width (2.5 metres)..Reg 8
- brake efficiencies..Regs 16, 18
- wings ....Reg 63
- overall width ....Reg 8
- wings ....Reg 63
- laden weight...Regs 75, 77
- weight ....Reg 79
- maintenance of brakes.......................................Reg18

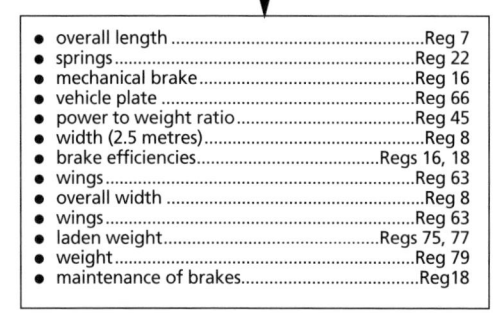

(K) SPECIAL TYPES VEHICLES
VEHICLES CARRYING OR DRAWING ABNORMAL LOADS
(ART 18)

Vehicles carrying or drawing an abnormal load are exempt from the below requirements provided the conditions on facing page are met: ---> Vehicles must comply with the conditions of an appropriate category:

Total weight of vehicle not exceeding	Category (see table below)
46,000kg	**Category 1**
80,000kg	**Category 2**
150,000kg	**Category 3**

Type of vehicle	Regulations exempt from	
Heavy motor car manufactured before 1.10.89	Springs	REG 22
	Parking brake	REG 16
	Power to weight ratio	REG 45
	Width	REG 8
	Brakes	REGS 15,18 (except 18(1))
	Tyres	REG 24
	Tyre loads and speed ratings	REG 25
	Wings	REG 63
	Weight	REGS 75-80
	Width of load	REG 82
	Number of trailers	REG 83(1)
Locomotive or tractor manufactured before 1.10.89	Springs	REG 22
	Tyre loads and speed ratings	REG 25
	Power to weight ratio	REG 45
	Width	REG 8
	Weight of vehicle & trailer	REGS 75(3), 76
Trailer manufactured before 1.10.89	Length	REG 7
	Springs	REG 22
	Diameter of wheels	REG 21
	Width	REG 8
	Brakes	REGS 15,18 (except 18(1))
	Tyres	REG 24
	Tyre loads and speed ratings	REG 25
	Wings	REG 63
	Spray suppression	REG 64
	Weight	REGS 75-80
	Width of load	REG 82
	Number of trailers	REG 83(1)
Category 1: vehicle or combination of vehicles whenever manufactured	Length	REG 7
	Width	REG 8
	Weight	REG 80
	Width of load	REG 82
Categories 2 and 3: vehicle or combination of vehicles manufactured after 1.10.89	Length	REG 7
	Width	REG 8
	Brakes	REGS 15,16,18 (except 18(1))
	Tyre loads and speed ratings	REG 25
	Power to weight ratio	REG 45
	Spray suppression	REGS 64,65
	Weight	REGS 75-80
	Width of load	REG 82
	Number of trailers	REG 83(1)

K SPECIAL TYPES VEHICLES

VEHICLES CARRYING OR DRAWING ABNORMAL LOADS cont (ART 18)

CONDITIONS				
Use	Must not use a bridge if there is another abnormal load using it. Must not remain stationary on a bridge.			
Width	Heavy motor car or trailer, locomotive or motor tractor	Not to exceed 2.9 metres unless the load can only be safely carried on a vehicle or trailer which exceeds that width		
	Any vehicle	Not to exceed 6.1 metres including any projections.		
Length	Not to exceed 27.4 metres.			
Tyres	Must be wheeled vehicle with soft or elastic or pneumatic tyres.			
Max speed		Motorway	Dual Carriageway	Other Roads
	Cat 2 (total weight not exceeding 80,000kg)	40	35	30
	Cat 3 (total weight not exceeding 150,000kg)	30	25	20
Plate	Category 2 and 3 vehicles manufactured after 1.10.88 must have a plate showing the maximum weights of the vehicle and marked 'SPECIAL TYPES USE'.			
Identification sign	The vehicle (or drawing vehicle in a combination) shall be fitted with a sign to indicate the category. The sign must be fitted vertically on the front facing forwards, in the following form: Sign: 400 mm wide × 250 mm tall, black background with "STGO" (105 mm) above "CAT 3" (70 mm) in white lettering. Note: the category number 3 is shown as an example; the number could be 1, 2 or 3 depending upon the category of the vehicle or combination of vehicles.			

for weight see following pages and for general conditions see General Conditions 1-5 (post)

Part 1: Construction and use **79**

SPECIAL TYPES VEHICLES
MAXIMUM WEIGHT OF ABNORMAL LOADS

REGS 75, 76, 78 AND 79, C&U REGULATIONS APPLY (WEIGHT). ARTICULATED VEHICLES WITH LESS THAN FIVE AXLES MUST ALSO COMPLY WITH REG 77 (MAX WEIGHT)

Category 1 (total weight not exceeding 46,000kg)
(maximum permitted laden, wheel and axle weights)

Articulated vehicles with five or more axles:

Distance between rearmost axle on tractive unit and rearmost axle on trailer (metres)	Max weight (kg)
At least 6.5	40,000
" 7.0	42,000
" 7.5	44,000
" 8.0	46,000

Where a semi-trailer has a group of 4 axles, the outermost of which are 3.25 metres apart or less and distance between any two is at least 0.87 metres, then the max weight for any one axle is 6,000kg.

Categories 2 (total weight not exceeding 80,000kg) and 3 (total weight not exceeding 150,000kg)

	Category 2	**Category 3**
Min number of axles	5	6
Max weight for any one axle	12,500kg	16,500kg
Max weight for any one wheel	6,250kg	8,250kg
Where distance between two adjacent axles is between 1.1m and 1.35m:		
Max weight for any one axle	12,000kg	15,000kg
Max weight for any one wheel	6,000kg	7,500kg
Min distance between two adjacent axles	1.1m	1.1m

SPECIAL TYPES VEHICLES
MAXIMUM WEIGHT OF ABNORMAL LOADS CONT (K)

REGS 75, 76, 78 AND 79, CONSTRUCTION AND USE REGS APPLY (WEIGHT). ARTICULATED VEHICLES WITH LESS THAN FIVE AXLES MUST ALSO COMPLY WITH REG 77 (MAX WEIGHT)

Categories 2 and 3 continued from previous page

	Category 2		**Category 3**	
	Distance between foremost and rearmost axles (metres)	**Max weight (kg)**	**Distance between foremost and rearmost axles (metres)**	**Max weight (kg)**
Total max weight	5.07 5.33 6.0 6.67 7.33 8.0 8.67 9.33 10.0 10.67	38,000 40,000 45,000 50,000 55,000 60,000 65,000 70,000 75,000 80,000	5.77 6.23 6.68 7.14 7.59 8.05 8.50 8.95 9.41 9.86 10.32 10.77 11.23 11.68 12.14	80,000 85,000 90,000 95,000 100,000 105,000 110,000 115,000 120,000 125,000 130,000 135,000 140,000 145,000 150,000
Max weight of a group of axles	Adjacent axles in group less than 2 m. and distance between groups is more than 2 metres	50,000	Adjacent axles in group less than 1.5 metres and distance between groups is more than 1.5 metres	100,000
			Distance between 2 axles in a group is less than 1.35 metres	90,000

Part 1: Construction and use **81**

SPECIAL TYPES VEHICLES
OTHER VEHICLES EXCEEDING 4.3 METRES IN WIDTH
(ART 20)

Vehicles plus any projection may exceed 4.3 metres in width provided:

- width does not exceed 6.1 metres.
- speed does not exceed 30mph on motorways, 25mph on dual carriageways or 20mph on other roads.
- conditions 1, 3 and 5 are complied with *(see later, General conditions)*
- all C&U Regulations are complied with except parts of Reg 82 (length of projections).

SPECIAL TYPES VEHICLES

ENGINEERING PLANT (ART 19)

M

Engineering plant is exempt from C&U Regulations — *other than the Regulations shown overleaf*

provided the conditions below are applied:

CONDITIONS	
speed	On roads other than motorways – 12mph. However, if the following conditions relating to abnormal loads under Article 18 (see earlier) are complied with, the speed limits are increased to the same as those applicable to abnormal loads under Article 18. The conditions are: weight; all C&U Regulations to be complied with except those from which Category 1, 2 or 3 vehicles are exempt; plate; and identification sign.
brakes	The vehicle and trailer shall be equipped with an efficient brake.
use	Only to proceed to or from, or when actually engaged in, engineering operations, demonstration, testing repair or maintenance.
load	No load except: engineering plant may carry materials for treatment whilst being carried, or which has been excavated by the vehicle's apparatus; and a mobile crane may transport or lift a load.
construction	Either wheeled or track-laying.
trailer	• Mobile cranes not allowed to draw a trailer. • Other engineering plant may draw engineering plant, an office hut or living van, unless vehicle exceeds 7.93 metres in width.
weight	Not to exceed 152,400kg.
length	Not to exceed 27.4 metres.
width	Not to exceed 6.1. metres.
plus	*General conditions, see later*

Part 1: Construction and use **83**

SPECIAL TYPES VEHICLES
ENGINEERING PLANT cont (ART 19)   Ⓜ

C&U Regulations which apply to engineering plant are:

- Compensating arrangement...................REG 23
- Dangerous parts, accessories and load....REG 100
- Gas containers ....REG 40
- General application ....REG 4
- Glass............................REGS 31, 32
- Maintenance of brakes ......REG 8
- Maintenance of glass........REG 30
- Maintenance of steering gear ....REG 29
- Marking of UW ....REG 10
- Noise ....REG 58
- Radio interference ....REG 60
- Silencer ....REG 54
- Smoke or vapour...............REG 61
- View to front ....REG 30
- Warning instrument ....REG 37
- Washers/wipers ....REGS 27, 28

SPECIAL TYPES VEHICLES
VEHICLES PROPELLED BY NATURAL GAS (ART 17A)

(N)

Construction and Use requirement which need not be complied with	Conditions to be complied with
Reg 40 Gas propulsion systems and gas-fired appliances to comply with Scheds 4 or 5 (security, pipe lines, unions, reducing valves, valves & cocks, pressure gauges, charging connections, trailers, etc) **Reg 94 (2)** restricted to using only liquefied petroleum gas. **Reg 94 (3)** gas container not to be carried on a trailer. **Reg 96** gas fired appliances restricted to engineering plant, a bus or refrigerated appliances and the same to comply with Sched. 5 (as above).	All other construction and use requirements. **Shed 5A of STGO:** suitability of container; capable of working pressure of 200 bar; undamaged; have isolation valve; not more than 30 years old; marked 'CNG ONLY'; specify month and year of expiry; date of testing; positioning; no leakage; ventilation; written information re-installation requirements, pressure relief devices, inspection intervals and inspection procedures; fitted with pressure relief devices; pipelines protected from heat vibration etc.; filling connectors to have flow-back prevention, dust cap and be outside the vehicle; regulators to be fitted; vehicle fitted with metal identification plate stating it is constructed or adapted to run on national gas and the maximum filling pressure. **Sched. 5B** – tested in accordance with requirements every 3 years.

SPECIAL TYPES VEHICLES
VEHICLES CONSTRUCTED FOR USE OUTSIDE THE UK OR NEW OR IMPROVED VEHICLES OR EQUIPMENT FOR TEST OR TRIAL (ART 16)

(P)

Applies to wheeled motor vehicles and trailers but not if covered in sections K or M (abnormal loads or engineering plant) which are motor vehicles and trailers

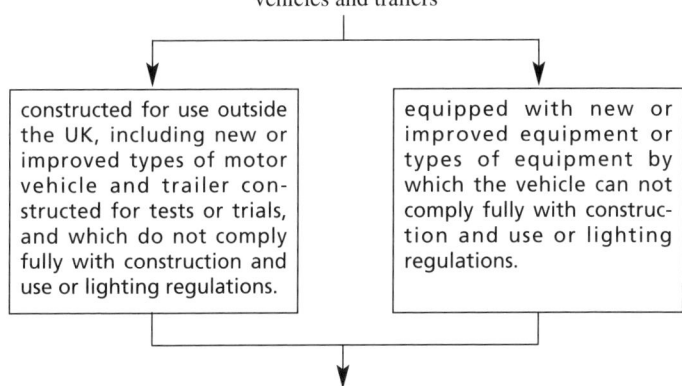

- constructed for use outside the UK, including new or improved types of motor vehicle and trailer constructed for tests or trials, and which do not comply fully with construction and use or lighting regulations.

- equipped with new or improved equipment or types of equipment by which the vehicle can not comply fully with construction and use or lighting regulations.

Provided the following provisions are complied with:

1986 Construction & Use Regs		1989 Lighting Regs	
Reg		Reg	
10	Indication of overall travelling height	11	Colour of lights (lamps & reflectors)
16	Braking systems	13	Lamps to show steady lights
18(1)	Maintenance & efficiency of brakes	16	Restriction on fitting blue warning beacons, special warning lamps, etc
20	Wheels & tracks		
27	Condition & maintenance of tyres	17	Obligatory warning beacons
29	Maintenance of steering gear	18	Obligatory lamps, reflectors, rear markings and devices (but not the markings of lamps etc; angles of visibility; dim-dip device or running lamp; nor positioning of lamps etc., which are allowed an extra 5% on minimum and maximum measurements)
30	View to front		
34	Windscreen wipers & washers		
37	Audible warning instruments		
53	Mascots		
54	Silencers		
61	Emissions		
62	Closets, etc		
81	Vehicles carrying wide or long loads		
82			
83	Number of trailers		

Continued on following page

86 The Traffic Officer's Companion

Provisions to be complied with (cont)			
1986 Construction & Use Regs		1989 Lighting Regs	
Reg		Reg	
84	Trailers drawn by motor cycles	19	Obstruction of certain lamps and reflectors
86	Distance between motor vehicle and trailers	21	Projecting trailers and vehicles carrying overhanging or projecting loads or equipment
89	Leaving trailers at rest		
90	Passengers in trailers		
92	Sidecars	22	Additional side marker lamps (But not the markings of lamps; angles of visibility; and the measurements for positioning of lamp is increased by 5% for both maximum and minimum measurements)
97	Excessive noise		
98	Stopping engine when stationary		
99	Use of warning instrument		
100	Maintenance & use so as not be be a danger		
101	Parking in darkness		
102	Passengers on motor cycles		
103	Obstruction		
104	Driver's control		
105	Opening of doors		
106	Reversing		
107	Leaving vehicle unattended		
108	Securing suspended implements		
109	TV sets		

OTHER CONDITIONS TO BE COMPILED WITH

The vehicle may only be used:
- (a) for testing or demonstration of the vehicle;
- (b) for delivery on sale;
- (c) for going to or from a manufacturer or repairer for construction, repair or overhaul; (The above 3 conditions will not apply if the vehicle is registered in the name of an approved person and used by him for the purpose of evaluating the vehicle; or the approved person has lent the vehicle for such purpose (S.I. 1998/2249))
- (d) by a person authorised by the Secretary of State, when the vehicle is registered in the name of that person, for the purpose of evaluation by himself or a borrower;
- (e) when not carrying a load except ballast etc, necessary for testing, etc. (unless all construction and use weight requirements are compiled with);
- (f) if width exceeds 2.9 metres or length exceeds that laid down in Reg 7 Construction & Use Regs, when 2 days' notice is given to the police and used in compliance with the agreed route and timings; or
- (g) if construction and use weights are not complied with, 2 days' notice is given to the highway or bridge authority.

GENERAL CONDITIONS

(ART 22) **CONDITION 1 – attendant to be carried if:**	
width	Of vehicle plus any projection exceeds 3.5 metres.
length	Of vehicle plus any projection exceeds 18.3 metres, or if the combination of vehicle and trailer plus any projection exceeds 25.9 metres.
projection	Exceeds 1.83 metres to the front or 3.5 metres to the rear.

(ART 23) **CONDITION 2 – marking of projections if:**	
Forward or rearward exceeding 1.83 metres.	In accordance with C&U Regulations *(see Projection markers, Part 3, later)*.
Rearward between 1.07 and 1.83 metres.	Rendered clearly visible.

(ART 25) **CONDITION 3 - two days' notice to police if:**	
width	Of vehicle and any projection exceeds 2.9 metres.
length	Of vehicle and any projection exceeds 18.3 metres.
	Of combination of vehicle and trailer plus any projection exceeds 25.9 metres.
projection	Forward or rearward exceeds 3.05 metres.
weight	Of combination of vehicle, trailer (if any) and load exceeds 80,000kg.

(ART 26) **CONDITION 4 – notification to highway authority**	
weights exceeds 80,000kg	Five days' notice, plus an indemnity must be given to Highway Authority.
C&U weight limits exceeded	Two days' notice, plus an indemnity must be given to Highway Authority.

(ART 24) **CONDITION 5 – approval of minister required in writing if width exceeds 5 metres.**

SIDEGUARDS

REG 51 ROAD VEHICLES (CONSTRUCTION AND USE) REGULATIONS 1986

The following vehicles are to be fitted with sideguards to give protection on any side of the vehicle – no sideguard to be outside vehicle's normal width nor more than 30 mm inboard of outer wall of rearmost tyre.

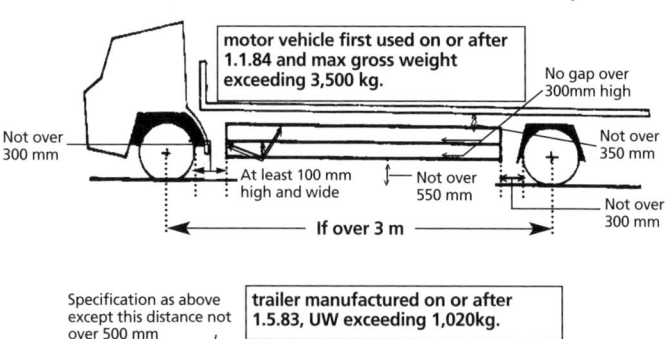

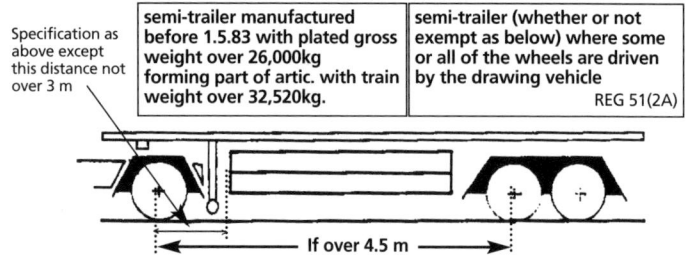

motor vehicle first used on or after 1.1.84 and max gross weight exceeding 3,500 kg.

- Not over 300 mm
- No gap over 300mm high
- Not over 350 mm
- At least 100 mm high and wide
- Not over 550 mm
- Not over 300 mm
- If over 3 m

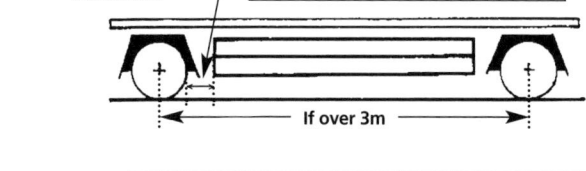

trailer manufactured on or after 1.5.83, UW exceeding 1,020kg.

Specification as above except this distance not over 500 mm

If over 3m

semi-trailer manufactured before 1.5.83 with plated gross weight over 26,000kg forming part of artic. with train weight over 32,520kg.

semi-trailer (whether or not exempt as below) where some or all of the wheels are driven by the drawing vehicle
REG 51(2A)

Specification as above except this distance not over 3 m

If over 4.5 m

Exemptions

- Incapable of over 15mph on flat
- Agricultural trailer
- Engineering plant
- Fire engine
- Agricultural motor vehicle
- Rear and side tippers
- Defence
- Chassis for testing or fitting
- Used for fitting sideguards
- Street cleaning etc
- Trailer for lengthy beams etc
- Articulated tractive unit
- Vehicle for carrying vehicles
- Trailers not over 750mm high
- Trailer temporarily in GB within 12 months of entry

Shall be maintained free from any defect likely to affect effectiveness.
REG 52

Part 1: Construction and use **89**

REARGUARDS

REG 49 ROAD VEHICLES (CONSTRUCTION AND USE) REGULATIONS 1986

Rearguards generally consists of a cross-member and linking components connected to the chassis side-members or whatever replaces them.

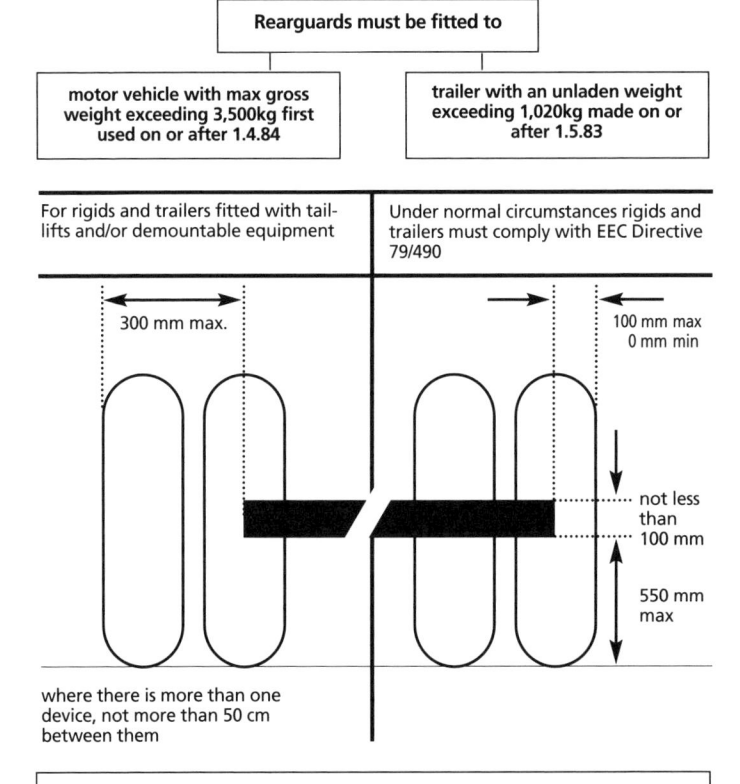

Rearguards must be fitted to
- motor vehicle with max gross weight exceeding 3,500kg first used on or after 1.4.84
- trailer with an unladen weight exceeding 1,020kg made on or after 1.5.83

For rigids and trailers fitted with tail-lifts and/or demountable equipment

300 mm max.

where there is more than one device, not more than 50 cm between them

Under normal circumstances rigids and trailers must comply with EEC Directive 79/490

100 mm max
0 mm min

not less than 100 mm

550 mm max

Rearguards need not be fitted to

- Incapable of over 15mph on flat
- Articulated tractive unit
- Engineering plant
- Fire engine
- Agricultural motor vehicle
- Agricultural trailer
- Road spreader
- Rear tipper
- Defence
- Chassis for testing or fitting
- For fitting guards
- For carrying other vehicles
- Trailer for lengthy beams etc
- Tail lifts over one metre long
- Concrete carrier/mixer
- Trailer temp. in GB within 12 months of entry

Must be maintained free from any obvious defect which would be likely to adversely affect performance in the event of an impact from the rear.
REG 50

SPRAY SUPPRESSION DEVICES

REG 64 ROAD VEHICLES (CONSTRUCTION AND USE) REGULATIONS 1986

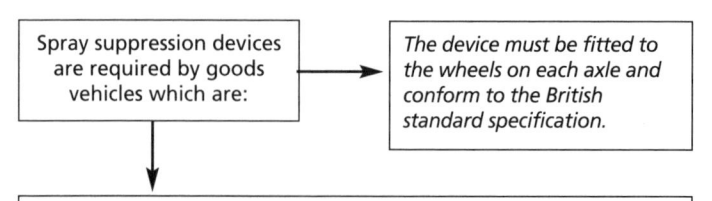

Spray suppression devices are required by goods vehicles which are: → *The device must be fitted to the wheels on each axle and conform to the British standard specification.*

1. motor vehicles first used on or after 1.4.86 with max gross weight exceeding 12,000kg
2. trailers manufactured on or after 1.5.85 with max gross weight exceeding 3,500kg
3. trailers whenever manufactured with max gross weight exceeding 16,000kg and 2 or more axles.

Exemptions

- Motor vehicles of which no part in the area consisting the middle 80% of the width (measured between the insides of the wheels) and the entire length is less than 400mm above the ground.

- Agricultural motor vehicle
- Agricultural trailed appliance
- Agricultural trailer
- Broken down vehicles
- Concrete mixer
- Engineering plant
- Fire engine
- Four-wheel drive vehicles
- Max speed not exceeding 30mph
- Military etc vehicles
- Refuse vehicle
- Tipper vehicles (side or rear)

- Trailer leased outside GB which has been in this country in previous 12 months.
- Vehicle being taken for spray suppression device to be fitted. Vehicle already fitted with spray-suppression device in accordance with EC Directive 91/226.
- Vehicle without a body being taken for testing, body fitting or delivery to a dealer.
- Works trailers
- Works trucks

At all times when the vehicle is on a road the device must be maintained free from defects which would adversely affect the efficiency of the device.

REG 65

Part 1: Construction and use **91**

MISCELLANEOUS CONSTRUCTION AND USE OFFENCES

MASCOTS (REG 53)
No mascot, emblem or other ornamental object shall be carried by a motor vehicle first used on or after 1.10.37 in any position where it is likely to strike any person with whom the vehicle may collide unless the mascot is not liable to cause injury.

MOTOR CYCLE SIDESTANDS (REG 38)
No motorcycle first used on or after 1.4.86 shall be fitted with any sidestand which is capable of:
1. disturbing stability or direction when in motion; or
2. closing automatically if the angle of inclination of the motor cycle is inadvertently altered when it is stationary.

RADIO INTERFERENCE SUPPRESSION (REG 60)
Every wheeled motor vehicle first used on or after 1.4.74 which is propelled by a spark ignition engine shall comply at the time of its first use with EEC or Community Directives relating to suppression. This does not apply to vehicles constructed or assembled by persons not normally in the business of manufacturing such vehicles.

STOPPING OF ENGINE WHEN STATIONARY (REG 98)
The driver of a vehicle shall, when the vehicle is stationary, stop the action of any machinery attached to or forming part of the vehicle so far as may be necessary for the prevention of noise or of exhaust emissions. Does not apply when stationary due to traffic, working of the machinery is necessary for other than driving the vehicle, or gas propelled vehicle producing gas.

MISCELLANEOUS CONSTRUCTION AND USE OFFENCES cont

AVOIDANCE OF EXCESSIVE NOISE (REG 97)
No motor vehicle shall be used on a road in such a manner as to cause any excessive noise which could have been avoided by the exercise of reasonable care on the part of the driver.

PARKING IN DARKNESS (REG 101)
A motor vehicle must, between sunset and sunrise, when standing on a road, have the nearside of the vehicle as close as may be to the edge of the carriageway. This does not apply with permission of a police officer in uniform; fire, police, ambulance or defence purposes; building, demolition repair of buildings or roads etc; on a one-way street; parking place or taxi or bus stand; or setting down or picking up passengers in accordance with regulations.

MOTOR CYCLES – FOOTRESTS (REG 102)
Footrests shall be available for any passenger carried astride a two-wheeled motor cycle (whether a sidecar is attached or not).

OBSTRUCTION (REG 103)
No person in charge of a motor vehicle or trailer shall cause or permit the vehicle to stand on a road so as to cause any unnecessary obstruction of the road.

MISCELLANEOUS CONSTRUCTION AND USE OFFENCES cont

DRIVER'S CONTROL (REG 104)
No person shall drive or cause or permit any other person to drive, a motor vehicle on a road if he is in such a position that he cannot have proper control of the vehicle or have a full view of the road and traffic ahead.

OPENING OF DOORS (REG 105)
No person shall open, or cause or permit to be opened, any door of a vehicle on a road so as to injure or endanger any person.

REVERSING (REG 106)
No person shall drive, or cause or permit to be driven, a motor vehicle backwards on a road further than may be requisite for the safety or reasonable convenience of the occupants of the vehicle or other traffic, unless for road repairs, etc.

LEAVING VEHICLE UNATTENDED (REG 107)
No person shall leave, or cause or permit to be left, on a road a motor vehicle which is unattended by a licensed driver unless the engine is stopped and the parking brake is set. This does not apply to police, ambulance or fire, or if the engine is needed to drive machinery, etc.

TELEVISION SETS (REG 109)
The driver must not be in a position to see, whether directly or by reflection, any television or other like apparatus used to display anything other than information about the state of the vehicle, location, to assist the driver to see the adjacent road, or to assist the driver to reach his destination.

Mobile telephones
At the time of going to press, the Department of Transport has announced its intention to introduce a new offence of driving whilst using a hand-held mobile phone, to take effect from 1st December 2003. The new offence will be created by a new regulation to be added to the Road Vehicles (Construction and Use) Regulations 1986.

PART 2

DOCUMENTATION

This part of the book aims to highlight the various types of formal documentation required, including driving licences, insurance, operator's licences, vehicle excise duty, registration plates, plating and testing, trade licences, the operation of passenger carrying vehicles, and foreign vehicles.

HGV DOCUMENTATION

The following 'check list' may prove to be a guide to the legal requirements for the use of a heavy goods vehicle. Depending on the type of vehicle, reference should be made to the relevant pages as indicated.

	PAGE
records of work	217
hours of work	212 - 215
operators' licence	123 - 126
LGV and PCV driving licences	104
ordinary driving licences	100 - 118
plating and testing of vehicles	138 - 144
certificate of insurance	122
excise licence	127 - 131
manufacturer's plate	141-142
Ministry plate	141
trailer disc	140
plating certificate	140
trailer plate	140 - 142
unladen weight markings	124
rear reflective markers	195 - 198

DRIVING LICENCES - DEFINITIONS
MOTOR VEHICLES (DRIVING LICENCES) REGULATIONS 1999

LARGE MOTOR BICYCLE
(a) If without sidecar, the bicycle engine has a maximum net power exceeding 25 kilowatts or a power-to-weight ratio exceeding 0.16 kilowatts per kilogram, or
(b) if with sidecar, the combination has a power-to-weight ratio exceeding 0.16 kilowatts per kilogram.

STANDARD MOTOR BICYCLE
Not a large motor bicycle.

PASSENGER CARRYING VEHICLE RECOVERY VEHICLE
A vehicle other than an articulated goods vehicle which:
(a) has unladen weight not exceeding 10.2 tonnes
(b) is being operated by the holder of a PSV Operator's Licence, and
(c) is proceeding to, returning from or giving assistance to, a damaged or disabled passenger-carrying vehicle.

INCOMPLETE LARGE VEHICLE
(a) Typically consisting of a chassis and a complete or incomplete cab which, when complete, is capable of becoming a medium-sized or large goods vehicle or a passenger-carrying vehicle, or
(b) a vehicle which would be an articulated goods vehicle but for the absence of a 5th wheel coupling.

WORKING WEIGHT
The weight of a vehicle in working condition on a road but exclusive of the weight of any liquid coolant and fuel used for its propulsion.

MAXIMUM AUTHORISED MASS
(a) in relation to a goods vehicle means its permissible maximum weight (as marked on the plate of the vehicle, or the notional maximum gross weight (see general definitions)),
(b) in relation to an incomplete large vehicle, means its working weight,
(c) in relation to any other motor vehicle or trailer, its maximum gross weight as shown on the Ministry plate or (if none), manufacturer's plate or (if none), the design weight.

Continued on following page

DEFINITIONS cont

MOTOR VEHICLES (DRIVING LICENCES) REGULATIONS 1999

AMBULANCE

A motor vehicle which –
(a) is constructed or adapted for, and used for no other purpose than, the carriage of sick, injured or disabled people to or from welfare centres or places where medical or dental treatment is given, and
(b) is readily identifiable as such a vehicle by being marked "Ambulance" on both sides.

EXEMPTED GOODS VEHICLE (S51)

Steam-driven vehicle; road construction vehicle for conveying built-in road construction machinery (with or without articles or materials used for the purpose of the machinery); engineering plant (other than a mobile crane); works truck; industrial tractor; agricultural motor vehicle (not being an agricultural or forestry tractor); digging machine; vehicle not used on public roads or, if so used, is only passing between pieces of land in the occupation of the person keeping the vehicle and not used for more than 9.7km in any calendar week; any vehicle – not being an agricultural motor vehicle – only used for agriculture, horticulture or forestry and used on public roads for not more than 1.5 km to pass between different areas of land occupied by the same person; vehicle for hauling lifeboats; unladen vehicle manufactured before 1.1.60 not drawing a trailer; articulated goods vehicle with UW not over 3.05 tonnes; visiting Forces vehicles; vehicle driven by a constable to protect life and property, etc; vehicle with UW not over 3.05 tonnes for raising and drawing disabled vehicles, used solely for that purpose and not carrying goods other than those required for its operation; passenger-carrying vehicle recovery vehicle; and a mobile project vehicle. 'Public road' in this definition means a road repairable at public expense (or in Scotland, as defined in the Roads (Scotland) Act 1984).

EXEMPTED MILITARY VEHICLE

Defence fire vehicle, urgent national defence work, and defence armoured vehicle not being a tracked vehicle.

MOBILE PROJECT VEHICLE

Vehicle having a maximum authorised mass exceeding 3.5 tonnes, constructed or adapted to carry not more than 8 persons in addition to the driver, carrying
(a) play or educational equipment, or

DEFINITIONS cont

(b) articles required for the purposes of display or of an exhibition,
and the primary purpose when stationary is recreational, educational or instructional.

QUALIFIED DRIVER
For the purpose of supervising a provisional licence holder must:
(a) be over 21 years of age (unless member of the Armed Forces acting as such)
(b) Hold a <u>relevant licence</u> (includes the Northern Ireland or Community Licence)
(c) Have the <u>relevant driving experience</u> (unless member of the Armed Forces acting such),
and
(d) In the case of supervising a disabled driver in a category B vehicle, be able in an emergency to take control of the steering and braking of the vehicle.

"relevant licence" means:
(i) in the case of a disabled driver a full licence for a Category B licence (other than B1 or B1 (invalid carriages)), and
(ii) in any other case a full licence for the class of vehicle.

"relevant driving experience" means:
(i) has held the relevant licence for not less than 3 years, or
(ii) supervising in Category C, D, C + E, D + E and held the relevant licence on 6.4.98 and continuously for 3 years since then and has held a full Category B licence continuously or in aggregate for 3 years. ("relevant licence" above includes a provisional licence with a test pass certifcate for that class of vehicle)

100 The Traffic Officer's Companion

DRIVING LICENCES – GRANTING
REG 5 MOTOR VEHICLES (DRIVING LICENCES) REGULATIONS 1999

A driving licence may be granted to a person entitled to drive by virtue of:

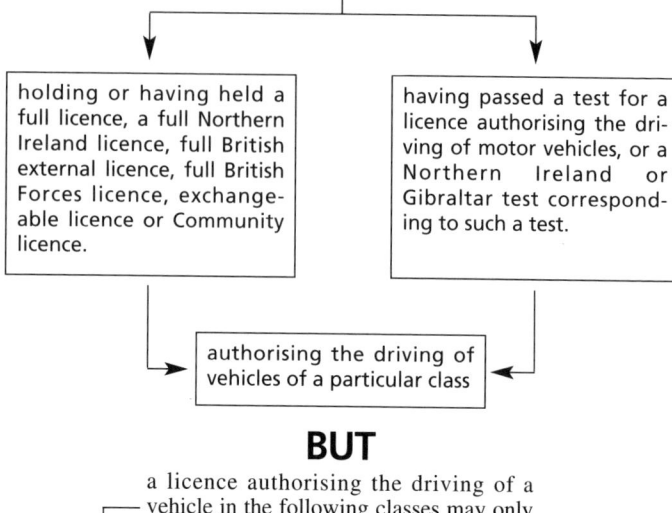

- holding or having held a full licence, a full Northern Ireland licence, full British external licence, full British Forces licence, exchangeable licence or Community licence.

- having passed a test for a licence authorising the driving of motor vehicles, or a Northern Ireland or Gibraltar test corresponding to such a test.

authorising the driving of vehicles of a particular class

BUT

a licence authorising the driving of a vehicle in the following classes may only be granted to persons who, before 1st January 1997
(a) <u>for full licence</u>
  (i) held a full licence for that class, or
  (ii) passed a test authorising the driving of a vehicle in that class
(b) <u>for provisional licence</u>
  held a provisional licence for that class.

CLASSES

1. **C1 + E** (8.25 tonnes)
2. **D1** (not for hire or reward)
3. **D1 + E** (not for hire or reward)
4. **L**

A Sub-category B1 (Invalid Carriages) licence may not be granted unless before 12.11.99
(a) in an application for a full licence, a full B1 (Invalid Carriages) licence (or corresponding sub-category) was held, or
(b) in the case of a provisional licence application he held a provisional B1 (Invalid Carriages) Licence (or corresponding sub category)

CATEGORIES & SUB-CATEGORIES OF VEHICLE FOR LICENSING PURPOSES

REGS 4, 40 AND SCHED 2 MOTOR VEHICLES (DRIVING LICENCES) REGULATIONS 1999

Category or sub-category	Classes of vehicle included
A	Motor bicycles but excluding any motor vehicle in category K.
A1	A sub-category of category A comprising learner motor bicycles.
B	Any motor vehicle, other than a vehicle included in category A, F, K or P, having a maximum authorised mass not exceeding 3.5 tonnes and not more than 8 seats in addition to the driver's seat, including: (i) a combination of such a vehicle and a trailer where the trailer has a maximum authorised mass not exceeding 750kg, and (ii) a combination of such a vehicle and a trailer where the maximum authorised mass of the combination does not exceed 3.5 tonnes and the maximum authorised mass of the trailer does not exceed the UW of the tractor vehicle.
B1	A sub-category of category B comprising motor vehicles having three or four wheels and an UW not exceeding 550kg.
B1 (invalid carriages)	A sub-category of category B comprising motor vehicles which are invalid carriages.
B + E	Combination of a motor vehicle and trailer where the tractor vehicle is in category B but the combination does not fall within that category.
C	Any motor vehicle having a maximum authorised mass exceeding 3.5 tonnes, other than a vehicle falling within category D, F. G or H, including such a vehicle drawing a trailer having a maximum authorised mass not exceeding 750 kilograms.
C1	A sub-category of category C comprising motor vehicles having a maximum authorised mass exceeding 3.5 tonnes but not exceeding 7.5 tonnes, including such a vehicle drawing a trailer having a maximum authorised mass not exceeding 750kg.
D	Any motor vehicle constructed or adapted for the carriage of passengers having more than 8 seats in addition to the driver's seat, including such a vehicle drawing a trailer having a maximum authorised mass not exceeding 750kg.
D1	A sub-category of category D comprising motor vehicles having more than 8 but not more than 16 seats in addition to the driver's seat and including such a vehicle drawing a trailer with a maximum authorised mass not exceeding 750kg.

continued on following page

CATEGORIES & SUB-CATEGORIES OF VEHICLE FOR LICENSING PURPOSES cont

MOTOR VEHICLES (DRIVING LICENCES) REGULATIONS 1999

Category or sub-category	Classes of vehicle included (cont from previous page)
C + E	Combination of a motor vehicle and trailer where the tractor vehicle is in category C but the combination does not fall within that category.
C1 + E	A sub-category of category C + E comprising any combination of a motor vehicle and trailer where: (a) the tractor vehicle is in sub-category C1, (b) the maximum authorised mass of the trailer exceeds 750kg but not the UW of the tractor vehicle, and (c) the maximum authorised mass of the combination does not exceed 12 tonnes.
D + E	Combination of a motor vehicle and trailer where the tractor vehicle is in category D but the combination does not fall within that category.
D1 + E	A sub-category of category D + E comprising any combination of a motor vehicle and trailer where: (a) the tractor vehicle is in sub-category D1, (b) the maximum authorised mass of the trailer exceeds 750 kilograms but not the UW of the tractor vehicle, (c) the maximum authorised mass of the combination does not exceed 12 tonnes, and (d) the trailer is not used for the carriage of passengers.
F	Agricultural or forestry tractor, but excluding any motor vehicle included in category H.
G	Road roller.
H	Track-laying vehicle steered by its tracks.
K	Mowing machine or vehicle controlled by a pedestrian.
P	Moped.
C1 + E (8.25 tonnes)	A sub-category of category C + E comprising any combination of a motor vehicle and trailer in sub-category C1 + E the maximum authorised mass of which does not exceed 8.25 tonnes.
D1 (not for hire or reward)	A sub-category of category D comprising motor vehicles in sub-category D1 driven otherwise than for hire or reward.
D1 + E (not for hire or reward)	A sub-category of category D + E comprising motor vehicles in sub-category D1 + E driven otherwise than for hire or reward.
L	Motor vehicle propelled by electrical power.

NOTE:

Persons authorised to drive the former groups M (trolley vehicles with not more than 16 seats) and N (vehicles used for short distances) will be able to continue to drive those vehicles (Regs 71 & 71A)

LICENCES ISSUED BEFORE 1.1.97
REG 76 MOTOR VEHICLES (DRIVING LICENCES) REGULATIONS1999

A person who before 1st January 1997 passed a test in respect of a class in an old category shall be regarded as having passed a test in the new category as shown in the table below:
("Old category" includes those groups in existence before 1st January 1990.)

Old Category or Class	Corresponding New Category or Class
A	A
B1	B1
B1, limited to invalid carriages	B1, (invalid carriages)
B	B
B plus E	B + E
C1	C1
C1 plus E	C1 + E (8.25 tonnes)
C	C
C plus E	C+ E
C plus E, limited to drawbar trailer combination only	Vehicles in cat C + E which are drawbar trailer combinations
D1	D1 (not for hire or reward)
D1 plus E	D1 plus E (not for hire or reward)
D, limited to 16 seats	D1
D, limited to vehicles not more than 5.5 metres in length	D1 and vehicles in cat. D not more than 5.5 metres in length
D, limited to vehicles not driven for hire or reward	Vehicles in cat. D which are either driven while being used in accordance with a Section 19 permit or, if not being so used, driven otherwise than for hire or reward
D	D
D plus E	D + E
F	F
G	G
H	H
K	K
L	L
P	P

LICENCES – LGV/PCV EXEMPTIONS

REG 50 MOTOR VEHICLES (DRIVING LICENCE) REGULATIONS 1999

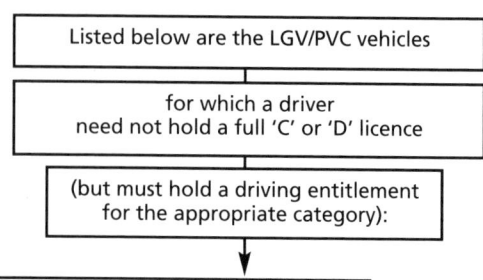

Listed below are the LGV/PVC vehicles

for which a driver need not hold a full 'C' or 'D' licence

(but must hold a driving entitlement for the appropriate category):

large goods vehicles *
1. included in categories
   F – agricultural or forestry tractor;
   G – road roller;
   H – track-laying vehicle steered by its tracks;
   C1 + E (8.25 tonnes) – motor vehicle and trailer;
2. which are exempted goods vehicles or exempted military vehicles: **

* see definition at the start of the book

** see definitions page at start of this section

passenger-carrying vehicles *
1. manufactured more than 30 years before the date when driven and not used for hire or reward or for the carriage of more than 8 passengers; or
2. driven by a constable for the purpose of removing or avoiding obstructions, or protecting life or property, etc.

* see definition at the start of the book

dual purpose vehicles *
These are treated for the purpose of LGV/PCV licences as PCVs
except:
(a) adapted to carry not more than 24 persons in addition to the driver,
(b) driven by a member of the armed forces of the crown, and
(c) carrying passengers for naval, military or airforce purposes
will be regarded as LGVs.

* see definition at the start of the book

DRIVING LICENCES – ADDITIONAL ENTITLEMENTS

Regs 19, 43, 44A and Sched. 2 Motor Vehicles (Driving Licences) Regulations 1999

- The holder of a full licence for a category specified in the table below is also authorised to drive vehicles in the column alongside as if he held a provisional licence to do so.
- In addition the classes of vehicle mentioned alongside in the 3rd column may be driven as if a full licence for that category was held.
- For convenience, the corresponding old groups are shown.

CATEGORY ENTITLEMENT	PROVISIONAL ENTITLEMENT	ADDITIONAL FULL ENTITLEMENT	OLD GROUP
A	B & F	B1 (but see note below), K & P	D
A1	A, B, F & K	P (but see note below)	
B	A, B + E, G & H	F, K & P	A
B1	A, B & F	K & P	C, J
B1 (inv.)			
B + E			A
C	C1 + E, C + E		HGV 2 & 3
C1			A
D	D1 + E, D + E		PSV
D1	D1 + E		PSV
C + E		B + E	HGV 1 & 2
C1 + E		B + E	A
D + E		B + E	PSV
D1 + E		B + E	PSV
F	B & P	K	F
G	H		G
H	G		H
K			K
P (but see note below)	A, B, F + K		E
L			L

DRIVING LICENCES – ADDITIONAL ENTITLEMENTS cont

● Where a full licence authorises only vehicles with automatic transmission, it will act as a provisional licence for manual vehicles in that category.

● Category entitlement A - will not include additional category B1 if test passed on or after 1.2.2001.

● If a licence authorises only A1 category motor cycles or standard motor cycles, large motor cycles may not be driven by a person under 21.

● Category entitlement B - only includes additional category P if - (a) test was passed before 1.2.2001; (b) at the time test was passed he had completed an approved course for motor cycles. Where the approved course was for 3-wheeled mopeds, the category P authorisation only covers such vehicles.

● Similarly, where a test is passed for category P on a 3-wheeled moped the authorisation is restricted to such vehicles..

● For provisional entitlement of LGV trainee driver's licence, see that section, later.

● The holder of a Community licence may claim the provisional entitlements in the table above as if he held a full licence of the appropriate category.

ADDITIONAL CLASSES COVERED BY EXISTING LICENCE
REG 6 AND SCHED 2. MOTOR VEHICLES (DRIVING LICENCES) REGULATIONS 1999

Licence Held	Additional Classes Covered
'C' for at least 2 years (other than C1)	Vehicles in Category 'D' (a) damaged or defective and being driven to a place for repair or being road tested following repair, and (b) not carrying any person not connected with its repair or road testing. But if licence is restricted to automatic transmission, may only drive automatic vehicles.
'C' (other than C1)	Dual Purpose Vehicle if (a) a member of the Armed Forces of the Crown; and (b) the vehicle is adapted to carry not more than 24 persons in addition to the driver, and being used for naval, military or air force purposes. Incomplete large vehicle with working weight exceeding 7.5 tonnes (unless licence restricts driving to automatic transmission in which case vehicle must be automatic.)
C1	Incomplete large vehicles with working weight exceeding 3.5 tonnes but not exceeding 7.5 tonnes (unless licence restricts driving to automatic transmission in which case vehicle must be automatic.
Full 'D' licence (other than D1 or D1 (not for hire or reward))	Passenger-carrying vehicle recovery vehicle. (But if licence is restricted to automatic vehicles then recovery vehicle must be automatic.)
'B' except if restricted to B1 and B1 (invalid carriages)	Exempted goods vehicle other than a passenger-carrying vehicle recovery vehicle, or a mobile project vehicle. Exempted military vehicle. Passenger carrying vehicle (a) manufactured more than 30 years ago and not used for hire or reward or for the carriage of more than 8 passengers; or (b) being driven by a constable for removing or avoiding obstruction, protecting life or property or other similar purposes. (Unless licence is restricted to automatic transmission, in which case the above vehicles must also be automatic.) B+E if trailer is damaged or defective and presenting hazard or obstruction, driven only to remove it and no consideration is received.
'B' except if restricted to B1 and B1 (invalid carriages), has held the licence for not less than 2 years and aged 21 or over	Mobile project vehicle for a non-commercial body: (a) to or from a place where the equipment, display or exhibition is used, or (b) to or from a place where a defect is being remedied, or (c) vehicle is exempt from excise duty due to it being subject to a compulsory test or weight test. (Unless licence is restricted to automatic transmission, in which case above vehicles must also be automatic.)

ADDITIONAL CLASSES COVERED BY EXISTING LICENCE cont

Licence Held	Additional Classes Covered
'B' except if restricted to B1 and B1 (invalid carriages), and has held the licence for not less than 2 years, aged 21 years or over, aged 70 years or over and not suffering from any relevant disability which would result in refusal of a licence to drive this category of vehicle, and receives no payment except expenses	D1 without trailer and maximum authorised mass not exceeding: (a) 3.5 tonnes (excluding specialised equipment for disabled passengers), and (b) 4.25 tonnes otherwise. (But if licence is restricted to automatic transmission, the above vehicles must also be automatic.) Vehicles must be driven for a non-commercial body for social purposes but not for hire or reward.

NOTE:

If a test is passed,
(a) on a vehicle with automatic transmission, only classes of vehicle with automatic transmission are authorised to be driven (except where the additional category is F, K or P);
(b) on an invalid carriage, only they are authorised; and
(c) on a vehicle adapted for a disabled person, only vehicles so adapted are authorised.

The above additional classes covered may be claimed by persons holding a full licence granted under the Road Traffic Act, a corresponding Northern Ireland licence or a Community licence.

DUAL PURPOSE VEHICLES - ARMED FORCES DRIVING
Reg 8 Motor Vehicles (Driving Licences) Regulations 1999

A member of the armed forces may drive a dual purpose vehicle whilst carrying passengers for armed forces purposes provided -
(a) vehicle does not exceed 3.5 tonnes maximum authorised mass and a full Category B licence is held,
(b) if maximum authorised mass is over 3.5 tonnes but under 7.5 tonnes, a full sub-category C1 licence is held,
(c) in any other case, a full Category C licence is held.
If authorised only for automatic transmission, may only drive such vehicles.

PROVISIONAL LICENCES – CONDITIONS
REG 16 MOTOR VEHICLES (DRIVING LICENCES) REGULATIONS 1999

Provisional licence-holders must comply with the following conditions:

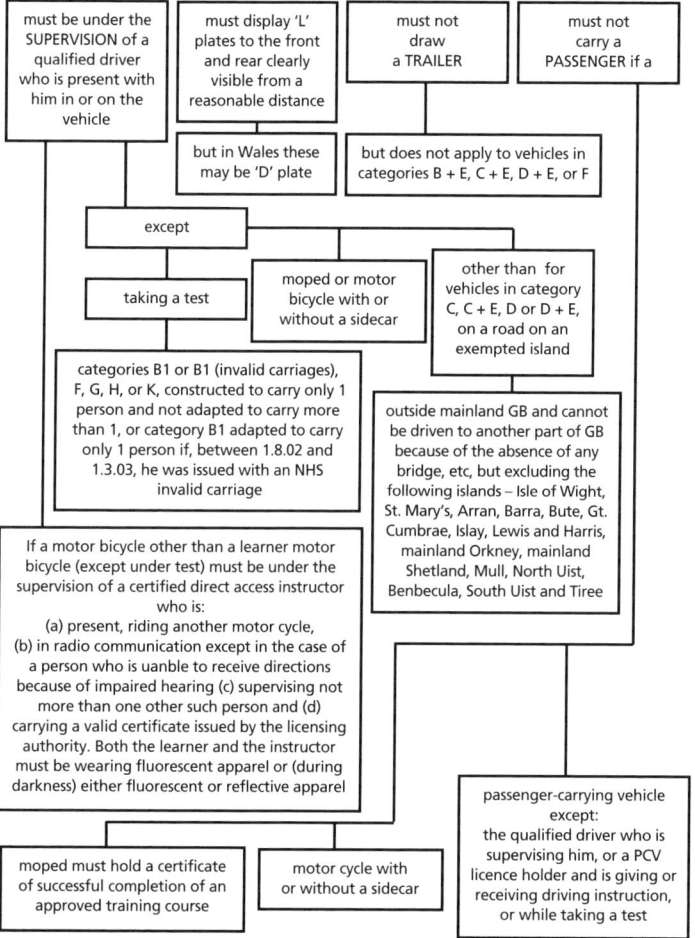

- must be under the SUPERVISION of a qualified driver who is present with him in or on the vehicle
- must display 'L' plates to the front and rear clearly visible from a reasonable distance
  - but in Wales these may be 'D' plate
- must not draw a TRAILER
  - but does not apply to vehicles in categories B + E, C + E, D + E, or F
- must not carry a PASSENGER if a

except
- taking a test
- moped or motor bicycle with or without a sidecar
- other than for vehicles in category C, C + E, D or D + E, on a road on an exempted island

categories B1 or B1 (invalid carriages), F, G, H, or K, constructed to carry only 1 person and not adapted to carry more than 1, or category B1 adapted to carry only 1 person if, between 1.8.02 and 1.3.03, he was issued with an NHS invalid carriage

outside mainland GB and cannot be driven to another part of GB because of the absence of any bridge, etc, but excluding the following islands – Isle of Wight, St. Mary's, Arran, Barra, Bute, Gt. Cumbrae, Islay, Lewis and Harris, mainland Orkney, mainland Shetland, Mull, North Uist, Benbecula, South Uist and Tiree

If a motor bicycle other than a learner motor bicycle (except under test) must be under the supervision of a certified direct access instructor who is:
(a) present, riding another motor cycle,
(b) in radio communication except in the case of a person who is uanble to receive directions because of impaired hearing (c) supervising not more than one other such person and (d) carrying a valid certificate issued by the licensing authority. Both the learner and the instructor must be wearing fluorescent apparel or (during darkness) either fluorescent or reflective apparel

- moped must hold a certificate of successful completion of an approved training course
- motor cycle with or without a sidecar
- passenger-carrying vehicle except: the qualified driver who is supervising him, or a PCV licence holder and is giving or receiving driving instruction, or while taking a test

- The holder of a provisional licence for a motor cycle or moped must take Compulsory Basic Training before they may ride on a road. Upon successful completion, a certificate will be issued and must be produced to the police if requested. (S 164(4A) RTA 1988)
- When motor cyclists pass their test, they are restricted to standard motor cycles for the first 2 years unless, if over 21 years, they take a further test.

MOTOR CYCLE/MOPED LICENCES – IN A NUTSHELL

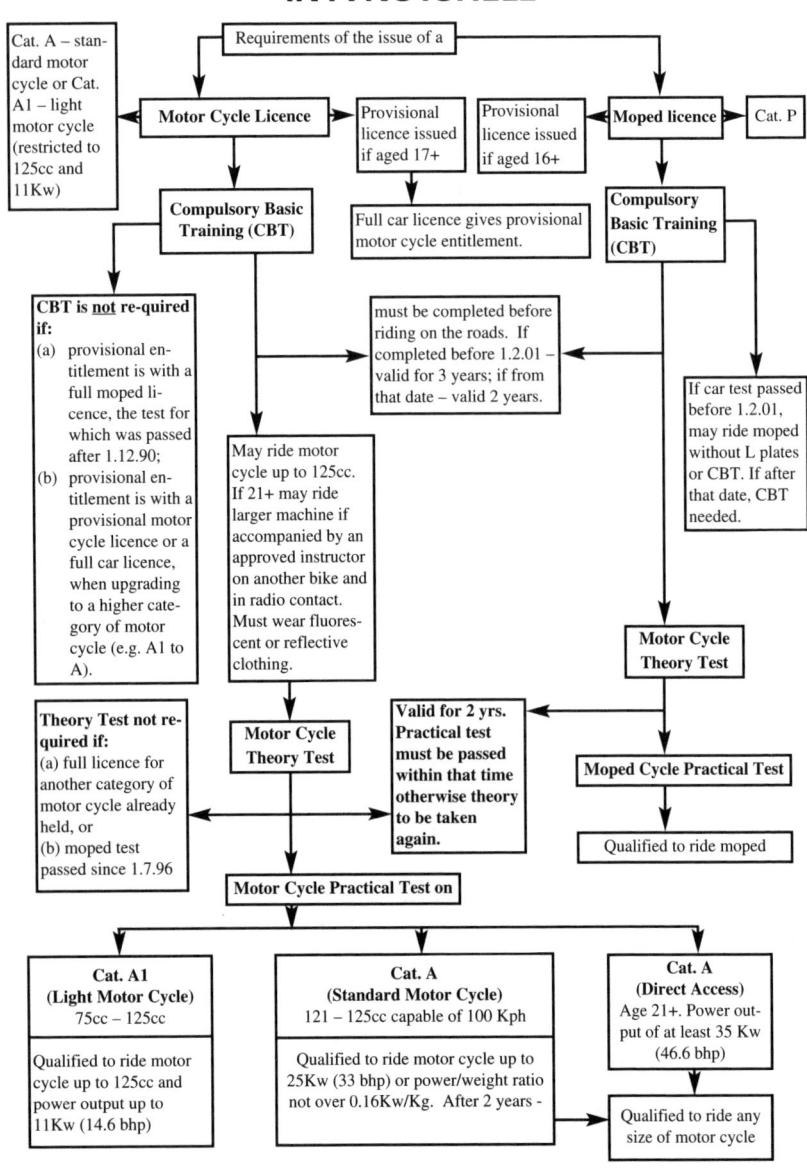

Requirements of the issue of a **Motor Cycle Licence** or **Moped licence**.

- Cat. A – standard motor cycle or Cat. A1 – light motor cycle (restricted to 125cc and 11Kw)
- Moped licence: Cat. P
- Provisional licence issued if aged 17+
- Provisional licence issued if aged 16+
- Full car licence gives provisional motor cycle entitlement.

Motor Cycle Licence route

Compulsory Basic Training (CBT)

CBT is not re-quired if:
(a) provisional entitlement is with a full moped licence, the test for which was passed after 1.12.90;
(b) provisional entitlement is with a provisional motor cycle licence or a full car licence, when upgrading to a higher category of motor cycle (e.g. A1 to A).

CBT must be completed before riding on the roads. If completed before 1.2.01 – valid for 3 years; if from that date – valid 2 years.

May ride motor cycle up to 125cc. If 21+ may ride larger machine if accompanied by an approved instructor on another bike and in radio contact. Must wear fluorescent or reflective clothing.

Theory Test not re-quired if:
(a) full licence for another category of motor cycle already held, or
(b) moped test passed since 1.7.96

Motor Cycle Theory Test

Valid for 2 yrs. Practical test must be passed within that time otherwise theory to be taken again.

Motor Cycle Practical Test on:

Cat. A1 (Light Motor Cycle)	Cat. A (Standard Motor Cycle)	Cat. A (Direct Access)
75cc – 125cc	121 – 125cc capable of 100 Kph	Age 21+. Power output of at least 35 Kw (46.6 bhp)
Qualified to ride motor cycle up to 125cc and power output up to 11Kw (14.6 bhp)	Qualified to ride motor cycle up to 25Kw (33 bhp) or power/weight ratio not over 0.16Kw/Kg. After 2 years –	Qualified to ride any size of motor cycle

Moped Licence route

Compulsory Basic Training (CBT)

If car test passed before 1.2.01, may ride moped without L plates or CBT. If after that date, CBT needed.

Motor Cycle Theory Test

Moped Cycle Practical Test

Qualified to ride moped

110 The Traffic Officer's Companion

PROVISIONAL LICENCES – PREREQUISITES FOR ISSUE

REG 11 MOTOR VEHICLES (DRIVING LICENCES) REGS 1999

● Before a provisional licence for a particular category of vehicle can be issued, a relevant full licence must be held in the appropriate category.

● The table below shows the category of full licence needed for a particular provisional licence.

● Licences for sub-categories D1 (not for hire or reward), D1 + E (not for hire or reward) and C1 + E (8.25 tonnes) shall not be treated as a licence authorising the driving motor vehicles of a class included in sub-categories D1, D1 +E and C1 + E.

CATEGORY OF LICENCE APPLIED FOR	FULL LICENCE NEEDED
B + E	B
C	B
C1	B
D	B
D1	B
C1 + E	C1
C + E	C
D1 + E	D1
D + E	D
G	B
H	B

NOTE: The above provisions do not apply to full-time members of the armed forces.

LARGE GOODS VEHICLE LICENCES – TRAINEE DRIVERS

REG 54 MOTOR VEHICLES (DRIVING LICENCES) REGULATIONS 1999.
(AS SUBSTITUTED BY THE MOTOR VEHICLES (DRIVING LICENCES)
(AMENDMENT) (NO.3) REGULATIONS 2003

An LGV driver's licence authorising the driving of vehicles in category C may be issued to a person who is under the age of 21 provided that:

- the driver is a registered employee of a registered employer

- the vehicle is of a class to which his training agreement applies and is owned or operated by the registered employer or by a registered training establishment

or

in the case of a member of the armed forces, the vehicle is owned by the defence secretary and used for navy, military or air force purposes.

An LGV trainee driver's full licence is subject to the condition that the holder:

(a) must be a registered employee of a registered employer;

(b) may drive only vehicles of a class to which his training agreement applies and which is owned by that registered employee or registered training establishment;

(c) may not draw a trailer otherwise than under the supervision of the holder of a full LGV licence for that class of vehicle; and

(d) may only drive C + E as a provisional licence holder after 6 months from passing the category C test. (Does not apply to C1 + E if max. authorised mass does not exceed 7.5 tonnes).

LICENCES – NEWLY QUALIFIED DRIVER
ROAD TRAFFIC (NEW DRIVERS) ACT 1995

- A driver who acquires 6 or more penalty points within two years of passing his test may have his driving licence revoked and will then have to take another driving test. Newly qualified drivers are on a 2-year probationary period starting from the day on which the driving test is passed.

    SECTION 1

- If a newly qualified driver acquires 6 or more penalty points, the Secretary of State will be informed by the convicting court and must revoke the licence by notice to the driver which will state the date of revocation (cannot be earlier than the date of service of the notice). There is provision for the licence to be restored without re-testing where the driver successfully appeals against the conviction and where he gives notice of appeal.

    SECTION 5

- Until the driver passes a driving test he is in the position of a learner driver.

    SECTION 4

LICENCES – MINIMUM AGES

REG 9 MOTOR VEHICLES (DRIVING LICENCES) REGULATIONS 1999
AND SECTION 101 ROAD TRAFFIC ACT 1988

CATEGORY	AGE	REMARKS
A	21 (17)	Large motor bicycle, 21 years. But will not apply if: (a) If test passed on or after 1.1.97 for category A (but not A1), and 2 years have elapsed since passing the test, or (b) large motor bicycle owned by defence secretary or being driven subject to the orders of the armed forces, and being used for naval, military or air force purposes, 17 years, or (c) test passed for large motor bicycle before 1.1.97
A1	17 years	Other motor cycles, 17 years.
B B + E B1 B1 (invalid carriages)	17 (16) 17 years 17 years 16 years	Generally 17 but if in receipt of a disability living allowance and no trailer drawn, then 16.
C1, C1 + E and C1 + E (8.25 tonnes)	21 years (17, 18)	Generally 21 years except: (a) max authorised mass not over 7.5 tonnes (18 years), or (b) owned by defence secretary or being driven under orders of the armed forces (17 years).
C and C + E	21 years (17, 18)	Generally 21 but if on LGV training scheme, 18 years. If owned by defence secretary and driven under orders of the armed forces, 17 years. If incomplete large vehicle (a) with working weight not exceeding 3.5 tonnes, 17 years, (b) with working weight exceeding 3.5 tonnes but not exceeding 7.5 tonnes, 18 years.
D1 (not for hire or reward) D1 + E (not for hire or reward)	21 (18) 21 years	Generally 21 but if an ambulance which is a category D1 vehicle owned or operated by a health service, national health service trust, or primary care trust, 18 years
D1, D1 + E, D and D + E	21 years (17, 18)	Generally 21 except: (a) provisional licence and not carrying passengers except supervisor and other trainees, 18 years. (b) used under PSV operator's licence or community bus permit and (i) carrying passengers on a regular service with route not over 50km, or (ii) where not carrying passengers as aforementioned and the vehicle is in category D1, 18 years, or (c) vehicle owned by defence secretary and driven subject to the orders of the armed forces, 17 years.
F	17 (16)	Agricultural or forestry tractor generally 17 but if a wheeled vehicle with overall width not over 2.45 metres and not drawing a trailer other than one which is either 2-wheeled or close-coupled 4 wheeled in either case with width not over 2.45 metres; and used only in connection with a category 'F' test, 16 years
G	17 - 21	Road roller which is not steam propelled, does not have pneumatic soft or elastic tyres, unladen weight does not exceed 11.69 tonnes, is not constructed or adapted to carry a load other than water, fuel or accumulator used for propulsion, loose tools and objects for increasing the weight of the vehicle – 17 years. Otherwise 21 years.
H K L P	21 years 16 years 17 years 16 years	

LICENCES – UNDER AGE
ROAD TRAFFIC ACT 1988

● A person who drives under age may be prosecuted for driving otherwise in accordance with the conditions of a licence.   S 87 RTA 1988

DRIVING LICENCES – MISCELLANEOUS
RENEWAL
A person may drive even when he has not received his licence provided that a valid application for the grant or renewal of the licence has been received by the driving licence computer centre at Swansea, except where the application relates to:
(a) the first provisional licence
(b) further classes of vehicle not covered in existing licence
(c) a replacement more than 10 years after the expiry of the previous one
(d) an applicant suffering from a relevant disability and this is declared in the application
(e) an applicant disqualified until he passes a test of competence
S 88 (1-2) RTA 1988

PHOTOCARD LICENCES
From July 2001 all UK licences will be of this type but they are already being phased in. The licence includes details of driver number, signature, name and address, date of birth and categories of vehicle. A paper counterpart shows categories for provisional entitlement, previous history, endorsements, penalty points and disqualification period.

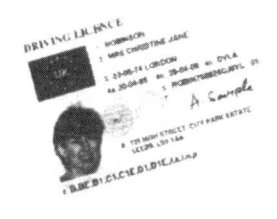

Both photocard and paper counterpart must be produced when required by a police officer or other authorised person.

SIGNATURE
Every person to whom a licence is granted shall forthwith sign it in ink with his usual signature
REG 20 MV (DL.) REGS 1999

PRODUCTION OF DRIVING LICENCE etc

ROAD TRAFFIC ACT 1988, S 164

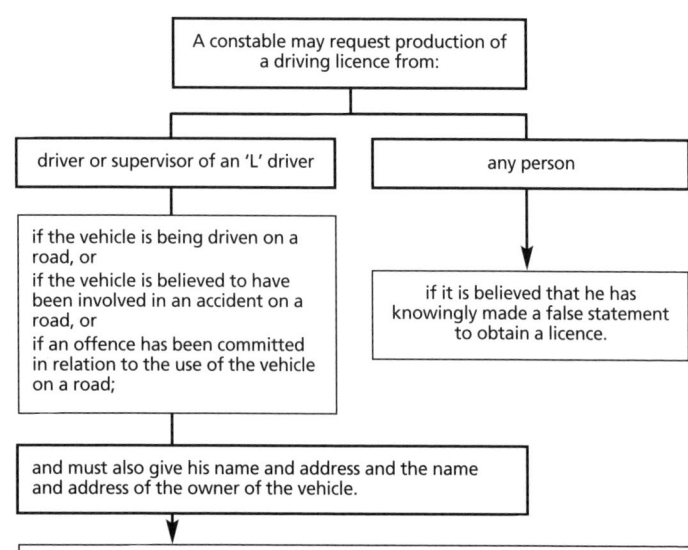

```
A constable may request production of
a driving licence from:
```

driver or supervisor of an 'L' driver

if the vehicle is being driven on a road, or
if the vehicle is believed to have been involved in an accident on a road, or
if an offence has been committed in relation to the use of the vehicle on a road;

any person

if it is believed that he has knowingly made a false statement to obtain a licence.

and must also give his name and address and the name and address of the owner of the vehicle.

If a driving licence is not produced; suspected not to be granted to him; granted in error; or altered with intent to deceive, where the driver number has been altered, removed or defaced; or (if supervising a provisional licence holder) he is suspected to be under 21 years of age, he must also give his date of birth

REG 83 MV (DL) REGS 1999

The driver must also produce Insurance, Test certificate, Plating certificate and this includes where an accident has occurred on a road or <u>other public place.</u>

S 165

NOTE:

- If licence not produced at the time, may be at a police station within seven days S 164(8)

- Upon a licence being granted it must be signed in ink forthwith

  REG. 20 MV(DL) REGS 1999

- The owner of a mechanically propelled vehicle shall produce the registration document when requested by a constable at any reasonable time

  REG. 11 RV(R&L) REGS 2002

DRIVING LICENCES –
VISITORS AND NEW RESIDENTS IN G.B.
MOTOR VEHICLE (DRIVING LICENCES) REGULATIONS 1999. REG 80
MOTOR VEHICLES (INTERNATIONAL CIRCULATION) ORDER 1975

The rules governing driving in the GB by persons from foreign countries depends upon the country from which the person originated and whether visiting or a new resident.

Originating countries may be conveniently grouped as follows:

> European Community and the European Economic Area (EC/EEA)
> Northern Ireland
> Gibraltar and Designated Countries
> Jersey, Guernsey and Isle of Man
> All other countries

European Community Countries:
Austria, Belgium, Denmark, Finland, France, Germany, Greece, Ireland, Italy, Luxembourg, Netherlands, Portugal, Spain, Sweden, UK

European Economic Area Countries:
All EC countries, Iceland, Liechtenstein, Norway.

Ordinary Licence
Generally cars up to 3.5 tonnes and motor cycles.

Vocational Licence
Generally medium/large goods vehicles, Minibuses and Buses.

Where authorised, the use of a non-GB licence is subject to it remaining valid and containing the appropriate group/category of vehicle.

THE CHART ON THE FOLLOWING PAGE EXPLAINS THE DRIVING ENTITLEMENT FOR VISITORS/RESIDENTS FROM EACH OF THE ABOVE COUNTRIES.

VISITORS AND NEW RESIDENTS cont

	VISITORS		RESIDENTS	
	ORDINARY LICENCE	VOCATIONAL LICENCE	ORDINARY LICENCE	VOCATIONAL LICENCE
EC/EEA	Provided licence issued in EC/EEA may drive any vehicle shown on licence.		May drive until 70 years of age or 3 years after becoming resident whichever is longer. After these periods a British licence must be obtained, but may apply for one at any time.	May drive until age 45 or for 5 years after becoming resident, whichever longer. If aged 45 but under 65 may drive until 66th birthday or for 5 years after becoming resident whichever shorter. Aged 65 or over – for 12 months after becoming resident.
NORTHERN IRELAND	May use licence until it expires or may exchange for British one.			
GIBRALTAR AND DESIGNATED COUNTRIES	May drive for up to 12 months from date of last entering GB.	May only drive temporarily imported vehicles for 12 months but may travel in and out indefinitely.	May drive for up to 12 months from date of becoming resident but may exchange for GB one.	Must exchange for GB licence before driving.
JERSEY, GUERNSEY, ISLE OF MAN	May drive for 12 months.	May drive GB registered or temporarily imported vehicle for up to 12 months Guernsey licence restricted to temporary imports.	May drive for 12 months from becoming resident but may exchange for GB one.	May drive for 12 months and may exchange for GB one.
ALL OTHER COUNTRIES	May drive for 12 months from date of entering GB.	May drive only temporarily imported vehicles.	May drive for 12 months. To drive continually must pass test within 12 months. If not must comply with provisional licence conditions.	Must take relevant GB test.

COMMUNITY DRIVING

DRIVING LICENCES (COMMUNITY DRIVING LICENCE) REGS. 1996

Exchange for British Licence

The holder of a licence issued within the European Economic Area (EEA) – a 'Community Licence', who become resident in G.B. need not now exchange it for a British one within 12 months. There remains, however, a right to exchange. But exchange of licences is mandatory for the purpose of periods of validity, health standards and disqualification, where applicable.

Period of Validity of licence held by British residents

Community licences held by Britons are valid for the same period as a British licence unless it would have expired earlier had the holder remained in the State of issue or would otherwise have become invalid in that State.

Health and Fitness

Community licence holders resident in G.B. are subject to the same health and fitness standards and medical checks as persons holding British licences.

LGV and PCV Licences

Resident community licence holders who are entitled to drive large goods and passenger carrying vehicles are subject to the requirements of Part IV of the Road Traffic Act (hours of work and records, etc.) For certain classes, details must be submitted to the Secretary of State within 1 year of becoming resident.

Endorsements

Counterpart licences will be issued to provide evidence of convictions and fixed penalties.

Modification of Vehicle Categories and Ages

Provision is made in the Road Traffic Act for the re-categorisation of vehicles for licensing purposes and for changes to the minimum age for driving motor cycles.

Right to Issue of British Licence

This is restricted to persons normally resident in GB or the UK

Other Benefits

Certain statutory benefits such as taxi and community bus licences are extended to the holders of community motor car licences.

EXCHANGEABLE LICENCES
Road Traffic Act 1988 S108
Driving Licences (Exchangeable Licences) Order 1999

An exchangeable licence is a document (not being a Community Licence) issued by

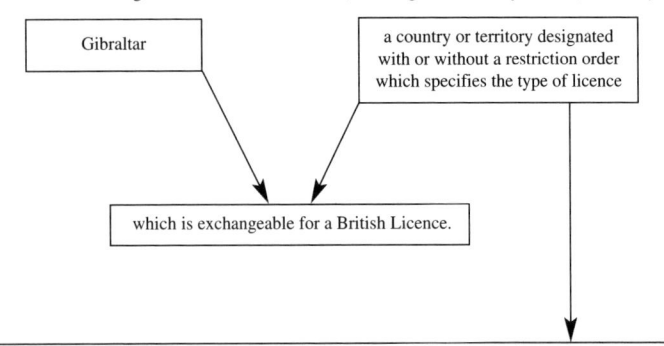

- Gibraltar
- a country or territory designated with or without a restriction order which specifies the type of licence

which is exchangeable for a British Licence.

The following countries or territories have so far been designated:
Australia, Barbados, British Virgin Isles, Canada, Cyprus Republic, Guernsey, Hong Kong, Isle of Man, Japan, Jersey, Malta, New Zealand, Singapore, South Africa Republic, Switzerland and Zimbabwe.

DRIVING WHILST DISQUALIFIED
ROAD TRAFFIC ACT 1988, SS. 87, 101 & 103

A person is guilty of an offence if, while disqualified for holding or obtaining a licence, he-
a) obtains a licence ; or
b) drives a motor vehicle on a road. (S.103)

However, the above provision does not apply to persons disqualified by reason of their age. Such persons should be dealt with under S.87 (driving otherwise than in accordance with a licence).

Minimum ages for driving are as follows (S.101)-

Class of Vehicle	Age
Invalid carriage (Specially designed and constructed for disabled person and not over 254kg.)	16
Moped (Less than 4 wheels and (a) if first used before 1.8.77, has pedals and not over 50cc, or (b) otherwise, has max. speed not over 50 kph and not over 50cc.).	16
Motor bicycle (2 wheels, max. speed over 50 kph and over 50cc. Includes side-car combinations).	17
Agricultural or forestry tractor (2 or more axles; constructed for agricultural or forestry work off road; and primarily used as such)	17
Small vehicle (Not an invalid carriage, moped or motor bicycle. Not constructed to carry more than 9 persons incl. driver, and max. weight not over 3.5 tonnes)	17
Medium sized goods vehicle (Constructed or adapted to haul or carry goods; not adapted to carry more than 9 passengers, incl. driver; and max. weight over 3.5 but not over 7.5 tonnes. Includes combinations where trailer is not over 750kg.).	18
Other motor vehicle	21

INSURANCE
SECTION 143 ROAD TRAFFIC ACT 1988

> No person shall use, or cause or permit to be used

> a motor vehicle on a road or other public place

> unless there is in force a policy of insurance or security in respect of third party risks.

Defence

It shall be a defence if a person proves that he was not the owner of the vehicle, nor had he hired the vehicle and it was used in the course of his employment and he did not know or have reason to believe there was no insurance in force.

Exemptions:
The following vehicles are exempt from the requirements of section 143 above:
S 144 RTA 1988

- Vehicles where owner has deposited £500,000 with Supreme Court
  Note – vehicle only exempted when being driven under owner's control.
- Invalid carriages not exceeding 254kg
- Local authority vehicles
- Police authority vehicles
- Vehicles owned by official receiver of Metropolitan Police
- Vehicles being driven for police purposes or under the direction of PC for police purposes
- Crown vehicles
- Vehicles being used for salvage purposes under Merchant Shipping Act 1894
- Vehicles requisitioned by army or air force
- London Transport Executive Vehicles
- Tramcars and trolley vehicles
- Visiting Forces Vehicles
- Vehicles made available under National Health Service Acts when used for NHS purposes
- Vehicles owned by health service body when driven under owner's control
- Ambulances owned by NHS Trust when driven under owner's control

---

Green card

Vehicles temporarily in Great Britain for which a Green Card has been issued may use the card the same as insurance. Insurance certificates issued in Community Member States (Austria, Belgium, Denmark, France, Finland, Germany, Greece, Ireland, Italy, Luxembourg, Netherlands, Portugal, Spain, Sweden, UK) provide third-party cover throughout all other Member States – there is no need for a Green Card.
S 143 RTA 1988

Part 2: Documentation **123**

OPERATORS' LICENCES

GOODS VEHICLES (LICENSING OF OPERATORS) ACT 1995
GOODS VEHICLES (LICENSING OF OPERATORS) REGULATIONS 1995

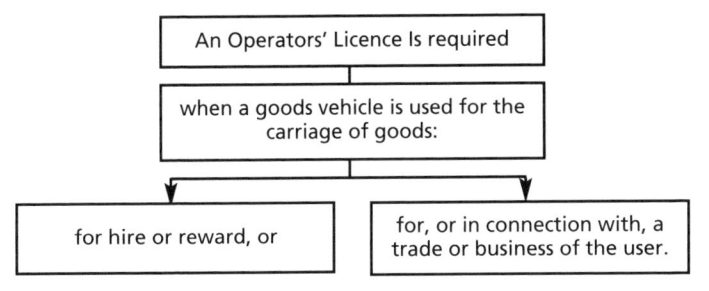

```
            ┌─────────────────────────────────────┐
            │   An Operators' Licence Is required │
            └─────────────────────────────────────┘
            ┌─────────────────────────────────────┐
            │   when a goods vehicle is used for  │
            │          the carriage of goods:     │
            └─────────────────────────────────────┘
              ↓                                ↓
┌──────────────────────────┐   ┌──────────────────────────────────┐
│  for hire or reward, or  │   │  for, or in connection with, a   │
│                          │   │  trade or business of the user.  │
└──────────────────────────┘   └──────────────────────────────────┘
```

S2 GV (L OF O) ACT 1995

Vehicles covered

Any vehicle or trailer in the lawful possession of the licence-holder (whether that motor vehicle is specified or not). However a licence may impose maximum weights for motor vehicles and trailers, may prohibit the use of trailers, or may prohibit the use of motor vehicles which are not specified in the licence.

S5 GV (L OF O) ACT 1995

To avoid making application for the authorisation of motor vehicles temporarily in the operator's possession, the original licence may authorise the use of additional vehicles. If such vehicles are acquired, the Licensing Authority must be notified within one month of acquisition of the vehicle.

TYPE	S 3 GOODS VEHICLES (LICENSING OF OPERATORS) ACT 1995	
(I)	**Standard (International)**	For hire or reward or in connection with any trade or business carried on by the holder in both national and international transport.
(N)	**Standard (National)**	For hire or reward etc in UK.
(R)	**Restricted**	For carrying goods only in connection with operator's trade or business, other than carrying goods for hire or reward.

S5(6) GV (L OF O) ACT 1995

Displaying operator's disc

All motor vehicles used under a licence must display a disc in a waterproof container on the nearside near the lower edge of the windscreen with the obverse side facing forwards (or, if not fitted with a windscreen, in a conspicuous position on the front or nearside of the vehicle)

REG 23 GV (L OF O) REGULATIONS 1995

124 The Traffic Officer's Companion

OPERATORS' LICENCES – EXEMPTIONS

GOODS VEHICLES (LICENSING OF OPERATORS) ACT 1995
GOODS VEHICLES (LICENSING OF OPERATORS) REGULATIONS 1995

A Goods Vehicle Operators' licence is not required for the following

---

small goods vehicles:

rigid vehicles not forming part of a combination

1. with relevant **plated** weight of not more than 3.5 tonnes, or
2. if **unplated**, an unladen weight of not more than 1,525kg;

rigid vehicles forming part of a combination

1. if all the vehicles (except any small trailer with unladen weight not exceeding 1,020 kg) **have relevant plated weights** the aggregate of which does not exceed 3.5 tonnes
2. if any are **not plated**, the aggregate of the unladen weight (excluding and small trailer with unladen weight not exceeding 1,020kg) does not exceed 1,525kg;

articulated vehicles

1. if the aggregate of the unladen weight of the tractive unit, together with the **plated weight** of semi-trailer is not more than 3.5 tonnes
2. if semi-trailer unplated, the aggregate unladen weight of tractive unit and semi-trailer is not more than 1,525kg;

---

goods vehicle used for international carriage

1. a goods vehicle for international carriage by a haulier established in a member State other than the UK and not established in the UK;
2. a goods vehicle for international carriage by a haulier established in Northern Ireland and not established in Great Britain.

Part 2: Documentation **125**

OPERATORS' LICENCES – EXEMPTIONS cont

GOODS VEHICLES (LICENSING OF OPERATORS) ACT 1995
GOODS VEHICLES (LICENSING OF OPERATORS) REGULATIONS 1995

cont from previous page

A Goods Vehicle Operators' licence is not required for the following

For fuller details consult Sched 3 to the Regulations.

- agricultural machinery and trailers taxed at the concessionary excise rate and being used for an authorised purpose (SEE PART II, SCHED 3)
- civil defence vehicles
- dual-purpose vehicles (such as Land Rovers) and trailers
- electric vehicles
- fire-fighting and rescue vehicles used in mines
- hearses and other vehicles used for funerals
- local authority vehicles for weights & measures etc enactments
- pre-1977 vehicles not over 1,525kg unladen, plated between 3.5 tonnes and 3.5 tons
- police, fire brigade and ambulance vehicles
- RNLI and Coastguard vehicles
- recovery vehicles
- road maintenance trailers
- road rollers and trailers
- showmen's goods vehicles and trailers
- snow clearing vehicles and gritters etc
- steam-propelled vehicles
- tower wagons and trailers carrying only goods used in connection with its work
- uncompleted vehicles on test or trial
- vehicle allowed to carry out cabotage in the UK under EC Regs
- vehicles and their trailers using the roads for less than six miles a week while moving between parts of private premises
- vehicles carrying a load for the purposes of the examination of that vehicle
- vehicles constructed or adapted primarily for the carriage of passengers and their effects, and trailers drawn thereby
- vehicles used by highway authorities for weighing vehicles
- vehicles used by or under the control of HM UK Forces
- vehicles used solely on aerodromes
- vehicles with special fixed equipment (such as road sweepers and feedmobiles)
- vehicles with trade plates
- visiting Forces' vehicles
- water, electricity, gas or telephone vehicles held ready for use in emergencies.

OPERATORS' LICENCES cont

GOODS VEHICLES (LICENSING OF OPERATORS) ACT 1995
GOODS VEHICLES (LICENSING OF OPERATORS) REGULATIONS 1995

FORGERY (S 38)

A person is guilty of an offence if with intent to deceive, he:

- forges alters or uses
- lends to, or allows to be used by, any other person
- makes or has in his possession any document or other thing so closely resembling any of the following as to be calculated to deceive

any operators' licence; any document plate, mark or other thing by which a vehicle is to be identified as being authorised to be used under an operators' licence; any document evidencing the authorisation of any person for the purpose of inspecting maintenance facilities or the seizure or disposal of documents etc.; any certificate of qualification to be engaged in road transport undertakings; or any certificate or diploma of professional competence.

PRODUCTION OF LICENCE (REG 26)
An officer or police constable may require the production of an operator's licence by the holder of such within 14 days at an operating centre or (in the case of the requirement being made by a police officer) at a police station chosen by the licence holder.

Failure to comply is an offence. (REG 32)

POWER TO INSPECT (S 40)
An officer or police constable may, at any reasonable time, enter the premises of an applicant for, or holder of, an operator's licence and inspect any facilities on those premises for maintaining vehicles in a fit and serviceable condition. Any obstruction in the exercise of these powers constitutes an offence.

POWER TO SEIZE DOCUMENTS ETC (S 41)
If an officer or police constable has reason to believe that:
a. a document or article carried on or by the driver of a vehicle, or
b. a document produced to him in pursuance of this Act, is a document or article in relation to which an offence under S 38 (forgery etc) or S 39 (false statement to obtain) relates, he may seize that document or article.

Part 2: Documentation **127**

EXCISE LICENCES

VEHICLE EXCISE AND REGISTRATION ACT 1994

Excise licences are required by all mechanically propelled vehicles used or kept on a public road maintainable at public expense. Tax rates for goods vehicles depend on the vehicle weight. For HGVs subject to plating and testing this means the maximum weight. For other vehicles it means the weight at which the vehicle can be operated under Construction and Use Regulations. For HGVs the tax rate depends upon not only its weight, but also the number of axles and whether it is rigid or articulated. There are also reduced rates for engines which reduce pollution.

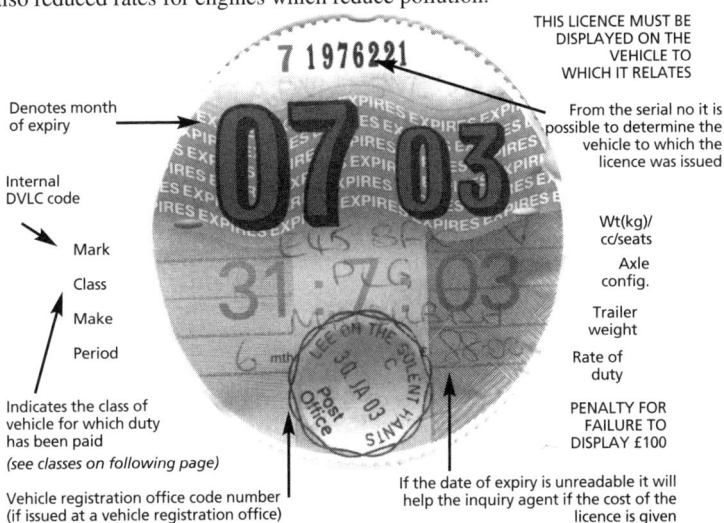

THIS LICENCE MUST BE DISPLAYED ON THE VEHICLE TO WHICH IT RELATES

Denotes month of expiry

From the serial no it is possible to determine the vehicle to which the licence was issued

Internal DVLC code

Mark

Class

Make

Period

Wt(kg)/cc/seats

Axle config.

Trailer weight

Rate of duty

Indicates the class of vehicle for which duty has been paid
(see classes on following page)

PENALTY FOR FAILURE TO DISPLAY £100

Vehicle registration office code number (if issued at a vehicle registration office)

If the date of expiry is unreadable it will help the inquiry agent if the cost of the licence is given

Exemptions

Electrically assisted pedal cycles	Vehicles being imported by members of foreign armed forces, etc.
Fire and ambulance vehicles and health service vehicles	Vehicles for export
Invalid carriages weighing less than 508kg	Vehicles carrying disabled persons and registered in name of disabled driver
Lifeboat haulage vehicles	Veterinary ambulances
Mine rescue vehicles	Vehicles not constructed, adapted or used to carry any person
Trams	
Vehicles being taken to or from annual test or retest by prior appointment or being driven for the purposes of the test, or being taken to or from a place for relevant work to be carried out on the vehicle following refusal of a certificate.	Vehicles used for agriculture, horticulture or forestry purposes, passing between different areas of land occupied by the same person and not travelling on public roads (or more than 1.5km per journey
Old vehicles (more than 25 years old)	SECTION 5 AND SCHED 2

128 The Traffic Officer's Companion

EXCISE DUTY CLASSES

SCHED 1 VEHICLES EXCISE AND REGISTRATION ACT 1994

The following details the classes of vehicle as described in the above-mentioned Act and Schedule

Private/light goods
Applies to vehicle not otherwise mentioned in Schedule 1

Motor bicycles and tricycles
The rate of duty is calculated according to the cc of the engine

Buses
The rate of duty is calculated according to the seating capacity. "Bus" means a PSV which is not 'excepted' (less than 9 seats, community bus, or used with educational permit) nor a 'special concessionary vehicle' (see later).

Recovery vehicles.
The rate payable depends on the revenue weight. It is restricted to vehicles constructed or permanently adapted for lifting, towing or transporting a disabled vehicle. It must not be used for any other purpose and may only carry passengers or goods which are being conveyed in the disabled vehicle.

Vehicles used for exceptional loads
These are taxed at the Heavy Tractive Unit rate. An exceptional load is one which by reason of its weight or dimensions cannot be carried in compliance with construction and use regulations and is being carried under special types order.

Haulage vehicles
If a showman's vehicle the rate is the same as the basic goods vehicle, otherwise the general haulage rate applies. A 'haulage vehicle' is one, not being a 'special vehicle', 'special concessionary vehicle', or 'exceptional load', which is constructed and used solely for haulage and not for carrying a load.

Goods vehicles
The rate applicable depends upon revenue weight, the number of axles and whether rigid or articulated. Different scales apply to rigid vehicles over 7,500kg, tractive units exceeding 7,500kg, vehicles with reduced plated weights, vehicles for conveying machines, and island goods vehicles.

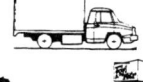

Part 2: Documentation **129**

Special vehicles
The duty applicable is the basic goods vehicle rate. It includes a vehicle over 3,500kg revenue weight which is not a 'special concessionary vehicle' (see later) and which is a digging machine, mobile crane, works truck, road roller, vehicle not used to carry goods or burden for hire or reward or in connection with a trade or business, and a vehicle designed for use with a semi-trailer but which does not carry goods or burden.

Special concessionary vehicles
The duty payable is 25% of the general rate (private/light goods rate).
Vehicles included in this category are:
(a) Agricultural tractor used for agriculture, horticulture, forestry, or cutting verges/hedges etc
(b) Off road tractor not being an agricultural tractor designed and constructed for use off-roads and not exceeding 25mph.
(c) Light agricultural vehicle not over 1,000kg with only 1 seat and used only for agriculture, horticulture or fishery purposes.
(d) Agricultural engine
(e) Mowing machine
(f) Steam powered vehicle
(g) Electrically powered vehicle (not being a motorcycle)
(g) Vehicle used/kept only for snow clearing or salt/grit spreading

Statutory Off-Road Notification
Where a vehicle licence is surrendered, or is not renewed, or the vehicle is kept unlicenced the holder of the licence (or keeper) must declare the address at which the vehicle is being kept. Reg. 26 Road Vehicles (Registration and Licensing) Regulations 2002.

IMMOBILISATION AND REMOVAL OF UNLICENSED VEHICLES

VEHICLE EXCISE DUTY (IMMOBILISATION, REMOVAL AND DISPOSAL OF VEHICLES) REGULATIONS 1997

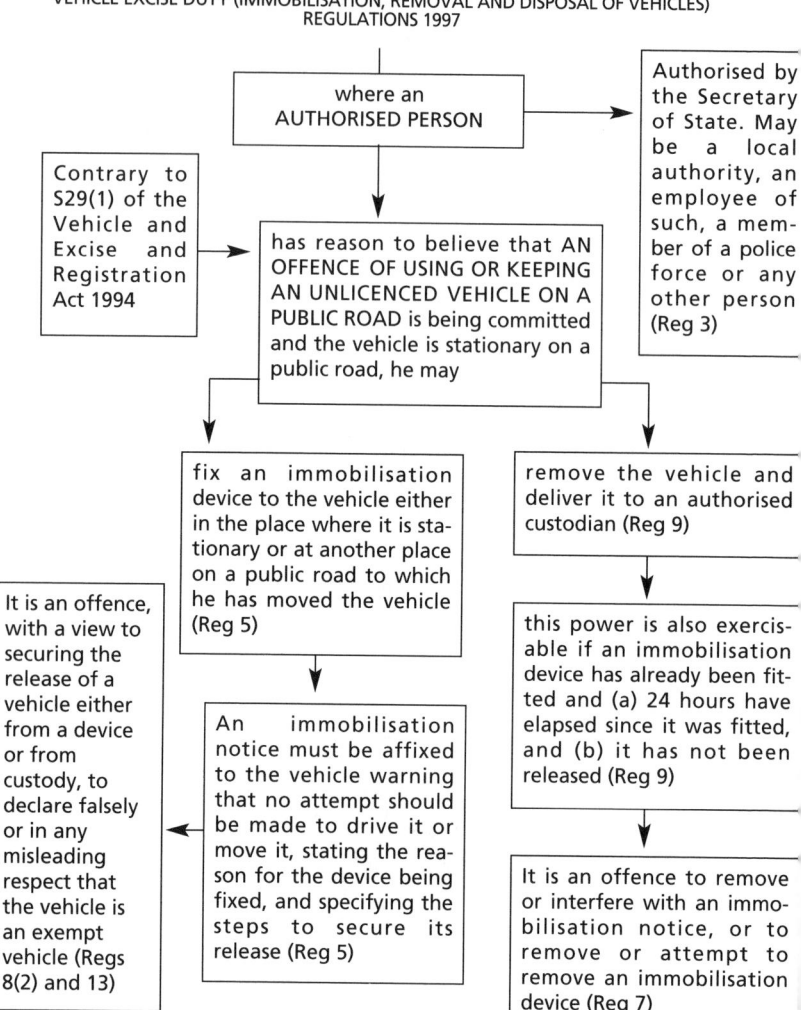

where an **AUTHORISED PERSON**

Authorised by the Secretary of State. May be a local authority, an employee of such, a member of a police force or any other person (Reg 3)

Contrary to S29(1) of the Vehicle and Excise and Registration Act 1994

has reason to believe that AN OFFENCE OF USING OR KEEPING AN UNLICENCED VEHICLE ON A PUBLIC ROAD is being committed and the vehicle is stationary on a public road, he may

fix an immobilisation device to the vehicle either in the place where it is stationary or at another place on a public road to which he has moved the vehicle (Reg 5)

remove the vehicle and deliver it to an authorised custodian (Reg 9)

this power is also exercisable if an immobilisation device has already been fitted and (a) 24 hours have elapsed since it was fitted, and (b) it has not been released (Reg 9)

It is an offence, with a view to securing the release of a vehicle either from a device or from custody, to declare falsely or in any misleading respect that the vehicle is an exempt vehicle (Regs 8(2) and 13)

An immobilisation notice must be affixed to the vehicle warning that no attempt should be made to drive it or move it, stating the reason for the device being fixed, and specifying the steps to secure its release (Reg 5)

It is an offence to remove or interfere with an immobilisation notice, or to remove or attempt to remove an immobilisation device (Reg 7)

THE REGULATIONS DO NOT APPLY:

(a) if disabled person's badge is displayed (b) exempt vehicle and 'nil' licence displayed, (c) B.M.A. badge is displayed (d) vehicle abandoned, (e) PSV used to carry passengers, (f) construction, maintenance, etc vehicle (g) Post Office or Royal Mail vehicle delivering or collecting, (h) less than 24 hours since immobilised vehicle was released. (Reg 4)

Part 2: Documentation **131**

EXHIBITION OF EXCISE LICENCES

VEHICLE EXCISE AND REGISTRATION ACT 1994
THE ROAD VEHICLES (REGISRATION AND LICENSING) REGULATIONS 2002

> Excise licences must be fixed to and exhibited on vehicle in a manner prescribed by the regulations
> S 33

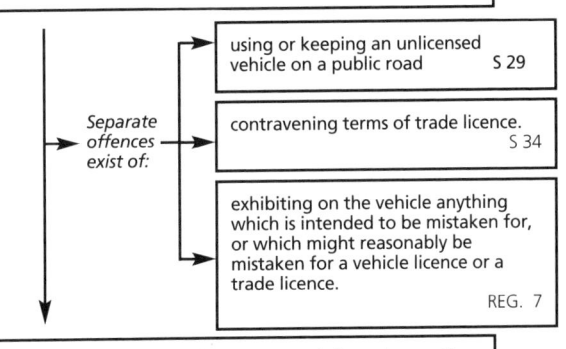

Separate offences exist of:

- using or keeping an unlicensed vehicle on a public road S 29
- contravening terms of trade licence. S 34
- exhibiting on the vehicle anything which is intended to be mistaken for, or which might reasonably be mistaken for a vehicle licence or a trade licence. REG. 7

and must be displayed in a holder to protect it from the weather and must be clearly visible from the nearside of the road.

no licence need be displayed if the licence has been returned to the secretary of state for the issue of a replacement.

Motor bicycle, tricycle or invalid carriage

Position: nearside of vehicle

Motor bicycle with sidecar attached or drawing a sidecar

Position: nearside of handlebars or nearside of sidecar

Any vehicle fitted with glass windscreen extending to the nearside

Position: on or adjacent to the nearside of the windscreen

Any other vehicle

- If fitted with cab having nearside window – on that window and not less than 760mm and not more than 1.8m above the road surface

132 The Traffic Officer's Companion

REGISTRATION MARKS - FIXING AND LIGHTING

Road Vehicles (Display of Registration Marks) Regulations 2001

Exempt Vehicles (Reg.3)
- Invalid carriage not over 254 kg. unladen
- Pedestrian controlled vehicle not over 450 kg. unladen

Fixing of Plates (Regs. 5 – 8)
- **Vehicles registered on or after 1.10.38 (or 1.1.48 in Northern Ireland)**
  (Except works trucks, road rollers and agricultural machines)

  Rear

  Must be fixed to the rear of the vehicle or, if towing a trailer, the trailer. If there is more than 1 trailer, must be fixed to the rearmost.
  Unless fixed in accordance with a type approval directive, it must be fixed as follows:
  Vertically or, where this is not practicable, as near to vertical as possible, and
  In such position that in normal daylight the characters are easily distinguishable from every part of a square having a diagonal length of:

Width of Characters	Diagonal Length
At least 57mm	22 metres
50mm	21.5 metres
44mm	18 metres

  Front

  Must comply with above vertical and diagonal length requirements.
  A motor cycle or tricycle which does not have a 4-wheeled vehicle type body **need not** have a front registration plate if first registered before 1.9.01. If after this date, **must not** have one.

- **Vehicles registered before the above dates**
  (Except works trucks, road rollers and agricultural machines)

  Must be fixed on the front of the vehicle. Also on the rear of the vehicle or trailer. If more than 1 trailer, must be fixed to the rearmost trailer.
  Must be vertical or, if not possible, as near to vertical as practicable.
  In normal daylight the characters must be clearly distinguishable from in front and behind the vehicle respectively.
  A motor cycle or tricycle which does not have a 4-wheeled vehicle type body need not have a front registration plate.

- **Works trucks, road rollers and agricultural machines**
  Must be fixed vertically or, where that is not possible, as close to vertical as practicable-
  1. on both sides of the vehicle, characters easily distinguishable from both sides, or
  2. on the rear so as to be easily distinguishable from the behind, or
  3. if a trailer or trailers are being drawn and plates not fixed on the sides of the vehicle, on the trailer or the rearmost if more than one, easily distinguishable from behind.

  If the towing vehicle is an agricultural machine, the plate fixed on the trailer may bear the registration mark of any agricultural machine belonging to the keeper.

Lighting of Rear Plates (Reg. 9)
(Does not apply to works trucks, road rollers, agricultural machines and vehicles first registered before 1.10.38 (or 1.1.48 in Northern Ireland))

Between sunset and sunrise the rear plate, unless lit by light complying with the relevant type approval directive, must be lit so that it is easily distinguishable from every part of a square having a diagonal length of:

Width of Characters	Diagonal Length
44mm	15 metres
Any other case	18 metres

Part 2: Documentation **133**

REGISTRATION MARKS - SPECIFICATIONS
Road Vehicles (Display of Registration Marks) Regulations 2001, Reg. 10 & Sch. 2

Vehicles registered and new registration plates fitted on or after 1st September 2001
- Must be made of retroreflecting material which complies with BS AU 145d, or
- Any other relevant standard or specification recognised for use in a EEA State and which is of equivalent performance to the BS specification,
 and which in either case is marked with the identification number or mark of that standard or specification.
- The front plate must have black characters and a white background.
- The rear plate must have black characters on a yellow background.

Vehicles registered on or after 1st January 1973 and before 1st September 2001
(Optional – may instead comply with previous section)
- Must be of reflex-reflecting material which complies with BS AU 145a, or
- Any other relevant standard or specification recognised for use in a EEA State and which is of equivalent performance to the BS specification,
 and which in either case is marked with the identification number or mark of that standard or specification.
- The front plate must have black characters and a white background.
- The rear plate must have black characters on a yellow background

---

Vehicles registered before 1st January 1973
(Optional – may comply instead with previous 2 sections)

(a) (where the mark may be illuminated from behind by virtue of the translucency of the characters)
- Must be formed of white translucent characters on a black background.
- When illuminated during the hours of darkness the characters must appear white against a black background.

(b) (where the mark is not so constructed)

EITHER:
- Must be made of reflex-reflecting material which complies with BS AU 145.
- Front plate to be black characters on a white background
- Rear plate to be black characters on a yellow background

OR:
- White, silver or grey characters on a black surface
- Characters either indelibly inscribed or attached so that they cannot readily be detached
- May be either
    1. made of cast or pressed metal with raised characters, or
    2. consist of plate to which separate characters are attached, or
    3. consist of a plastic plate having either reverse engraved characters or characters of a foil type, or
    4. consist of an unbroken rectangular area on the surface of the vehicle which is either flat or, if there is no flat area, almost flat.

Other restrictions   (Reg 11)

No reflex-reflecting material may be added, nor must the plate be treated so characters become retroreflective, less easily distinguishable, or less accurately photographed. The plate must not be fixed to the vehicle in a way (eg screws or bolts) which changes the appearance of the characters, makes them less distinguishable or prevents or impairs any photographic image. The surface must not comprise or incorporate any design, pattern or texture, or be treated in any way which gives the appearance of such.

134 The Traffic Officer's Companion

REGISTRATION MARKS - LAYOUT

Road Vehicles (Display of Registration Marks) Regulations 2001
Reg. 13 & Sch. 3

A registration mark must be laid out in conformity with one of the diagrams specified below:

Description	Permitted Layouts		
2 letters and 2 numbers followed by a group of 3 letters	**DE51 ABC**	**DE51** **ABC**	-
A single letter and not more than 3 numbers followed by a group of 3 letters	**A123 ABC**	A123 ABC	**A** **123** **ABC**
3 letters followed by a group of not more than 3 numbers and a single letter	**ABC 123A**	ABC 123A	**ABC** **123** **A**
A group of 4 numbers followed by a single letter or a group of 2 letters	**1234 AB**	12 34 **AB**	-
A group of not more than 3 numbers followed by a group of not more than 3 letters	**123 AB**	123 **AB**	-
A group of not more than 3 letters followed by a group of not more than 3 numbers	**AB 123**	**AB** 123	-
A single letter or group of 2 letters followed by a group of 4 numbers	**AB 1234**	**AB** **12** **34**	-
A group of 3 letters followed by a group of 4 numbers (Northern Ireland)	**ABZ 1234**	**ABZ** **1234**	-
A group of 4 numbers followed by a group of 3 letters (Northern Ireland)	**1234 ABZ**	**1234** **ABZ**	-

Motor Cycles may not use a layout in this column

Vehicles first registered or replacement plates fitted (except if vehicle first registered before 1.1.73) on or after 1.9.01 may not use these layouts

Part 2: Documentation **135**

REGISTRATION MARKS - SIZE AND SPACING

Road Vehicles (Display of Registration Marks) Regulations 2001
Reg. 14 & Sch. 3

Height

Each character in a registration mark must be **79mm** high except:
- Vehicle first registered before 1.9.01 – may be **89mm** high unless:
    1. vehicle was first registered on or after 1.1.73 and fitted with a new registration plate to replace a previous one, or
    2. the vehicle is a motor cycle, motor tricycle, quadricycle, agricultural machine, works truck or road roller.
- REGISTRATION MARK ON A MOTOR CYCLE, MOTOR TRICYCLE, QUADRICYCLE, AGRICULTURAL MACHINE, WORKS TRUCK OR ROAD ROLLER, MAY BE **64MM** HIGH.

Width of Character

Each character other than the letter "I" and the figure "1" must be:
- If vehicle first registered on or after 1.9.01,
- a new registration plate fitted on or after that date to replace a previous plate (except if vehicle was first registered before 1.1.73),

the width shown in **line 1** of the table below.

In any other case, that shown in **line 2** of the table below.

Width of Stroke forming a Character

Must be that shown in **line 3** of the table below.

Spacing between Characters in a Group

Must be that shown in **line 4** of the table below except:
1. where the characters are 79mm or 89mm high,
2. on a vehicle first registered before 1.9.01,
3. registration mark was fitted to vehicle before 1.9.01, or the vehicle was first registered before 1.1.73, and
4. plate is made of cast or pressed metal with raised characters, then
- spacing between two characters, one of which is "I" or "1" must be within limits shown in **line 8** of the table below
- spacing between two characters both of which are "I" or "1" must be within the limits shown in **line 9** of the table below

but where 1 or more characters in a group is "I" or "1" all the characters within that group must be evenly spaced.

Horizontal and Vertical Spacing between Groups of Characters

Must be that shown in **line 5** and **line 6** respectively of the table below.

Width of Margin between Mark and Edge of Plate

Must be that shown in line 7 of the table below.

Imported Vehicles - see Registration Marks - Miscellaneous

DIMENSION	CHARACTER HEIGHT		
	89mm	**79mm**	**64mm**
1. Character width	-	50mm	44mm
2. Character width	64mm	57mm	44mm
3. Stroke width	16mm	14mm	10mm
4. Space between characters	13mm	11mm	10mm
5. Horizontal space	38mm	33mm	30mm
6. Vertical space	19mm	19mm	13mm
7. Margin	13mm	11mm	11mm
8. Space between characters	13-37mm	11-33mm	-
9. Space between characters	13-60mm	11-54mm	-

136 The Traffic Officer's Companion

REGISTRATION MARKS – SYSTEM

The registration mark is made up of seven characters divided into three parts:

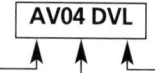

AV04 DVL

- Local memory tag. 1st letter represents the region; 2nd letter relates to a local DVLA office. See list below. In this example 'AV' would be Ipswich.
- Age identifier. See list below. In this example '04' would be March 2004.
- Three random letters. These make the registration mark unique.

\multicolumn{6}{c	}{MEMORY TAGS}
Local Memory Tag	DVLA Office	Local Identifier	Local Memory Tag	DVLA Office	Local Identifier
A	Peterborough	ABCDEFGHJKLMN	M	Manchester	A-Y
	Norwich	OPRSTU	N	Newcastle	ABCDEFGHJKLMNO
	Ipswich	VWXY		Stockton	RSTUVWXY
B	Birmingham	A-Y	O	Oxford	A-Y
C	Cardiff	ABCDEFGHJKLMNO	P	Preston	ABCDEFGHJ KLMNOPRST
	Swansea	PRSTUV		Carlisle	UVWXY
D	Bangor	WXY	R	Reading	A-Y
	Chester	ABCDEFGHJK	S	Glasgow	ABCDEFGHJ
	Shrewsbury	LMNOPRSTUVWXY		Edinburgh	KLMNO
E	Chelmsford	A-Y		Dundee	PRST
F	Nottingham	ABCDEFGHJKLMNP		Aberdeen	UVW
	Lincoln	PSTVWXY		Inverness	XY
G	Maidstone	ABCDEFGHJKLMNO	V	Worcester	A-Y
	Brighton	PRSTUVWXY	W	Exeter	ABCDEFGHJ
H	Bournemouth	ABCDEFGHJ		Truro	KL
	Portsmouth	KLMNOPRSTUVWXY		Bristol	MNOPRSTUVWXY
	'HW' reserved for the Isle of Wight		Y	Leeds	ABCDEFGHJKL
K	Luton	ABCDEFGHJKL		Sheffield	MNOPRSTUV
	Northampton	MNOPRSTUVWXY		Beverley	WXY
L	Wimbledon	ABCDEFGHJ			
	Stanmore	KLMNOPRST			
	Sidcup	UVWXY			

\multicolumn{6}{c	}{AGE IDENTIFIERS}
Year	March	Sept	Year	March	Sept
2001	-	51	2005	05	55
2002	02	52	2006	06	56
2003	03	53	2007	07	57
2004	04	54	2008	08	58

REGISTRATION MARKS - MISCELLANEOUS
ROAD VEHICLES (DISPLAY OF REGISTRATION MARKS) REGULATIONS 2001

Style of Characters (Reg. 15)
There are 2 prescribed fonts and these are described in Schedule 4 of the Regulations, one for characters 79mm high and another for those being 64mm high.
A prescribed font must be used
- for vehicles which are first registered on or after 1.9.01
- for new plates fixed to a vehicle on or after 1.9.01 to replace a previous one

(except where the vehicle was first registered before 1.1.73).

For all other vehicles, either a prescribed font must be used or a style which is substantially similar so that the characters are easily distinguishable. However, characters must not be formed in any of the following ways:
- italic script
- a font in which the characters are not vertical
- a font in which the curvature or alignment of the lines of the stroke is substantially different from the prescribed font
- using multiple strokes
- using a broken stroke
- in such a way as to make a character appear like a different character

Other Materials on Registration Plate (Reg. 16)
Other than a standards mark (see Reg. 10) and the registration mark, no material may be displayed on a registration plate.
However, **Dual Purpose Plates** which conform to Council Regulation (EC) No. 2411/98 (which recognises distinguishing signs of member states) may display both the registration mark and the international distinguishing sign of the U.K. In this case, no material other that the U.K. sign may be placed in the space provided for that purpose, nor may the sign encroach beyond its margins.
Unless forming part of a dual purpose plate a plate may not be combined with a plate or device containing material which would not be permitted to be displayed on a dual purpose plate.

Culpability (Reg. 19)
The person responsible for complying with these Regulations is the person driving or, where it is not being driven, the person keeping it.

Imported vehicles (Reg. 14A) which do not have European type approval and are constructed in a way which precludes the display of registration marks conforming with Reg. 14 (see previous page), must comply as follows:
Height of characters - 64mm
Width of characters except 'I' & '1' - 44mm
Width of stroke of characters - 10mm
Spacing between any 2 characters in group - 10mm
Vertical spacing between groups - 5mm
Width of top and side margins not less than - 5mm
Space between bottom of mark and bottom of plate not less than - 13mm
Space between bottom of mark and top of suppler's details not less than - 5mm

REGISTRATION PLATE SUPPLIERS
VEHICLES (CRIME) ACT 2001
VEHICLES CRIME (REGISTRATION OF REGISTRATION PLATE SUPPLIERS) (ENGLAND AND WALES) REGULATIONS 2002

Registration (S.17)
Any person who carries on a business as a registration plate supplier in England and Wales must be registered with the Secretary of State. Failure to do so is an offence.

'Carrying on a business' means wholly or partly selling registration plates but does not include a dealer selling a vehicle which is fitted with registration plates, who has arranged its first registration in the UK on behalf of the intending purchaser. (Reg. 3)

Keeping of records (S.24 & Reg.7)
For each sale the supplier must keep records on his premises for 3 years. The records must contain details of-
a) information required to be supplied by the purchaser (see below);
b) method of payment, including credit/debit card/bank account details as appropriate;
c) details of the document used to verify the purchaser's name and address; and
d) details of the document used to verify the connection of the registration mark or the vehicle.

Failure to keep such records is an offence

Provision of information (S.25 & Reg.6)
The supplier must obtain the following details from the purchaser-
a) name and address;
b) registration number;
c) where the vehicle is being repaired at the request of an insurance company, the relevant insurance policy number; and
d) the connection of the purchaser with the registration mark or the vehicle to which it is to be attached.

Failure to obtain such information is an offence

REGISTRATION PLATE SUPPLIERS – cont
VEHICLES (CRIME) ACT 2001
VEHICLES CRIME (REGISTRATION OF REGISTRATION PLATE SUPPLIERS) (ENGLAND AND WALES) REGULATIONS 2002

Police powers (S.26)
A constable may at any reasonable time enter and inspect premises which have been registered for the supply of registration plates. He may require production of, and inspect, any registration plates kept on the premises and any records required to be kept, and may take copies. Force may not be used to enter premises unless a warrant has been issued by a justice. Before exercising these powers, the constable must, if required, produce evidence of his identity and authority for entry (if applicable). The above powers are also exercisable by a person authorised by the local authority.

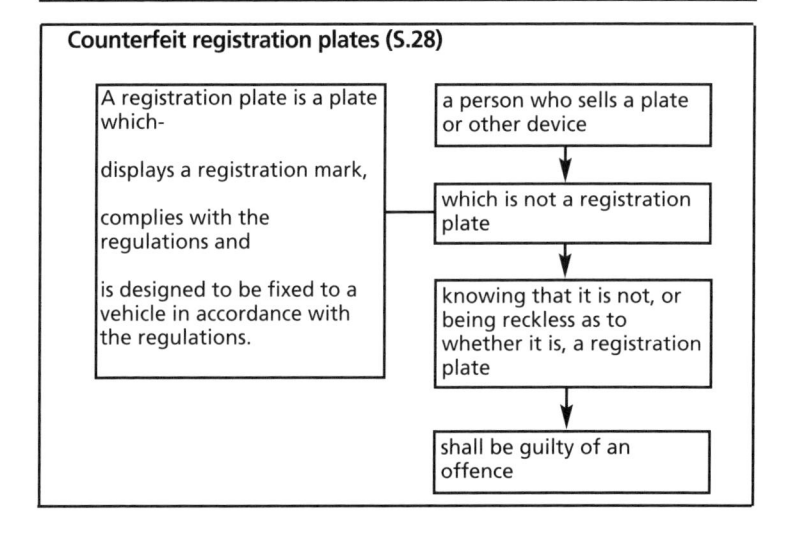

Counterfeit registration plates (S.28)

A registration plate is a plate which-

displays a registration mark,

complies with the regulations and

is designed to be fixed to a vehicle in accordance with the regulations.

↓

a person who sells a plate or other device

↓

which is not a registration plate

↓

knowing that it is not, or being reckless as to whether it is, a registration plate

↓

shall be guilty of an offence

Supplying to unregistered persons (S.29)
A person who –
a) supplies a plate, device or other object to an unregistered person (other than an exempt person) who carries on a business of selling registration plates; and
b) knows or reasonably suspects that the plate, etc., will be used for the purposes of that person's business as a registration plate;
shall be guilty of an offence.

PLATING AND TESTING OF GOODS VEHICLES

GOODS VEHICLES (PLATING AND TESTING) REGULATIONS 1988

The following goods vehicles are required to be tested annually, the first examination being not later than the end of the calender month in which falls the first anniversary of the date of registration (or, in the case of a trailer, the date of being sold or supplied by retail).

REG 9

Heavy motor cars and motor cars constructed or adapted for the purpose of forming part of an articulated vehicle

Other motor cars the design gross weight of which exceeds 3,500kg

Other heavy motor cars semi trailers; converter dollies manufactured or or after 1.1.79

Other trailers, the weight of which, unladen exceeds 1,020kg

REG 4

- A test certificate is issued and, in the case of a trailer, a test disc is also issued. The disc must be displayed on the trailer in a position where it is conspicuous, readily accessible and clearly visible from the nearside.

Light vehicles

- Goods vehicles under the above weights, private cars and dual-purpose vehicles under 2,040kg must be submitted for an annual test to an approved garage, starting on the third anniversary of first registration.

- However, certain vehicles have to be tested by the time they are **one year old**: taxis, ambulances, minibuses and other passenger vehicles with more than 8 seats (excluding the driver's).

S 47 ROAD TRAFFIC ACT 1988

Part 2: Documentation **141**

PLATING OF GOODS VEHICLES

REGS 66, 70 AND 70A ROAD VEHICLES (CONSTRUCTION AND USE) REGULATIONS 1986
GOODS VEHICLES (PLATING AND TESTING) REGULATIONS 1988

There are two basic types of plate:

Manufacturer's Plate and Ministry Plate

MANUFACTURER'S PLATE
REG 66 OF THE 1986 REGS

Contains details of maximum permitted weights. Must be fitted to:

(a) heavy motor cars and motor cars first used on or after 1.1.68.

> **Exceptions:** dual-purpose vehicles, agricultural vehicles, works trucks, pedestrian controlled, or passenger vehicles.

(b) buses first used on or after 1.4.82.
(c) wheeled locomotives and motor tractors first used on or after 1.4.73.

> **Exceptions:** agricultural vehicles, industrial tractors, works trucks, engineering plant, or pedestrian controlled vehicles.

(d) wheeled trailers manufactured after 1.1.68 exceeding 1,020kg UW

> **Exceptions:** those not constructed or adapted to carry a load other than permanent or essentially permanent fixtures – and not exceeding 2,290kg in total; living van not exceeding 2,040kg UW; works trailer; trailers for street cleaning or agricultural purposes; broken down vehicle; gritting trailer, trailers manufactured and used initially outside GB.

(e) converter dolly manufactured on or after 1.1.79.

MINISTRY PLATE
REGS 17-22 OF THE 1988 REGS
Purpose of examination

Upon submission of the vehicle for its first Goods Vehicle test, the vehicle is also examined for plating. The examination seeks to determine whether:

(a) the vehicle is of a make, model and type to which the standard lists apply. These lists are published by the Goods Vehicle Centre and show, in relation to vehicles of certain constructional particulars, the gross weight, axle weight, and train weight for that type of vehicle;
(b) the constructional particulars relating to that type of vehicle are substantially complied with; and
(c) the weights shown in the standard lists are applicable to the vehicle.

PLATING OF GOODS VEHICLES cont

Production of evidence of conformity

In conjunction with the plating examination, the driver must produce either a certificate of conformity issued by the manufacturer or a Minister's approval certificate as required under the National Type Approval for Goods Vehicles Regulations. This certificate is treated as a plating certificate.

The examination

The examiner ensures that the particulars on the certificate are appropriate for the vehicle; and the vehicle has not been altered. If the examiner is satisfied, that certificate is then deemed to be the plating certificate issued for the purposes of these Regulations. If the examiner is not so satisfied the vehicle must be subject to a full examination and determination of the various weights.

Plating certificate

The plating certificate contains the maximum weights permissible for the vehicle. Once a plating certificate has been issued, a Ministry Plate must be securely affixed, so as to be legible at all times, in a conspicuous and readily accessible position, and in the cab of the vehicle if it has one.

REG 70 C&U REGULATIONS 1986

The certificate is retained by the operator. Following the plating examination, the vehicle may undergo a goods vehicle test. Vehicles submitted for test are examined by a goods vehicle examiner for compliance with C&U Regulations. Following successful test, a goods vehicle test certificate is issued in relation to the vehicle.

DIMENSION PLATE

A vehicle which is not a goods vehicle fitted with a Ministry plate in accordance with Reg 70, and which is either (a) a bus or heavy motor car and which was manufactured after 31.5.98, or (b) a trailer used with such a vehicle and manufactured after 31.5.98, must be fitted with a plate in a conspicuous and readily accessible position containing the dimensions of the vehicle. Alternatively, those particulars may be shown in the manufacturer's plate fitted in accordance with Reg 66.

Part 2: Documentation **143**

PLATING & TESTING EXEMPTIONS

SCHED 2 GOODS VEHICLES (PLATING & TESTING) REGULATIONS 1988

> The following are exempt from the requirements of the regulations:

Agricultural motor vehicles and agricultural trailed appliances

Agricultural trailers and agricultural trailed appliances conveyors drawn by an agricultural motor vehicle

breakdown vehicles

converter dollies for agricultural, horticultural or forestry purposes

cranes (mobile)

dual purpose vehicles not constructed or adapted to form part of an articulated vehicle

electrically or steam propelled vehicles

engineering plant (not being moveable plant – being part of motor vehicle or trailer (not constructed to carry load)) designed and constructed for the special purposes of engineering operations

export – vehicles going to a port for export

funeral vehicles used solely for that purpose

heavy motor cars or motor cars constructed or adapted to form part of an articulated vehicle drawing a trailer which is (a) a living van not over 3,500kg, (b) permanently equipped with medical, dental, veterinary, health, educational, display, clerical or experimental laboratory purposes (but not involving sale hire or loan of goods from the vehicle, or for drain clearing or sewage or refuse collection), or (c) equipped only with automatic over-run brakes. The trailer/vehicle is itself exempt.

heavy motor cars and motor cars forming part of an articulated vehicle drawing a trailer which is being used under "Special Types" authorisation

licenced taxis

lifeboat vehicles

living vans not exceeding 3,500kg

police and fire vehicles

public service vehicles

road construction vehicles

play buses

snow ploughs and gritters

tower wagons

Vehicles, for street cleansing, refuse collection or disposal, or gully contents collection or disposal, in each case being 3 wheeled vehicles, incapable of exceeding 20mph, or have inside track width of less than 810mm

track-laying vehicles

trailers designed for the production of tar-macadam etc

trailers with only over-run brakes

vehicles for servicing, loading, unloading or controlling aircraft, or used on an aerodrome for road cleansing, refuse collection or disposal or gully (or cesspool) contents collection or disposal

motor vehicles first used before 1.1.60 and trailers manufactured before 1.1.60 used unladen

vehicles temporarily in GB for no more than 12 months

vehicles licensed in Northern Ireland and those based on certain specified Scottish Islands

Vehicles and trailers on public roads passing between areas of land in the occupation of the same person and not used for more than 6 miles on public roads in that calendar week

vehicles used for test or trial of new vehicles or equipment

visiting Forces

works trucks and works trailers

MOTORCYCLE PLATES

REG.69 AND SCHED 9 ROAD VEHICLES (CONSTRUCTION AND USE) REGULATIONS 1986

Every motor cycle first used on or after 1.8.77

which is not

a. propelled by an internal combustion engine with a cylinder capacity exceeding:
   i) 150cc if first used before 1.1.82, or
   ii) 125cc if first used on or after 1.1.82, or

b. a mowing machine; or

c. a pedestrian-controlled vehicle

---

must have a conspicuous and readily accessible plate securely fixed to the vehicle stating whether the machine is a

---

standard motor cycle

means a motor cycle which is not a moped.

moped

means a motorcycle which has:
(a) maximum design speed not in excess of 30mph
(b) kerbside weight not exceeding 250kg
(c) engine not exceeding 50cc

The plate must also include:

- manufacturer's name
- engine capacity
- kerbside weight (mopeds only)
- maximum design speed (mopeds only)
- manufacturer's vehicle identification number
- power to weight ratio (standard motor cycle)
- maximum engine power (standard motor cycle).

TRADE LICENCES
VEHICLE EXCISE AND REGISTRATION ACT 1994
ROAD VEHICLES (REGISTRATION AND LICENSING) REGULATIONS 2002

Trade licences are issued to motor traders, vehicle testers and persons who intend to commence business as such. More than 1 trade licence may be held at a time.

Vehicles covered by the licence (S.11)

1. <u>Motor trader who is a vehicle manufacturer</u> - covers all vehicles temporarily in his possession in the course of his business, all vehicles kept and used by him for research and development, and all vehicles submitted to him by other manufacturers for testing on roads;
2. <u>Any other motor trader</u> - covers all vehicles temporarily in his possession in the course of his business; and
3. <u>Vehicle tester</u> - covers all vehicles submitted to him for testing in the course of his business.

Definition of 'Motor Trader' (S.62)

A person who
a) manufactures, repairs or deals in, vehicles;
b) modifies vehicles, whether by the fitting of accessories or otherwise; or
c) valets vehicles.

Use of vehicles (S.12)
1. Not more than 1 vehicle may be used at a time;
2. May only be used for the purposes described on the following page;
3. May not be kept on a road unless being used on a road;
4. May not carry goods or burden other than:
    - A load carried solely for testing the vehicle or its accessories or equipment and which is returned to the place of loading without being unloaded,
    - Where a vehicle is being delivered or collected, a load consisting of a vehicle to be used for travel to or from the place of delivery or collection,
    - A load built in as part of the vehicle or permanently attached to it,
    - Parts, accessories or equipment designed to be fitted to the vehicle, and tools for such fitting,
    - A trailer other than a disabled vehicle;
5. A vehicle and semi-trailer is regarded as a single vehicle.

TRADE LICENCES cont

Purposes for which a licence may be used (Sched. 6)

1. No person may be carried on the vehicle or any trailer except a person carried in connection with such purposes; and
2. Goods or burden of any description (except specified loads) may not be carried.

A motor trader may use a vehicle (other than a vehicle kept by a vehicle manufacturer solely for research and development) only for the following business purposes:

(a) test or trial or the test or trial of its accessories or equipment;
(b) proceeding to or from a public weighbridge for ascertaining its weight or to or from any place for its registration or inspection;
(c) test or trial for the benefit of a prospective purchaser;
d) test or trial for the benefit of a person interested in promoting publicity in regard to it;
(e) delivering it to the place where the purchaser intends to keep it;
(f) demonstrating its operation or the operation of its accessories or equipment when it is being handed over to the purchaser;
(g) delivering it to or removing it from one part of the licence holder's premises to another part of his premises, or to those of another manufacturer, repairer or dealer;
(h) proceeding to or returning from a workshop for fitting, painting, valeting or repair;
(i) proceeding to or from the premises of a manufacturer or repairer of or dealer in vehicles to a place from which it is to be transported by train, ship or aircraft;
(j) proceeding to or from any garage, auction room or other place for storage or sale;
(k) proceeding to or from a place of inspection or testing; or
(l) proceeding to a place where it is to be broken up or otherwise dismantled.

Display of Licence (Reg.42)

The trade licence must be exhibited to the front of the vehicle by means of the trade plates issued for the vehicle.

Part 2: Documentation **147**

PUBLIC SERVICE VEHICLES

PUBLIC PASSENGER VEHICLES ACT 1981

Definition
A public service vehicle is a motor vehicle (other than a tram car) which is either:

- adapted to carry more than eight passengers and used for carrying passengers for hire or reward

- not adapted to carry more than eight passengers and used for carrying passengers at separate fares in the course of a business of carrying passengers

However, a small bus (not more than 8 seats) provided for hire with the services of a driver for the purposes of carrying passengers otherwise than at separate fares will not be regarded as a public services vehicle, but may need to be licenced as a private hire vehicle. but this will not apply if the business mainly operates large buses (over 8 seats). (S79A)

See over for fuller explanation

For 'Minibuses', see later this section

PUBLIC SERVICE VEHICLES – DEFINITIONS

PUBLIC PASSENGER VEHICLES ACT 1981

Adapted

There must be sufficient seating for more than eight passengers.

Used

Includes periods when temporarily used without passengers, but its use for such purpose has not been permanently discontinued.

Hire or reward

Would not cover an isolated occasion, nor a social arrangement between friends where contributions are made towards the expenses of the journey. There must be a systematic carrying of passengers beyond the bounds of mere social kindness.

But it would cover the case of payments made by members of an association in respect of a vehicle owned by that association.

Separate fares

Will not be treated as being a PSV (unless adapted to carry more than 8 passengers) if:
(a) the agreement to pay separately must not have been initiated by the driver, owner, person making the vehicle available, or receiving remuneration;
(b) no previous advertisement of separate fares (except under local authority approval);
(c) all passengers going to same destination;
(d) no differentiation of fares on the basis of distance or time.

Bearing in mind the exceptions already mentioned, it includes the case where a number of passengers are carried and one of them pays the total cost of the journey to the driver and then collects a share from the other passengers.

In the course of a business

Where passengers are carried at separate fares it shall not be in the course of a business of carrying a passenger if:
- the total fare for the journey does not exceed the running costs of the vehicle for that journey (including depreciation and general wear) and
- the arrangement for the payment of the fares was made before the journey began.

Terminology (PSVs/PCVs)

The change in terminology from PSV to PCV only relates to new issues of driving licences. Old driving licences still refer to a PSV and for other purposes the term PSV remains valid.

Taxis

TRANSPORT ACT 1985

A licensed taxi may carry passengers at separate fares without becoming a PSV if hired in an area where the licensing authority has made a scheme under this section, provided the hiring falls within the terms of the scheme. S 10

Similarly, a licensed taxi or licensed hire car may carry passengers at separate fares without becoming a PSV if all passengers booked their journeys in advance and each consented, when booking, to share the use of the vehicle.

PSVs – LOCAL SERVICES

SECTIONS 3 AND 6 TRANSPORT ACT 1985

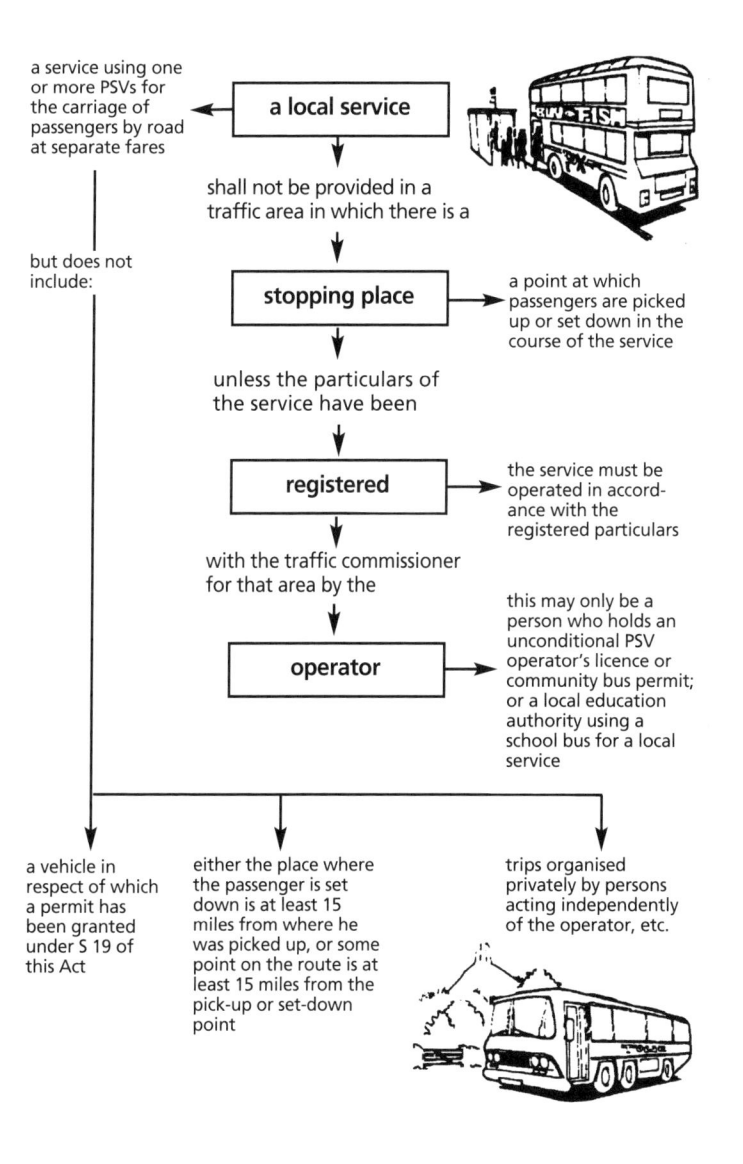

a local service ← a service using one or more PSVs for the carriage of passengers by road at separate fares

shall not be provided in a traffic area in which there is a

stopping place → a point at which passengers are picked up or set down in the course of the service

unless the particulars of the service have been

registered → the service must be operated in accordance with the registered particulars

with the traffic commissioner for that area by the

operator → this may only be a person who holds an unconditional PSV operator's licence or community bus permit; or a local education authority using a school bus for a local service

but does not include:

- a vehicle in respect of which a permit has been granted under S 19 of this Act
- either the place where the passenger is set down is at least 15 miles from where he was picked up, or some point on the route is at least 15 miles from the pick-up or set-down point
- trips organised privately by persons acting independently of the operator, etc.

PSV DOCUMENTATION

PUBLIC PASSENGER VEHICLES ACT 1981
PUBLIC SERVICE VEHICLES (OPERATOR'S LICENCE) REGULATIONS 1995

OPERATOR NEEDS:

Registration
In an area where there are stopping places for the services, the holder of an 'unconditional PSV operator's licence' or a 'community bus permit' or an education authority using a free school bus to transport fare-paying passengers, must register particulars of the service with the Traffic Commissioners for that area.
S 6 TRANSPORT ACT 1985

PSV operator's licence S 12(1)
Permits the operator to run a specified number of vehicles. There are 2 types of licence:
standard authorises the use of any PSV;
restricted authorises the use of
(a) PSVs not adapted to carry more than eight passengers
and
(b) PSVs not adapted to carry more than 16 passengers being operated either
  (i) other than in the course of a business of carrying passengers, or
  (ii) by a person who does not normally operate PSVs adapted to carry more than eight passengers.
S 13(1)

DRIVER NEEDS:

PSV DRIVER'S LICENCE
In addition to an ordinary driving licence, the driver of a PSV requires a PCV Driving Licence. The driver need only be 18 years' old if either:
- he is not carrying passengers and either he or his supervisor holds a PCV Licence, or
- he holds a PCV Licence and is carrying passengers either on a route which is less than 50km. or on a national route but the vehicle is constructed to carry not more than 14 passengers.

A constable may request production within 5 days at an address nominated by the driver.

VEHICLE NEEDS:

CERTIFICATE OF INITIAL FITNESS
A PSV adapted to carry more than 8 passengers requires a certificate indicating that the prescribed conditions as to vehicle fitness are fulfilled.
S 6(1)

Test certificate
All PSVs which are 3 years' old require a test certificate in the same manner as a car.

Operator's disc
Issued in respect of each vehicle run by the holder of an Operators' Licence. It must be exhibited on the vehicle
S 18(1)
The disc and operators licence must be produced within 14 days if so required by a police constable.
REG 1

See also 'Passenger carrying vehicle licences' early in this section

MINIBUSES
TRANSPORT ACT 1985

Defined as a motor vehicle adapted to carry more than 8 but not more than 16 seated passengers in addition to the driver. (S19)

Lawful operation depends upon whether the vehicle is being used for hire or reward. If not being so used there is no need for an operator's licence or permit, and may be driven on a D1 restricted licence.

If used for hire or reward, it will need to be operated on:
(a) Section 19 permit (see following page)
    granted to bodies concerned with education, religion, social welfare, or other activities of benefit to the community
(b) Section 22 permit (see later),
    this concerns "community bus services", being local services provided by voluntary bodies, or
(c) Full operator's licence (see previous pages)
    needed for a profit-making service provided to the general public or for private hire. Drivers are paid.

MINIBUSES – S19 PERMITS

SECTION 19 MINIBUS AND OTHER SECTION 19 PERMIT BUSES REGULATIONS 1987
TRANSPORT ACT 1985 – Ss19 & 20

This provision allows permits to be issued to educational and other bodies. Exempt from being classified as PSVs, therefore do not need PCV operator's or driver's licence, if:

- adapted to carry more than eight and not more than 16 passengers
- specified in the permit
- not used for members of the public
- not used for profit
- used only by permit holder
- used in accordance with permit conditions.
- comply with the conditions of fitness:

    a. first used on or after 1.4.88

    REGS 41-43 ROAD VEHICLES (C&U) REGULATIONS 1986

    (locks, doors, seats, fire extinguishers, first aid kit etc)

    b. before 1.4.88, either as (a) above, or

    REGS 5 -28 MINIBUS (CONDITIONS OF FITNESS,EQUIPMENT AN USE) REGULATIONS 1977

- Permits are granted to bodies concerned with
  - activities for the benefit of the community
  - education
  - recreation
  - religion
  - social welfare.

- Every authorised minibus shall carry a disc and a driver's notice setting out the conditions which have been imposed.

- Drivers must be over 21. On reaching the age of 70, drivers holding only a 'B' licence must comply with the medical standards applicable to D1 licences.

MINIBUSES – COMMUNITY BUS SERVICES

COMMUNITY BUS REGULATIONS 1986. TRANSPORT ACT 1985, SS 22 & 23

This allows for "Community bus services" to be granted permits for a local service operated by voluntary bodies. Permits may also be granted for a community bus service and (other than in the course of a local service) which *carries passengers for hire or reward* if this will directly assist by providing financial support for it.

"Community bus service" means a local service provided
(a) by a body concerned with the social and welfare needs of a community;
(b) not profit making either for the body or anyone else
(c) by means of a public service vehicle adapted to carry more than 8 but not more than 16 passengers

Conditions:
(1) Driver receives no payment except expenses
(2) Driver holds either a PCV driver's licence, a PCV Community Licence, a corresponding Northern Ireland PCV licence, or fulfils the following conditions:
 (a) holds a B (other than B1) licence,
 (b) has held the licence for an aggregate of not less than 2 years
 (c) is 21 years of age or over, and
 (d) if 70 years or over is not suffering from any disability which would result in the refusal of a D1 licence
(3) If unable to fulfil 2(a) (b) (c) & (d) above, must comply with the following:
 (a) granted licence before 1.1.97
 (b) holds licence authorising category B other than B1 vehicles, and D1 (not for hire or reward), and
 (c) is 21 years or over

A *permit disc* will be issued and must be affixed inside the vehicle so that it can be read in daylight from outside the vehicle (Reg 4).

A PSV *certificate of initial fitness* is not required provided the vehicle complies with the requirements contained on the following page (S 23(7)).

COMMUNITY BUSES – CONDITIONS OF FITNESS FOR USE

TRANSPORT ACT 1985 S23(7) COMMUNITY BUS REGULATIONS 1986 REG 6 COMMUNITY BUS REGULATIONS 1978 REGS 5-28 ROAD VEHICLES (CONSTRUCTION AND USE) REGULATIONS 1986 REGS 41-43

A Certificate of Initial Fitness is not required for a Community Bus provided it complies with the following conditions.

	First used on or after 1.4.88 (Construction & Use Regs)	First used before 1.4.88 (Community Bus Regs)
FIRE EXTINGUISHERS	Must comply with BS5423 (1977, 1980 or 1987) min. rating 8A or 21B. Readily available, maintained and marked with BS No.	Must comply with BS740/1 1948, 740/2 1952, 138 1948, 1382 1948, 1721 1968, 5423 1977 or 5423 1980. min rating 8A or 21B
FIRST AID	Contents as laid down in the schedule to the relevant regs, in receptacle maintained, suitable, available and prominently marked.	
EXHAUST PIPES	Outlet at rear or offside	Outlet at rear or offside. Not likely to cause fire.
DOORS	One on rearside and one emergency door at rear or offside. No door on offside other than driver's or emergency	If fuel tank behind rear wheels, one on rearside and an emergency door at rear or offside, if not, rear door may be emergency. No door on offside other than driver's or emergency. Unobstructed
EMERGENCY DOORS	Clearly marked as such on inside and outside. Means of operation clearly indicated	
POWER OPERATED DOORS (IF FITTED)	Have windows, operable by driver, operable from inside or outside, soft edges, closing resistance mechanism, not linked to braking system	
LOCKS ETC	Unlockable from inside, prevent accidental operation, open from inside or outside, closing catch, hinged to front, slam locking or warning to driver when opened	
VIEW OF DOORS	Driver to be able to see every door by mirrors, etc	
ACCESS TO DOORS	Unobstructed access from every passenger seat	
GRAB HANDLES	To be fitted to doors to assist passengers entry and exit	
SEATS	Wheelchair anchorages not to be side-facing. No seat to be side facing if immediately in front of rear doors unless protected	
	Not fitted to any door. Securely fixed to vehicle. Not less than 400mm wide. Fitted with guards to prevent passengers being thrown through doorway	
ELECTRICAL	Current not greater than that for which designed. Cables insulated and protected from damage Fused or circuit breaker fitted. Not exc-eeding 100V unless isolating switch fitted	To be guarded against shock or fire. Voltages exceeding 100v and not earthed must have isolating switch (except HT leads)
FUEL TANKS	No part of fuel system to be in driver or passenger accommodation. Before 1.4.88 must have fuel cut-off and not to carry flammable material unless in suitable packaging.	
STEP LIGHTING	All exits of gangways to be lit	
CONSTRUCTION	To be sound, of suitable materials, properly maintained and designed to withstand stresses	In addition to provisions on left, length not to exceed 7m and to be single decked.
STABILITY		Able to tilt to 35° without overturning
SUSPENSION		Must prevent excessive body sway
STEERING		No overlock possible
NUTS		All nuts subject to vibration to be locked

HACKNEY CARRIAGES

TRANSPORT ACT 1980

LOCAL AUTHORITY LICENCE

If the vehicle stands or plies for hire in an area to which the Town Police Clauses Act 1847 applies, a local authority licence is required.

PRIVATE HIRE

If the vehicle does not stand or ply for hire a local authority licence is not required, but the vehicle must still display the hackney carriage plate.

TAXI ROOF SIGNS – VEHICLES OTHER THAN TAXIS

Taxis are defined as vehicles which are licensed as such by the local authority.

Any vehicle which is not such a 'taxi' if carrying passengers for hire or reward must **not display** on or above the roof any sign which consists of or includes the word *Taxi* or *Cab* or any word of similar meaning or appearance; or any sign, notice, mark, illumination or other feature which may suggest that the vehicle is a taxi.

S 64

NOTE: (England and Wales only) the 1980 Act does not apply in Scotland

156 The Traffic Officer's Companion

SIGNS ON BUSES CARRYING CHILDREN

REGS 11, 17A AND SCHED 21A ROAD VEHICLES LIGHTING REGULATIONS 1989

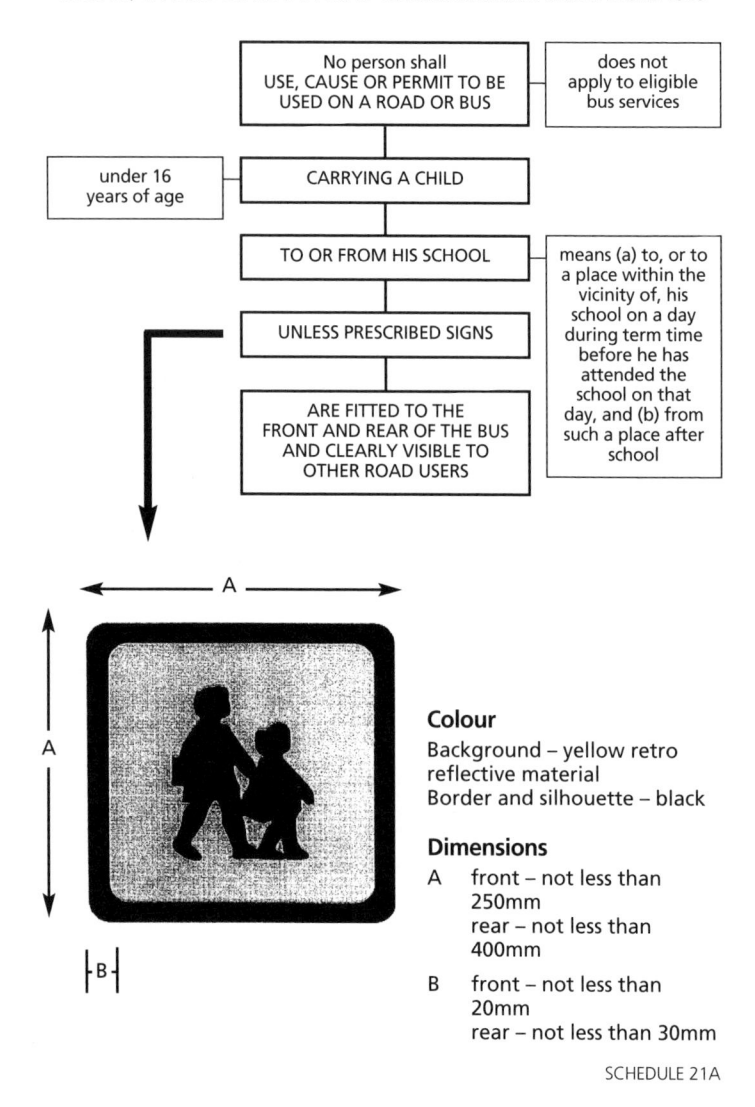

```
┌─────────────────────────────┐  ┌──────────────┐
│      No person shall         │  │   does not   │
│ USE, CAUSE OR PERMIT TO BE   │──│ apply to eligible │
│    USED ON A ROAD OR BUS     │  │ bus services │
└─────────────────────────────┘  └──────────────┘
                │
┌──────────┐    │
│ under 16 │────┤ CARRYING A CHILD
│ years of │
│   age    │
└──────────┘
                │
         TO OR FROM HIS SCHOOL ──── means (a) to, or to
                │                    a place within the
                │                    vicinity of, his
         UNLESS PRESCRIBED SIGNS     school on a day
                │                    during term time
                │                    before he has
         ARE FITTED TO THE           attended the
         FRONT AND REAR OF THE BUS   school on that
         AND CLEARLY VISIBLE TO      day, and (b) from
         OTHER ROAD USERS            such a place after
                                     school
```

Colour

Background – yellow retro reflective material
Border and silhouette – black

Dimensions

A   front – not less than 250mm
    rear – not less than 400mm

B   front – not less than 20mm
    rear – not less than 30mm

SCHEDULE 21A

Part 2: Documentation **157**

GOODS VEHICLES - INTERNATIONAL OPERATIONS

The following list may serve as a guide to the documentation which may be expected to be carried by the driver of a goods vehicle involved in the international carriage of goods

International freight permit
Issued to operators running services from countries with which Britain has entered an agreement.

TIR carnet
Intended to simplify customs procedures and avoid liability to pay customs duty. It is not mandatory but if used the carrying space is sealed by customs and a certificate must be carried in the vehicle. A plate must be displayed on the front and rear showing 'TIR' in white on a blue background. A separate carnet is required for each load carried.

'T' form
Not mandatory. There are two types of certificate. The first is a form T2L which merely establishes the origin of the goods. It is normally used in conjunction with the TIR system to secure lower rates of duty. The second type is an alternative to the TIR system and a form T1 or T2, certified by customs must be carried on the vehicle.

'ATA' carnet
Goods such as samples and display items which are only temporarily imported can receive customs clearance if an 'ATA' carnet is carried.

'ADR' certificate
When dangerous goods are transported, an 'ADR' certificate must be carried to signify that the vehicle and load conform with safety standards. If a tank vehicle or carrying tank containers a Vocational Certificate of Training is needed. A 'Tremcard' should also be carried, together with 'Consignor Declaration'.

Insurance
Although not mandatory, a green card may be carried providing the necessary evidence of cover. In the event of an accident, the police may retain the duplicate page, endorsing the front cover accordingly.
REG 5 MOTOR VEHICLES (INTERNATIONAL MOTOR INSURANCE CARD) REGS 1971

Insurance (cont)
Note that drivers of vehicles from EU Member States will be covered by the insurance issued in that Member State and do not have to produce a green card (see Insurance, earlier).
COUNCIL DIRECTIVE 72/166.

'CMR' consignment note
Operators carrying goods for hire or reward must ensure that a copy of the 'CMR' consignment note is carried on the vehicle, giving all particulars of sender, addressee and load, where goods are carried on the operator's own account (not for hire or reward) only a simple consignment note giving brief particulars is required.
ARTICLE 6, COUNCIL REG 11/1960

Public service vehicles
When used for the international carriage of passengers must carry an authorisation issued by the country of registration.
(ROAD TRANSPORT INTERNATIONAL PASSENGER SERVICES) REGS 1984

PSV Community licences
Council Regulation (EC) No. 11/98 established a community wide licence allowing PSV operators access to the international market for the carriage of passengers. Such carriage between Member States is prohibited without a Community Licence. Current holders of Standard National or International Licences, or Restricted Licences are entitled to be issued with Community Licences.
It is an offence to use, cause or permit a vehicle to be used on a road for UK cabotage operations without a Community licence; or for the driver of the vehicle to fail to produce the licence when requested to do so by an authorised inspecting officer (includes uniformed police officers)
(PUBLIC SERVICE VEHICLES (COMMUNITY LICENCES) REGS 1999
ROAD TRANSPORT (PASSENGER VEHICLES CABOTAGE) REGS 1999

INTERNATIONAL OPERATIONS cont

Registration document
The document (or copy of it) must be carried on the vehicle. If the vehicle is hired, a form VE103 is required.

Driving licence
This may be either an international driving permit or a driving permit issued in the country of origin (domestic driving permit).
ART 2 MOTOR VEHICLES (INTERNATIONAL CIRCULATION) ORDER 1955

Excise Form 115E
This is the authorisation for the vehicle to be in this country. It gives the date by which the vehicle should have returned to its place of origin.

ATP Certificate or Plate
Issued for refrigerated vehicles carrying perishable foodstuffs.

Community Authorisation
For hauliers within the EU. A certified copy must be carried on the vehicle. This is in place of the 'O' licence which is peculiar to the UK.

Letter of Attestation
Where tachograph charts for current week and last day of the previous week are not available due to e.g. holiday, a letter from the employer is needed.

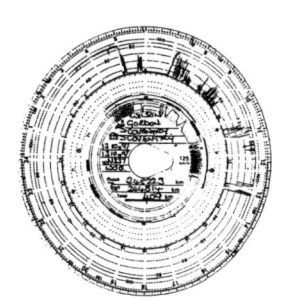

Letter of Authority
Where the driver is not the owner a letter of authority to drive the vehicle is needed from the owner.

Nationality Sign
The plate appertaining to the country of origin should be affixed to the vehicle.

Tachograph Chart
If vehicle is over 3.5 tonnes.

Passport
Full standard passport is required.

Plating and Testing
Foreign vehicles are exempt from UK requirements for up to 12 months in the UK. However, prohibitions may be issued if defects are discovered following a roadside check.

PART 3

LIGHTING AND MARKING

This section looks at obligatory lights, direction indicators, reflectors and the use and movement of lamps. It then moves on to consider the need for fog lights, reversing lights, warning lights and beacons. Finally it considers various apsects applicable to goods vehicles, eg marker lamps and reflectors, and the marking of projecting loads.

OBLIGATORY LAMPS ETC DEFINITIONS

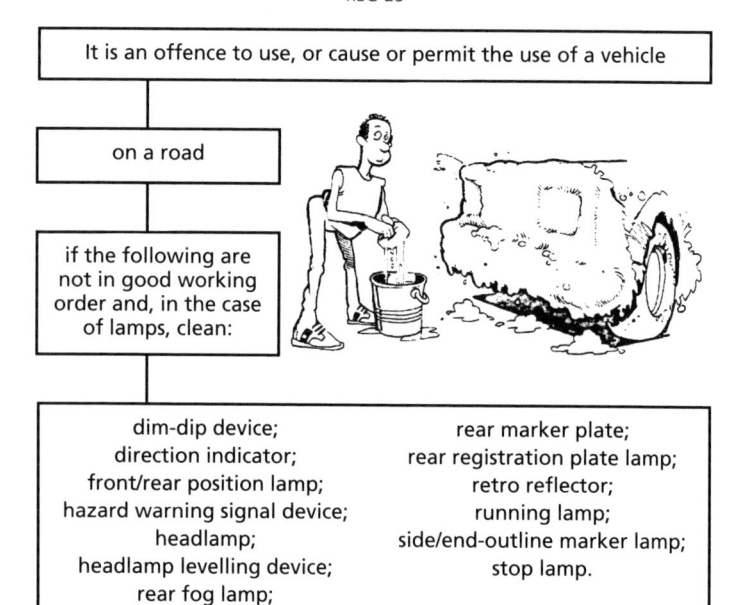

REG 18 AND SCHED 1 ROAD VEHICLE LIGHTING REGULATIONS 1989

POSITION LAMP – FRONT OR REAR

A lamp used to indicate the presence and width of a vehicle when viewed from the front or rear.

HEADLAMP

A lamp used to illuminate the road in front of a vehicle and which is not a front fog lamp.

HOURS OF DARKNESS

Means the time between half an hour after sunset and half an hour before sunrise.

MAINTENANCE
REG 23

It is an offence to use, or cause or permit the use of a vehicle

on a road

if the following are not in good working order and, in the case of lamps, clean:

dim-dip device;
direction indicator;
front/rear position lamp;
hazard warning signal device;
headlamp;
headlamp levelling device;
rear fog lamp;
rear marker plate;
rear registration plate lamp;
retro reflector;
running lamp;
side/end-outline marker lamp;
stop lamp.

Part 3: Lighting and marking

OBLIGATORY LAMPS ETC cont

REG 18 AND SCHED 1 ROAD VEHICLE LIGHTING REGULATIONS 1989

A SOLO MOTOR BICYCLE OR COMBINATION

Type	Vehicle exemptions
Front position lamp	Solo m/cycle fitted with headlamp
Dipped beam headlamp	First used before 1.1.31
Main beam headlamp	1. Max speed n/e 25mph. 2. Less than 50cc and first used before 1.1.72 3. First used before 1.1.31. 4. Constructed or adapted for use off roads and can carry only 1 person (If combination, 1 person plus 1 in sidecar)
Direction indicator	1. Max speed n/e 25mph 2. First used before 1.4.86 3. Constructed or adapted for use off roads and can carry only 1 person. (If combination, 1 person plus 1 in sidecar)
Rear position lamp	None
Stop lamp	1. Max speed n/e 25mph 2. Less than 50cc and first used before 1.4.86 3. First used before 1.1.36
Rear reg plate lamp	Vehicle not required to have reg plate
Rear retro reflector	None

A PEDAL CYCLE

Type	exemptions
Front position lamp	None
Rear position lamp	None
Rear retro reflector	None
Pedal retro reflector	Manufactured before 1.10.85

OBLIGATORY LAMPS ETC

REG 18 & SCHED 1 ROAD VEHICLE LIGHTING REGULATIONS 1989

A MOTOR VEHICLE, HAVING 3 OR MORE WHEELS

not being
a motor cycle (or combination), pedal cycle, pedestrian-controlled vehicle, horse-drawn vehicle, track-laying vehicle, or trailer drawn by a motor vehicle

shall be fitted with lamps, reflectors, rear markings and devices which are stated below unless exempted:

Exemptions are shown in the following tables

Type	Vehicle exemptions
Front position lamp	none
Dim-dip or running lamp device	1. Max speed n/e 40mph 2. First used before 1.4.87 3. Home forces' vehicle 4. Vehicles in respect of certain conditions being satisfied re the fitting of lighting and light-signalling devices as per requirements of EEC Directive 76/756 as amended, and alignment of dipped beam headlamps
Dipped beam headlamps	1. Max speed n/e 15mph 2. Agricultural vehicle or works truck first used before 1.4.86 3. First used before 1.1.31
Main beam headlamp	1. Max speed n/e 25mph 2. Agricultural vehicle or works truck first used before 1.4.86 3. First used before 1.1.31
Direction indicator	1. Max speed n/e 15mph 2. Invalid carriage n/e 4mph 3. Agricultural vehicle, industrial tractor or works truck first used before 1.4.86 4. First used before 1.1.36.
Hazard warning signal device	1. As for 'direction indicators' above 2. First used before 1.4.86
Rear position	None
Rear fog lamp	1. Max speed n/e 25 mph 2. Agricultural vehicle or works truck first used before 1.4.86 3. First used before 1.4.80 4. Width n/e 1,300mm

Part 3: Lighting and marking **163**

OBLIGATORY LAMPS ETC cont

REG 18 AND SCHED 1 ROAD VEHICLE LIGHTING REGULATIONS 1989

Continued from previous page

Type	Vehicle exemptions cont...
Stop lamp	1. Max speed n/e 25mph 2. Agricultural vehicle or works truck first used before 1.4.86 3. First used before 1.1.36
Rear registration plate lamp	1. Vehicle not requiring registration plate 2. Works truck
Side retro reflector	1. Max speed n/e 25mph 2. Goods vehicle: length n/e 6 metres and first used on or after 1.4.86; or length n/e 8 metres and first used before 1.4.86 3. Passenger vehicle 4. Incomplete vehicle going for completion, storage or display 5. Excavator (special types vehicle) 6. Mobile crane or engineering plant
Rear retro reflector	None
Rear marking	1. Max speed n/e 25mph 2. UW n/e 3,050kg and first used before 1.8.82 3. Max gross weight n/e 7,500kg 4. Passenger vehicle not being articulated bus 5. Articulated tractive unit 6. Incomplete vehicle going for completion, storage or display for sale 7. Agricultural vehicle, works truck or engineering plant first used before 1.4.86 8. First used before 1.1.40 9. Home forces' vehicle 10. Vehicle constructed or adapted for: fire fighting or salvage; or aircraft servicing or controlling; or road maintenance, dispensing tar etc; or transporter for 2 or more vehicles or boats
Side marker lamp	1. Max speed n/e 25mph 2. Passenger vehicles 3. Incomplete vehicle going for completion, storage or display for sale. 4. Overall length n/e 6 metres 5. Vehicle first used before 1.4.91 6. Vehicle first used after 1.4.96 in respect of which certain conditions are satisfied re fitting of lighting and light signalling devices as per EEC Directive 76/756 as amended, and alignment of dipped beam headlamps

OBLIGATORY LAMPS ETC cont

REG 18 & SCHED 1 ROAD VEHICLE LIGHTING REGULATIONS 1989

TRAILER DRAWN BY A MOTOR VEHICLE

shall be fitted with lamps, reflectors, rear markings and devices which are stated below unless exempted

Exemptions are shown in the following tables

Type	Vehicle exemptions
Front position lamp	1. Trailers for carrying or launching boats 2. Width n/e 1,600mm 3. Length n/e 2,300mm and manufactured before 1.10.85
Direction indicator	1. Manufactured before 1.9.65 2. Agricultural vehicle or works trailer manufactured before 1.10.90
Side marker lamp	1. Excluding any drawbar and any fitting, length n/e 6 metres or 9.15 metres, manufactured before 1.10.90 2. Incomplete trailer going for completion, storage or display for sale 3. Agricultural vehicle or works truck 4. Caravan 5. Trailer for carriage and launching boat 6. Trailer manufactured before 1.10.95 in respect of which certain conditions are satisfied re fitting of lighting and light signalling devices as per EEC Directive 76/756 as amended, and are installed and maintained as per requirements
Rear position lamp	None
Rear fog lamp	1. Manufactured before 1.4.80 2. Width n/e 1,300mm 3. Agricultural vehicle or works trailer
Stop lamp	Agricultural vehicle or works trailer.

Part 3: Lighting and marking **165**

OBLIGATORY LAMPS ETC cont

REG 18 AND SCHED 1 ROAD VEHICLE LIGHTING REGULATIONS 1989

Continued from previous page

Type	Vehicle exemptions cont...
End-outline marker lamp	1. Width n/e 2,100mm 2. Incomplete trailer going for completion, storage or display for sale 3. Agricultural vehicle or works trailer 4. Manufactured before 1.10.90
Rear reg plate lamp	Trailer not required to have a registration plate
Side retro reflector	1. Length n/e 5 metres excluding drawbar 2. Incomplete trailer going for completion, storage or display for sale 3. Engineering plant 4. Excavator trailer (Special types vehicle)
Front retro reflector	1. Manufactured before 1.10.90 2. Agricultural vehicle or works trailer
Rear retro reflector	None
Rear marking	1. UW n/e 1,020kg and manufactured before 1.8.82 2. Max gross weight n/e 3,500kg 3. Incomplete trailer going for completion storage or display 4. Agricultural vehicle, works trailer or engineering plant 5. Drawn by a bus 6. Home Forces' vehicle 7. Constructed or adapted for fire fighting; aircraft servicing etc; dispensing tar etc; carrying asphalt or macadam, being mixing or drying plant; transporting 2 or more vehicles or boats

LAMPS ETC – GENERAL EXEMPTIONS

ROAD VEHICLE LIGHTING REGULATIONS 1989

TOWING REG 6

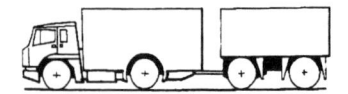

Type of Vehicle	Exemption
Motor vehicle first used before 1.4.86 and pedal cycle or trailer manufactured before 1.10.85.	Rear position lamp, stop lamp, rear direction indicator, rear fog lamp or rear reflector while a trailer fitted with such is attached to the rear.
Trailer manufactured before 1.10.85.	Front position lamp while being drawn by passenger vehicle.
Trailer manufactured on or after 1.10.85.	Stop lamp, rear fog lamp or rear direction indicator while being drawn by vehicle not requiring them.
Trailer manufactured before 1.10.90.	Stop lamp or direction indicator if towing vehicle is fitted with such and dimensions of trailer allow them to be seen from a point 6 metres behind the trailer (does not apply to trailers manufactured on or after 1.10.90).
Vehicle in combination	Rear marking if another vehicle in combination would obscure it.
Broken down vehicle being drawn.	Lamp, reflector or rear marking (except rear position lamps, and rear reflectors between sunset and sunrise).

Part 3: Lighting and marking **167**

LAMPS ETC – GENERAL EXEMPTIONS cont

ROAD VEHICLE LIGHTING REGULATIONS 1989

MASKING, ETC

A lamp shall not be treated as a lamp if:

1. Painted over or marked, so as not capable of immediate use or of readily being put to use; or
2. No wiring system to electrical source.

REG 4(4)

DURING DAYTIME

Lamps and reflectors need not be fitted during the daytime to:

1. Vehicle not fitted with any position lamps
2. Incomplete vehicle going for completion
3. Pedal cycle
3. Pedestrian-controlled vehicle
4. Horse-drawn vehicle
5. Vehicle drawn or propelled by hand, or
6. Combat vehicle.

REG 4 (3)

USE OF LAMPS

REGS 24 AND 25 ROAD VEHICLE LIGHTING REGULATIONS 1989

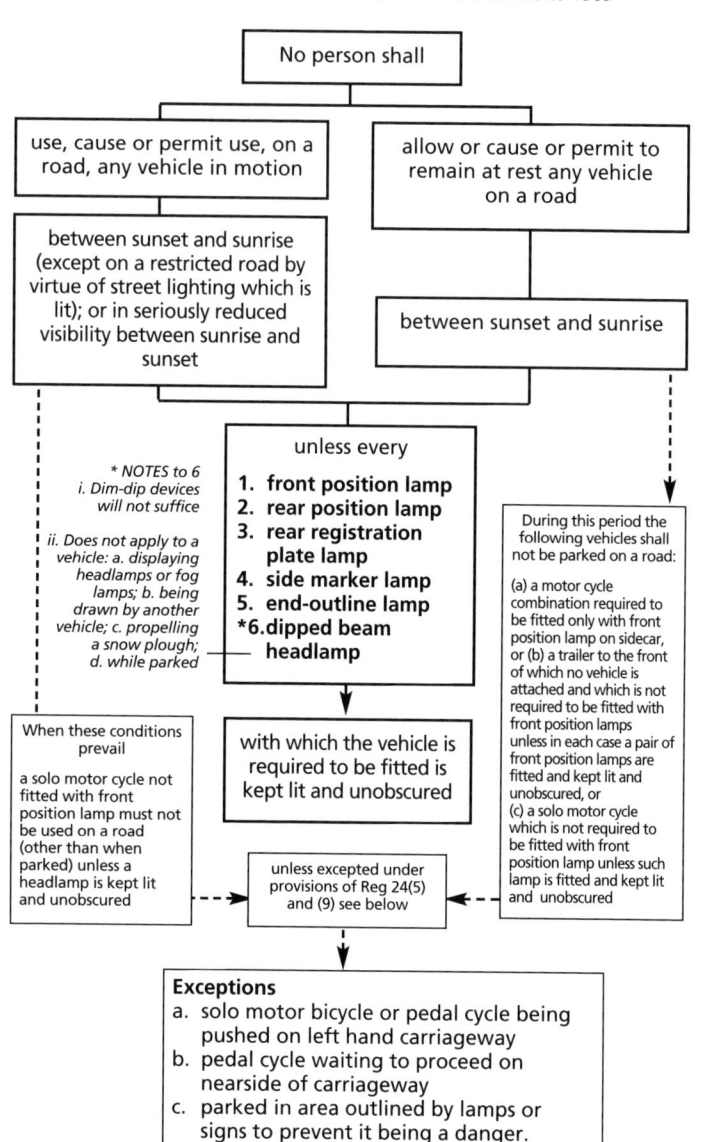

No person shall

- use, cause or permit use, on a road, any vehicle in motion
  - between sunset and sunrise (except on a restricted road by virtue of street lighting which is lit); or in seriously reduced visibility between sunrise and sunset
- allow or cause or permit to remain at rest any vehicle on a road
  - between sunset and sunrise

*NOTES to 6
i. Dim-dip devices will not suffice

ii. Does not apply to a vehicle: a. displaying headlamps or fog lamps; b. being drawn by another vehicle; c. propelling a snow plough; d. while parked

unless every
1. **front position lamp**
2. **rear position lamp**
3. **rear registration plate lamp**
4. **side marker lamp**
5. **end-outline lamp**
*6. **dipped beam headlamp**

with which the vehicle is required to be fitted is kept lit and unobscured

During this period the following vehicles shall not be parked on a road:

(a) a motor cycle combination required to be fitted only with front position lamp on sidecar, or (b) a trailer to the front of which no vehicle is attached and which is not required to be fitted with front position lamps unless in each case a pair of front position lamps are fitted and kept lit and unobscured, or (c) a solo motor cycle which is not required to be fitted with front position lamp unless such lamp is fitted and kept lit and unobscured

When these conditions prevail

a solo motor cycle not fitted with front position lamp must not be used on a road (other than when parked) unless a headlamp is kept lit and unobscured

unless excepted under provisions of Reg 24(5) and (9) see below

Exceptions
a. solo motor bicycle or pedal cycle being pushed on left hand carriageway
b. pedal cycle waiting to proceed on nearside of carriageway
c. parked in area outlined by lamps or signs to prevent it being a danger.

Part 3: Lighting and marking **169**

USE OF LAMPS cont

REG 24(5) ROAD VEHICLE LIGHTING REGULATIONS 1989

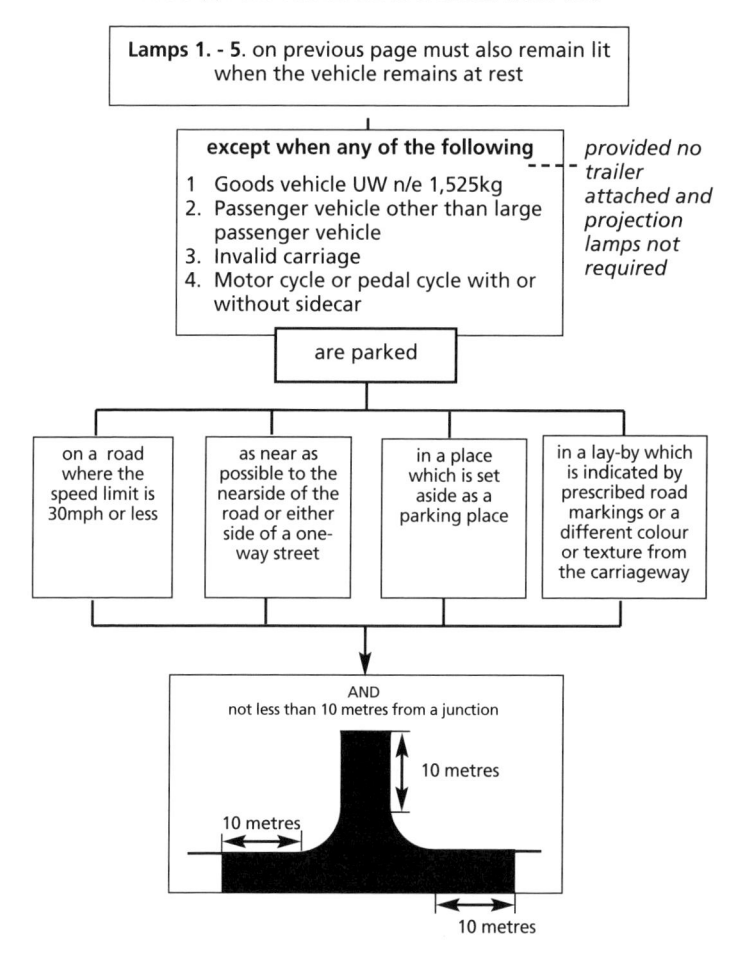

Lamps 1. - 5. on previous page must also remain lit when the vehicle remains at rest

except when any of the following

1. Goods vehicle UW n/e 1,525kg
2. Passenger vehicle other than large passenger vehicle
3. Invalid carriage
4. Motor cycle or pedal cycle with or without sidecar

provided no trailer attached and projection lamps not required

are parked

- on a road where the speed limit is 30mph or less
- as near as possible to the nearside of the road or either side of a one-way street
- in a place which is set aside as a parking place
- in a lay-by which is indicated by prescribed road markings or a different colour or texture from the carriageway

AND
not less than 10 metres from a junction

10 metres

10 metres

10 metres

OBSTRUCTION OF LIGHTS REG 19

At least part of the surface of any obligatory front and rear position lamp, front and rear direction indicator and rear reflector, must be visible when every door, boot or other movable part of the vehicle is in a fixed open position.

170 The Traffic Officer's Companion

MOVEMENT OF LAMPS

ROAD VEHICLE LIGHTING REGULATIONS 1989

REG 12

It is an offence to use, cause or permit use, on a road

a vehicle fitted with a

lamp, reflector or marking capable of being moved by swivelling, deflecting or otherwise while the vehicle is in motion

except:

amber pedal reflex indicator
direction indicator on vehicle first used before 1.4.86
headlamps adjustable to compensate for load
lamps/reflectors turning with steering wheels
movable dipping headlamps
reflex reflective material/reflector fitted to wheel or tyre of pedal
  cycle/sidecar solo motor bicycle/combination invalid carriage
retractable headlamps/front fog lights
warning beacon work lamp

REG 13

It is an offence to use, cause or permit use of

a vehicle fitted with a lamp which automatically emits a

flashing light

except:

direction indicator fitted for police purposes
green warning lamp used as anti-lock brake
indicator headlamp fitted to an emergency
vehicle lamps forming part of traffic sign
warning beacon/special warning lamp

FITTING BEACONS

Other than vehicles mentioned above, it is an offence to a fit warning beacon/special warning light – whether working or not – or device resembling such. REG 16

Part 3: Lighting and marking **171**

COLOUR OF LIGHT SHOWN BY LAMPS AND RETRO REFLECTORS

REG 11 ROAD VEHICLES LIGHTING REGULATIONS 1989

It is an offence to use, cause or permit use on a road a vehicle readily capable of showing a red light to the front:

except

1. Red and white chequered domed lamp or a red and white segmented mast mounted warning beacon fitted to a fire control vehicle, intended for use at scene of an emergency
2. Prescribed traffic sign attached to a vehicle; or side marker lamp, or side retro reflector;
3. Retro reflective material or reflector in wheels or tyres of
   a. pedal cycle and any sidecar attached
   b. solo motor bicycle or combination
   c. invalid carriage.

NOTE: For police control vehicle, read blue light and white light from chequered domed lamp fitted to vehicle; and in case of ambulance control vehicle, a green light and white light from chequered domed lamp fitted to vehicle

It is an offence to use, cause or permit use on a road a vehicle readily capable of showing a light other than a red light to the rear:

except

airport vehicle (yellow)
ambulance service control (green & white)
breakdown vehicle;
Customs and Excise fuel testing vehicle, surveying purposes, statutory removal or immobilisation of vehicles, escort purposes under 25 mph,
direction indicator and side marker lamp (amber)
emergency vehicle (blue)
fire service control vehicle (red & white)
illuminated rear registration plate
illumination of bus route indication
interior illumination
medical practitioner (green)
pedal reflectors (amber)
police control vehicle (blue & white)
prescribed traffic sign attached to vehicle (any colour)
rear markers reflex reflective (yellow)

reflective material incorporated in prescribed sign and fitted to the rear of a bus
reflected orange light to rear of vehicle carrying dangerous substances
registration plates reflex reflective (yellow)
retro reflective material as above (any col)
retro reflective (amber)
reversing lamp (white)
road clearance vehicle
taxi meter illumination
vehicle having max speed of 25mph,
vehicle over 2.9 metres wide,
warning beacon (amber) fitted to: refuse collection vehicle; road clearance vehicle; road cleansing etc vehicle; road apparatus cleansing etc vehicle, special types vehicles etc – S 44 RTA 1988,
work lamp (white)

172 The Traffic Officer's Companion

HEADLAMPS

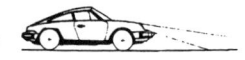

REG 18 AND SCHEDS 1, 4 AND 5 ROAD VEHICLES LIGHTING REGULATIONS 1989

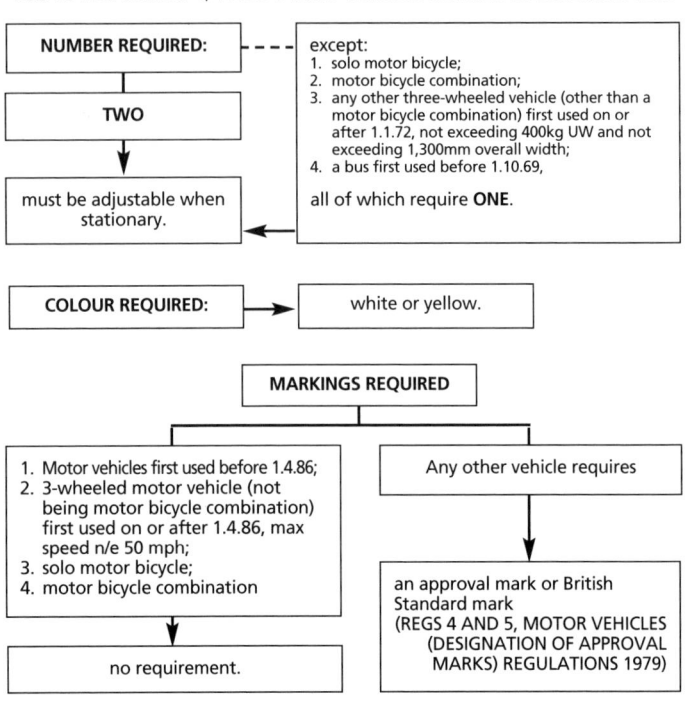

NUMBER REQUIRED: **TWO**

except:
1. solo motor bicycle;
2. motor bicycle combination;
3. any other three-wheeled vehicle (other than a motor bicycle combination) first used on or after 1.1.72, not exceeding 400kg UW and not exceeding 1,300mm overall width;
4. a bus first used before 1.10.69,

all of which require **ONE**.

must be adjustable when stationary.

COLOUR REQUIRED: white or yellow.

MARKINGS REQUIRED

1. Motor vehicles first used before 1.4.86;
2. 3-wheeled motor vehicle (not being motor bicycle combination) first used on or after 1.4.86, max speed n/e 50 mph;
3. solo motor bicycle;
4. motor bicycle combination

no requirement.

Any other vehicle requires

an approval mark or British Standard mark
(REGS 4 AND 5, MOTOR VEHICLES (DESIGNATION OF APPROVAL MARKS) REGULATIONS 1979)

WATTAGE REQUIRED

Motor vehicle	Minimum wattage	
	Dipped	Main
four or more wheels		
1. first used on or after 1.4.86	NR*	NR*
2. first used before 1.4.86	30	30
three wheels (not combination)		
1. first used on or after 1.4.86		
a. max 50mph	15	NR*
b. over 50 mph	NR*	NR*
2. first used before 1.4.86	24	30
solo motor bicycle (incl combination)		
a. n/e 250cc and n/e 25mph	10	15
b. n/e 250cc over 25mph	15	15
c. over 250cc	24	30

Must be capable of being dipped, and motor vehicles first used on or after 1.4.86 must be fitted with a circuit-closed tell-tale.

Must not cause undue dazzle or discomfort, or be lit while parked
REG 27

Must be kept clean and in good working order
REG 23

Part 3: Lighting and marking **173**

HEADLAMPS cont

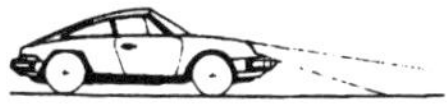

REG 18 AND SCHEDS 1, 4 AND 5 ROAD VEHICLES LIGHTING REGULATIONS 1989

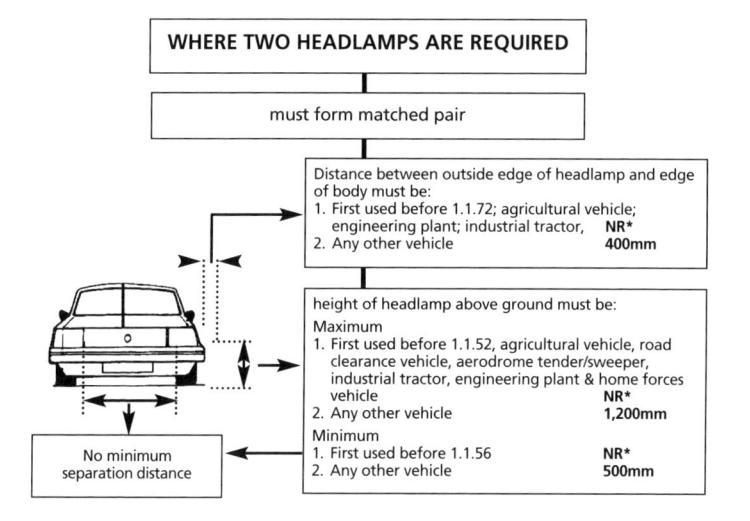

WHERE TWO HEADLAMPS ARE REQUIRED

must form matched pair

Distance between outside edge of headlamp and edge of body must be:
1. First used before 1.1.72; agricultural vehicle; engineering plant; industrial tractor, **NR***
2. Any other vehicle **400mm**

height of headlamp above ground must be:
Maximum
1. First used before 1.1.52, agricultural vehicle, road clearance vehicle, aerodrome tender/sweeper, industrial tractor, engineering plant & home forces vehicle **NR***
2. Any other vehicle **1,200mm**
Minimum
1. First used before 1.1.56 **NR***
2. Any other vehicle **500mm**

No minimum separation distance

WHERE ONE HEADLAMP IS REQUIRED

should be on centre line of vehicle (disregarding any sidecar)

or
any distance from side of vehicle (disregarding sidecar)
provided
another is fitted making a pair. Both then are obligatory.

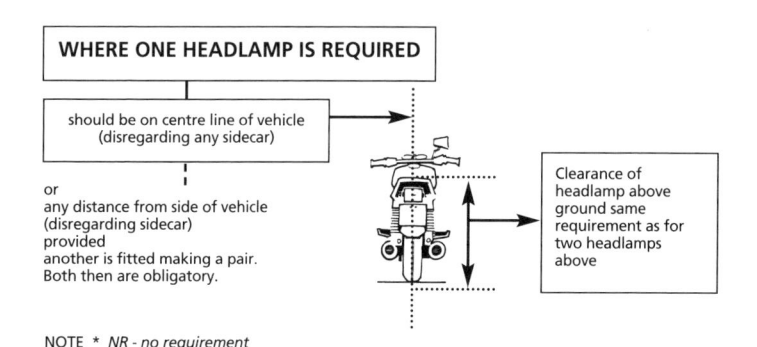

Clearance of headlamp above ground same requirement as for two headlamps above

NOTE * *NR - no requirement*

OPTIONAL LAMPS.

● Any number may be fitted but must comply with vertical fitting and colour requirements.

If first used after 1.4.91 only one pair of dipped headlamps may be shown at a time. Two pairs may be fitted only if one pair is for driving in other countries on the right of the road.

174 The Traffic Officer's Companion

FRONT POSITION LAMPS

REG 18 AND SCHEDS 1 AND 2 ROAD VEHICLES LIGHTING REGULATIONS 1989

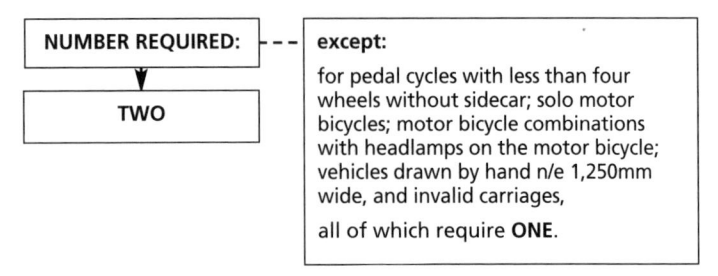

NUMBER REQUIRED: → **TWO**

except:

for pedal cycles with less than four wheels without sidecar; solo motor bicycles; motor bicycle combinations with headlamps on the motor bicycle; vehicles drawn by hand n/e 1,250mm wide, and invalid carriages,

all of which require **ONE**.

COLOUR REQUIRED: WHITE

unless incorporated in headlamp which is yellow.

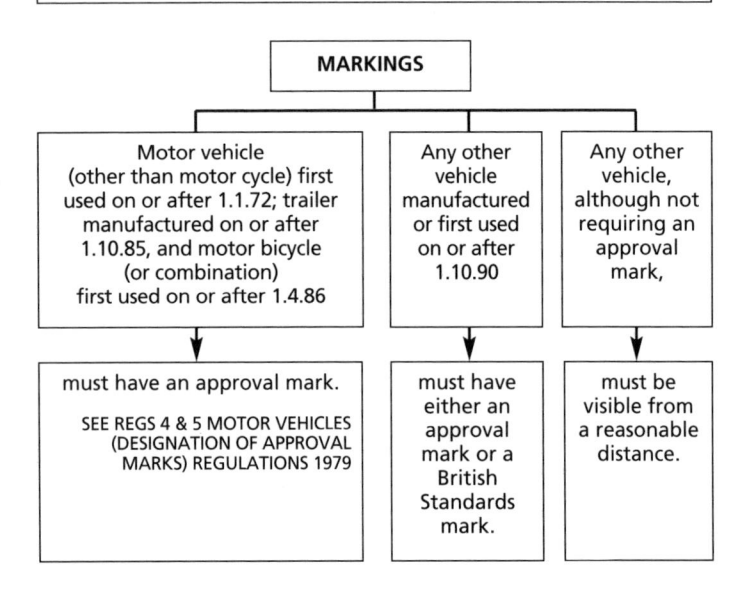

MARKINGS

- Motor vehicle (other than motor cycle) first used on or after 1.1.72; trailer manufactured on or after 1.10.85, and motor bicycle (or combination) first used on or after 1.4.86

  ↓

  must have an approval mark.

  SEE REGS 4 & 5 MOTOR VEHICLES (DESIGNATION OF APPROVAL MARKS) REGULATIONS 1979

- Any other vehicle manufactured or first used on or after 1.10.90

  ↓

  must have either an approval mark or a British Standards mark.

- Any other vehicle, although not requiring an approval mark,

  ↓

  must be visible from a reasonable distance.

Must be kept clean and in good working order.   REG 23

Optional Lamps

Any number may be fitted – apart from for solo motor bicycles first used after 1.4.91, which can have a maximum of two.   SCHED. 2.

Part 3: Lighting and marking **175**

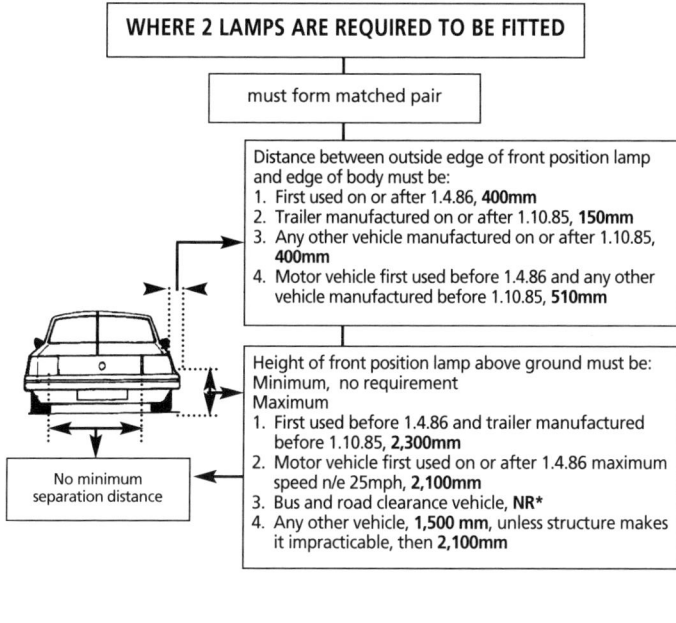

FRONT POSITION LAMPS cont

REG 18 AND SCHEDS 1 AND 2 ROAD VEHICLES LIGHTING REGULATIONS 1989

WHERE 2 LAMPS ARE REQUIRED TO BE FITTED

must form matched pair

Distance between outside edge of front position lamp and edge of body must be:
1. First used on or after 1.4.86, **400mm**
2. Trailer manufactured on or after 1.10.85, **150mm**
3. Any other vehicle manufactured on or after 1.10.85, **400mm**
4. Motor vehicle first used before 1.4.86 and any other vehicle manufactured before 1.10.85, **510mm**

Height of front position lamp above ground must be:
Minimum, no requirement
Maximum
1. First used before 1.4.86 and trailer manufactured before 1.10.85, **2,300mm**
2. Motor vehicle first used on or after 1.4.86 maximum speed n/e 25mph, **2,100mm**
3. Bus and road clearance vehicle, **NR***
4. Any other vehicle, **1,500 mm**, unless structure makes it impracticable, then **2,100mm**

No minimum separation distance

WHERE ONE FRONT LAMP IS REQUIRED TO BE FITTED

For any vehicle other than motor bicycle combination

lamp must be on centre-line or offside of vehicle

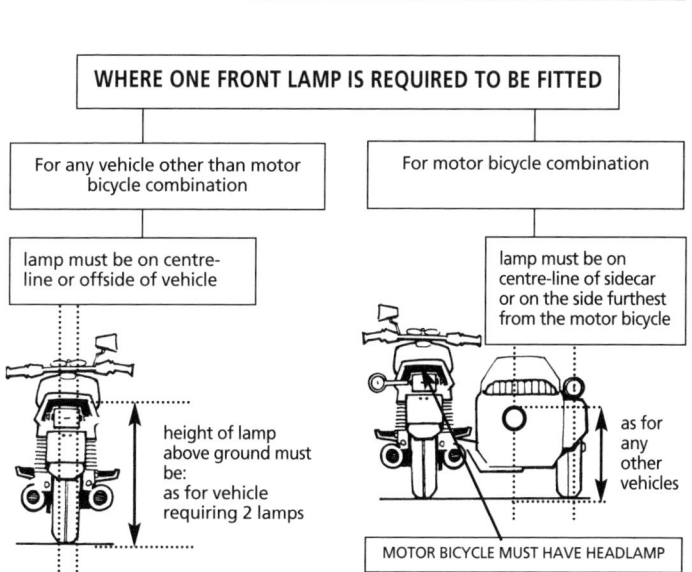

height of lamp above ground must be:
as for vehicle requiring 2 lamps

For motor bicycle combination

lamp must be on centre-line of sidecar or on the side furthest from the motor bicycle

as for any other vehicles

MOTOR BICYCLE MUST HAVE HEADLAMP

176 The Traffic Officer's Companion

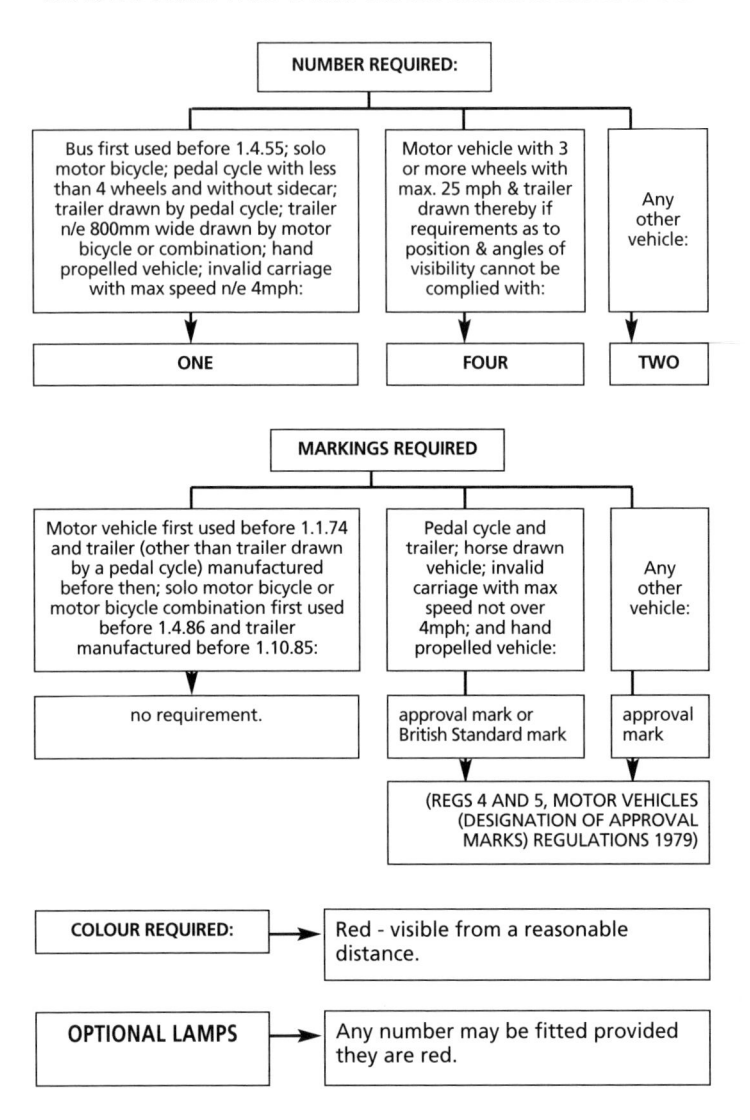

REAR POSITION LAMPS

REG 18 AND SCHEDS 1 AND 10 ROAD VEHICLES LIGHTING REGULATIONS 1989

NUMBER REQUIRED:

Bus first used before 1.4.55; solo motor bicycle; pedal cycle with less than 4 wheels and without sidecar; trailer drawn by pedal cycle; trailer n/e 800mm wide drawn by motor bicycle or combination; hand propelled vehicle; invalid carriage with max speed n/e 4mph:	Motor vehicle with 3 or more wheels with max. 25 mph & trailer drawn thereby if requirements as to position & angles of visibility cannot be complied with:	Any other vehicle:
ONE	**FOUR**	**TWO**

MARKINGS REQUIRED

Motor vehicle first used before 1.1.74 and trailer (other than trailer drawn by a pedal cycle) manufactured before then; solo motor bicycle or motor bicycle combination first used before 1.4.86 and trailer manufactured before 1.10.85:	Pedal cycle and trailer; horse drawn vehicle; invalid carriage with max speed not over 4mph; and hand propelled vehicle:	Any other vehicle:
no requirement.	approval mark or British Standard mark	approval mark

(REGS 4 AND 5, MOTOR VEHICLES (DESIGNATION OF APPROVAL MARKS) REGULATIONS 1979)

COLOUR REQUIRED: → Red - visible from a reasonable distance.

OPTIONAL LAMPS → Any number may be fitted provided they are red.

- Must be kept clean and in good working order   REG 23

Part 3: Lighting and marking **177**

REAR POSITION LAMPS cont

REG 18 AND SCHEDS 1 AND 10 ROAD VEHICLES LIGHTING REGULATIONS 1989

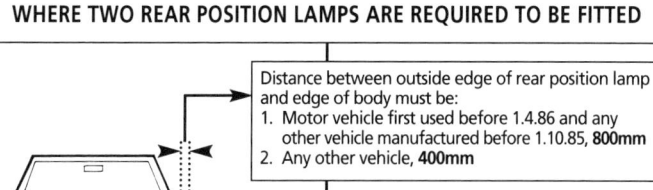

WHERE TWO REAR POSITION LAMPS ARE REQUIRED TO BE FITTED

Distance between outside edge of rear position lamp and edge of body must be:
1. Motor vehicle first used before 1.4.86 and any other vehicle manufactured before 1.10.85, **800mm**
2. Any other vehicle, **400mm**

Height of rear position lamp above ground must be:
Maximum
1. Large passenger vehicle first used before 1.4.86, **NR***
2. Motor vehicle first used before 1.4.86 not being large passenger vehicle, **2,100mm**
3. Trailer manufactured before 1.10.85, **2,100mm**
4. Agricultural vehicle, horse drawn vehicle, industrial tractor and engineering plant, **2,100mm**
5. Any other vehicle, **1,500mm** (unless impracticable), then, **2,100mm**

Minimum
1. Motor vehicle first used before 1.4.86 and any other vehicle manufactured before 1.10.85, **NR***
2. Any other vehicle, **350mm**

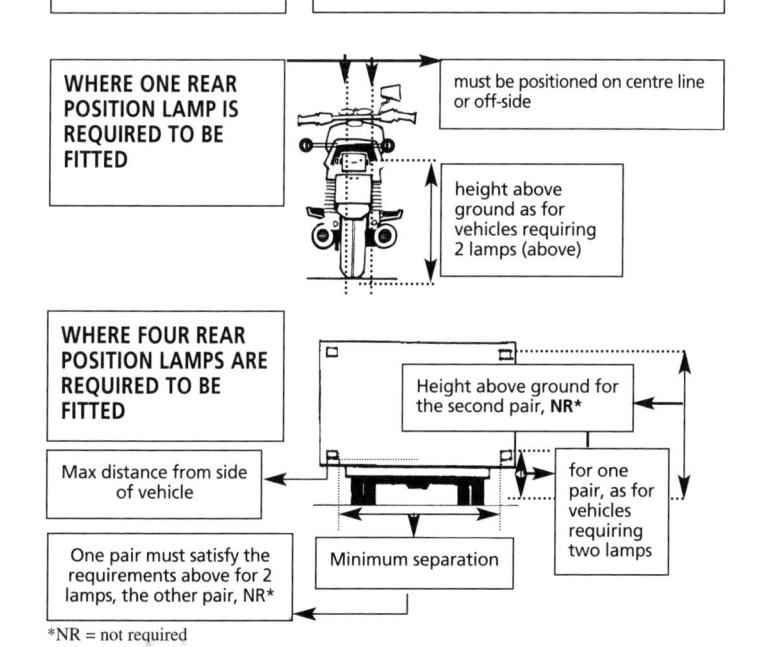

Minimum separation
1. Motor vehicle first used before 1.4.86 and any other vehicle manufactured before 1.10.85, **NR***
2. Any other vehicle, width n/e 1,400mm, **400mm**
2. Any other vehicle, **500mm**

WHERE ONE REAR POSITION LAMP IS REQUIRED TO BE FITTED

must be positioned on centre line or off-side

height above ground as for vehicles requiring 2 lamps (above)

WHERE FOUR REAR POSITION LAMPS ARE REQUIRED TO BE FITTED

Max distance from side of vehicle

Height above ground for the second pair, **NR***

for one pair, as for vehicles requiring two lamps

One pair must satisfy the requirements above for 2 lamps, the other pair, NR*

Minimum separation

*NR = not required

REAR RETRO REFLECTORS

REG 18 AND SCHEDS 1 AND 18 ROAD VEHICLES LIGHTING REGULATIONS 1989

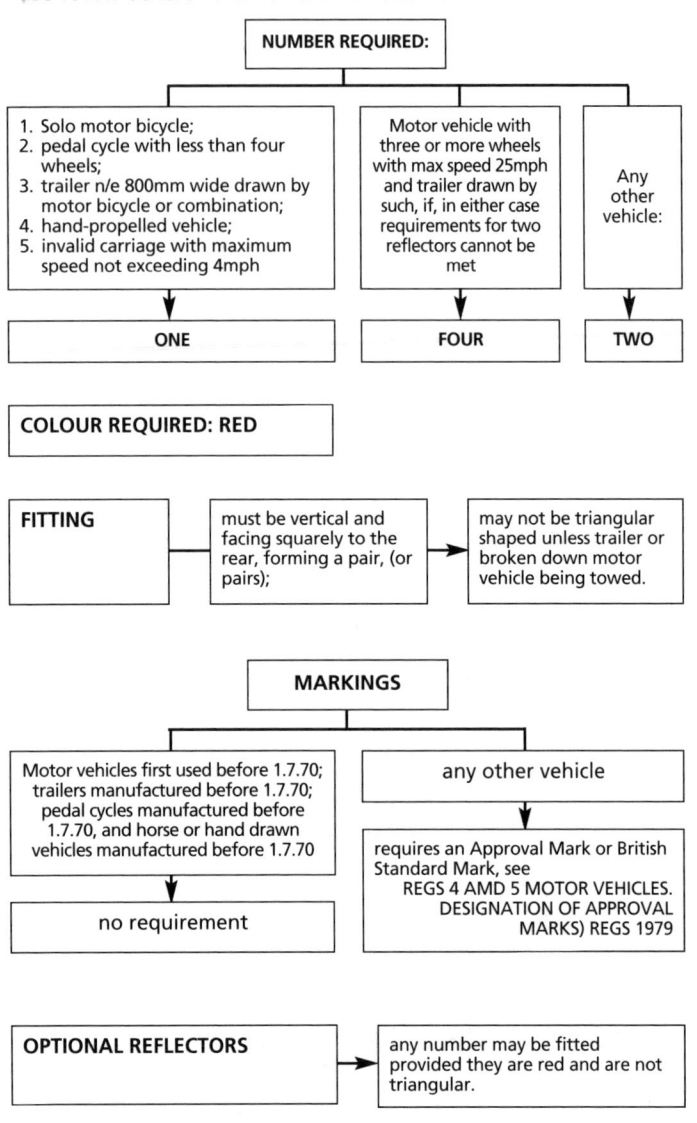

NUMBER REQUIRED:

1. Solo motor bicycle; 2. pedal cycle with less than four wheels; 3. trailer n/e 800mm wide drawn by motor bicycle or combination; 4. hand-propelled vehicle; 5. invalid carriage with maximum speed not exceeding 4mph	Motor vehicle with three or more wheels with max speed 25mph and trailer drawn by such, if, in either case requirements for two reflectors cannot be met	Any other vehicle:
ONE	FOUR	TWO

COLOUR REQUIRED: RED

FITTING	must be vertical and facing squarely to the rear, forming a pair, (or pairs);	may not be triangular shaped unless trailer or broken down motor vehicle being towed.

MARKINGS

Motor vehicles first used before 1.7.70; trailers manufactured before 1.7.70; pedal cycles manufactured before 1.7.70, and horse or hand drawn vehicles manufactured before 1.7.70	any other vehicle
no requirement	requires an Approval Mark or British Standard Mark, see **REGS 4 AMD 5 MOTOR VEHICLES. DESIGNATION OF APPROVAL MARKS) REGS 1979**

OPTIONAL REFLECTORS	any number may be fitted provided they are red and are not triangular.

- Must be kept clean and in good working order   REG 23

Part 3: Lighting and marking **179**

REAR RETRO REFLECTORS cont

REG 18 AND SCHEDS 1 AND 18 ROAD VEHICLES LIGHTING REGULATIONS 1989

WHERE TWO RETRO REFLECTORS ARE REQUIRED TO BE FITTED

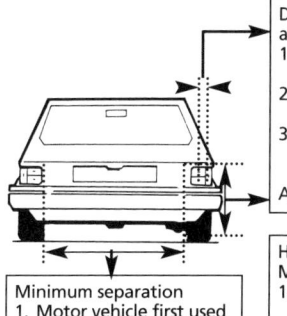

Distance between outside edge of retro reflectors and edge of body must be:
1. Bus first used before 1.10.54 and horse-drawn vehicle manufactured before 1.10.85, **NR***
2. Vehicle constructed or adapted to carry round timber, **765mm**
3. Any other motor vehicle first used before 1.4.86 and any other vehicle manufactured before 1.10.85, **610mm**

Any other vehicle, **400mm**

Minimum separation
1. Motor vehicle first used before 1.4.86 and any other vehicle manufactured before 1.10.85, **NR***
2. Any other vehicle n/e 1,300mm wide, **400mm**
3. Any other vehicle, **600mm**

Height of retro reflectors above ground must be:
Maximum
1. Motor vehicle first used before 1.4.86 and any other vehicle manufactured before 1.10.85, **1,525mm**
2. Any other vehicle, **900mm**, (unless impracticable), then **1,200mm**

Minimum
1. Motor vehicle first used before 1.4.86 and any other vehicle manufactured before 1.10.85, **NR***
2. Any other vehicle, **350mm**

* NR = no requirement

WHERE ONE REAR RETRO REFLECTOR IS REQUIRED TO BE FITTED

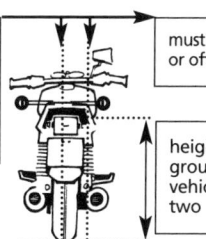

must be positioned on centre line or off-side

height above ground as for vehicles requiring two (above)

WHERE FOUR REAR RETRO REFLECTORS ARE REQUIRED TO BE FITTED

Height above ground for the second pair, **2,100mm**

for one pair, as for vehicles requiring 2 reflectors

Minimum separation: one pair as per vehicle requiring two, the other pair, no requirement.

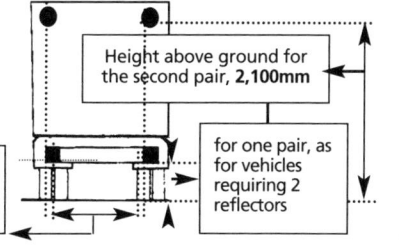

180 The Traffic Officer's Companion

FRONT RETRO REFLECTORS

REG 18 AND SCHEDS 1 AND 21 ROAD VEHICLES LIGHTING REGULATIONS 1989

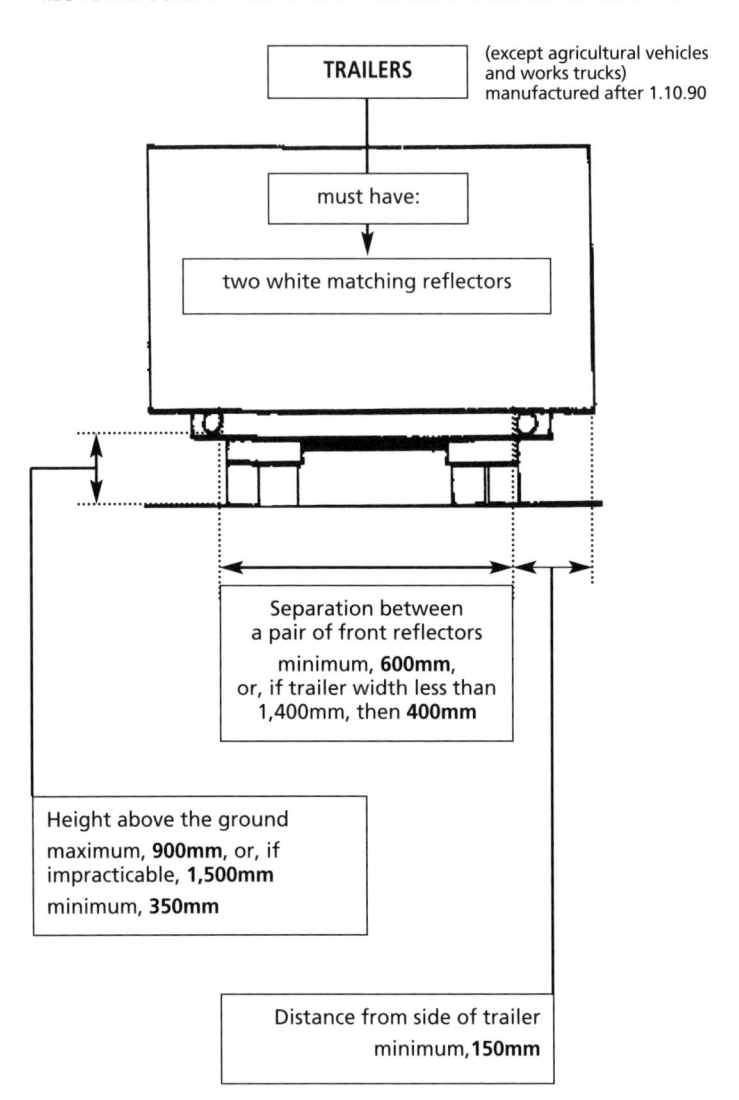

TRAILERS (except agricultural vehicles and works trucks) manufactured after 1.10.90

must have:

two white matching reflectors

Separation between a pair of front reflectors

minimum, **600mm**, or, if trailer width less than 1,400mm, then **400mm**

Height above the ground

maximum, **900mm**, or, if impracticable, **1,500mm**

minimum, **350mm**

Distance from side of trailer
minimum, **150mm**

Part 3: Lighting and marking **181**

SIDE RETRO REFLECTORS

REG 18 AND SCHEDS 1 AND 17 ROAD VEHICLES LIGHTING REGULATIONS 1989

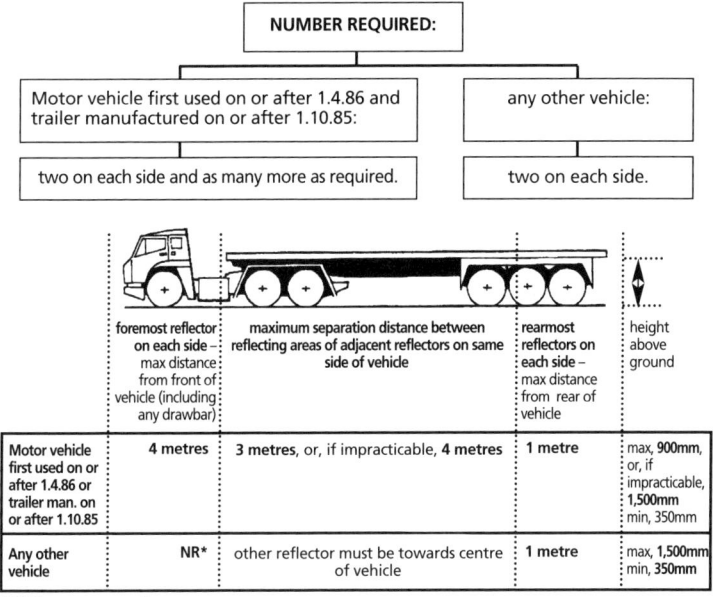

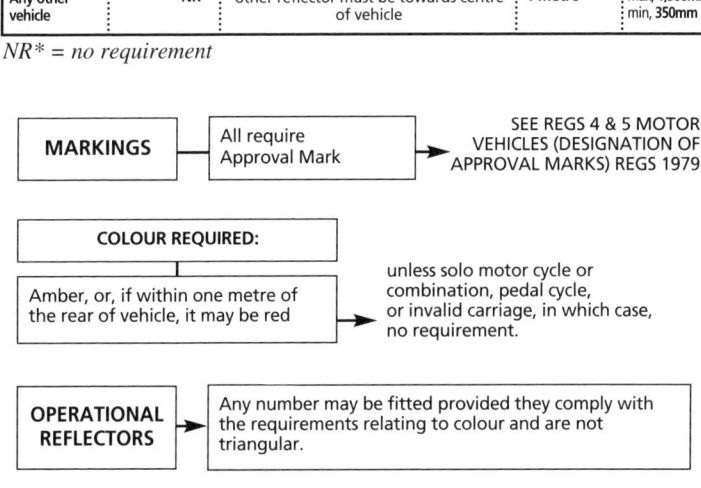

NUMBER REQUIRED:

Motor vehicle first used on or after 1.4.86 and trailer manufactured on or after 1.10.85:

two on each side and as many more as required.

any other vehicle:

two on each side.

	foremost reflector on each side – max distance from front of vehicle (including any drawbar)	maximum separation distance between reflecting areas of adjacent reflectors on same side of vehicle	rearmost reflectors on each side – max distance from rear of vehicle	height above ground
Motor vehicle first used on or after 1.4.86 or trailer man. on or after 1.10.85	4 metres	**3 metres**, or, if impracticable, **4 metres**	1 metre	max, **900mm**, or, if impracticable, **1,500mm** min, 350mm
Any other vehicle	NR*	other reflector must be towards centre of vehicle	1 metre	max, **1,500mm** min, **350mm**

NR* = no requirement

MARKINGS — All require Approval Mark → SEE REGS 4 & 5 MOTOR VEHICLES (DESIGNATION OF APPROVAL MARKS) REGS 1979

COLOUR REQUIRED:

Amber, or, if within one metre of the rear of vehicle, it may be red → unless solo motor cycle or combination, pedal cycle, or invalid carriage, in which case, no requirement.

OPERATIONAL REFLECTORS — Any number may be fitted provided they comply with the requirements relating to colour and are not triangular.

- Must be kept clean and in good working order.
- Must be vertical and facing squarely to the side.
- May not be triangular.

REG 23

DIRECTION INDICATORS

REG 18 AND SCHEDS 1 AND 7 ROAD VEHICLES LIGHTING REGULATIONS 1989

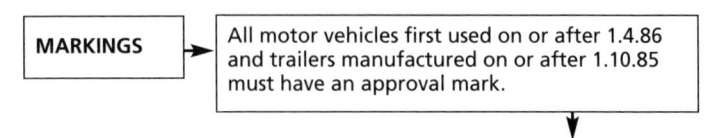

MARKINGS → All motor vehicles first used on or after 1.4.86 and trailers manufactured on or after 1.10.85 must have an approval mark.

SEE REGS 4 AND 5 MOTOR VEHICLES (DESIGNATION OF APPROVAL MARKS) REGS 1979

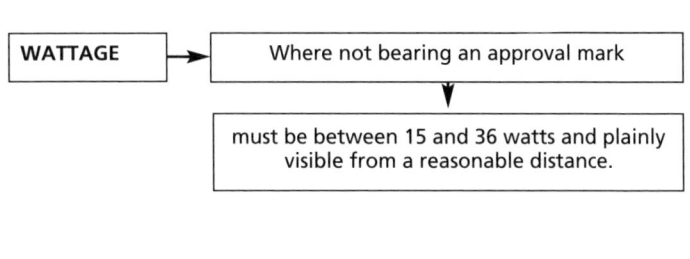

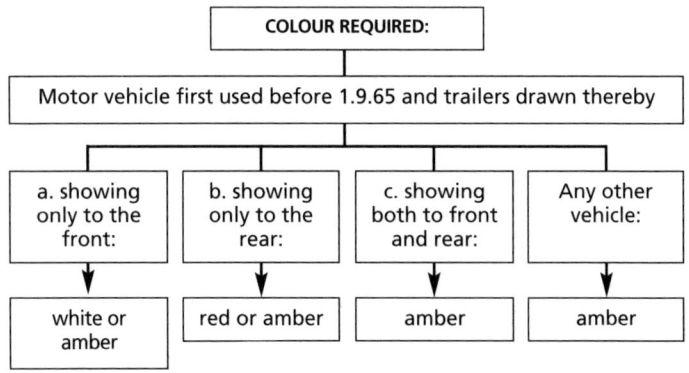

WATTAGE → Where not bearing an approval mark

must be between 15 and 36 watts and plainly visible from a reasonable distance.

COLOUR REQUIRED:

Motor vehicle first used before 1.9.65 and trailers drawn thereby

a. showing only to the front:	b. showing only to the rear:	c. showing both to front and rear:	Any other vehicle:
white or amber	red or amber	amber	amber

FITTING

- All indicators on one side should be operated by one switch, and shall flash in phase (except motor cycles and pedal cycles which may flash alternately).

- Must be an operational tell-tale unless the driver can see the indicators from the driving position.

- Must flash between 60 and 120 flashes per minute. Must form a pair (or if more than 2 – 2 pairs).

Part 3: Lighting and marking **183**

DIRECTION INDICATORS cont

REG 18 AND SCHEDS 1 AND 7 ROAD VEHICLES LIGHTING REGULATIONS 1989

Minimum separation distance between indicators on opposite sides of vehicle

A motor vehicle (other than solo motor bicycle or motor bicycle combination or invalid carriage having maximum speed not exceeding 8mph) first used on or after 1.4.86; a trailer manufactured on or after 1.10.85; a horse-drawn vehicle, pedestrian controlled vehicle and vehicle drawn or propelled by hand, **500mm**

or, if the overall width of vehicle is less than 1,400mm, **400mm**

Before above date, **NR***

Height above ground

Maximum
motor vehicle first used before 1.4.86 & trailer manufactured before 1.10.85, NR* maximum speed n/e 25mph , NR*
any other vehicle, **1,500mm** unless impracticable, then, **2,300mm**

Minimum, **350mm**

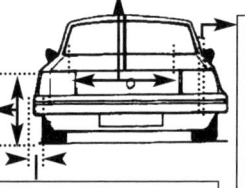

Minimum separation distance between front indicator and any headlamp or front fog lamp

Motor vehicle not being solo motor bicycle or motor bicycle combination first used on or after 1.4.95
CAT 1 indicator, **40mm**;
CAT 1a indicator, **20mm**;
CAT 1b indicator, **NR***

Before above date, **NR***

Maximum distance from side of vehicle

Motor vehicle first used before 1.4.86; trailer manufactured before 1.10.85;
solo motor bicycle, pedal cycle, horse-drawn vehicle or vehicle drawn by hand, **NR***

Before the above dates, **NR***

Any other vehicle, **400mm**

Minimum separation distance between front indicator and headlamp or foglamp

for solo motor bicycles or motor bicycle combination first used on or after 1.4.86 (includes combinations), **100mm**

before above date, **NR***

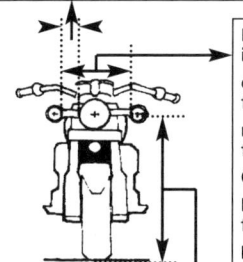

Minimum separation distance between indicators on opposite sides of vehicle

over 50cc and first used on or after 1.4.86:
front, **300mm**; rear, **240mm**; side, **NR***

n/e 50 cc and first used on or after 1.4.86 and pedal cycle:
front, **240mm**; rear, **180mm**; side, **NR***

Combination first used on or after 1.4.86, **400mm**

Invalid carriage maximum speed n/e 8mph:
front, **240mm**; rear, **300mm**

Before the above dates – **NR***

Height above ground as shown for above

* NR = no requirement

- Must be kept clean and in good working order.

REG 23

STOP LAMPS

REG 18 AND SCHEDS 1 AND 12 ROAD VEHICLES LIGHTING REGULATIONS 1989

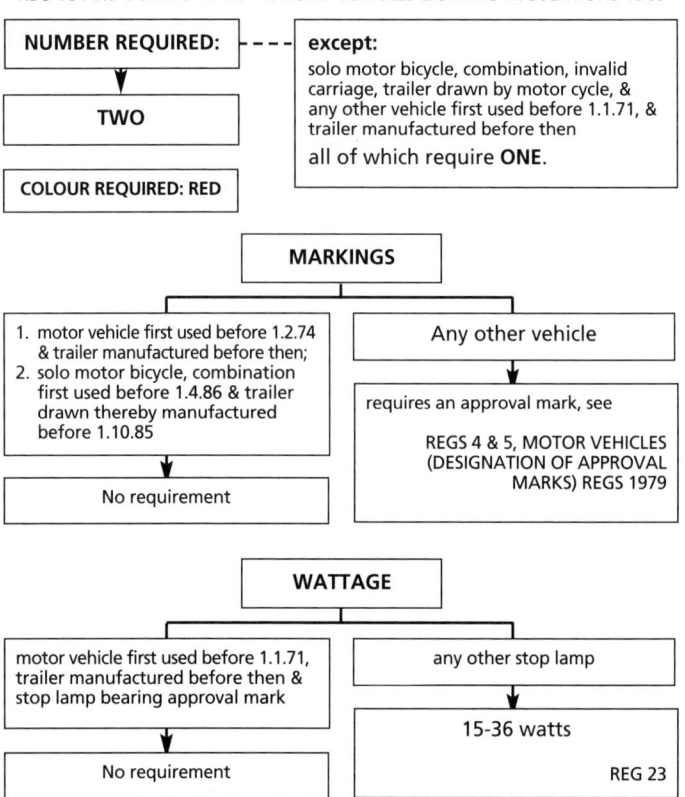

NUMBER REQUIRED: ---- **except:**
solo motor bicycle, combination, invalid carriage, trailer drawn by motor cycle, & any other vehicle first used before 1.1.71, & trailer manufactured before then

TWO

all of which require **ONE**.

COLOUR REQUIRED: RED

MARKINGS

1. motor vehicle first used before 1.2.74 & trailer manufactured before then;
2. solo motor bicycle, combination first used before 1.4.86 & trailer drawn thereby manufactured before 1.10.85

No requirement

Any other vehicle

requires an approval mark, see

REGS 4 & 5, MOTOR VEHICLES (DESIGNATION OF APPROVAL MARKS) REGS 1979

WATTAGE

motor vehicle first used before 1.1.71, trailer manufactured before then & stop lamp bearing approval mark

No requirement

any other stop lamp

15-36 watts

REG 23

ELECTRICAL CONNECTIONS

A motor bicycle (including combination) first used on or after 1.4.86 must be capable of operating the stop lamp by both front and back brakes.

Every other vehicle and trailer must operate the stop lamp by the braking system.

OPTIONAL LAMPS

Any number may be fitted but they must comply with all other requirements relating to obligatory stop lamps except minimum separation distance between 2 stop lamps.

| Must be kept clean & in good working order | Reg 23 |

Part 3: Lighting and marking **185**

STOP LAMPS cont

REG 18 AND SCHEDS 1 AND 12 ROAD VEHICLES LIGHTING REGULATIONS 1989

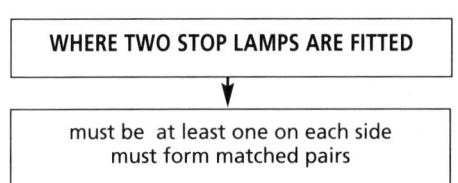

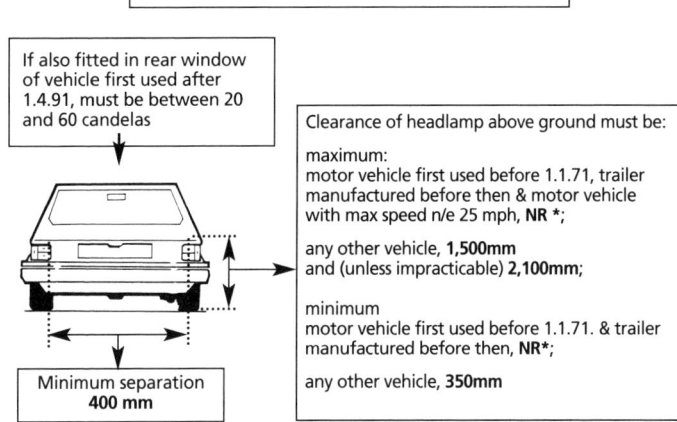

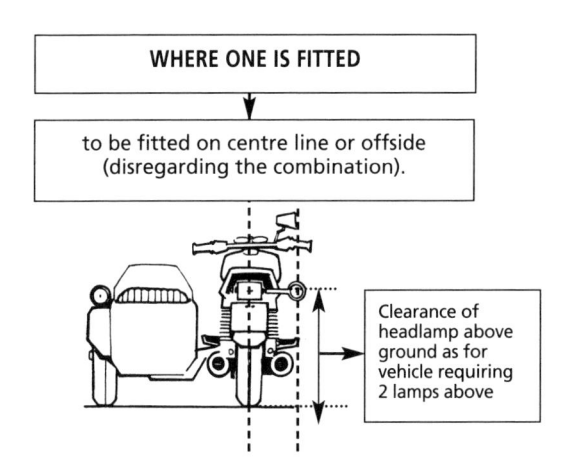

WHERE TWO STOP LAMPS ARE FITTED

↓

must be at least one on each side
must form matched pairs

If also fitted in rear window of vehicle first used after 1.4.91, must be between 20 and 60 candelas

Clearance of headlamp above ground must be:

maximum:
motor vehicle first used before 1.1.71, trailer manufactured before then & motor vehicle with max speed n/e 25 mph, **NR ***;

any other vehicle, **1,500mm**
and (unless impracticable) **2,100mm**;

minimum
motor vehicle first used before 1.1.71. & trailer manufactured before then, **NR***;

any other vehicle, **350mm**

Minimum separation
400 mm

WHERE ONE IS FITTED

↓

to be fitted on centre line or offside
(disregarding the combination).

Clearance of headlamp above ground as for vehicle requiring 2 lamps above

* *NR - no requirement*

186 The Traffic Officer's Companion

REAR FOG LAMPS

REG. 18 SCHEDS. 1 AND 11
ROAD VEHICLES LIGHTING REGULATIONS 1989

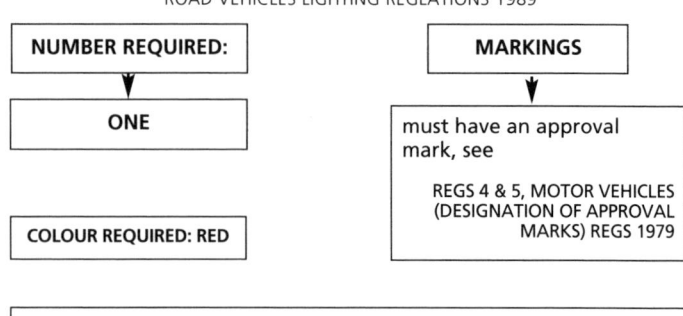

NUMBER REQUIRED:
↓
ONE

COLOUR REQUIRED: RED

MARKINGS
↓
must have an approval mark, see

REGS 4 & 5, MOTOR VEHICLES (DESIGNATION OF APPROVAL MARKS) REGS 1979

ELECTRICAL CONNECTIONS
Must not be capable of being operated by braking systems. A circuit-closed tell-tale must be fitted.

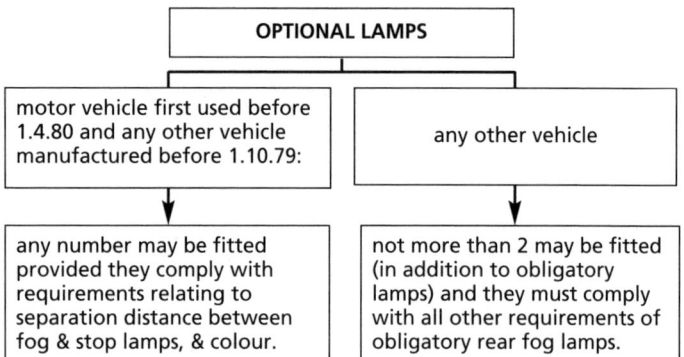

OPTIONAL LAMPS

motor vehicle first used before 1.4.80 and any other vehicle manufactured before 1.10.79:
↓
any number may be fitted provided they comply with requirements relating to separation distance between fog & stop lamps, & colour.

They must not be capable of being operated by the braking system.

any other vehicle
↓
not more than 2 may be fitted (in addition to obligatory lamps) and they must comply with all other requirements of obligatory rear fog lamps.

Must not cause undue dazzle or discomfort, be lit when parked, nor be used except in seriously reduced visibility
REG 27

Part 3: Lighting and marking **187**

REAR FOG LAMPS cont
REG. 18 SCHEDS. 1 AND 11
ROAD VEHICLES LIGHTING REGLATIONS 1989

WHERE TWO REAR FOG LAMPS ARE FITTED

Laterally there is no fitting requirement, but must form a matching pair if vehicle first used on or after 1.4.86, or trailer manufactured on or after 1.10.85.

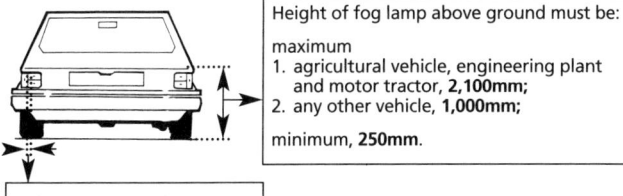

Height of fog lamp above ground must be:

maximum
1. agricultural vehicle, engineering plant and motor tractor, **2,100mm**;
2. any other vehicle, **1,000mm**;

minimum, **250mm**.

Minimum separation distance between fog lamp and stop lamp, **100mm**

WHERE ONE REAR FOG LAMP IS FITTED

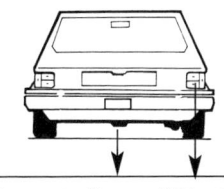

Fitted on centre line or offside of the vehicle (disregarding any sidecar forming part of motor bicycle combination)

Must be kept clean, in good working order and maintained so as not to cause undue dazzle or inconvenience

REG 23

188 The Traffic Officer's Companion

FRONT FOG LAMPS
REG. 20 AND SCHED. 6
ROAD VEHICLES LIGHTING REGULATIONS 1989

These lamps are not obligatory, but must comply with the following:

NUMBER:

motor vehicles (other than motor bicycle or motor bicycle combination) first used on or after 1.4.91 – not more than two.

Any other vehicle, no requirement

COLOUR: white or yellow

MARKINGS:

first used before 1.4.86, no requirement

any other vehicle needs an approval mark, see:
REGS 4 & 5, MOTOR VEHICLES (DESIGNATION OF APPROVAL MARKS) REGULATIONS 1979

When used as a pair in seriously reduced visibility in place of obligatory head lights, **400 mm**

Any other case, **no requirement**

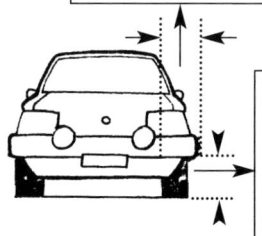

Maximum height above the ground:
1. agricultural vehicle, road clearance vehicle aerodrome fire tender or runway sweeper, industrial tractor, engineering plant & home forces vehicle, **no requirement**
2. any other vehicle, **1,200 mm**

Minimum height above the ground, **no requirement**

● Must not cause undue dazzle or discomfort, be lit when parked, nor be used except in seriously reduced visibility

REG 27

● Must be kept clean, in good working order and maintained so as not to cause undue dazzle or inconvenience

REG 23

Part 3: Lighting and marking **189**

REVERSING LIGHTS

REG. 20 AND SCHED 14
ROAD VEHICLES LIGHTING REGULATIONS 1989

These lamps are not obligatory, but must comply with the following:

NUMBER: not more than two

COLOUR: white

POSITION: no requirement

MARKINGS

Motor vehicle first used on or after 1.4.86 and trailer manufactured on or after 1.10.85 requires an approval mark. See
REGS 4 AND 5 OF THE MOTOR VEHICLES (DESIGNATION OF APPROVAL MARKS) REGS 1979

Any other vehicle, no requirement

WATTAGE

Lamp bearing approval mark, no requirement

All other lamps n/e 24 watts each.

TELL-TALE

Motor vehicle first used on or after 1.7.54 with automatic switching of lamp upon selection of reverse gear, no requirement

A motor vehicle first used before 1.7.54, no requirement

Any other motor vehicle first used on or after 1.7.54 requires a circuit-closed tell-tale.

A vehicle which is not a motor vehicle, no requirement

- Must be kept clean, in good working order and maintained so as not to cause undue dazzle or inconvenience
  REG 23

- Must only be lit for reversing.
  REG 27

HAZARD WARNING

REG 18 AND SCHEDS 1 AND 8 ROAD VEHICLES LIGHTING REGULATIONS 1989

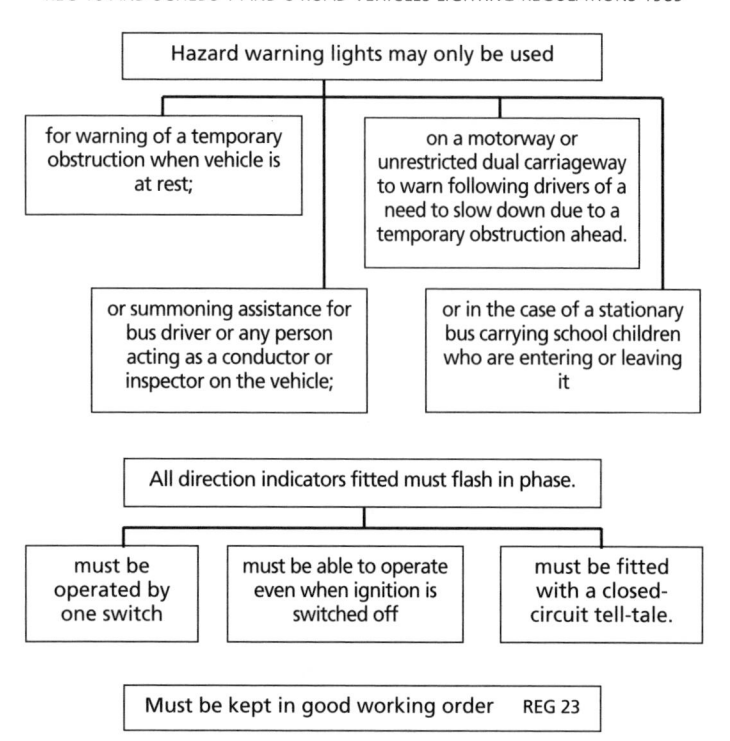

Hazard warning lights may only be used

- for warning of a temporary obstruction when vehicle is at rest;
- on a motorway or unrestricted dual carriageway to warn following drivers of a need to slow down due to a temporary obstruction ahead.
- or summoning assistance for bus driver or any person acting as a conductor or inspector on the vehicle;
- or in the case of a stationary bus carrying school children who are entering or leaving it

All direction indicators fitted must flash in phase.

- must be operated by one switch
- must be able to operate even when ignition is switched off
- must be fitted with a closed-circuit tell-tale.

Must be kept in good working order   REG 23

REAR REGISTRATION PLATE LAMP

REG 18 AND SCHED 1 ROAD VEHICLES LIGHTING REGULATIONS 1989

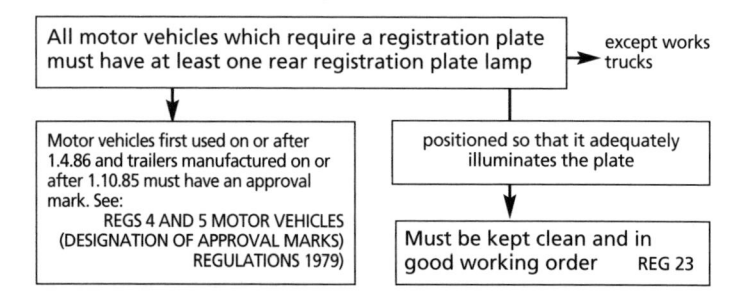

All motor vehicles which require a registration plate must have at least one rear registration plate lamp → except works trucks

Motor vehicles first used on or after 1.4.86 and trailers manufactured on or after 1.10.85 must have an approval mark. See:
REGS 4 AND 5 MOTOR VEHICLES (DESIGNATION OF APPROVAL MARKS) REGULATIONS 1979)

positioned so that it adequately illuminates the plate

Must be kept clean and in good working order   REG 23

Part 3: Lighting and marking **191**

WARNING BEACONS

ROAD VEHICLES LIGHTING REGULATIONS 1989

Except for emergency vehicles — REG 16

it is an offence to fit a blue warning beacon — or special warning lamp or device resembling such

whether working or not

- *For improper use of beacons see Reg 27*
- *See also Reg 11 (colour of light)*

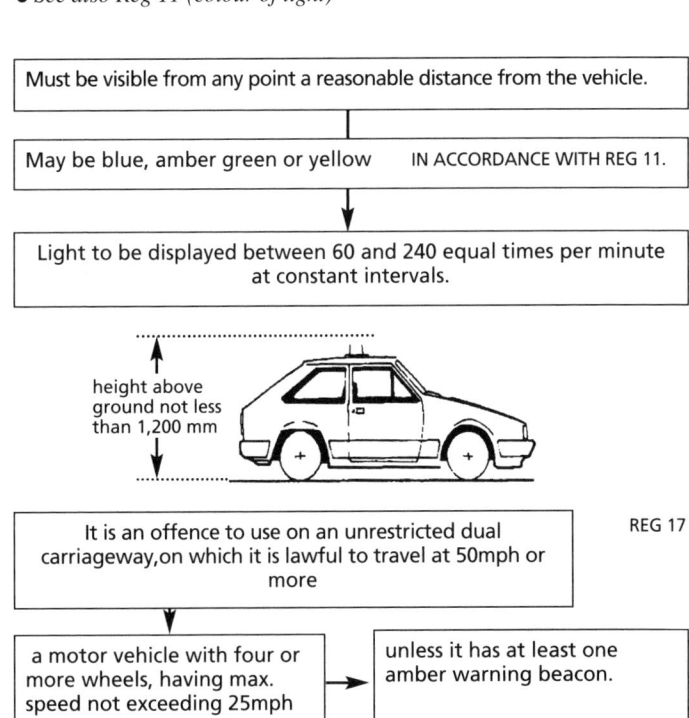

Must be visible from any point a reasonable distance from the vehicle.

May be blue, amber green or yellow — IN ACCORDANCE WITH REG 11.

Light to be displayed between 60 and 240 equal times per minute at constant intervals.

height above ground not less than 1,200 mm

It is an offence to use on an unrestricted dual carriageway, on which it is lawful to travel at 50mph or more — REG 17

a motor vehicle with four or more wheels, having max. speed not exceeding 25mph → unless it has at least one amber warning beacon.

But this does not apply to a vehicle first used before 1.1.47 or to a vehicle or trailer only quickly crossing the carriageway

192 *The Traffic Officer's Companion*

SIDE MARKER LAMPS

REGS 18, 20, 22 AND SCHEDS 1 AND 9 ROAD VEHICLES LIGHTING REGS 1989

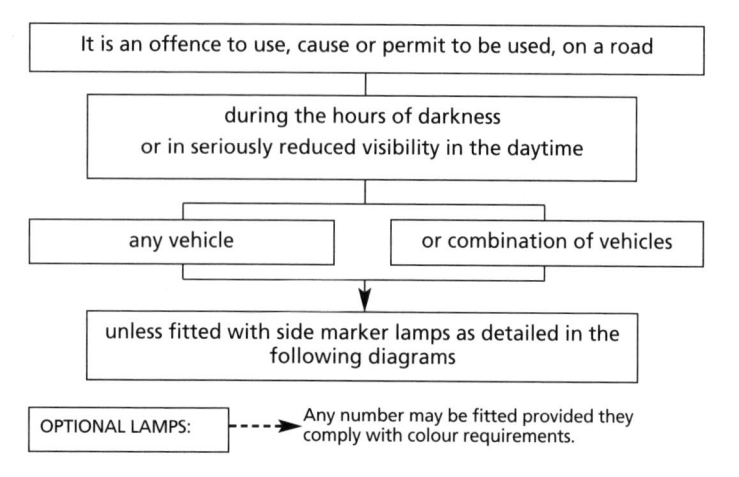

It is an offence to use, cause or permit to be used, on a road

during the hours of darkness
or in seriously reduced visibility in the daytime

any vehicle — or combination of vehicles

unless fitted with side marker lamps as detailed in the following diagrams

OPTIONAL LAMPS: ----> Any number may be fitted provided they comply with colour requirements.

1. Vehicle or combination overall length (including load) exceeding 18.3 m

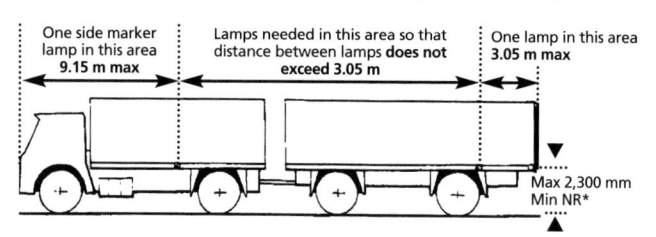

One side marker lamp in this area **9.15 m max**

Lamps needed in this area so that distance between lamps **does not exceed 3.05 m**

One lamp in this area **3.05 m max**

Max 2,300 mm
Min NR*

2. Combination of vehicles overall length (including load) exceeding 12.2 m but not exceeding 18.3 m and carrying a load supported by any two of the vehicles but not including a load carried by an articulated vehicle.

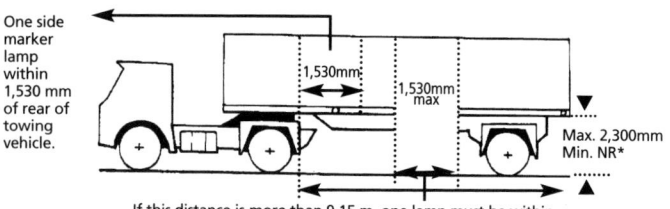

One side marker lamp within 1,530 mm of rear of towing vehicle.

1,530mm

1,530mm max

Max. 2,300mm
Min. NR*

If this distance is more than 9.15 m, one lamp must be within 1,530 mm behind centre point of overall length of load. This also applies to any other trailer.

NR = no requirement

Part 3: Lighting and marking **193**

SIDE MARKER LAMPS cont

REGS 18, 20, 22 AND SCHEDS 1 AND 9 ROAD VEHICLES LIGHTING REGS 1989

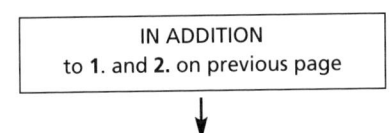

IN ADDITION
to **1.** and **2.** on previous page

3. Motor vehicles first used after 1.4.91 and trailers manufactured after 1.10.90 must also comply with the following:

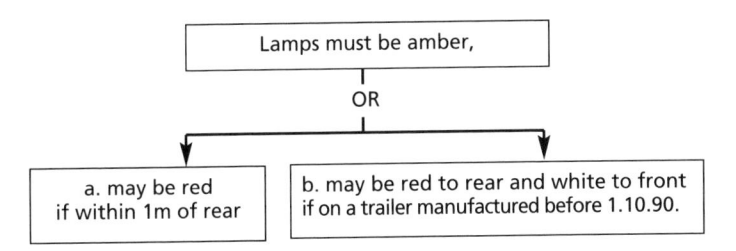

Lamps must be amber,

OR

a. may be red if within 1m of rear

b. may be red to rear and white to front if on a trailer manufactured before 1.10.90.

At least 2 on each side

Foremost not more than 4 m from front

Max separation 3 m, unless not practicable, then 4 m.

Rearmost not more than 1 m from rear

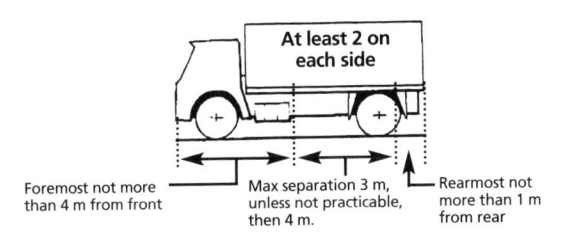

Exceptions:

1. Agricultural or works trailers;
2. caravan;
3. length n/e 6 metres and first used before 1.4.91. (but if trailer manufactured before 1.10.90 n/e 9.15 metres);
4. max speed n/e 25mph;
5. passenger vehicle;
6. proceeding for completion or sale;
7. vehicle for carrying or launching boat.

END-OUTLINE MARKER LAMPS

REGS 18, 20, AND SCHEDS 13 ROAD VEHICLES LIGHTING REGULATIONS 1989

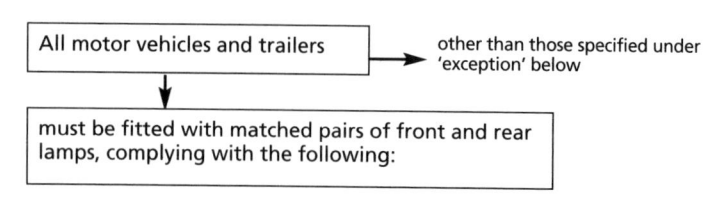

All motor vehicles and trailers → other than those specified under 'exception' below

↓

must be fitted with matched pairs of front and rear lamps, complying with the following:

Distance between end-outline marker and side of vehicle not more than **400mm**

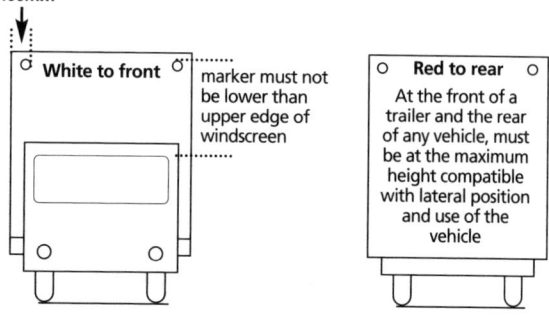

White to front — marker must not be lower than upper edge of windscreen

Red to rear — At the front of a trailer and the rear of any vehicle, must be at the maximum height compatible with lateral position and use of the vehicle

The white front and rear red lamps may be combined to form a single lamp.

OPTIONAL LAMPS: → Any number of optional lamps may be fitted but must comply with colour requirements.

Exceptions

Motor vehicles
1. First used before 1.4.91.
2. Incomplete vehicle going for completion, storage or display for sale.
3. Maximum speed n/e 25mph.
4. Overall width n/e 2,100mm.

Trailers
1. Agricultural vehicle.
2. Incomplete trailer going for completion, storage or display for sale.
3. Manufactured before 1.10.90
4. Overall width n/e 2,100 mm.
5. Works trailer.

Part 3: Lighting and marking **195**

REAR REFLECTIVE MARKERS - REQUIREMENTS

The following vehicles are required to be fitted with the type of reflector indicated (and illustrated on the following pages).

	Motor vehicles first used before 1.4.96 and trailers manufactured before 1.10.95	Any motor vehicles regardless of date of first use, and any trailer regardless of date of manufacture
	TYPE	TYPE
motor vehicle not over 13 m long	1, 2 or 3	A, B, C or D
motor vehicle over 13 m long	4 or 5	E, F, G or H
trailer forming part of a combination of vehicles not over 11 m overall length	1, 2 or 3	A, B, C or D
trailer forming part of a combination of vehicles over 11 m but not over 13 m overall length	1, 2, 3, 4 or 5	Any of types A - H
trailer forming part of a combination of vehicles over 13 m overall length	4 or 5	E, F, G or H

196 *The Traffic Officer's Companion*

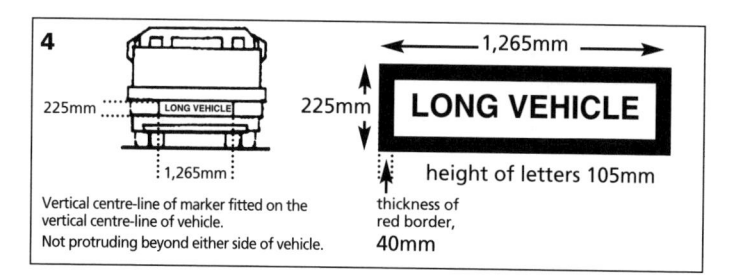

REAR REFLECTIVE MARKERS - TYPES

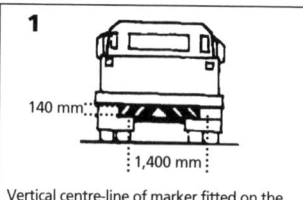

1
140 mm
1,400 mm
Vertical centre-line of marker fitted on the vertical centre-line of vehicle.
Not protruding beyond either side of vehicle

2
140 mm
700 mm
Of equal size and shape
Fitted as near as possible to outer edge of vehicle but not protruding beyond.

For 1 and 2: angle of bars, **46 °**
width and distance apart of bar, **140mm**

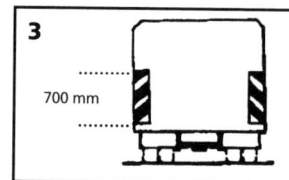

3
700 mm
Equal size and shape
Fitted as near as possible to outer edge of vehicle but not protruding beyond.

4
225mm
1,265mm
225mm
LONG VEHICLE
1,265mm
height of letters 105mm
Vertical centre-line of marker fitted on the vertical centre-line of vehicle.
Not protruding beyond either side of vehicle.
thickness of red border, **40mm**

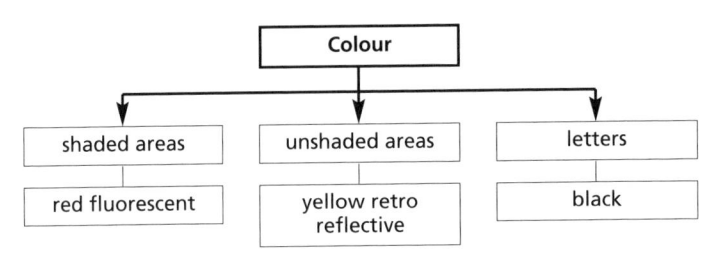

REAR REFLECTIVE MARKERS - TYPES cont

5

250mm — 525mm

Equal size and shape
Fitted as near as possible to outer edge of vehicle but not protruding beyond.

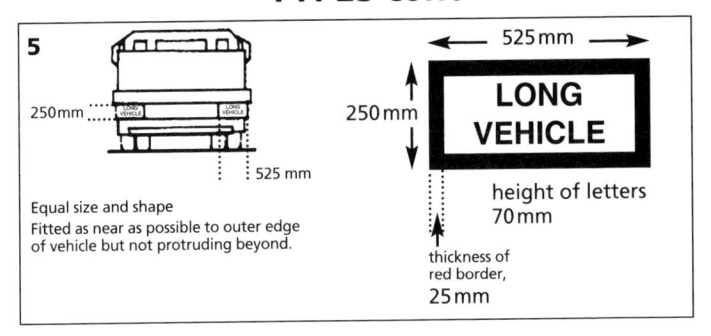

LONG VEHICLE

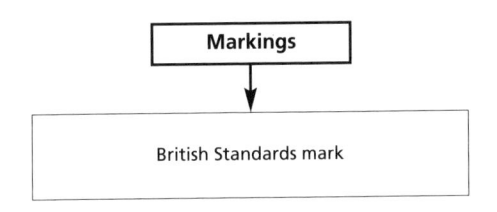

525mm × 250mm

height of letters 70mm

thickness of red border, 25mm

Colour

- shaded areas → red fluorescent
- unshaded areas → yellow retro reflective
- letters → black

Markings

British Standards mark

198 *The Traffic Officer's Companion*

REAR REFLECTIVE MARKERS
- TYPES cont

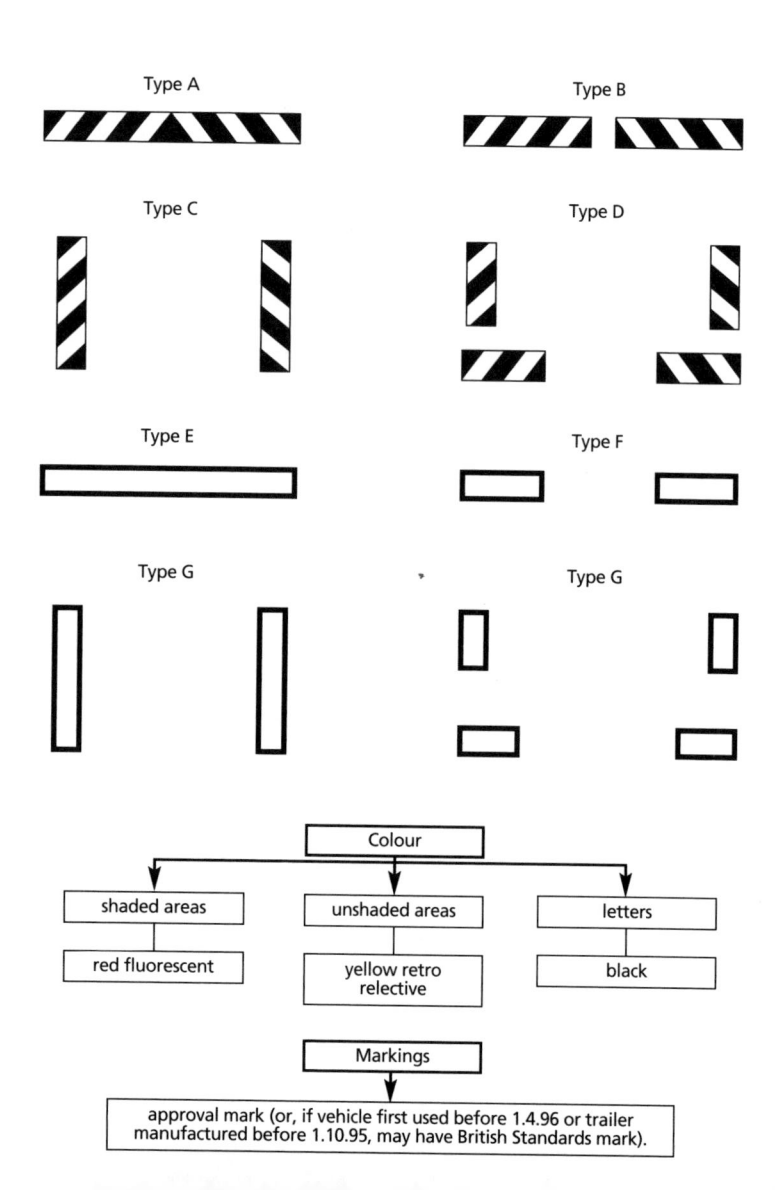

Type A

Type B

Type C

Type D

Type E

Type F

Type G

Type G

Colour		
shaded areas	unshaded areas	letters
red fluorescent	yellow retro relective	black

Markings

approval mark (or, if vehicle first used before 1.4.96 or trailer manufactured before 1.10.95, may have British Standards mark).

Part 3: Lighting and marking **199**

LAMPS ON PROJECTING LOADS
REG 21 ROAD VEHICLE LIGHTING REGULATIONS 1989

Offence to use, cause or permit use of vehicle during hours of darkness or in seriously reduced visibility unless it complies with the following:

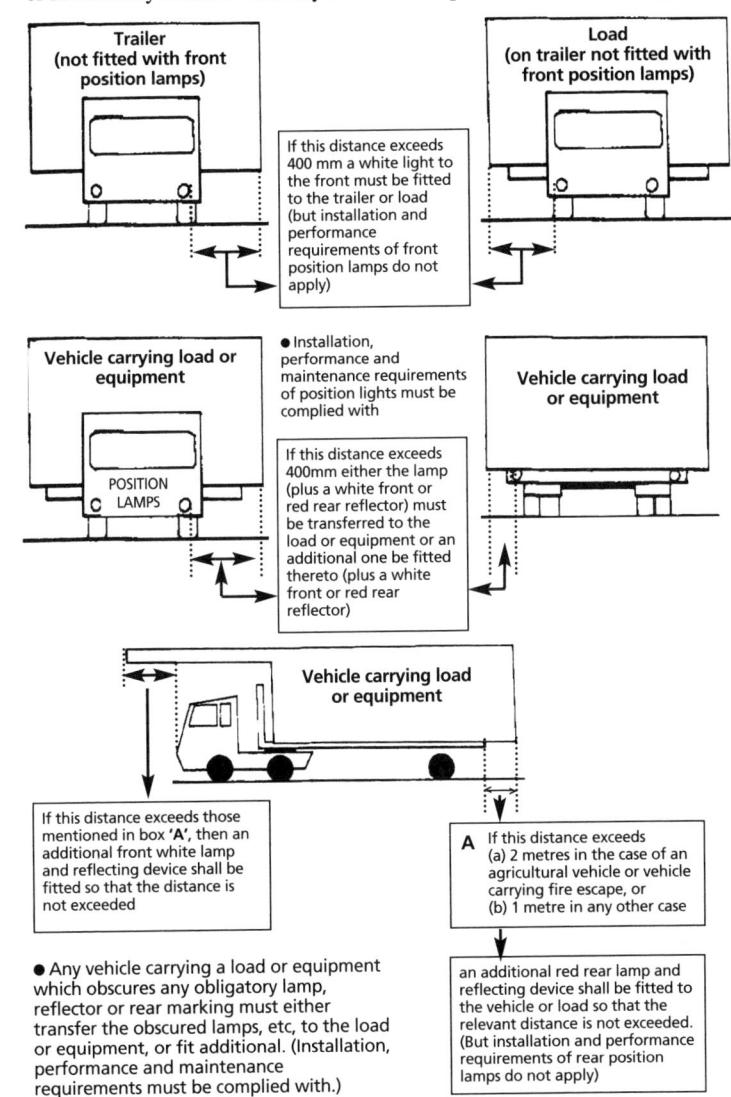

Trailer (not fitted with front position lamps)

If this distance exceeds 400 mm a white light to the front must be fitted to the trailer or load (but installation and performance requirements of front position lamps do not apply)

Load (on trailer not fitted with front position lamps)

Vehicle carrying load or equipment

- Installation, performance and maintenance requirements of position lights must be complied with

If this distance exceeds 400mm either the lamp (plus a white front or red rear reflector) must be transferred to the load or equipment or an additional one be fitted thereto (plus a white front or red rear reflector)

Vehicle carrying load or equipment

Vehicle carrying load or equipment

If this distance exceeds those mentioned in box '**A**', then an additional front white lamp and reflecting device shall be fitted so that the distance is not exceeded

A If this distance exceeds
(a) 2 metres in the case of an agricultural vehicle or vehicle carrying fire escape, or
(b) 1 metre in any other case

- Any vehicle carrying a load or equipment which obscures any obligatory lamp, reflector or rear marking must either transfer the obscured lamps, etc, to the load or equipment, or fit additional. (Installation, performance and maintenance requirements must be complied with.)

an additional red rear lamp and reflecting device shall be fitted to the vehicle or load so that the relevant distance is not exceeded. (But installation and performance requirements of rear position lamps do not apply)

PROJECTION MARKERS

ART 23 MOTOR VEHICLES (AUTHORISATION OF SPECIAL TYPES) GENERAL ORDER 1979

SCHED 12 ROAD VEHICLES (CONSTRUCTION AND USE) REGULATIONS 1986

Projection	Requirement
Forward or rearward projection exceeding 1.83m	End markers unless rear marking is in accordance with the Lighting Regs
Forward projection exceeds 2m or rearward exceeds 3m	One side marker on each side
Forward projection exceeds 4.5m that or rearward exceeds 5m	Extra side markers on each side so that horizontal distance between marker and end of projection or between adjacent markers on the same side, does not exceed: forward projection - 2.5m rearward projection - 3.5m

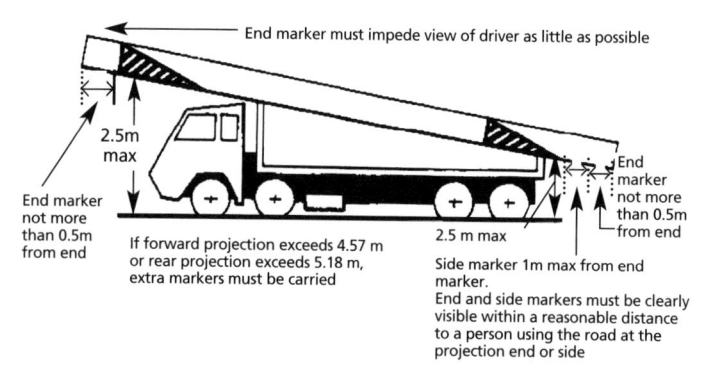

End marker must impede view of driver as little as possible

2.5m max

End marker not more than 0.5m from end

If forward projection exceeds 4.57 m or rear projection exceeds 5.18 m, extra markers must be carried

2.5 m max

Side marker 1m max from end marker.
End and side markers must be clearly visible within a reasonable distance to a person using the road at the projection end or side

End marker not more than 0.5m from end

Markers must have alternating red and white stripes 100 mm wide, with 50 mm wide red border. Each not less than 610 mm high

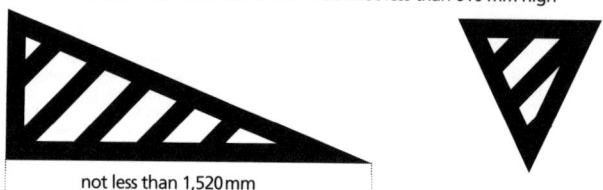

not less than 1,520mm

side marker

front or rear end marker

- Must be kept illuminated between sunset and sunrise.
- End projection markers are not required if reflective rear markings are carried on the load.

TRAILER PLATES – REAR REFLECTORS

REG 18 AND SCHEDS 1 AND 18 ROAD VEHICLES LIGHTING REGULATIONS 1989

REG 3 EEC DIRECTIVE 76/757

A trailer (other than a broken down motor vehicle) manufactured on or after 1.7.70 must have a pair of reflex reflectors of one of the following types:

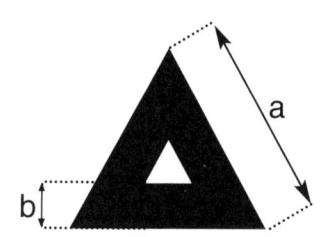

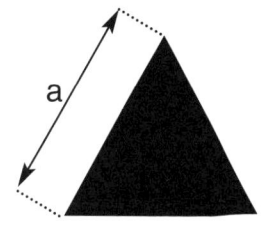

a must be 150mm or over but must not exceed 200mm

b must be at least $\frac{9}{5}$ (ie greater than or equal to)

c must not exceed 15mm (ie less than or equal to)

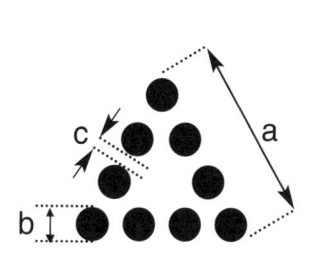

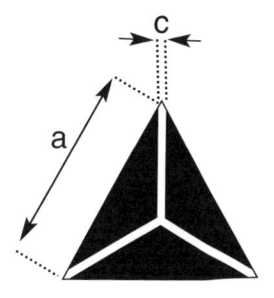

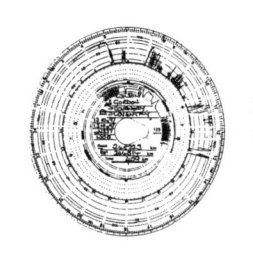

PART 4

DRIVER'S HOURS
AND RECORDS

Here we discuss the need to comply with
drivers' hours and the keeping of records.
The use of the tachograph and possible
malpractices are then considered.
Both community and domestic rules
are explained.

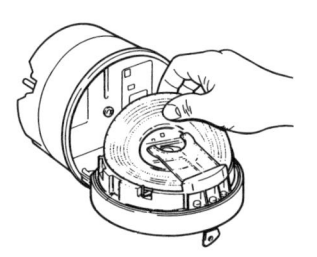

DRIVER'S HOURS AND RECORDS (GENERAL)

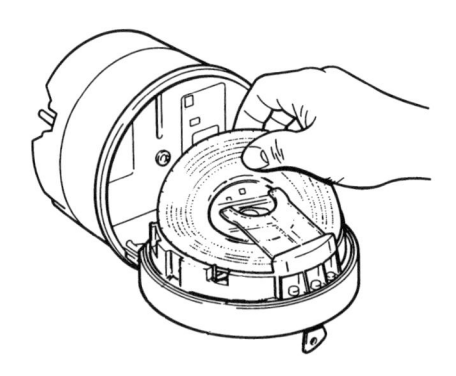

The set of rules to be followed depends upon the type of vehicle and the work being carried out. Unless totally exempt, vehicles will have to comply with:

- **Community Rules**
  (COUNCIL REGULATIONS (EEC) 3820/85 AND 3821/85)

  or

- **Domestic Rules** (TRANSPORT ACT 1968)

(1) These rules apply to journeys made by vehicles, whether laden or not, used for the carriage of passengers or goods within the Community.

(2) The same rules relating to hours apply to operations to, from or through countries which are not in the European Union but which have entered an agreement to comply. The rules also apply to operations to or from countries which are not party to the AETR agreement where the journey is made within the European Union by a vehicle registered in one of those countries.

(3) However, certain types of operation within the UK are exempt from the EC rules but may be required to comply with domestic rules.

To decide which type of rule is applicable follow the flow chart opposite:

Part 4: Driver's hours and records **205**

DRIVER'S HOURS AND RECORDS
SELECTOR

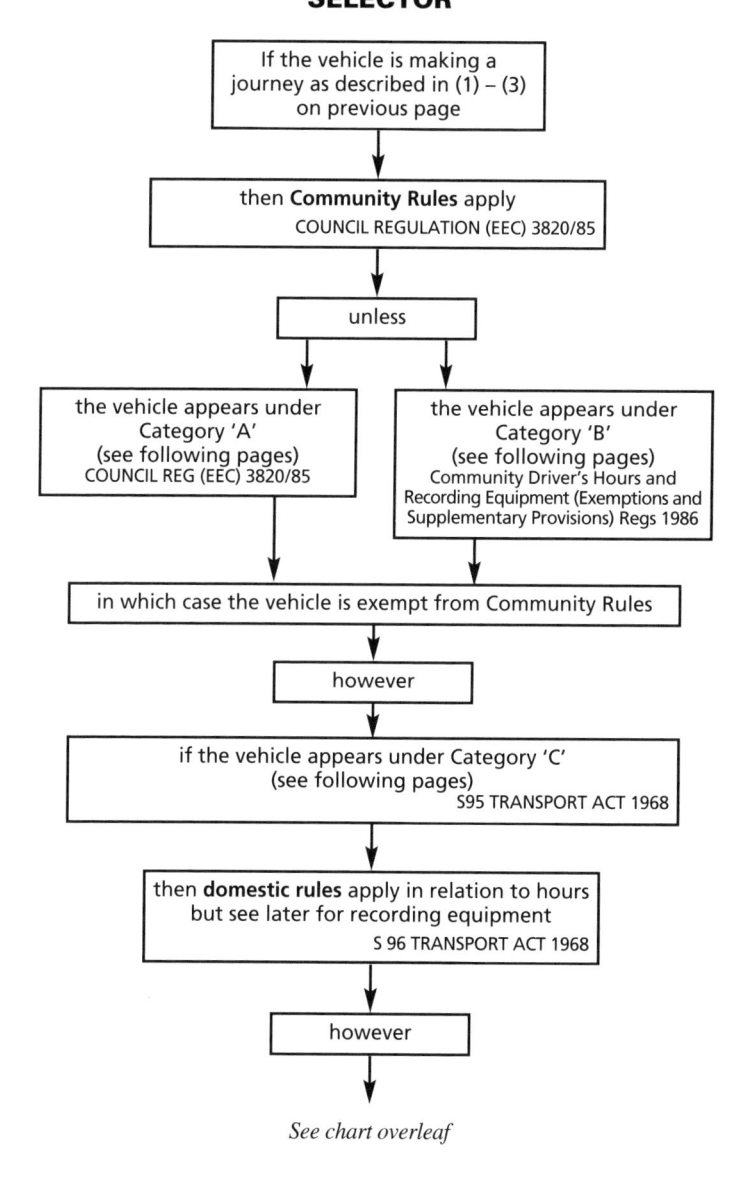

```
If the vehicle is making a
journey as described in (1) – (3)
on previous page
            ↓
then Community Rules apply
COUNCIL REGULATION (EEC) 3820/85
            ↓
         unless
         ↙     ↘
the vehicle appears under        the vehicle appears under
     Category 'A'                     Category 'B'
 (see following pages)             (see following pages)
COUNCIL REG (EEC) 3820/85      Community Driver's Hours and
                               Recording Equipment (Exemptions and
                               Supplementary Provisions) Regs 1986
         ↘     ↙
in which case the vehicle is exempt from Community Rules
            ↓
         however
            ↓
if the vehicle appears under Category 'C'
(see following pages)
                    S95 TRANSPORT ACT 1968
            ↓
then domestic rules apply in relation to hours
but see later for recording equipment
                    S 96 TRANSPORT ACT 1968
            ↓
         however
            ↓
```

See chart overleaf

DRIVER'S HOURS AND RECORDS cont

SELECTOR cont

Domestic rules do not apply to driving to which the Community rules apply, but:

time spent on both **community** and **domestic driving** will be regarded as Domestic

REG 2 DRIVER'S HOURS (HARMONISATION WITH COMMUNITY RULES) REGS 1986

↓

When dealing with an **emergency** of a type listed under Category 'E' overleaf the driver is exempt from the daily driving limit and the working day limit provided that time spent on such duty does not (otherwise than dealing with the emergency) exceed 11 hours

REG 2 DRIVER'S HOURS (GOODS VEHICLES) (EXEMPTIONS) REGULATIONS 1986

↓

Where, during a working week, all or the greater part of the time is spent **driving goods vehicles**, the driver is exempt from breaks, daily rest, weekly duty and weekly rest. However, he may not extend the working day to $12\frac{1}{2}$ hours (see later for specific modifications to the basic domestic rules)

ARTICLE 2 DRIVER'S HOURS (GOODS VEHICLES) (MODIFICATIONS) ORDER 1986

↓

Where all driving time is spent **driving goods vehicles with maximum weight not exceeding 3.5 tonnes**, or dual purpose vehicles for a purpose listed under Category 'D' overleaf, the driver is exempt from all those items in the previous paragraph plus working day limits.

ARTICLE 3 DRIVER'S HOURS (GOODS VEHICLES) (MODIFICATIONS) ORDER 1986

↓

continued on following page

Part 4: Driver's hours and records

DRIVER'S HOURS AND RECORDS cont

SELECTOR cont

Drivers are exempt from the daily driving limit when driving elsewhere than on a road in the course of **agriculture, forestry, quarrying, construction etc. of buildings, or construction or civil engineering (including roads)**
TRANSPORT ACT 1968 AND DRIVER'S HOURS (GOODS VEHICLES) (MODIFICATIONS) ORDER 1970

Where a driver spends all or the greater part of a working day **driving passenger vehicles**, the basic domestic rules are modified (see later)

VEHICLE CATEGORIES

Category A (Exemptions from Community rules)
ARTICLE 4 COUNCIL REGULATION (EEC) 3820/85

Goods vehicle not exceeding 3.5 tonnes maximum permissible weight (including trailer or semi-trailer).

Passenger vehicle constructed and intended for not more than nine persons including driver.

Carrying passengers on scheduled services and route not exceeding 50 km.

Max authorised speed not exceeding 30 kph.

Armed services, civil defence, fire service and forces responsible for maintaining public order.

Sewerage, flood protection, water, gas, electricity, highway maintenance, refuse collection, telephone, post, radio, TV broadcasting/detecting.

Emergency/rescue/specialised medical vehicle.

Circus/funfair vehicles.

Specialised breakdown vehicles.

Vehicles undergoing road tests for technical development, etc.

Non-commercial carriage of personal goods.

Milk collection from farms.

Part 4: Driver's hours and records **209**

VEHICLE CATEGORIES cont

Category B (Exemptions from Community rules)
COMMUNITY DRIVER'S HOURS AND RECORDING EQUIPMENT
(EXEMPTIONS AND SUPPLEMENTARY PROVISIONS) REGULATIONS 1986

Passenger vehicle constructed and intended to carry not exceeding 17 persons including driver.

Public Authority Vehicles after 1.1.90 not in competition with professional road hauliers:
used by a health service body - as an ambulance under a statutory duty, or an ambulance service or carrying staff; patients or medical supplies; social services vehicle for the aged or physically or mentally handicapped; coastguard or lighthouse vehicles; harbour vehicle within harbour limits; airport vehicle within airport limits; railway maintenance vehicle; or British Waterways maintenance vehicle.

Being used by agricultural, horticultural, forestry or fishery undertaking (ie, carrying live fish or a catch of fish from where it was landed to place of processing), to carry goods within 50 km radius of its base.

Carrying animal waste or carcasses not intended for human consumption.

Carrying live animals between farm and market or between market and slaughterhouse.

Being used and specially fitted as a local market shop, door-to-door selling, mobile banking, worship, library or exhibitions.

Goods vehicle not over 7.5 tonnes carrying material or equipment for driver's use, within 50 km radius of base.

Operating exclusively on an island not over 2,300 sq km, not linked to Great Britian by bridge, ford or tunnel used by motor vehicles.

Goods vehicle not over 7.5 tonnes propelled by gas produced on the vehicle, or electricity.

Being used for driving instruction and not carrying goods for hire or reward.

Agricultural or forestry tractor after 1.1.90.

Used by RNLI for hauling lifeboats.

Vehicle manufactured before 1.1.47.

Steam propelled vehicle.

Vintage vehicle in rally etc.

Vehicle collecting sea coal and postal articles on national transport operations where max. weight of article does not exceed 3.5 tonnes or where vehicle is used by the Post Office to carry letters (exempt from recording equipment only).

VEHICLE CATEGORIES cont

Category C (Domestic Rules)
S 95 TRANSPORT ACT 1968
NONE OF THE BELOW WILL APPLY TO POLICE, FIRE BRIGADE, NAVY,
MILITARY OR AIR FORCE VEHICLES (S 102 TRANSPORT ACT 1968);
NOR TO TRAMCARS AND TROLLEY VEHICLES OPERATED UNDER
STATUTORY POWERS (S 102A TRANSPORT ACT 1968)

Vehicles and persons in the public service of the crown (S 102).

Public service vehicle (S 95).

Vehicle (not PSV) constructed or adapted to carry more than 12 passengers (S 95).

Goods vehicles, ie, heavy locomotive, light locomotive, motor tractor, other motor vehicles so constructed that a trailer may by partial superimposition be attached to the vehicle in such a manner as to cause a substantial part of the weight of the trailer to be borne by the vehicle, and any other goods vehicle constructed or adapted to carry goods other than effects of passengers.

Vehicles not included in the above category will nevertheless have to comply unless exempt by Catergory A or B (see previous pages).

Community Drivers Hours and Recording Equipment (Amendment) Regulations 1998.

The effect of the above is that by attaching a trailer to a vehicle for the purpose of carrying goos, this would make the vehicle "adapted, to carry goods".

Part 4: Driver's hours and records **211**

VEHICLE CATEGORIES cont

Category D (Modification of Driver's Hours)
DRIVER'S HOURS (GOODS VEHICLES) (MODIFICATIONS) ORDER 1986

Carrying on by him or his employer the profession of medical practitioner, nurse, midwife, dentist or veterinary surgeon.

Carrying out a service of inspection, cleaning, maintenance, repair, installation or fitting.

Commercial traveller only carrying goods for soliciting orders.

In course of employment by AA, RAC, or RSAC (Royal Scottish Automobile Club).

Carrying on by him or his employer the business of cinematography or radio or TV broadcasting.

Category E (Emergencies)
DRIVER'S HOURS (GOODS VEHICLES) (EXEMPTIONS) REGULATIONS 1986

Events which cause or are likely to cause such:
a) danger to life or health of one or more individuals or animals,
b) a serious interruption in the maintenance of public services for the supply of water, gas, electricity or drainage or of telecommunication or postal services, or
c) a serious interruption in the use of roads, railways, ports or airports, as to necessitate the taking of immediate action to prevent the occurrence or continuance of such danger or interruption.

Events which are likely to cause such serious damage to property as to necessitate the taking of immediate action to prevent the occurrence of such damage.

DRIVER'S HOURS – COMMUNITY RULES

COUNCIL REGULATION (EEC) 3820/85

DAILY DRIVING: 9 hours
- May be extended twice in any one week to 10 hours.

WEEKLY REST: 45 hours
- Must be taken after no more than six daily driving periods.
- Periods may be reduced to minimum of 36 hours if taken where vehicle or driver normally based; or minimum of 24 hours if taken elsewhere. Such reductions must be compensated by an equivalent rest period taken en bloc before end of third week following, attached to another rest of at least 8 hours to be taken at the vehicle's parking place or driver's base, if requested.
- Weekly rest may be postponed until end of sixth day if total driving is no more than six daily periods.
- But on national or international passenger services other than regular services:
    may be postponed to the end of twelfth day if total driving is no more than 12 daily periods, or
    may be postponed until the week following and added on to that week's rest period.
- Weekly rest periods beginning in one week and continuing into the following week may be attached to either week.

FORTNIGHTLY DRIVING: 90 hours   ARTICLE 6

BREAK DURING DRIVING: 45 minutes   ARTICLE 7
- Must be taken after four and a half hours' driving unless beginning a rest period. May be replaced by 15-minute breaks during the driving period or immediately afterwards provided basic rule is complied with.
- For regular national passenger services in a 'relevant area' if it is not possible to take a break of at least 15 minutes, he may take 30 minutes immediately after a driving period of four hours maximum instead of the basic rule. The 'relevant areas' are the Boroughs of Camden, Kensington and Chelsea, Islington, and the cities of Westminster, Birmingham, Bristol, Leeds, Leicester, Nottingham and Oxford. During any driving break the driver may not carry out other work.
- Breaks may not be regarded as daily rest periods.
- During breaks the driver may not carry out other work. Waiting time and time travelling (not driving) in a vehicle, ferry or train is not regarded as 'other work'.

Part 4: Driver's hours and records **213**

DRIVER'S HOURS – COMMUNITY RULES
cont COUNCIL REGULATION (EEC) 3820/85

DAILY REST: 11 consecutive hours ARTICLE 8
- To be taken in each period of 24 hours.
- May be reduced to nine hours not more than three times per week provided an equivalent rest period in compensation is taken before the end of the following week but must be attached to another rest, of at least 8 hours at the vehicle's parking place or driver's base, if requested.
- If not reduced, the period may be taken on two or three separate occasions but one must be at least eight hours and total is increased to 12 hours.
- Eight hours are to be taken where there are two drivers, by each driver, during each period of 30 hours.
- May be taken in a stationary vehicle if fitted with a bunk.

INTERUPTION OF DAILY REST ARTICLE 9
- If being transported by ferryboat or train rest period may be interrupted not more than once provided land rest period taken before or after that taken on board; period between the two portions of the rest period not to exceed 1 hour before embarkation or after disembarkation; driver must have access to bunk or couchette during both portions of the rest period; daily rest period is increased by 2 hours.

DEPARTURE FROM PROVISIONS ARTICLE 12
- Provided road safety is not jeopardised, and to enable him to reach a suitable stopping place, the driver may depart from the above provisions to the extent necessary to ensure the safety of persons, of the vehicle or of its load. Such departures must be recorded on the record sheet or duty roster.

DRIVER'S HOURS – DOMESTIC RULES

TRANSPORT ACT 1968, S 96

DAILY DRIVING: 10 hours

BREAKS: 30 minutes
Must be taken after five and a half hours' duty (or aggregate of five and a half hours if not continuous) unless taken during that period.

WORKING DAY: 11 hours
May be extended to up to 12.5 hours if during that day he is off duty for a period (or cumulation of periods) of not less than the amount by which the actual hours worked exceed 11 hours. And may be extended to 14 hours if:
a) all driving time is spent driving express or contract carriages; and
b) he is able to obtain not less than 4 hours rest.

DAILY REST: 11 hours
If all or greater part of the time is spent driving passenger vehicles, on one occasion during each working week may be reduced to nine and a half hours – does not apply in a week when each day's driving is not more than 4 hours.

WEEKLY DUTY: 60 hours
Does not apply in a week when each day's driving is not more than 4 hours.

WEEKLY REST: 24 hours
May fall wholly in that week or beginning in that week and ending in the next.
Does not apply in a week when each day's driving is not more than 4 hours.

Refer to selector to ascertain whether these rules are applicable.

DRIVER'S HOURS – DOMESTIC RULES cont

DRIVER'S HOURS (PASSENGER AND GOODS VEHICLES) (MODIFICATIONS) ORDER 1971

MODIFICATIONS FOR DRIVERS OF PASSENGERS VEHICLES (ART.4)

The basic domestic rules on the previous page are modified where a driver spends all or the greater part of a working day driving passenger vehicles. The modified rules are:

Daily Driving – 10 hours
This includes any driving under EC or AETR rules.

Continuous Driving – 5½ hours
Following this a break of at least 30 minutes must be taken and the driver must be able to obtain rest and refreshment. However, within any period of 8½ hours total breaks amounting to at least 45 minutes are taken, (therefore driver drives for not more than 7¾ hours). The driver must also have a break of at least 30 minutes at the end of this period unless that is the end of the working day.

Working Day – 16 hours
This includes 'other work' and off-duty periods.

Daily Rest – 10 hours
This may be reduced to 8½ hours but only for 3 times a week.

Fortnightly Rest – 24 hours
This must be taken in any 2 weeks (Monday to Sunday)

Weekly Duty – no restrictions

MODIFICATIONS FOR DRIVERS OF PASSENGERS VEHICLES (ART.2)

The basic domestic rules mentioned earlier are modified where the greater part of the time during a working week is spent driving goods vehicles. The modified rules are:

Daily driving – 10 hours

Working day – 11 hours

DEFINITIONS

ARTICLE 1 COUNCIL REGULATION (EEC) 3820/85

PERMISSIBLE MAXIMUM WEIGHT

Means the maximum authorised operating weight of the vehicle fully laden.

DRIVER

Means any person who drives the vehicle even for a short period, or who is carried in the vehicle in order to be available for driving if necessary.

WEEK

Means the period between 00.00 hours on Monday and 24.00 hours on Sunday.

REGULAR PASSENGER SERVICES

Means national and international services which provide for the carriage of passengers at specified intervals along specified routes, passengers being taken up and set down at predetermined stopping points.

REST

Means any uninterrupted period of at least one hour during which the driver may freely dispose of his time.

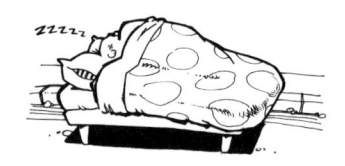

CARRIAGE BY ROAD

Means any journey made on roads open to the public of a vehicle, whether laden or not, used for the carriage of passengers or goods.

GOODS VEHICLE

Following the case of the National Trailer and Towing Association Ltd, v Chief Constable of Hampshire (which decided that a Daihatsu 4 wheel drive vehicle was not a goods vehicle and therefore, when towing a goods trailer bringing the combined weight to over 3.5 tonnes, did not need to be fitted with a tachograph even though used for commercial purposes), the Community Driver's Hours and Recording Equipment (Amendment) Regulations 1998 were introduced. These effectively reversed the decision by clarifying that the regulations would include vehicles used for the carriage of goods.

Part 4: Driver's hours and records

RECORDS

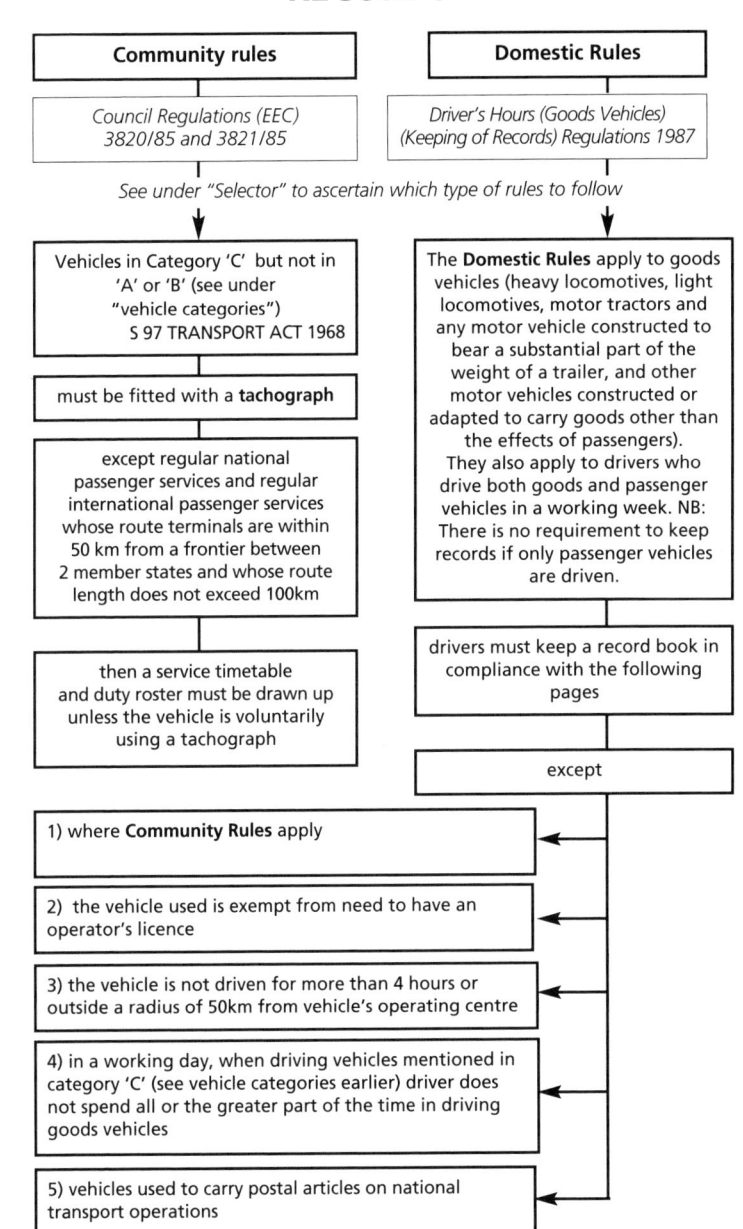

Community rules	**Domestic Rules**
Council Regulations (EEC) 3820/85 and 3821/85	*Driver's Hours (Goods Vehicles) (Keeping of Records) Regulations 1987*

See under "Selector" to ascertain which type of rules to follow

Community rules branch:

Vehicles in Category 'C' but not in 'A' or 'B' (see under "vehicle categories") S 97 TRANSPORT ACT 1968

↓

must be fitted with a **tachograph**

↓

except regular national passenger services and regular international passenger services whose route terminals are within 50 km from a frontier between 2 member states and whose route length does not exceed 100km

↓

then a service timetable and duty roster must be drawn up unless the vehicle is voluntarily using a tachograph

Domestic Rules branch:

The **Domestic Rules** apply to goods vehicles (heavy locomotives, light locomotives, motor tractors and any motor vehicle constructed to bear a substantial part of the weight of a trailer, and other motor vehicles constructed or adapted to carry goods other than the effects of passengers). They also apply to drivers who drive both goods and passenger vehicles in a working week. NB: There is no requirement to keep records if only passenger vehicles are driven.

↓

drivers must keep a record book in compliance with the following pages

↓

except

1) where **Community Rules** apply

2) the vehicle used is exempt from need to have an operator's licence

3) the vehicle is not driven for more than 4 hours or outside a radius of 50km from vehicle's operating centre

4) in a working day, when driving vehicles mentioned in category 'C' (see vehicle categories earlier) driver does not spend all or the greater part of the time in driving goods vehicles

5) vehicles used to carry postal articles on national transport operations

218 The Traffic Officer's Companion

RECORD BOOKS

DRIVER'S HOURS (GOODS VEHICLES) (KEEPING OF RECORDS) REGULATIONS 1987

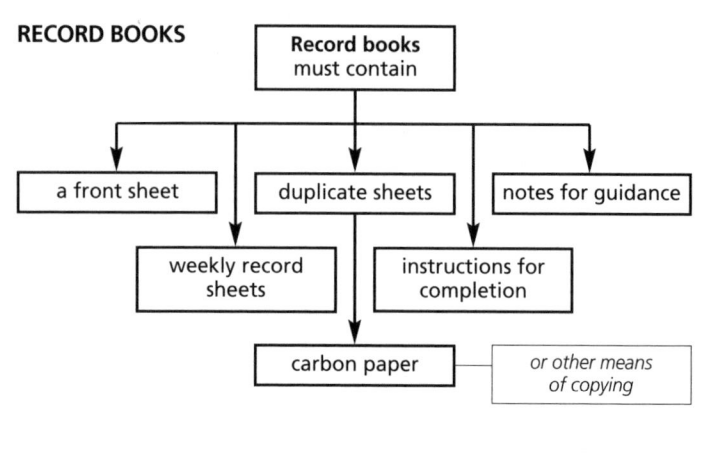

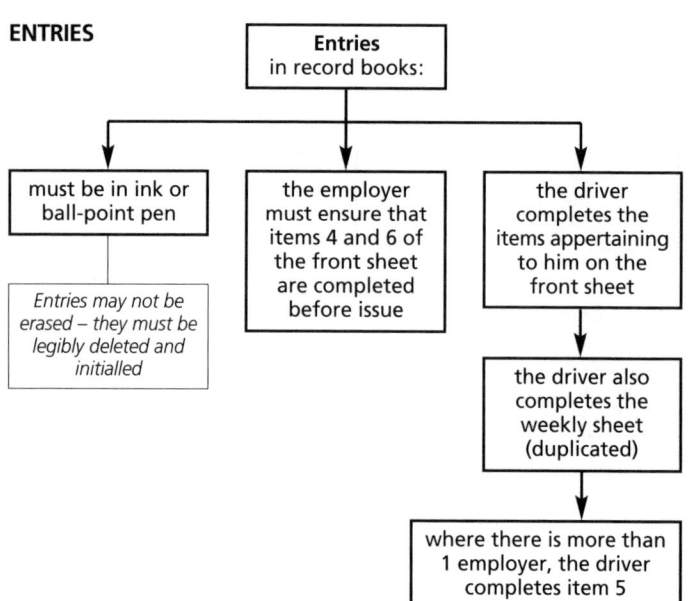

RECORD BOOKS

Record books must contain:
- a front sheet
- duplicate sheets
  - weekly record sheets
  - instructions for completion
  - carbon paper — *or other means of copying*
- notes for guidance

ENTRIES

Entries in record books:

- must be in ink or ball-point pen
  - *Entries may not be erased – they must be legibly deleted and initialled*
- the employer must ensure that items 4 and 6 of the front sheet are completed before issue
- the driver completes the items appertaining to him on the front sheet
  - the driver also completes the weekly sheet (duplicated)
  - where there is more than 1 employer, the driver completes item 5

Part 4: Driver's hours and records **219**

RECORD BOOKS cont

DRIVER'S HOURS (GOODS VEHICLES) (KEEPING OF RECORDS)
REGULATIONS 1987

Model For Driver's Record Book
a. Front sheet

RECORD BOOK FOR DRIVERS IN ROAD TRANSPORT

1. Date book first used ....

2. Date book last used ....

3. Surname, first name(s), and address of holder of book ....
....
....

4. Name, address, telephone number and stamp (if any) of
employer/under-taking ....
....
....

5. Name, address, telephone number and stamp (if any) of any other
employer(s) ....
....
....

6. Operator's Licence No. (Nos) ....

---

b. Weekly sheet

WEEKLY SHEET							
1. DRIVER'S NAME				2. PERIOD COVERED BY SHEET WEEK COMMENCING (DATE)............................. TO WEEK ENDING (DATE)..................................			
DAY ON WHICH DUTY	*REGISTRATION NO OF VEHICLE(S)*	*PLACE WHERE VEHICLE(S) BASED*	*TIME OF GOING ON DUTY*	*TIME OF GOING OFF DUTY*	*TIME SPENT DRIVING*	*TIME SPENT ON DUTY*	*SIGNA-TURE OF DRIVER*
MONDAY							
TUESDAY							
WEDNESDAY							
THURSDAY							
FRIDAY							
SATURDAY							
SUNDAY							
10. CERTIFICATION BY EMPLOYER			I HAVE EXAMINED THE ENTRIES IN THIS SHEET SIGNATURE..				

220 The Traffic Officer's Companion

TACHOGRAPHS

COUNCIL REGULATION 3821/85

In EC countries the tachograph chart replaces the driver's log sheet.

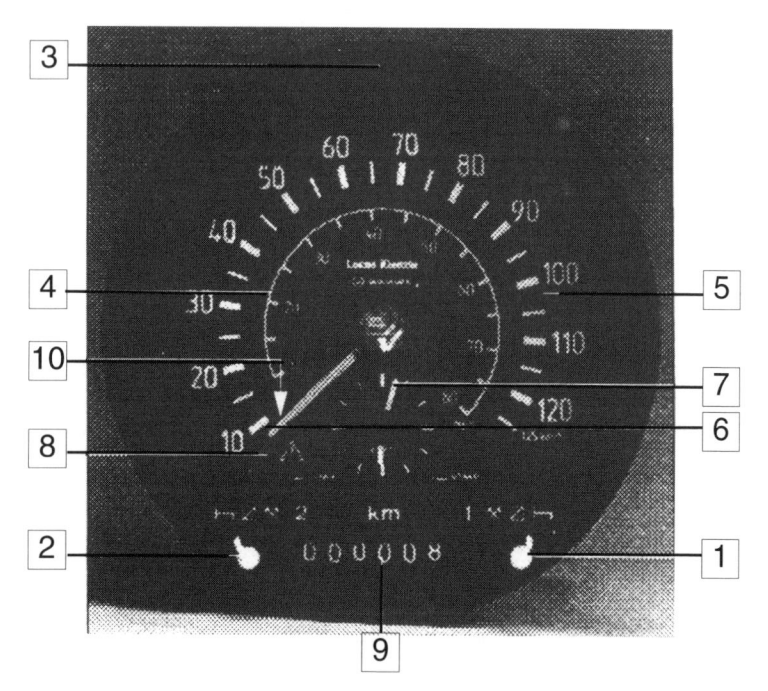

1. Driver work mode selector **2.** Crew work mode selector **3.** Lock
4. Miles/hour speed scale **5.** Kilometres/hour Speed scale
6. Speedometer pointer **7.** Clock **8.** Clock operating Indicator
9. Odometer **10.** RPM pointer

How the tachograph works

A tachograph is a speedometer and mileage counter fitted with a clock and recording mechanism. Instead of filling in a log sheet, the driver writes his name, the date and any other information onto a 'chart' and inserts it into a tachograph which then does the rest. The chart, in the form of a circular disc, is rotated by the clock mechanism and is marked by three sapphire-tipped styli which bear against it.

Part 4: Driver's hours and records 221

CHART ANALYSIS

1. Hours divisions 2. Speed trace 3. Driver mode: When the stylus is in the drive position and the vehicle is moving, the trace is broader than when the vehicle is stationary 4. Distance trace: Each complete zig-zag represents 10 km 5. Chart centre 6. End of duty/driving 7. Delay on route 8. Delivery 9. Work other than driving 10.Rest period 11.Start of duty/driving 12.Name of driver 13.Start place 14.Finish place 15. Start date 16.Finish date 17. Vehicle registration number 18. Finish odometer reading 19. Start odometer reading 20.Total distance travelled (km)

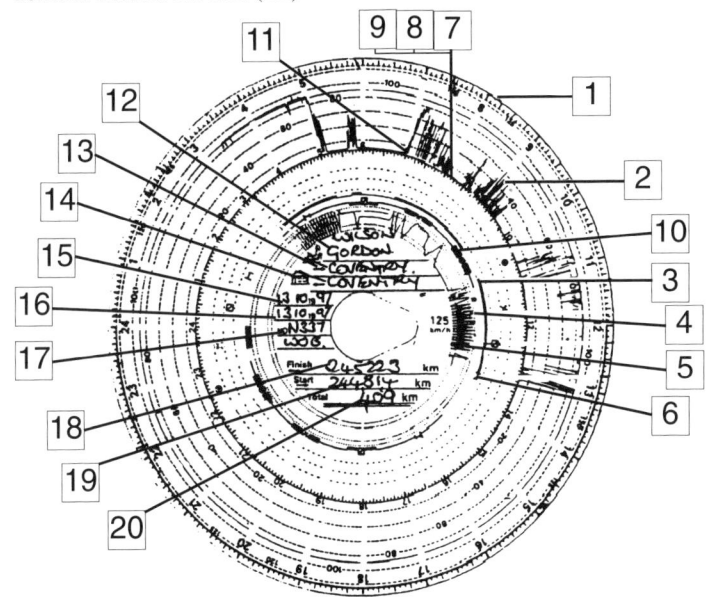

Distance Travelled
This is recorded by the innermost stylus. Every 10 km the stylus oscillates once, so that by counting the peaks, the journey length is measured.

Vehicle Movement
The middle stylus indicates when the vehicle is moving and hence records the hours at the wheel. By turning a knob, the driver can also record how the rest of his time has been apportioned between other work, eg loading and rest periods.

Speed
This is indicated by the outermost stylus and a jagged – as opposed to a smooth – trace indicates heavy use of the break and accelerator. A warning light goes on when a pre-selected speed is exceeded.

222 The Traffic Officer's Companion

TACHOGRAPHS – FITTING/USE

COUNCIL REGULATION (EEC) 3821/85

Requirement

The requirement to install tachographs is brought about by Article 3 of Council Regulation (EEC) 3821/85 on recording equipment in road transport. They must be fitted to all EEC vehicles carrying passengers or goods, to which EU drivers' hours are applicable. They are not required for exempt vehicles (see under "selector" and "vehicle categories", earlier); regular national passenger services, and regular international services whose route terminals are within 50km of a frontier between 2 member states and whose route length does not exceed 100km; vehicles never used on public roads; vehicles not used for carrying passengers or goods (fixed plant or machinery are not 'goods'); and vehicles collecting sea coal.

Type Approval is given by member states for tachographs and model record sheets, and an EC approval mark is issued. *(ARTS 5 & 6)*

Fitting

Tachographs may only be installed or repaired by fitters or workshops approved by the Secretary of State, and each has its special seal, a record of which is kept on a central registry. An installation plaque is then fitted which consists of the letter 'e' followed by the number designated to the member state. *(ART 12)*

Use

Both employers and drivers are responsible for ensuring the equipment works correctly. *(ART 13)*

The employer must issue sufficient suitable record sheets to drivers and the sheets must be kept by the employer for 1 year after their use. The sheets must be produced and handed over if requested by an authorised inspecting office. *(ART 14)*

Record sheets must be used at all times, starting as soon as the vehicle is taken over. Dirty or damaged sheets must not be used. If they become damaged they must be attached to the spare sheets after use. All times must be accurately recorded. *(ART 15)*

Crew members must also complete record sheets with their names, dates and places where the sheet begins and ends, registration number(s) of vehicle(s), odometer reading at the start and end of each journey and of both vehicles if he changes vehicles and the time of such change. *(ART 15(5))*

Where the driver is away from the vehicle and unable to operate the equipment, information relating to 'other periods of work', 'other periods of availability' (waiting time, time beside the driver or in a bunk whilst vehicle in motion) and break and daily rest periods, must be entered on the sheet either manually or automatically. *(ART 15 (2))*

Part 4: Driver's hours and records 223

TACHOGRAPHS – FITTING/USE cont

Tachographs and charts in use must be:

Calibrated	by DoT-approved calibration station
Re-calibrated/ inspected	every six years or after repair and a simple check every two years
Sealed	by calibration centre's seal. The cables connecting the recording transmitter must be protected by a continuous plastic-coated stainless sheath with crimped ends.
Certified	that it is calibrated by affixing a plaque on or near the tachograph
Produced	by the driver for the current week and the last day of the previous week
Returned	to employer when completed within 21 days
Filed	by employer and kept for 12 months
Repaired	as soon as possible after becoming defective – once it has returned to base, not to be used until repaired. Drivers must mark on the record sheet or on a temporary sheet to be attached to the record sheet, all information not properly recorded by the equipment

Practical points

- Identify the record sheet in such a manner that it can be readily recognised in the future.
- Note odometer reading.
- Note details of calibration plaque.
- Note tyre sizes of tachograph drive axle.
- Check lead seals, note the numbers.
- Be sure, where charts are seized, that they are carefully preserved.
- Note time on tachograph clock, compare it with the true time and note any difference.
- Ensure that the chart has been inserted properly and the **chart** time is not 12 hours out.
- Check that the disc is of the correct type for the tachograph and the correct speed range.

TACHOGRAPH OFFENCES – DRIVER

Offence	Explanation
1. Not fitted	Using a motor vehicle requiring a tachograph on a road when not fitted with a tachograph in accordance with the regulations, or which has been repaired otherwise than in accordance with 3821/85.
CONTRARY TO ARTICLE 3, COUNCIL REGULATION (EEC) 3821/85 AND S 97(1)(B) TRANSPORT ACT 1968 AS AMENDED BY PASSENGER AND GOODS VEHICLES (RECORDING EQUIPMENT) REGULATIONS 1979 AND 1989.	
2. Dirty/damaged sheets	Crew member using dirty or damaged record sheet.
CONTRARY TO ART 15 (1) COUNCIL REGULATION (EEC) 3821/85 AND S 97 (1)(B) TRANSPORT ACT 1968 AS AMENDED BY PASSENGER AND GOODS VEHICLES (RECORDING EQUIPMENT) REGULATIONS 1979.	
3. Dirty/damaged sheets	Driver failing to attach dirty or damaged record sheet to duplicate Record Sheet.
CONTRARY TO ARTICLE 15, COUNCIL REGULATIONS (EEC) 3821/85 AND S 97 (1)(B) TRANSPORT ACT 1968, AS AMENDED	
4. Not running	Driver failing to ensure that Recording Equipment is running continuously from the time he took over the vehicle until relieved of responsibility.
CONTRARY TO ARTICLE 15(2), COUNCIL REGULATION (EEC) 3821/85 AND S 97 (1)(B) TRANSPORT ACT 1968, AS AMENDED	
5. Time incorrect	Driver failing to ensure that the time on the clock is correct for the country in which the vehicle is registered.
CONTRARY TO ARTICLE 15(3), COUNCIL REGULATION (EEC) 3821/85 AND S 97(1)(B) TRANSPORT ACT 1968 AS AMENDED	
6. Improperly operated	Driver failing to operate the switch mechanism to change to: – driving time – other periods of work – breaks from work and rest periods – other periods of availability – delete which is not applicable
CONTRARY TO ARTICLE 15(3), COUNCIL REGULATION (EEC) 3821/85 AND S 97 (1)(B) TRANSPORT ACT 1968 AS AMENDED	

continued on next page

TACHOGRAPH OFFENCES – DRIVER cont

Offence	Explanation
7. Entering information	Driver failing to enter information of any of the following details on the face of the record sheet: – surname and first name of driver – date and place sheet is first used also where it ends and date – registered number of vehicle and other vehicles used – odometer reading, start and end, and time of any change of vehicle.
CONTRARY TO ARTICLE 15 (5) REGULATION (EEC) 3821/85 AND S 97 (1) (B) TRANSPORT ACT 1968 AS AMENDED	
8. Production	Driver failing to produce record sheets of the current week and the last day of the previous week.
CONTRARY TO ARTICLE 15(7), COUNCIL REGULATION (EEC) 3821/85 AND S 97 (1)(B) TRANSPORT ACT 1968, AS AMENDED	
9. Written records	Crew member failing to keep a written record if tachograph is unserviceable or defective.
CONTRARY TO ARTICLE 16(2), COUNCIL REGULATION (EEC) 3821/85 AND S 97 (1)(B) TRANSPORT ACT 1968, AS AMENDED	
10. Written records	Driver failing to keep records.
CONTRARY TO ARTICLE 15(2), COUNCIL REGULATION (EEC) 3821/85 AND S. 97(1)(C) TRANSPORT ACT 1968, AS AMENDED	
11. Handing in	Driver failing to hand in previous record sheets after 21 days.
CONTRARY TO S 97A (1)(A), TRANSPORT ACT 1968, AS AMENDED	
12. Notification	Driver who was employed by two or more employers failing to notify each or all of the other employers detailed.
CONTRARY TO S 97A (1)(B), TRANSPORT ACT 1968, AS AMENDED	
13. Inspection	Driver failing to allow record sheets to be examined by Inspecting Officer.
CONTRARY TO S 99(4)(A), TRANSPORT ACT 1968 AS AMENDED	
14. Inspection	Driver failing to allow Inspecting Officer entry into vehicle for the purpose of examining record sheets.
CONTRARY TO S 99(4)(A), TRANSPORT ACT 1968, AS AMENDED	
15. Seals etc	Driver failing to ensure that equipment functions correctly and seals remain intact.
CONTRARY TO ARTICLE 13, COUNCIL REGULATION (EEC) 3821/85 AND S 97 (1) (B) TRANSPORT ACT 1968, AS AMENDED	

226 The Traffic Officer's Companion

TACHOGRAPH OFFENCES – EMPLOYER

Offence	Explanation
1. Use etc	*Use, cause or permit any of offences 1 – 11 (see previous pages) committed by a driver.*
2. Supply	*Employer failing to issue sufficient number of record sheets (2 days' supply).*
CONTRARY TO ARTICLE 14 (1) COUNCIL REGULATION (EEC) 3821/85 AND S 97 (1)(B) TRANSPORT ACT 1968, AS AMENDED	
3. Retain	*Employer failing to retain record sheets (discs) for period of 12 months after use.*
CONTRARY TO ARTICLE 14(2), COUNCIL REGULATION (EEC) 3821/85 AND S 97(1)(B) TRANSPORT ACT 1968, AS AMENDED	
4. Inspection	*Employer failing to produce or hand over for inspection any records required to be kept.*
CONTRARY TO ARTICLE 14(2), REGULATION (EEC) 3851/85 AND S 97 (1)(B) TRANSPORT ACT 1968, AS AMENDED	
5. Not fitted	*Employer failing to fit tachograph in accordance with Regulations, or which has been repaired otherwise than in accordance with Art 16(1) of Council Regulation (EEC) 3821/85.*
CONTRARY TO S 97 (1)(A), TRANSPORT ACT 1968, AS AMENDED	
6. Inspection	*Employer failing to allow Inspecting Officer (including PC) to enter premises for the purpose of examining records, sheets, discs or vehicles.*
CONTRARY TO S 99(4), TRANSPORT ACT 1968, AS AMENDED	

Part 4: Driver's hours and records **227**

TACHOGRAPH OFFENCES – GENERAL

SECTION 97AA TRANSPORT ACT 1968

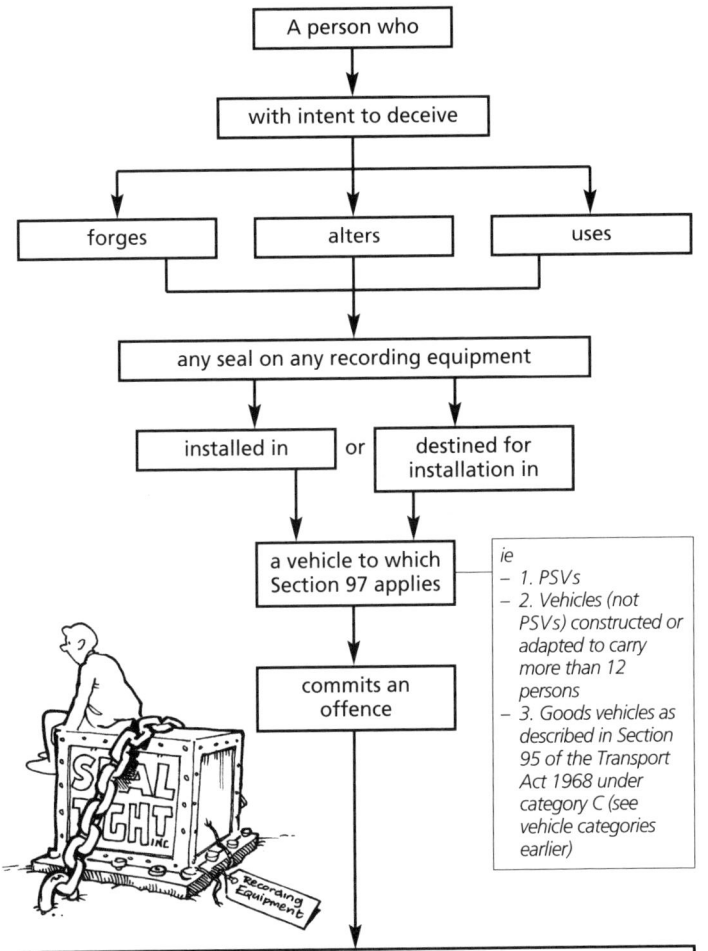

```
A person who
   ↓
with intent to deceive
   ↓
forges / alters / uses
   ↓
any seal on any recording equipment
   ↓
installed in   or   destined for installation in
   ↓
a vehicle to which Section 97 applies
   ↓
commits an offence
```

ie
- 1. PSVs
- 2. Vehicles (not PSVs) constructed or adapted to carry more than 12 persons
- 3. Goods vehicles as described in Section 95 of the Transport Act 1968 under category C (see vehicle categories earlier)

These are offences triable either way and the offender shall be liable on summary conviction to a fine not exceeding the statutory maximum (currently £5,000) or on conviction on indictment to imprisonment for a term not exceeding two years.

228 *The Traffic Officer's Companion*

TACHOGRAPH DEFENCES

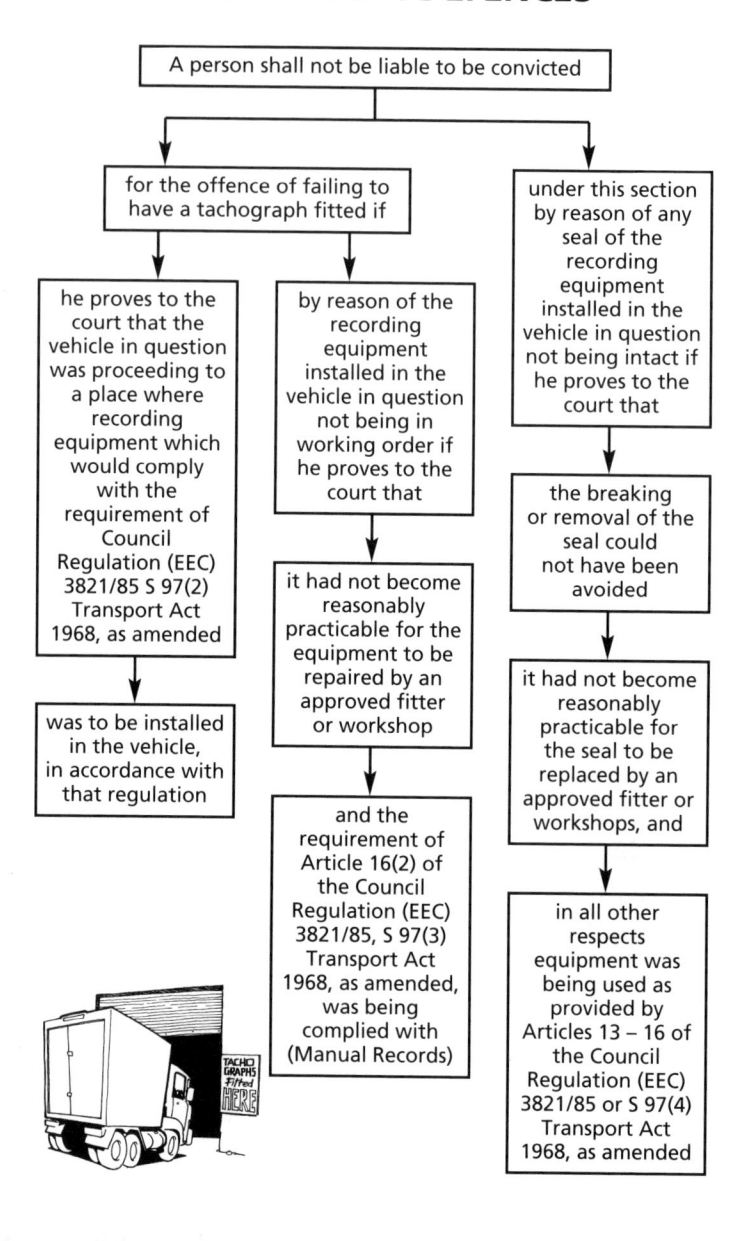

A person shall not be liable to be convicted

---

for the offence of failing to have a tachograph fitted if

- he proves to the court that the vehicle in question was proceeding to a place where recording equipment which would comply with the requirement of Council Regulation (EEC) 3821/85 S 97(2) Transport Act 1968, as amended
- was to be installed in the vehicle, in accordance with that regulation

---

by reason of the recording equipment installed in the vehicle in question not being in working order if he proves to the court that

- it had not become reasonably practicable for the equipment to be repaired by an approved fitter or workshop
- and the requirement of Article 16(2) of the Council Regulation (EEC) 3821/85, S 97(3) Transport Act 1968, as amended, was being complied with (Manual Records)

---

under this section by reason of any seal of the recording equipment installed in the vehicle in question not being intact if he proves to the court that

- the breaking or removal of the seal could not have been avoided
- it had not become reasonably practicable for the seal to be replaced by an approved fitter or workshops, and
- in all other respects equipment was being used as provided by Articles 13 – 16 of the Council Regulation (EEC) 3821/85 or S 97(4) Transport Act 1968, as amended

Part 4: Driver's hours and records 229

TACHOGRAPH IRREGULARITIES

Problem	Cause
Speed stylus records below base line	Stylus bent to obtain lower speed recording. To obtain correct readings add the k/m below the line.
Breaks in distance trace	Driven with head open.
Interrupted recordings	Instrument door has been opened. Blank spaces appear because styli were not making contact.
Speed and/or RPM recordings stay at same level for unusually long time	Stylus has been blocked to prevent recordings of high road and/or engine speeds.
	To calculate the average road speed, multiply the mileage by 60 and divide the answer by the travelling time in minutes. The average will be higher than the maximum speed as indicated on the chart.
Overtracing	The chart has been turned back to conceal long breaks, or has not been replaced when completed.
Distance travelled does not correspond with odometer	Change of tyre size, two-speed adaptor or rear axle ratio, without necessary adjustment in the cable drive adaptor.
	An incorrect speed indication will also be shown.
All recordings vertical in same spot	Power supply to clock interrupted or intentionally blocked.

POLICE POWERS
Transport Act 1968

Inspection of records (S.99)
An officer (includes Police Officer) may require the **production, inspection and copying** of any written records required to be kept by regulations made under S98 of the Transport Act 1968, or which he may reasonably require to inspect to ascertain whether Community rules have been complied with. He may require **production of the documents at a specified Traffic Commissioner's office** within a specified time (not being less than 10 days). He may also **enter any vehicle** and inspect it, the recording equipment and any record sheet. At any reasonable time he may, in addition, **enter any premises** on which he believes a vehicle is kept or where any record sheets, books or other such written documents may be found – and may inspect and copy such. He may **detain a** vehicle for the purpose of examining it and its equipment and records.

A person who **fails to comply** with a requirement to inspect, etc documents, **obstructs entry or inspection** of vehicles or premises or **makes any false entry** with intent to deceive shall be guilty of an offence.

Power to prohibit driving of vehicle (S.99A)
A constable authorised for the purposes of this section by the Chief Officer of Police may, upon giving written notice to the driver, **prohibit the driving** of a UK registered vehicle on a road and may require the driver to **remove it** (and any trailer) to such place and subject to such conditions as are specified in the direction. The power may be exercised in the following circumstances:

- If the driver obstructs the officer entering and inspecting any vehicle or premises as mentioned above or if he fails to allow the officer to detain the vehicle as above.

- If there has been a contravention of Ss. 96 –98 of this Act or regulations made hereunder (domestic hours, tachographs, record sheets, forgery, etc. of recording equipment seals, and record books) or that there will be such a contravention if the vehicle is driven on a road.

- If there has been a contravention of the applicable Community rules, or that there will be such a contravention if the vehicle is driven on a road.

- An offence under S 99(5) of the Act has been committed (making a record or entry on a record sheet, book, register or document (domestic or community) which he knows to be false, or alters such with intent to deceive).

Failure to comply with prohibition (S99C)

Any person who:
- drives a vehicle on a road in contravention of a prohibition
- causes or permits a vehicle to be so driven
- refuses or fails within a reasonable time to comply with a direction to remove the vehicle to a place or subject to conditions as specified

commits an offence.

PART 5

MISCELLANEOUS

This section is intended as a 'catch-all' to cater for those aspects of traffic law which do not readily fall within other parts of the book. The major aspects include vehicle testing, drink driving, speed limits and the carriage of dangerous goods.

TESTING ON ROADS

ROAD TRAFFIC ACT 1988, SS. 67, AND SCHED 2

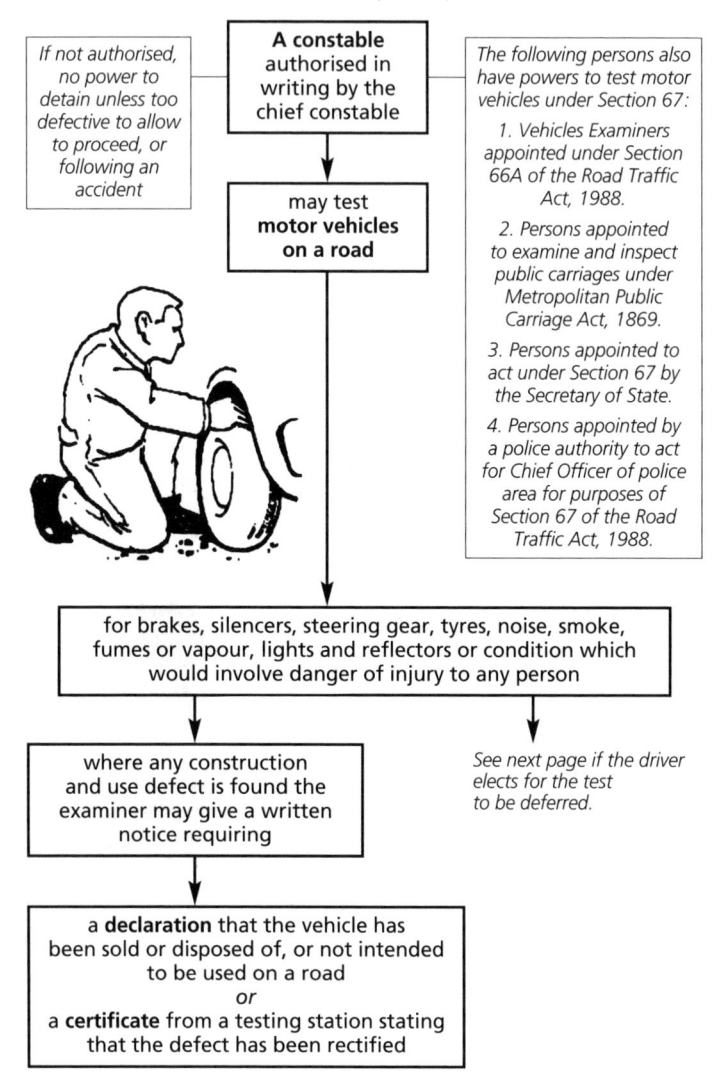

If not authorised, no power to detain unless too defective to allow to proceed, or following an accident

A constable authorised in writing by the chief constable

The following persons also have powers to test motor vehicles under Section 67:

1. Vehicles Examiners appointed under Section 66A of the Road Traffic Act, 1988.

2. Persons appointed to examine and inspect public carriages under Metropolitan Public Carriage Act, 1869.

3. Persons appointed to act under Section 67 by the Secretary of State.

4. Persons appointed by a police authority to act for Chief Officer of police area for purposes of Section 67 of the Road Traffic Act, 1988.

may test **motor vehicles on a road**

for brakes, silencers, steering gear, tyres, noise, smoke, fumes or vapour, lights and reflectors or condition which would involve danger of injury to any person

where any construction and use defect is found the examiner may give a written notice requiring

See next page if the driver elects for the test to be deferred.

a **declaration** that the vehicle has been sold or disposed of, or not intended to be used on a road
or
a **certificate** from a testing station stating that the defect has been rectified

Part 5: Miscellaneous **235**

Continued from previous page...

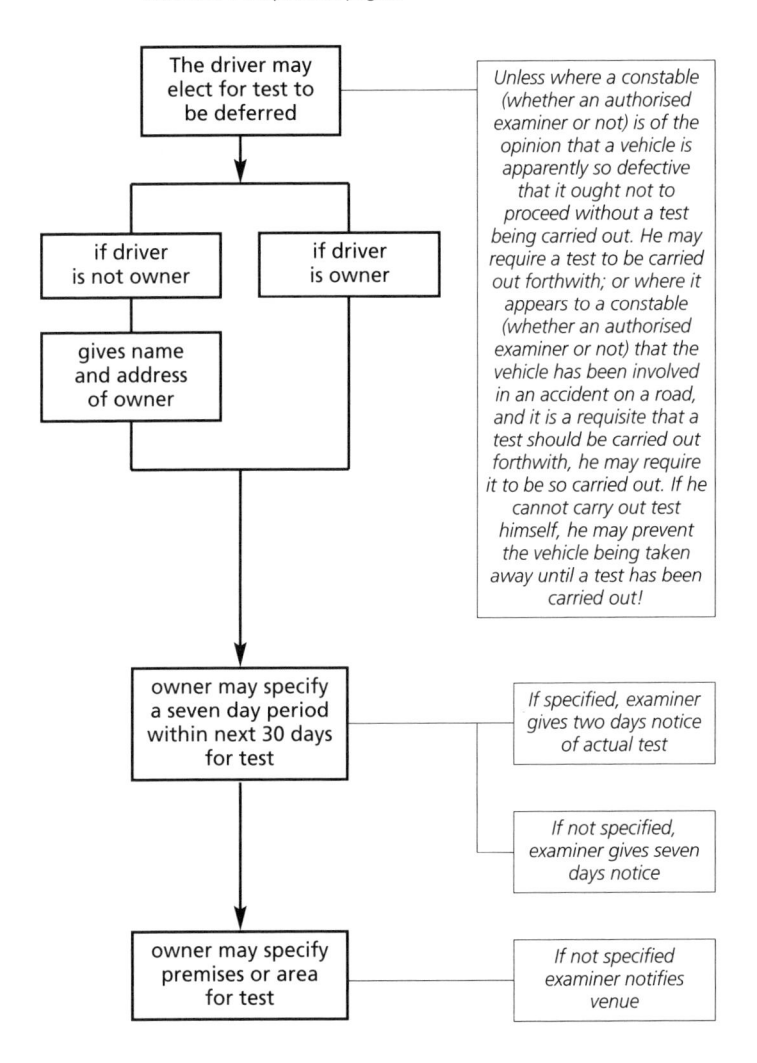

```
┌─────────────────┐
│ The driver may  │
│ elect for test  │──────  *Unless where a constable*
│  to be deferred │        *(whether an authorised*
└─────────────────┘        *examiner or not) is of the*
         │                 *opinion that a vehicle is*
         ▼                 *apparently so defective*
```

Unless where a constable (whether an authorised examiner or not) is of the opinion that a vehicle is apparently so defective that it ought not to proceed without a test being carried out. He may require a test to be carried out forthwith; or where it appears to a constable (whether an authorised examiner or not) that the vehicle has been involved in an accident on a road, and it is a requisite that a test should be carried out forthwith, he may require it to be so carried out. If he cannot carry out test himself, he may prevent the vehicle being taken away until a test has been carried out!

- if driver is not owner → gives name and address of owner
- if driver is owner

↓

owner may specify a seven day period within next 30 days for test

- *If specified, examiner gives two days notice of actual test*
- *If not specified, examiner gives seven days notice*

↓

owner may specify premises or area for test

- *If not specified examiner notifies venue*

It is an offence to obstruct an authorised constable,
(or authorised examiners) or to fail to comply with a lawful requirement.

236 *The Traffic Officer's Companion*

TESTING ON PREMISES

ROAD VEHICLES (CONSTRUCTION AND USE) REGULATIONS 1986, REG 74
ROAD VEHICLES LIGHTING REGULATIONS 1989, REG. 28

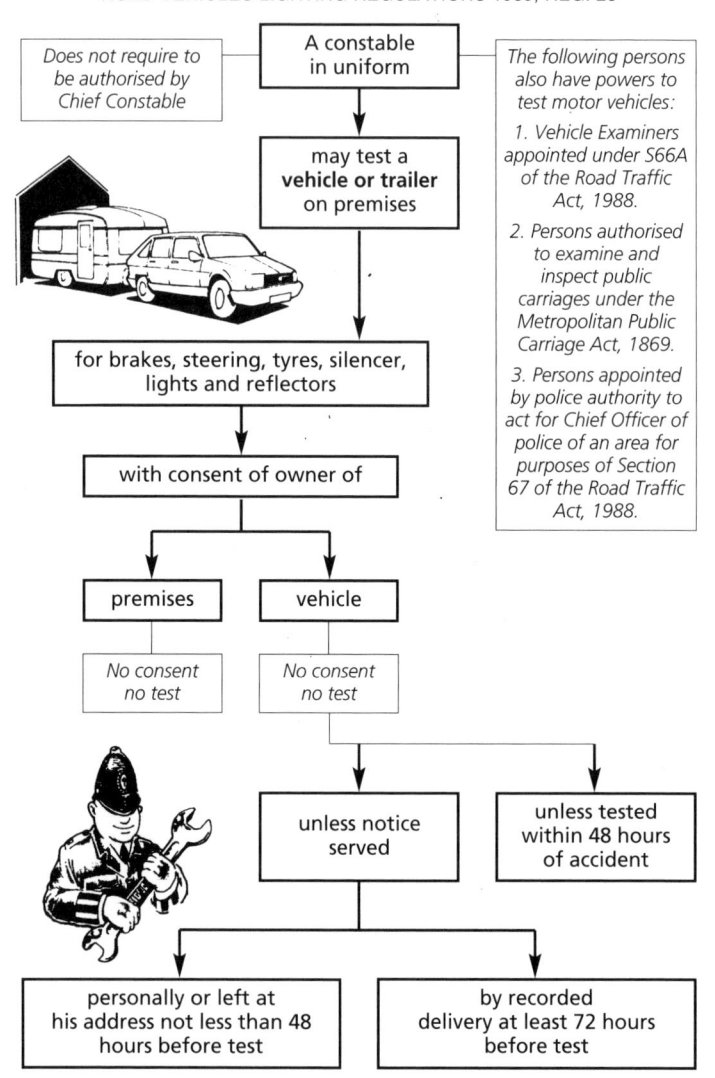

Does not require to be authorised by Chief Constable

A constable in uniform

The following persons also have powers to test motor vehicles:

1. Vehicle Examiners appointed under S66A of the Road Traffic Act, 1988.

2. Persons authorised to examine and inspect public carriages under the Metropolitan Public Carriage Act, 1869.

3. Persons appointed by police authority to act for Chief Officer of police of an area for purposes of Section 67 of the Road Traffic Act, 1988.

may test a **vehicle or trailer** on premises

for brakes, steering, tyres, silencer, lights and reflectors

with consent of owner of

premises	vehicle
No consent no test	*No consent no test*

unless notice served

unless tested within 48 hours of accident

personally or left at his address not less than 48 hours before test

by recorded delivery at least 72 hours before test

Part 5: Miscellaneous **237**

REMOVAL OF VEHICLES

REMOVAL AND DISPOSAL OF VEHICLES REGULATIONS 1986, REGS. 3 AND 4
ROAD TRAFFIC OFFENDERS ACT 1988, S. 91

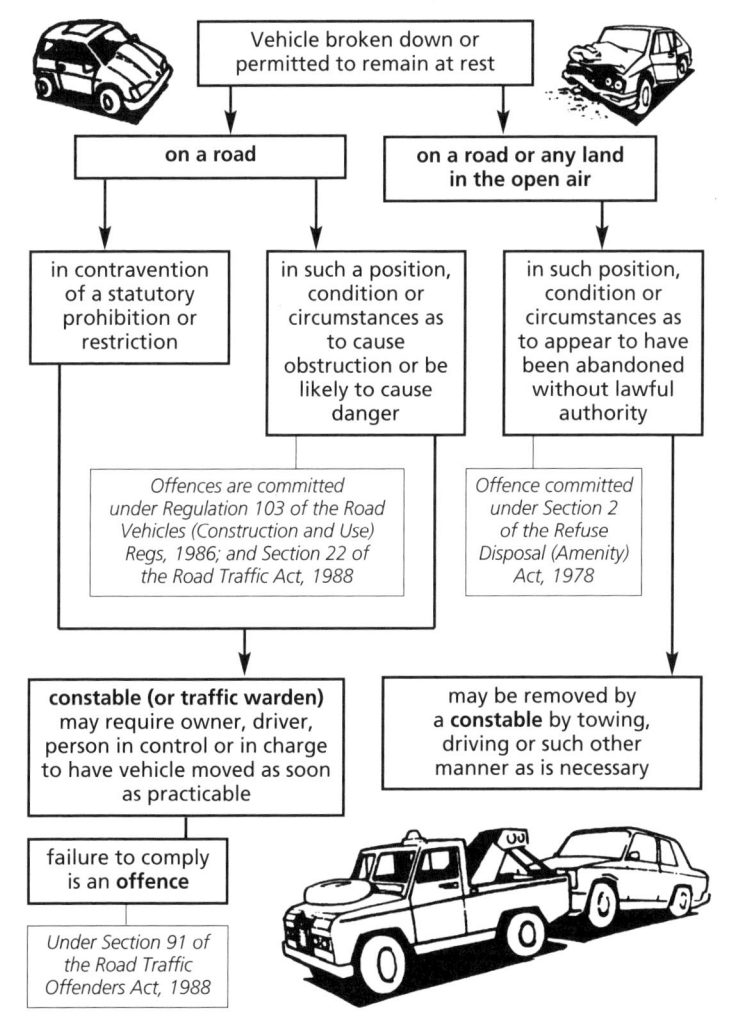

Vehicle broken down or permitted to remain at rest

- **on a road**
- **on a road or any land in the open air**

- in contravention of a statutory prohibition or restriction
- in such a position, condition or circumstances as to cause obstruction or be likely to cause danger
- in such position, condition or circumstances as to appear to have been abandoned without lawful authority

Offences are committed under Regulation 103 of the Road Vehicles (Construction and Use) Regs, 1986; and Section 22 of the Road Traffic Act, 1988

Offence committed under Section 2 of the Refuse Disposal (Amenity) Act, 1978

constable (or traffic warden) may require owner, driver, person in control or in charge to have vehicle moved as soon as practicable

may be removed by a **constable** by towing, driving or such other manner as is necessary

failure to comply is an **offence**

Under Section 91 of the Road Traffic Offenders Act, 1988

Note: Reference to traffic wardens having power under reg 3 (above) to require vehicle to be removed only applies in England and Wales.

MOTOR SALVAGE OPERATORS
VEHICLE (CRIME) ACT 2001

A motor salvage operator is a person who carries on a business which consists-
1. wholly or partly in recovery for re-use or sale of salvageable parts from motor vehicles and the subsequent sale or other disposal for scrap of the remainder of the vehicles;
2. wholly or mainly in the purchase of written-off vehicles and their subsequent repair and resale;
3. wholly or mainly in the sale or purchase of motor vehicles which are to be the subject of any of the above activities;
4. wholly or mainly in activities which fall within 2 or 3 above.

A person who carries out the business of a motor salvage operator must **register** with the local authority. It is an offence to make false statements in an application for registration.

Entry and Inspection of Premises

A constable may at any reasonable time enter and inspect **registered** premises which are occupied by an operator as a motor salvage yard. (Force may not be used in executing any warrant to enter)

Requirement to keep Records

Records (electronic or manual) must be kept at the premises of details relating to the vehicle, the supplier or person receiving (including proof of identity), condition of vehicle, date of transaction and date details were entered on the record.

Inspection of Records

A constable may at any reasonable time-
1. require production of, and inspect, any motor vehicles or salvageable parts kept on **registered** premises; and
2. require production of, inspect and take copies of or extracts from any records which the operator is required to keep.

Warrant to Enter Premises

In order to secure compliance with regulations, or to ascertain whether provisions are being complied with, a Justice of the Peace may issue a warrant authorising a constable to enter and inspect specified premises. (Other than as mentioned above, reasonable force may be used to execute a warrant). If required by the owner or occupier of the premises, the constable shall produce evidence of his identity and his authority for entering, before doing so.

Giving False Particulars

A person who sells a motor vehicle to a motor salvage operator commits an offence if he gives him a false name or address.

TAKING A CONVEYANCE WITHOUT AUTHORITY

THEFT ACT 1968

Without having the consent of the owner or other lawful authority, taking a conveyance for his own or another's use, or knowing that a conveyance has been taken without the consent of the owner or other lawful authority, drives it or allows himself to be carried in or on it.

The conveyance must be moved, however short the distance may be, merely trying to start an engine will not suffice. Also, it must be taken for use as a conveyance, merely pushing it around the corner for a prank will not satisfy this offence.

S 12(1)

Conveyance
Constructed or adapted for the carriage of a person by land, water or air.

- **This is an arrestable offence**

A similar offence exists in relation to pedal cycles but it is not an arrestable offence.

S 12(5)

AGGRAVATED VEHICLE-TAKING ACT 1992
adds S 12A TO THE THEFT ACT 1968.

Provides for obligatory disqualification and endorsement where the above offence under S 12(1) has been committed and, before the vehicle was recovered, the vehicle was driven dangerously or was damaged or was driven in a way which led to personal injury or damage to other property.

Note: These offences only apply in England and Wales (as Theft Act does not apply to Scotland) – Scots officers should consult Section 178 of the Road Traffic Act, 1988; Re: Taking of Motor Vehicles without Consent etc.

240 *The Traffic Officer's Companion*

VEHICLE INTERFERENCE

S 9 CRIMINAL ATTEMPTS ACT 1981

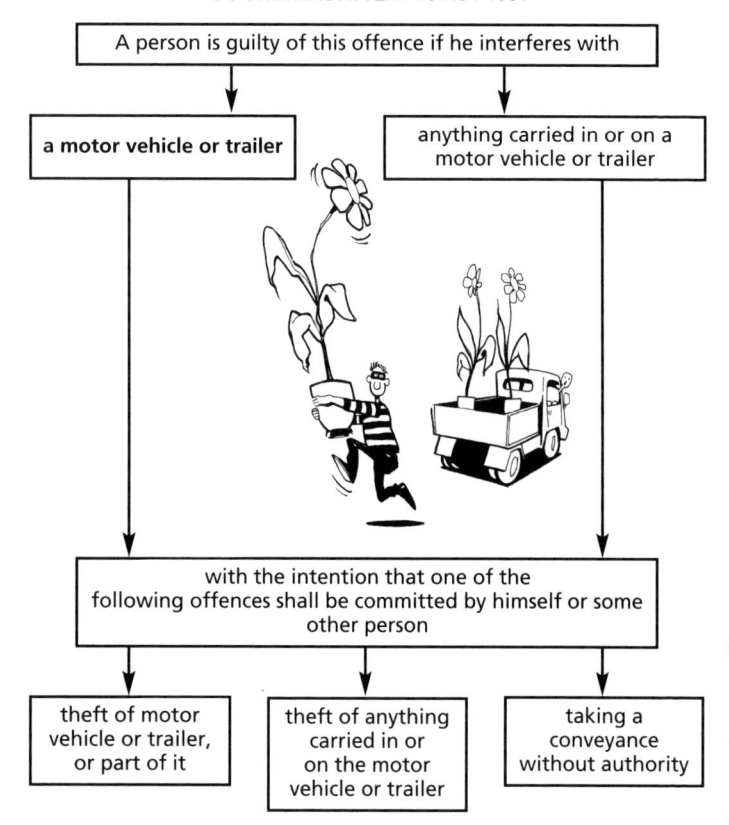

A person is guilty of this offence if he interferes with

- **a motor vehicle or trailer**
- anything carried in or on a motor vehicle or trailer

with the intention that one of the following offences shall be committed by himself or some other person

- theft of motor vehicle or trailer, or part of it
- theft of anything carried in or on the motor vehicle or trailer
- taking a conveyance without authority

Any arrest must be in accordance with the Police and Criminal Evidence Act 1984

Note:
1. The above legislation is only applicable to England and Wales.
2. A person may still be guilty of an offence under S 25 of the Road Traffic Act 1988, if, while a motor vehicle is on a road or local authority parking place, he gets onto the vehicle or tampers with the brakes or other parts of its mechanism.

DRINK/DRIVING

ROAD TRAFFIC ACT 1988, S.4 AND 5

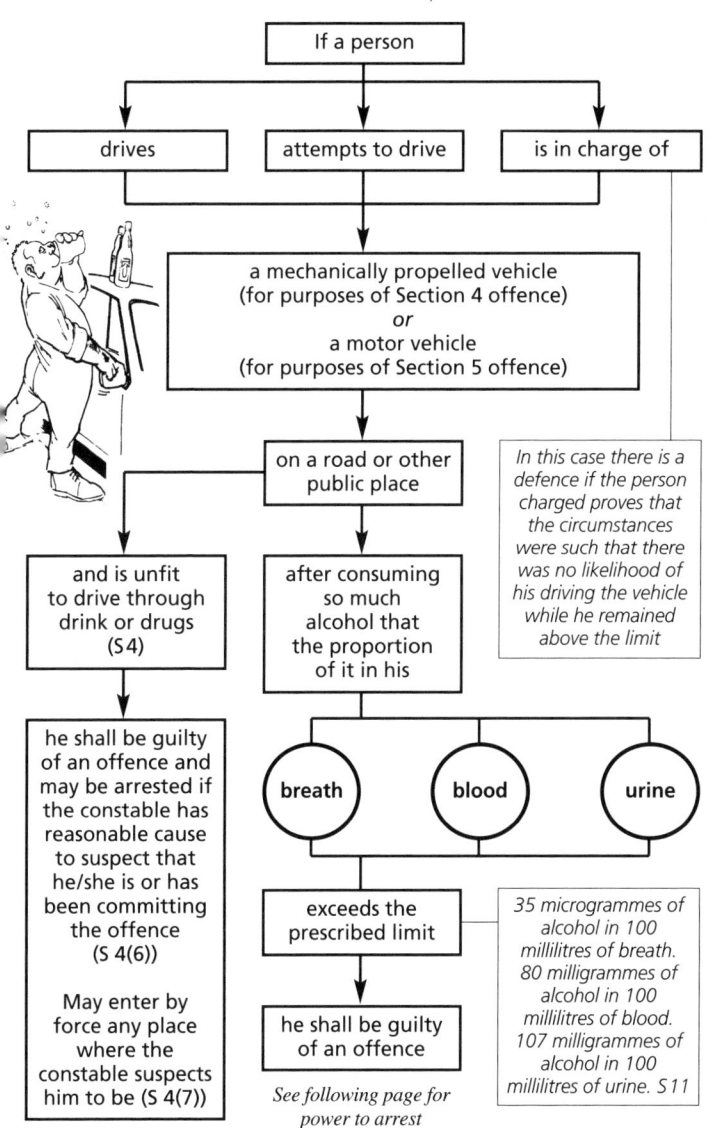

If a person

- **drives**
- **attempts to drive**
- **is in charge of**

a mechanically propelled vehicle
(for purposes of Section 4 offence)
or
a motor vehicle
(for purposes of Section 5 offence)

on a road or other public place

In this case there is a defence if the person charged proves that the circumstances were such that there was no likelihood of his driving the vehicle while he remained above the limit

and is unfit to drive through drink or drugs (S 4)

he shall be guilty of an offence and may be arrested if the constable has reasonable cause to suspect that he/she is or has been committing the offence (S 4(6))

May enter by force any place where the constable suspects him to be (S 4(7))

after consuming so much alcohol that the proportion of it in his

- **breath**
- **blood**
- **urine**

exceeds the prescribed limit

he shall be guilty of an offence

See following page for power to arrest

*35 microgrammes of alcohol in 100 millilitres of breath.
80 milligrammes of alcohol in 100 millilitres of blood.
107 milligrammes of alcohol in 100 millilitres of urine. S11*

242 The Traffic Officer's Companion

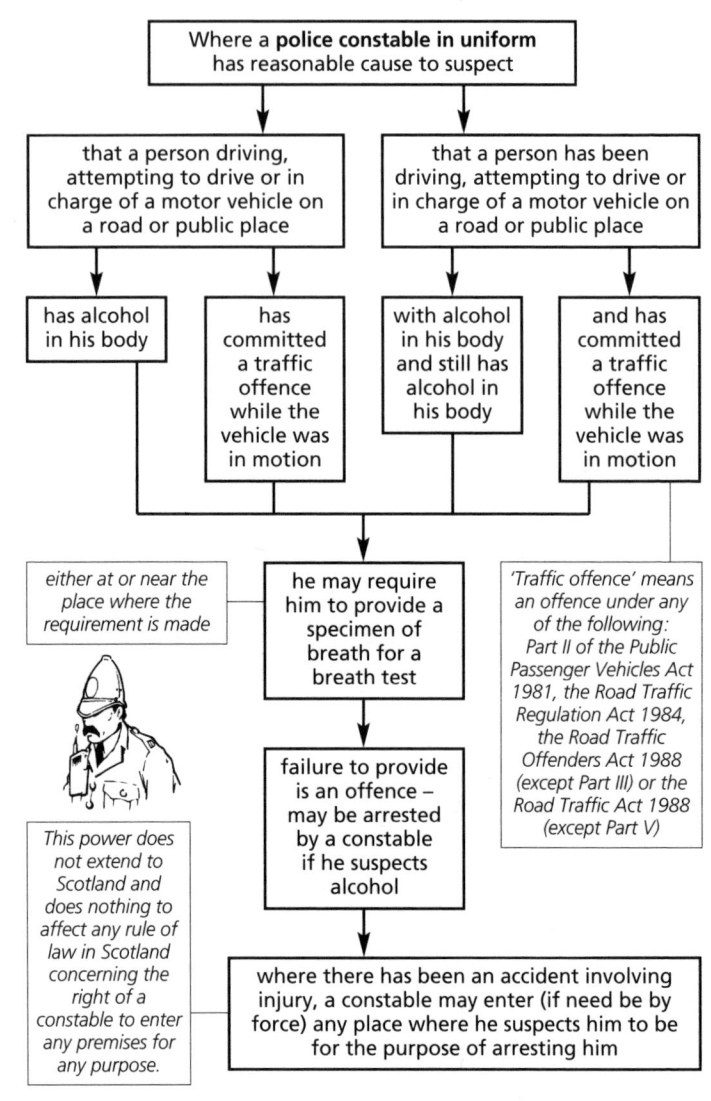

BREATH TESTS

ROAD TRAFFIC ACT 1988, S.6

Where a **police constable in uniform** has reasonable cause to suspect

- that a person driving, attempting to drive or in charge of a motor vehicle on a road or public place
  - has alcohol in his body
  - has committed a traffic offence while the vehicle was in motion

- that a person has been driving, attempting to drive or in charge of a motor vehicle on a road or public place
  - with alcohol in his body and still has alcohol in his body
  - and has committed a traffic offence while the vehicle was in motion

he may require him to provide a specimen of breath for a breath test

either at or near the place where the requirement is made

'Traffic offence' means an offence under any of the following: Part II of the Public Passenger Vehicles Act 1981, the Road Traffic Regulation Act 1984, the Road Traffic Offenders Act 1988 (except Part III) or the Road Traffic Act 1988 (except Part V)

failure to provide is an offence – may be arrested by a constable if he suspects alcohol

This power does not extend to Scotland and does nothing to affect any rule of law in Scotland concerning the right of a constable to enter any premises for any purpose.

where there has been an accident involving injury, a constable may enter (if need be by force) any place where he suspects him to be for the purpose of arresting him

BREATH TESTS cont

ROAD TRAFFIC ACT 1988, S.6

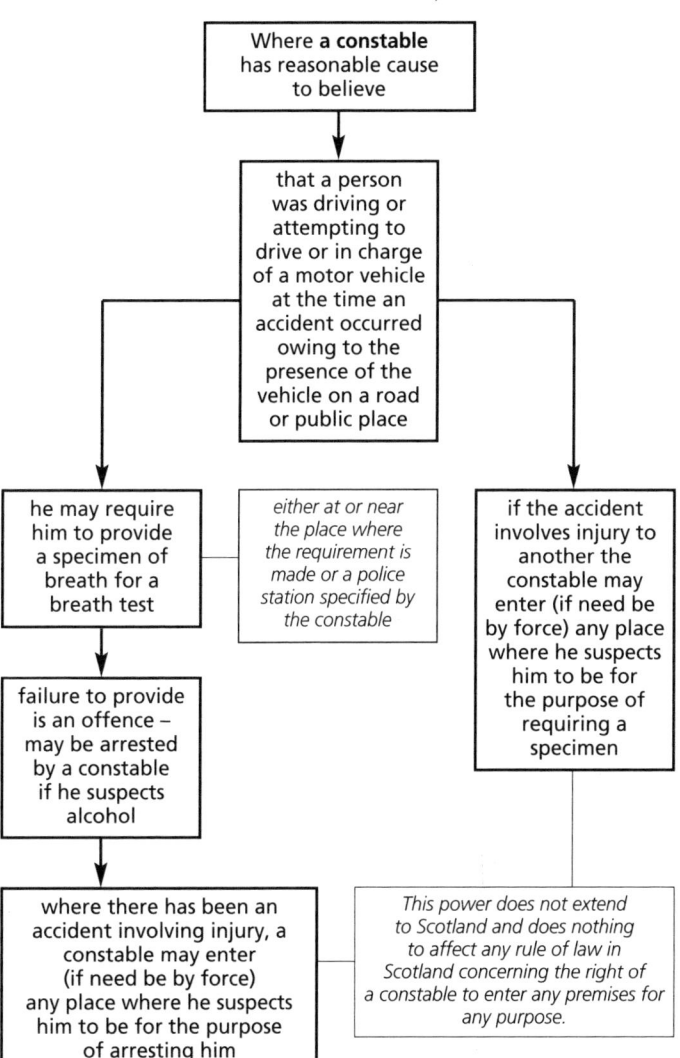

```
Where a constable has reasonable cause to believe
          ↓
that a person was driving or attempting to drive or in charge
of a motor vehicle at the time an accident occurred owing to
the presence of the vehicle on a road or public place
```

he may require him to provide a specimen of breath for a breath test

either at or near the place where the requirement is made or a police station specified by the constable

if the accident involves injury to another the constable may enter (if need be by force) any place where he suspects him to be for the purpose of requiring a specimen

failure to provide is an offence – may be arrested by a constable if he suspects alcohol

where there has been an accident involving injury, a constable may enter (if need be by force) any place where he suspects him to be for the purpose of arresting him

This power does not extend to Scotland and does nothing to affect any rule of law in Scotland concerning the right of a constable to enter any premises for any purpose.

244 The Traffic Officer's Companion

SPECIMENS – VENUE

ROAD TRAFFIC ACT 1988, S.7

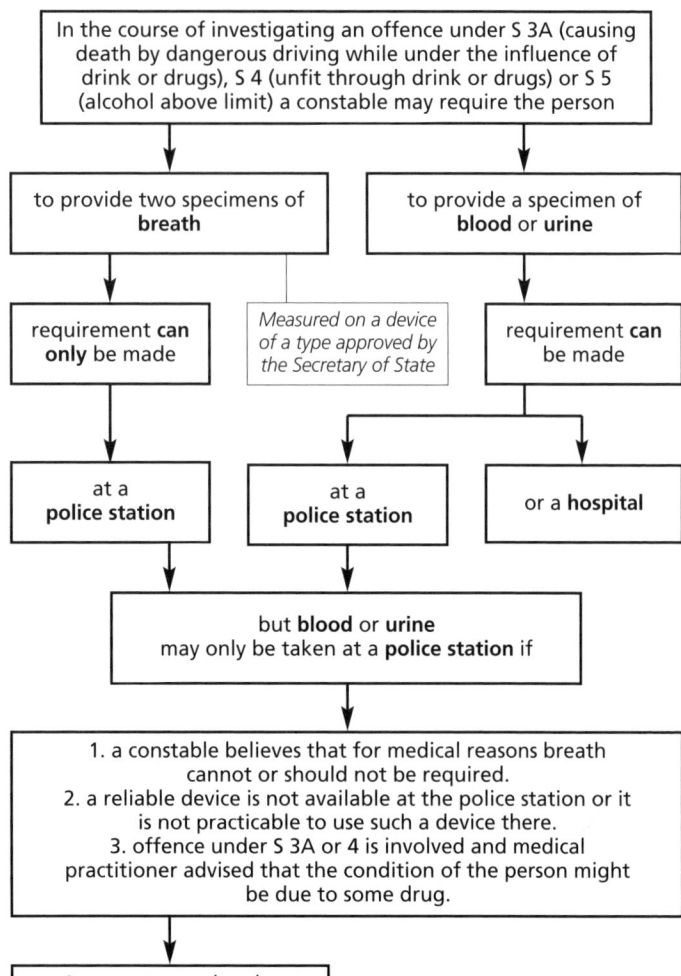

In the course of investigating an offence under S 3A (causing death by dangerous driving while under the influence of drink or drugs), S 4 (unfit through drink or drugs) or S 5 (alcohol above limit) a constable may require the person

- to provide two specimens of **breath**
- to provide a specimen of **blood** or **urine**

Measured on a device of a type approved by the Secretary of State

Breath: requirement **can only** be made at a **police station**

Blood/urine: requirement **can** be made at a **police station** or a **hospital**

but **blood** or **urine** may only be taken at a **police station** if

1. a constable believes that for medical reasons breath cannot or should not be required.
2. a reliable device is not available at the police station or it is not practicable to use such a device there.
3. offence under S 3A or 4 is involved and medical practitioner advised that the condition of the person might be due to some drug.

A request may then be made even where the person has already provided or been required to provide two specimens of breath.

Note: All motorists judged by the Intoximeter to be over the limit, and those who fail to give a sample of breath, have the option of giving a blood test.

Part 5: Miscellaneous **245**

SPECIMENS – PROCEDURE

ROAD TRAFFIC ACT 1988, Ss. 8 AND 9

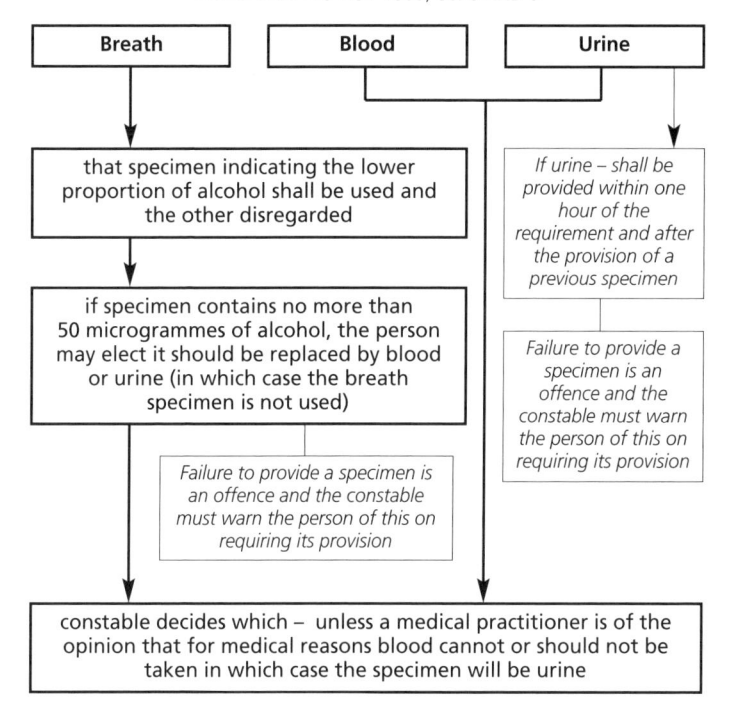

```
┌──────────┐   ┌──────────┐   ┌──────────┐
│  Breath  │   │  Blood   │   │  Urine   │
└──────────┘   └──────────┘   └──────────┘
```

that specimen indicating the lower proportion of alcohol shall be used and the other disregarded

if specimen contains no more than 50 microgrammes of alcohol, the person may elect it should be replaced by blood or urine (in which case the breath specimen is not used)

Failure to provide a specimen is an offence and the constable must warn the person of this on requiring its provision

If urine – shall be provided within one hour of the requirement and after the provision of a previous specimen

Failure to provide a specimen is an offence and the constable must warn the person of this on requiring its provision

constable decides which – unless a medical practitioner is of the opinion that for medical reasons blood cannot or should not be taken in which case the specimen will be urine

HOSPITALS

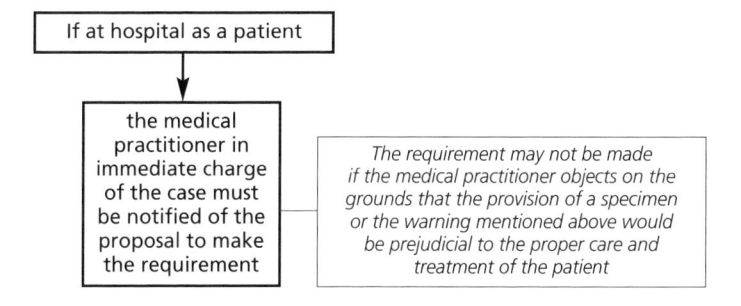

If at hospital as a patient

the medical practitioner in immediate charge of the case must be notified of the proposal to make the requirement

The requirement may not be made if the medical practitioner objects on the grounds that the provision of a specimen or the warning mentioned above would be prejudicial to the proper care and treatment of the patient

246 The Traffic Officer's Companion

SPEED LIMITS

ROAD TRAFFIC REGULATION ACT 1984

The maximum speed at which a vehicle can travel depends upon the road concerned and the type of vehicle

Road
If street lights are provided and are placed not more than 200 yards apart, speed is restricted to 30 mph
S 82

Vehicle
Section 86 makes it an offence to drive in excess of the speed specified on the following pages in relation to a vehicle of that class

In this case, evidence of the absence of derestriction signs shall be evidence that it was a restricted road
S 85(5)

In Scotland, if there is a system of carriageway lighting where lamps are placed not more than 185 metres apart, and road is of a class or type specified in regulations by Secretary of State, then speed is restricted to 30 mph

Evidence
Evidence of the opinion of one witness is not enough to secure a conviction
S 89(2)

If there is no system of street lighting not more than 200 yards (185 metres in Scotland) apart then there must be traffic signs

Employers
An employer may be guilty of procuring or inciting an employee to commit an offence if he publishes or issues a time-table or schedule or gives directions to complete a journey within such a time as cannot be achieved without exceeding the speed limit. S 89(4)

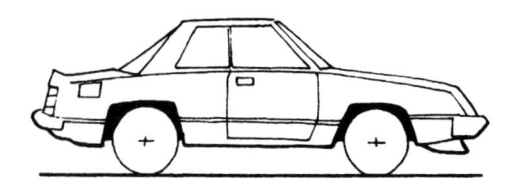

SPEED LIMITS cont

ROAD TRAFFIC REGULATION ACT 1984 S 86 AND SCHED. 6

motorway duel carriageway other road

Cars, small vans and dual-purpose vehicles

This limit was set by the 70 mph, 60 mph and 50 mph (Temporary Speed Limit) Order 1977, which was continued indefinitely by SI 1978 No 1548. The limit refers to all vehicles unless a lesser one applies.

(70) (70) (60)

Passenger vehicle, motor caravan or dual purpose vehicle without trailer

uw over 3.05 tonnes or adapted to carry more than 8 passengers.
a) Overall length n/e 12 metres

(70) (60) (50)

b) Overall length over 12 metres
Note: Coaches which could exceed the motorway limit must be fitted with a governor.

(60) (60) (50)

Invalid carriage

(N/A) (20) (20)

Passenger vehicle, motor caravan, car-derived van or dual purpose vehicle drawing one trailer

(60) (60) (50)

(A 'car-derived van' is a goods vehicle derivative of a passenger vehicle and which has a maximum laden weight not over 2000 kg.)

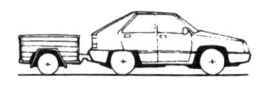

As above, drawing more than one trailer

(40) (20) (20)

SPEED LIMITS cont

ROAD TRAFFIC REGULATION ACT 1984 S 86 AND SCHED. 6

motorway   duel carriageway   other road

Goods vehicle

With max laden weight n/e 7.5 tonnes but which is not an articulated vehicle, or is not drawing a trailer, or is not a car-derived van.
(A 'car-derived van' is a goods vehicle derivative of a passenger vehicle and which has a maximum laden weight not over 2000 kg.)

(70) (60) (50)

Drawing 1 trailer (other than a car-derived van) – aggregate max. laden weight of both n/e 7.5 tonnes.

(60) (60) (50)

Goods vehicle other than a car-derived van drawing more than 1 trailer.

(40) (20) (20)

Goods vehicle max. laden weight over 7.5 tonnes not drawing trailer

(60) (50) (40)

Goods vehicle drawing 1 trailer with aggregate max. laden weight of vehicle and trailer over 7.5 tonnes.

(60) (50) (40)

Articulated goods vehicle

Max laden weight n/e 7.5 tonnes.

(60) (60) (50)

Max laden weight over 7.5 tonnes

(60) (50) (40)

Part 5: Miscellaneous **249**

SPEED LIMITS cont

ROAD TRAFFIC REGULATION ACT 1984 S 86 AND SCHED. 6

motorway   duel carriageway   other road

Motor tractor

Light or heavy locomotive with required springs and wings (other than industrial tractor).

(40) (30) (30)

As above drawing 1 trailer also complying with springs and wings.

(40) (30) (30)

Vehicle and/or trailer as above not complying with springs and wings.

(20) (20) (20)

Vehicle (and trailer if drawn) where at least one wheel has a resilient tyre and all other (if any) have pneumatic tyres.

(20) (20) (20)

Vehicle (or trailer if drawn) where any wheel has neither a pneumatic nor resilient tyre *(does not apply if track-laying)*.

(5) (5) (5)

Works truck

(18) (18) (18)

Industrial tractor

(N/A) (18) (18)

Agricultural motor vehicle

(40) (40) (40)

Vehicle displaying 'Low Platform Trailer' plate (LL).   *REG 100A RV (CON & USE) REGS 1986*

(40) (40) (40)

Vehicle displaying 'Restricted Speed Vehicle' plate (50).   *REG 100A RV (CON & USE) REGS 1986*

(50) (50) (50)

250 The Traffic Officer's Companion

SPEED LIMITERS

ROAD VEHICLES (CONSTRUCTION AND USE) REGULATIONS 1986, REGS 36A, 36B AND 70A

The following vehicles must be fitted with a device designed to limit the maximum speed by controlling its engine power

Coaches

First used on or after 1.4.74 and before 1.1.88 having a **maximum speed exceeding 112.65 Km/h**

or first used on or after 1.1.88, having max gross weight over 7.5 tonnes and **maximum speed exceeding 100 Km/h**

The limiter must be calibrated to a set speed **not exceeding 112.65 Km/h or 100 Km/h** as appropriate and **sealed**

Exemptions relate to a vehicle being taken for a speed limiter to be installed, calibrated, repaired or replaced, or completion of a journey after it has ceased to function

Goods Vehicles

Having gross weight over 7,500 kg but not over 12,000 kg, first used on or after 1.8.92 and **speed exceeding 60 mph**, must have a speed limiter fitted and calibrated to not exceed 60 mph.

If it has a gross weight over 12,000 kg first used on or after 1.1.88 and **speed exceeding 56 mph**, the limiter must be calibrated to not exceed 85 kmh and the stabilised speed of the vehicle must not exceed 90 kmh.

Exemptions relate, in addition to those on the left, to naval, military or air force vehicles; fire, ambulance or police vehicle; or only passing between private premises for not more than 6 miles per week

Note:
1. *The limiter must be maintained in good and efficient working order.*
2. *A plate must be displayed in the driving compartment in a conspicuous position clearly and indelibly marked with the speed at which it has been set.*
3. *The limiter must be sealed to prevent improper interference.*

Part 5: Miscellaneous **251**

CARRIAGE OF DANGEROUS GOODS
CARRIAGE OF DANGEROUS GOODS BY ROAD REGULATIONS 1996

Exemptions
Schedule 2 provides a number of exemptions from the regulations. The main ones are listed below but reference should be made to the schedule to ascertain specific technical details.

The regulations do not apply to:
1. A motor vehicle registered outside the U.K. where carriage is restricted to within G.B. and conforms to the provisions of the European Agreement concerning the International Carriage of Dangerous Goods by Road (ADR);
2. An international transport operation conforming with the provisions of ADR;
3. An international transport operation subject to a bilateral or multilateral agreement and the vehicle is owned by, or is under the control of, the armed forces of a country which is a contracting party to the ADR;
4. Certain dangerous goods being carried in an agricultural or forestry tractor, mobile machinery, a vehicle with fewer than 4 wheels, a vehicle with a design speed of 25 mph or less, or a vehicle owned by or under the control of the armed forces;
5. Explosives;
6. Flammable liquid carried in a tank or prover pipe used for the calibration of metering equipment or measurement of petroleum fuel deliveries;
7. Goods used solely in connection with the operation with the vehicle, container or tank;
8. Live animals;
9. Radioactive material;
10. A vehicle not being used for, or in connection with, work;
11. A vehicle used for the internal transfer of goods in private premises;
12. A road construction vehicle.

Definitions
Meaning of 'operator':
1. Of a container or vehicle:
    i) the person having a place of business in G.B. and at the time has the management of it; or
    ii) if no person satisfies the above, the driver of the vehicle.
2. Of a tank other than the carrying tank of a road tanker
    i) The person having a place of business in G.B. and who owns the tank;
    ii) If no person satisfies (i), the person having a place of business in G.B. and who acts as agent for the owner;
    iii) If no person satisfies (i) or (ii), the person who, having a place of business in G.B. has management of the tank at that time; or
    iv) if no person satisfies (i), (ii) or (iii), the driver of the vehicle.

Meaning of dangerous goods:
Any explosive, radioactive material, goods listed in a document approved by the Health and Safety Commission, and any other goods which have one or more dangerous properties as listed in Sched 1 to the 1994 Regs.

CARRIAGE OF DANGEROUS GOODS

Scope of regulations

Even though goods are deemed to be 'dangerous' as previously defined, they may not be fully regulated depending on the mode of transport. If they are being carried in a tanker, tank container or bulk they will be fully regulated irrespective of the quantity being carried. If, however, they are transported in packages (e.g. boxes or cylinders) the answer will depend upon the transport category, the receptacle size and the total quantity being carried in the vehicle (see below).

Transport category

Just as the dangerous goods themselves are listed in the approved carriage list, the 'transport category' can also be established from the document. Examples of the type of dangerous goods contained in the transport category are included in the following list:

Transport Category	Dangerous Goods
0	Highly infectious substances
1	Toxic gases, organic peroxide, self-reactive substances, infectious substances, goods in packing group 1
2	Flammable gases, goods in packing group 2, substances which are less infectious
3	Non-flammable, non-toxic gases, goods in packing group 3, life-saving appliances
4	Rubber scrap – Matches/firelighters – Empty unclean packages

Thresholds

Having established the transport category it is possible, using the table below to ascertain whether the dangerous goods in question are fully regulated and subject to the conditions of carriage (e.g. marking of the load, training of drivers).

Where the receptacle size in column 2 is not exceeded, then any quantity may be carried without regulation. However, once that 'threshold' is crossed the total quantity of goods must be established and if the 'threshold' appertaining to the total load in column 3 is exceeded then they will be fully regulated. If column 2 threshold is crossed but not that in column 3, then partial regulation is brought into play, requiring consigners to supply information about the load.

Column 1 Transport Category	Column 2 Receptacle size (Kg or litres as applicable)	Column 3 Total load (Kg or Litres as applicable)
0	All goods	All goods
1	1	20
2	10	200
3	25	500
4	unlimited	unlimited

CARRIAGE OF DANGEROUS GOODS – DUTIES OF THE OPERATOR

Suitability of Vehicles, etc.

Ensure that the requirements relating to the construction and design of vehicles and tanks, and the filling, examination, testing and certification of tanks are complied with. *REG. 6*

Ensure that the container, tank or vehicle is suitable for the carriage of the goods and has been adequately maintained. *REG. 10*

Ensure that the vehicle has no more than one trailer or semi-trailer; is suitably sheeted (or enclosed) if the packages are sensitive to moisture; and that the vehicle or container complies with specific requirements having regard to the type of goods carried. *REG. 10 AND SCHED. 7*

Shall not cause or permit the carriage of any dangerous goods in a tank unless a certificate has been issued stating that; the tank has been examined and tested, conforms to an approved design, and is suitable for the intended purpose. *REG. 11*

Consignor's Declaration

Shall not permit the carriage of dangerous goods unless he has obtained a declaration from the consignor stating that the goods are in a fit state to be carried. *REG. 12*

Transport Documentation

Ensure that the driver is in possession of the Transport Documentation, comprising:

a) Information relating to the goods, e.g. designation, classification code, UN* number, mass and number of any packages, mass of any container or tank, details of the consignor, and the consignor's declaration;
b) Details of the total mass or volume carried;
c) Emergency action code, where appropriate;
d) Prescribed temperature, where appropriate;
e) Emergency information regarding measures to be taken in the event of an accident. *REG. 14*

Must keep a copy of the information contained in the Transport Documentation (other than emergency information) for 3 months after completion of the journey. *REG. 16*

UN-United Nations

254 The Traffic Officer's Companion

CARRIAGE OF DANGEROUS GOODS – DUTIES OF THE OPERATOR cont

Display of Information

Ensure that the required information (orange-coloured panels, telephone number and danger signs) is displayed. *REG. 17*

Shall not cause or permit the display of information if dangerous goods are not being carried, or which would be likely to confuse the emergency services. *REG. 17*

Ensure that any panel or sign containing information is kept clean and free from obstruction. *REG. 17*

Ensure that any panel or sign which does not relate to the goods being carried is covered or removed. *REG. 17*

Health and Safety

Ensure the manner of loading, stowage and unloading does not create or increase the risk to health and safety of any person. *REG. 19*

Safety Advisers

Sufficent certificated advisers must be appointed to ensure adequate co-operation, time, means, information and facilities to perform his duties. Reports must be produced and kept.

Cleaning

Ensure that vehicles, tanks and containers are cleaned after use. *REG. 19*

Equipment

Ensure that the vehicle is equipped so that the driver can comply with the instructions contained in the emergency information, and that, if toxic gases are carried, the crew are supplied with suitable respiratory protective equipment. *REG. 21*

Ensure that the vehicle is equipped with suitable fire extinguishers. *REG. 23*

Parking

Ensure that when the vehicle is parked it is supervised by a person over 18 years of age or a member of the armed forces, or parked in an isolated position, having been properly secured. *REG. 24*

Part 5: Miscellaneous **255**

CARRIAGE OF DANGEROUS GOODS – DUTIES OF THE DRIVER

Carriage of Passengers
Shall not carry any person in the vehicle other than a crew member. *REG. 12*

Opening of Packages
Shall not open any package unless authorised by the operator. *REG.12*

Carrying Food
If carrying infectious substances, toxic goods or certain specified goods (including Blue or Brown Asbestos) (or if it has done so and has not yet been cleaned) shall not carry food (including fodder and feeding stuff for animals, birds and fish) in the vehicle unless it is effectively separated or adequately protected from the risk of contamination. *REG. 12*

Transport Documentation
Ensure that the Transport Documentation (see list under "Duties of Operator") is kept readily on the vehicle and produced on request to a police constable or goods vehicle examiner. *REG. 15*

Where a trailer is detached from the motor vehicle for parking, shall give the Transport Documentation (or copy) to the occupier of the premises and attach a copy to the trailer in a readily visible position. *REG. 15*

Any documentation relating solely to goods which are not being carried must be either removed from the vehicle or placed in a securely closed container clearly marked to show that it does not relate to goods being carried. *REG. 15*

Display of Information
Must not cause or permit any information (orange coloured panels, telephone number and danger sign) to be displayed if dangerous goods are not being carried or if it would be likely to confuse the emergency services.
REG. 17

Ensure that any panel or sign is kept clean and free from obstruction. *REG. 17*

Any panel or sign displayed which does not relate to the goods being carried must be covered or removed. *REG. 17*

Health and Safety
Ensure the manner of loading, stowage or unloading is not liable to create or increase the risk to health and safety of any person. *REG. 19*

CARRIAGE OF DANGEROUS GOODS – DUTIES OF THE DRIVER cont

Cleaning
Ensure that vehicles, containers and tanks are cleaned after use. *REG. 19*

Use of Tanks
Where a tank is used, it must not be overfilled, and all openings and valves must be securely closed before commencement and during the journey.

REG. 19

Emergencies
In the event of an accident or emergency must comply with any instructions laid down in the emergency information and if the situation cannot be brought under immediate control shall notify the emergency services by the quickest possible means. *REG. 22*

Parking
Ensure that when the vehicle is parked, it is supervised by a person over the age of 18 years or a member of the armed forces, or is parked in an isolated position, having been properly secured. When parked, the parking brake must be applied. *REG. 24*

CARRIAGE OF DANGEROUS GOODS – Display of Orange-Coloured Panels

TYPE OF VEHICLE	INFORMATION REQUIRED	REMARKS
Any vehicle carrying fully regulated (see earlier) dangerous goods (except a trailer not attached to a vehicle)	Orange-coloured panel conforming to fig.1	Displayed at the front of vehicle
a vehicle carrying fully regulated (see earlier) dangerous goods in packages	Orange-coloured panel confirming to fig. 1	Displayed at the rear of the vehicle
A vehicle carrying only one type of dangerous goods in a tank	Orange-coloured panel conforming to fig. 2 bearing the appropriate UN number and emergency action code	Displayed at the rear of the vehicle and on both sides of the tank, the frame of the tank, or the vehicle, provided it is immediately below the tank.
A vehicle carrying a multi-load in tanks	Orange-coloured panel conforming to fig.3 bearing the appropriate emergency action code.	Displayed at rear of the vehicle
	Orange-coloured panel conforming to fig. 2 bearing appropriate UN number and emergency action code.	Displayed on both sides of each tank or, where there is more than one compartment, each compartment.
	If diesel, gas oil, heating oil, light petrol, motor spirit, gasoline or kerosene are being carried, the vehicle will be treated as if it was carrying only one type of goods. The UN number and emergency action code will be those for the most hazardous of the goods being carried.	At least one on each side must conform to fig. 2 the remainder conform to fig. 4 bearing the appropriate UN number. They may be displayed on both sides of the frame of each tank or on both sides of the vehicle provided they are immediately below the tank or compartment
A vehicle carrying only one type of goods in bulk in the vehicle or a container.	As for a vehicle carrying only one type of goods in a tank.	
A vehicle carrying a multi load in bulk in the	As for a vehicle carrying a multi load in tanks.	

DISPLAY OF ORANGE-COLOURED PANELS cont

All panels must be rigid, vertical and in the form of a plate. But if a tank container or bulk container the panels may be replaced by orange-coloured self-adhesive sheets or orange-coloured paint provided the material used is weather resistant and durable.

Figure 1:
Orange-coloured panel

Height not less than 300mm

Base 400mm

All black borders 15mm or less

Figure 2:
Orange-coloured panel displaying the emergency action code and the UN number

The emergency action code shall be inscribed in the upper half, the UN number shall be inscribed in the lower half

2W
1832

Height not less than 300mm

Base 400mm

All black borders 15mm or less

Horizontal black line of 15mm stroke width

Figure 3:
Orange-coloured panel displaying the emergency action code

The emergency action code shall be inscribed in the upper half

2W

Height not less than 300mm

Base 400mm

All black borders 15mm or less

Horizontal black line of 15mm stroke width

Figure 4:
Orange-coloured panel displaying UN number

1832

Height not less than 150mm

Base 400mm

All black borders 15mm or less

Part 5: Miscellaneous **259**

CARRIAGE OF DANGEROUS GOODS
REG.17 & SCHED. 10

Display of Telephone Number

Where dangerous goods are being carried in a tank (or tanks) the telephone number shall be displayed:
a) at the rear of the vehicle;
b) on both sides of:
   i) the tank (or each tank in the case of a multi-load),
   ii) the frame of the tank(s), or
   iii) the vehicle; and
c) in the immediate vicinity of the orange coloured panels.

The telephone number shall be black, not less than 30mm high, and on an orange background.

However, the telephone number may be substituted by the words:
  "CONSULT LOCAL DEPOT" or "CONTACT LOCAL DEPOT"
provided:
a) the name of the operator is clearly marked on the tank or vehicle;
b) the chief fire officer of every area through which the goods will pass has been notified in writing of the address and telephone number of that local depot; and
c) each fire officer has agreed in writing to the arrangements.

Display of Danger Signs

Where a vehicle is carrying dangerous goods a danger sign appropriate to those goods (see following page) must be displayed:
a) if the goods are carried in packages in a container, on at least one side of the container;
b) if in a tank container or in bulk in a container, on each side of the container;
c) if in a tank other than a tank container, or if in bulk other than in a container, on each side and at the rear of the vehicle.

Display of Hazard Warning Panels

Instead of individually displaying the orange coloured panels, telephone number and danger signs, the information may be displayed on a hazard warning panel as per the below example.

The emergency action code shall be inscribed in the upper half, the UN number shall be inscribed in the lower half of the orange coloured panel and the telephone number (or text as the case may be) beneath the UN number

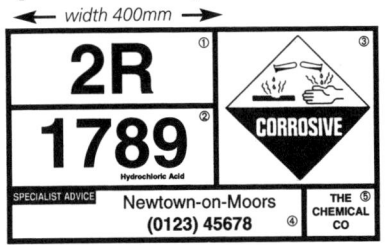

← width 400mm →

① 2R
② 1789
  Hydrochloric Acid
SPECIALIST ADVICE
Newtown-on-Moors
(0123) 45678 ④
③ CORROSIVE
⑤ THE CHEMICAL CO

Height not less than 300mm

Horizontal black line at mid height of 15mm stroke width

Height not less than 400mm

All black borders 15mm or less

Width not less than 700mm

DANGEROUS SUBSTANCE SIGNS

CLASSIFICATION	HAZARD WARNING SIGN	CLASSIFICATION	HAZARD WARNING SIGN
Non-flammable compressed gas	COMPRESSED GAS (Green background)	Toxic gas	TOXIC GAS (White background)
Flammable solid	(Red stripes on white)	Flammable gas	FLAMMABLE GAS (Red background)
Spontaneously combustible substance	SPONTANEOUSLY COMBUSTIBLE (White b/g upper) (Red b/g lower)	Flammable liquid	FLAMMABLE LIQUID (Red background)
Substance which in contact with water emits flammable gas	DANGEROUS WHEN WET (Blue background)	Toxic substance	TOXIC (White background)
Oxidising substance	OXIDIZING AGENT (Yellow background)	Harmful substance	(White background)
Organic peroxide	ORGANIC PEROXIDE (Yellow background)	Corrosive substance	CORROSIVE (Black and white)
Multi loads	(White background)	Other dangerous substance	(Black and white)

RADIOACTIVE SUBSTANCES
RADIOACTIVE MATERIAL (ROAD TRANSPORT) REGULATIONS 2002

These Regulations provide for the control of radiation, criticality and thermal hazards to persons, property and the environment whilst it is being transported by road. In particular they detail the requirements for radioactive materials and for packagings, packages and approval requirements for designs and shipments. Because of the detail involved it has only been possible to include a general description in this section.

Application of regulations (Regs. 5 & 6)
The regulations do not apply to radioactive material-
- a) that is an integral part of the means of transport;
- b) moved within an establishment and not on public roads;
- c) implanted into the body of a dead or alive person or a live animal for diagnosis or treatment;
- d) in approved consumer products;
- e) contained in natural material and ores with low activity concentration;
- f) with activity which does not exceed specified values;
- g) which forms part of an instrument of war, or the development of such, being transported by or on behalf of a UK government department or visiting force;
- h) transported by, or under the supervision of, the emergency services (including breakdown vehicles carrying vehicles which contain radioactive material);
- i) in emergency, to save human lives or to protect the environment, if carried out in complete safety;
- j) on an ADR journey and the UK is a signatory to the agreement;
- k) which conforms to the terms of derogations approved under Council Directive 94/55/EC; or
- l) which conforms to the International Maritime Dangerous Goods Code (IMDG) or the Technical Instructions for the safe Transport of Dangerous Goods by Air (ICAO Technical Instructions).

General exception (Reg. 17)
A person will not contravene these Regulations if he neither knew nor had reasonable grounds for believing that the material in question was radioactive.

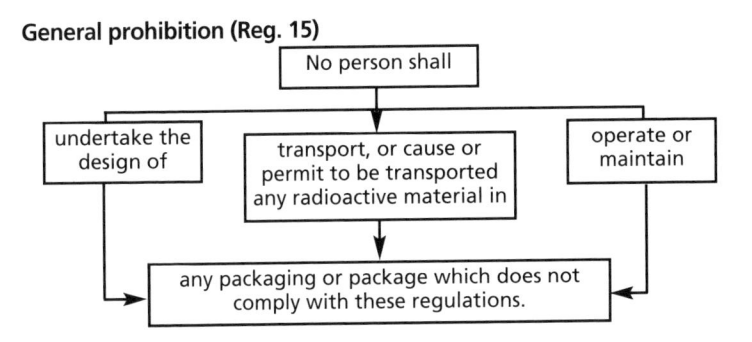

General prohibition (Reg. 15)

No person shall
- undertake the design of
- transport, or cause or permit to be transported any radioactive material in
- operate or maintain

any packaging or package which does not comply with these regulations.

RADIOACTIVE SUBSTANCES cont
RADIOACTIVE MATERIAL (ROAD TRANSPORT) REGULATIONS 2002

General duty of care (Reg. 16)
In addition to any other Regulation, the consignor, carrier and the driver of a consignment must exercise reasonable care to ensure that no injury to health or any damage to property or to the environment is caused.

Prohibition of passengers (Reg. 21)
No person except the driver and his assistant(s) may travel in a vehicle transporting packages, overpacks or freight containers bearing category II-YELLOW or III-YELLOW labels.

Categories of packages (Reg. 23 & Sched. 11)
Packages must be assigned to one of the following categories:
- I- WHITE
- II- YELLOW, or
- III- YELLOW

The maximum radiation level at any point on the external surface determines the category.

Segregation (Reg. 25)
Packages, etc. must be segregated from-
a) areas where persons have regular access;
b) undeveloped photographic film and mailbags;
c) workers in regularly occupied working areas; and
d) other dangerous goods.

RADIOACTIVE SUBSTANCES cont
RADIOACTIVE MATERIAL (ROAD TRANSPORT) REGULATIONS 2002

Responsibilities of Consignors (Reg. 48 & Sched. 6)

A 'consignor' is any person (or government) that prepares a consignment for transport and is named as consignor in the transport documents, or a freight forwarder acting as agent for such a person.

The consignor is responsible for the acts and omissions of his employees and any agents or other persons of whose services he makes use for the performance of transport. (Reg. 47)

Marking	Each package must be marked with- 1. Identification of consignor or consignee, or both, on outside; 2. United Nations number preceded by the letters 'UN', and the proper shipping name; 3. Gross mass if over 50kg. 4. Package type ("TYPE B(U)," "TYPE B(M)," "TYPE C", "TYPE IP-1", "TYPE IP-2", "TYPE IP-3" OR "TYPE A"). The first 3 must bear on the outside of the outermost receptacle, a fire and water proof trefoil as shown below. The latter 3, must bear the international vehicle registration code (VRI) and the name of the manufacturer or other identification.
Labelling	Each package, overpack and freight container must bear labels as shown below.
Placarding	Large freight containers (either an overall outer dimension of 1.5m or more, or an internal volume of 3 cu. m or more) carrying packages, and tanks, must bear 4 placards as shown below.
Particulars of consignment	The transport documents must include the following information- name, address and telephone number of consignor and consignee; proper shipping name; UN class no. "7"; UN material number; description of the material; category (eg "II-YELLOW"); and statement of contents of each package in an overpack or freight container.
Declaration	The transport documents must contain a consignor's declaration that the contents are fully and accurately described by the proper shipping name and are classified, packed, marked and labelled, and in all respects in proper condition for transport.
Removal/covering of labels	When empty packaging is being transported the previously displayed panels must not be visible.

RADIOACTIVE SUBSTANCES cont
RADIOACTIVE MATERIAL (ROAD TRANSPORT) REGULATIONS 2002

Responsibilities of Consignors cont

Information for carriers	The transport documents must contain a statement regarding actions to be taken by the carrier including the following requirements for loading, stowage, carriage, handling and unloading; restrictions on the mode of transport or conveyance and any instructions on routing; and emergency arrangements.
Notification of competent authorities	For certain shipments (mainly of high radioactivity) the competent authority through which it will pass must be notified.
Possession of certificates and instructions	Must have in his possession a copy of each certificate of approval and a copy of the instructions regarding the proper closing of the package and other preparations for shipment.
'ADR orange plate	Vehicles must be placarded in accordance with ADR.

Responsibilities of Carriers (Reg. 49 & Sched. 7)

A carrier is any person (or government) undertaking transport of the material and includes carriers for hire or reward and on their own account whether under contract or not.

Segregation	Packages, overpacks and freight containers must be segregated during transport or storage in transit from places occupied by persons, from undeveloped photographic film, or from other dangerous goods. Cat. II-YELLOW and III-YELLOW packages or overpacks must not be carried in compartments occupied by passengers, except specially authorised couriers. No persons other than the driver and his assistant(s) may be allowed in vehicles carrying cat. II-YELLOW or III-YELLOW labels.
Stowage	Must be secure and within the limits laid down for the total number of packages allowed
Fissile material	The total sum of the criticality safety indexes in any group of packages, overpacks or freight containers must not exceed 50. Where the total sum on board a vehicle exceeds this number, a spacing of at least 6 m must be maintained between groups.
Undeliverable consignments	Must be placed in a safe location and the Secretary of State must be informed as soon as possible, requesting details of further action.
Fire fighting equipment	Vehicles must be equipped in accordance with ADR requirements.

Part 5: Miscellaneous 265

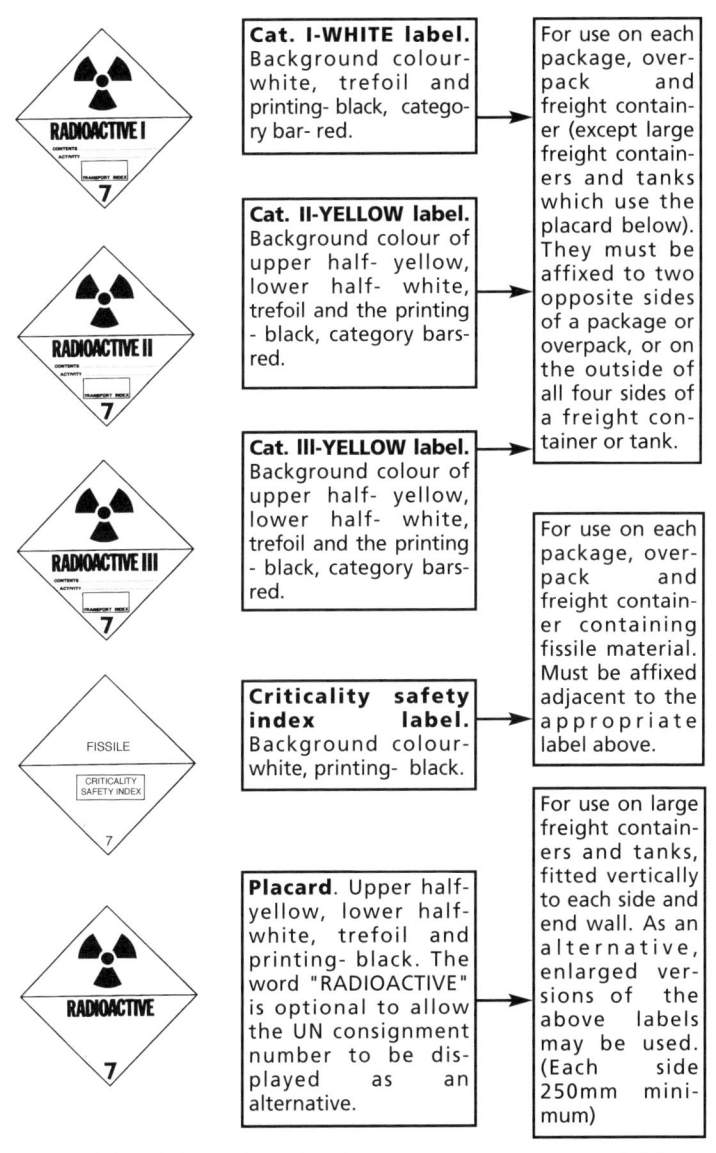

Cat. I-WHITE label. Background colour- white, trefoil and printing- black, category bar- red.

Cat. II-YELLOW label. Background colour of upper half- yellow, lower half- white, trefoil and the printing - black, category bars- red.

Cat. III-YELLOW label. Background colour of upper half- yellow, lower half- white, trefoil and the printing - black, category bars- red.

For use on each package, overpack and freight container (except large freight containers and tanks which use the placard below). They must be affixed to two opposite sides of a package or overpack, or on the outside of all four sides of a freight container or tank.

Criticality safety index label. Background colour- white, printing- black.

For use on each package, overpack and freight container containing fissile material. Must be affixed adjacent to the appropriate label above.

Placard. Upper half- yellow, lower half- white, trefoil and printing- black. The word "RADIOACTIVE" is optional to allow the UN consignment number to be displayed as an alternative.

For use on large freight containers and tanks, fitted vertically to each side and end wall. As an alternative, enlarged versions of the above labels may be used. (Each side 250mm minimum)

All labels (apart from the last) must be a minimum of 100mm square and have a border of 5mm.

RADIOACTIVE SUBSTANCES cont
RADIOACTIVE MATERIAL (ROAD TRANSPORT) REGULATIONS 2002

Duties in an Emergency (Reg. 69)
If a situation arises during the course of the transport of a consignment that requires urgent action in order to protect workers, members of the public or the population (either partially or as a whole) from exposure,

the driver, carrier and consignor must-
assist in preventing or decreasing the exposure of individuals to radiation.

In addition,

the driver must-
   a) immediately notify the police and, where appropriate, the fire brigade;
   b) immediately notify the consignor; and
   c) initiate the emergency arrangements,

the carrier must-
   a) immediately notify the police (unless the driver has already done so);
   b) immediately notify the Secretary of State; and
   c) as soon as reasonably practicable, arrange for the examination of the load so as to determine whether contamination has arisen and, if it has, to arrange for the safe disposal of it and the decontamination of the vehicle,

the consignor must-
   a) immediately notify the police and Secretary of State (unless either the driver or the carrier has already done so);
   b) provide the Secretary of State with details of the incident giving rise to the emergency; and
   c) notify the Secretary of State of any initiation of emergency arrangements.

Transport of Packages (Reg. 70)
A package that has been involved in a radiological emergency may not be transported unless the consignor or his agent is satisfied that it complies with the requirements of these regulations and he issues a certificate to that effect.

Production of Documents (Reg. 73)
An examiner, an inspector or a **constable in uniform** may require the carrier or driver transporting radioactive material to produce for inspection such documents as are required by these regulations.

Part 5: Miscellaneous **267**

THE EMERGENCY ACTION CODE (HAZCHEM CODE)

Hazchem card
front   back

	Hazchem / UN No	Issue No 2

1	JETS
2	JETS
3	FOAM
4	DRY AGENT

P	V	FULL	
R			
S	V	BA	DILUTE
S		BA for FIRE only	
T		BA	
T		BA for FIRE only	
W	V	FULL	
X			
Y	V	BA	CONTAIN
Y		BA for FIRE only	
Z		BA	
Z		BA for FIRE only	
E		CONSIDER EVACUATION	

Notes for Guidance

FOG
In the absence of fog equipment a fine spray may be used.

DRY AGENT
Water **must not** be allowed to come into contact with the substance at risk.

V
Can be violently or even explosively reactive.

FULL
Full body protective clothing with BA.

BA
Breathing apparatus plus protective gloves.

DILUTE
May be washed to drain with large quantities of water.

CONTAIN
Prevent, by any means available, spillage from entering drains or water course.

I.C.I. EMERGENCY TEL. -
I.C.I. C + P RUNCORN   01928 572000
I.C.I. C + P AVONMOUTH   01272 923601
I.C.I. C + P ESTON GRANGE 01642 452461

For your own protection the following points are worthy of note:

- 'V' is intended to warn against unexpected or possibly hazardous events which could occur due to the ignition of flammable gas, rapid acceleration of combustion due to the involvement of an oxidiser, or the reaction with water, which is itself violent – generating large quantities of steam or flammable gases which may subsequently ignite.

- 'FULL' indicates that the material presents hazards to the skin, eyes and respiratory system. Certain chemicals have the capability of inflicting severe poisoning which could prove fatal when splashed on the skin. If in doubt about a material, seek further advice before approaching too close.

- 'BA' it is probable that the substance will affect the respiratory system and/or eyes. Again – operations room have up-to-date information on most chemicals.

268 The Traffic Officer's Companion

Below is an example of a Tremcard. Such information is readily available in most operations rooms, and advice can be relayed to the officer at the scene of an incident within seconds.

TRANSPORT EMERGENCY CARD (Road)

Cargo **SODIUM CYANIDE (Solution)**

Usually colourless or yellow solution with perceptible odour.

Nature of Hazard Severe poisoning perhaps fatal when splashed on skin or swallowed

Contact with an acid may cause toxic fumes: hydrogen cyanide Heating will cause pressure rise with risk of bursting

Protective Devices Suitable respiratory protective device
Goggles giving complete protection to eyes

Plastic or rubber gloves and boots
Special first aid equipment

EMERGENCY ACTION Notify police and fire brigade immediately

Eyewash bottle with clean water

- Stop the engine
- Mark roads and warn other road users
- Keep public away from danger area
- Keep upwind

- Contain leaking liquid with sand or earth; consult an expert
- Prevent liquid entering sewers, vapour may create toxic atmosphere
- If substance has entered a water course or sewer or contaminated soil or vegetation advise police.

Fire
- Keep containers cool by spraying with water if exposed to fire

First aid
- Special treatment is required. Emergency kit in vehicle's first aid box
- If the substance has got into the eyes, immediately wash out with plenty of water for at least 15 minutes.
- Remove contaminated clothing immediately and wash affected skin with plenty of water
- Seek medical treatment when anyone has symptoms apparently due to swallowing, inhalation or contact with skin or eyes.
- Even if there are no symptoms send to doctor and show him this card.

Additional information provided by manufacturer or sender.

Part 5: Miscellaneous **269**

ANIMALS IN TRANSIT
WELFARE OF ANIMALS (TRANSPORT) ORDER 1997

Application (Art 2)
The order applies to the transport of:

(a) domestic animals: cattle, sheep, pigs, goats & horses
 transported in accordance with sections 1 & 2 following

(b) poultry, domestic birds and domestic rabbits
 transported in accordance with sections 1 and 3 following

(c) domestic dogs and cats
 transported in accordance with sections 1 & 4 following

(d) all other mammals (except man) and birds
 transported in accordance with sections 1 & 5 following

(e) other vertebrate animals and cold-blooded animals
 transported in accordance with section 6 following

The order does **not** apply to transport

(a) which is not of a commercial nature
(b) of an individual animal accompanied by a person having responsibility for it
(c) of pet animals accompanying their owner on a private journey

provided the manner of transport does not cause, or is not likely to cause, unnecessary suffering or injury.

ANIMALS IN TRANSIT
WELFARE OF ANIMALS (TRANSPORT) ORDER 1997
MISCELLANEOUS PROVISIONS

General Provisions (Art 4)
No animal shall be transported in a way which causes or is likely to cause injury or unnecessary suffering.

Space Allowance (Art 5)
Where a journey is over 50Km no animal is to be transported in a way which is likely to cause injury or unnecessary suffering because of the amount of space available to each animal, having regard to the limits set out in 'Council Directive 91/628/EEC, and the animal's weight, size and physical condition, the means of transport, the weather conditions and the likely journey time.

Fitness of animals to travel (Art 6)
Unless the nature of unfitness is only slight, an animal will not be considered fit to travel if it is ill, injured, infirm or fatigued. Suitable provision must be made for its care during the journey and on arrival at its destination.

Mammals are not considered fit if likely to give birth, have given birth during the preceding 48 hours or are newly born.

Infant mammals and infant birds not accompanied by their mother, are not considered fit unless they are capable of feeding themselves.

Cattle, sheep, pigs, goats and horses whilst unfit for veterinary treatment or diagnosis provided no unnecessary suffering is caused.

Authorisation of transporters (Art 12)
No person should transport vertebrate animals by sea, air or by any other means involving a journey over 50Km unless he is authorised by the Minister (or equivalent if from outside GB). Such persons shall also be registered as a transporter with the minister.

Animal transport certificate (Art 14)
Where a route plan is required (see later) a certificate must be carried stating the name and address of the transporter, name and address of animal owner, place of loading and final destination, date and time of both loading and departure, and the time and place rest periods were provided. A copy of the document must be kept for 6 months.

However a certificate not required:
(a) for poultry and domestic birds if (i) distance is not more than 50Km, and (ii) the number of birds is less than 50 or if the entire journey is on land occupied by the owner; and
(b) animals other than cattle, sheep, pigs, goats, horses or poultry and domestic birds, where the journey is not more than 50Km.

Accompaniment by competent person (Art 9)
All vertebrate animals on a journey over 50Km must be accompanied by at least one person who has either specific training or equivalent practical experience qualifying him to handle the animals and ensure their welfare.

Part 5: Miscellaneous **271**

ANIMALS IN TRANSIT cont
WELFARE OF ANIMALS (TRANSPORT) ORDER 1997

SECTION 1
(SCHED. 1)

General Construction and Maintenance Requirements and General Provisions

1. **Avoidance of injury** and unnecessary suffering and assurance of safety during transport, loading and unloading.

2. **Withstand action of weather** by being so constructed, maintained and operated.

3. **Adequate space** to lie down, unless unnecessary having regard to the species and nature of journey.

4. **Floors** to be strong enough to bear weight, prevent slipping and free of protrusions or spaces likely to cause injury.

5. **Protection from weather** i.e. inclement weather, sea conditions, air pressure, humidity, heat or cold.

6. **Free from projections and sharp edges** likely to cause injury or unnecessary suffering.

7. **Cleaning and disinfection** must be appropriately carried out to means of transport. Dead animals, soiled litter and droppings to be removed as soon as possible.

8. **Noise and vibration** not likely to cause injury or unnecessary suffering.

9. **Lighting** – sufficient natural or artificial to enable proper care and inspection.

10. **Partitions** – of suitable strength and used if necessary to provide support or prevent animals being thrown about. Partitions must be not less than
    (i) 1.27m high for cattle (not calves) and horses, and (ii) 76cm in any other case (Art 6(6) 1975 Order).

11. **Jolting** to be avoided.

ANIMALS IN TRANSIT cont

12. **Loading and unloading** to be carried out so as not to cause injury or unnecessary suffering by reason of excessive use of means of driving animals or contact with any part of the transport or receptacle.

13. **Emergency loading** – vehicle to carry means to unload animals in the event that there is no other suitable means of unloading.

14. **Segregation of animals and goods** – goods positioned so they do not cause injury or unnecessary suffering.

15. **Carcases** not to be carried in same vehicle unless it died on the journey.

16. **Litter** – sufficient to absorb droppings and urine unless alternative method available or regularly removed.

17. **Labelling** – all receptacles to indicate: that they contain live animals and the species; the upright position; and to be kept upright.

18. **Securing** – receptacles prevented from being displaced.

19. **Attendants** – at least one to be carried unless: receptacles secured ventilated and, where necessary, provide food and water; transporter performs function of attendant; or agent provided at stopping points.

ANIMALS IN TRANSIT cont
WELFARE OF ANIMALS (TRANSPORT) ORDER 1997

SECTION 2
(SCHEDS 2 AND 7 AND ART 9)

Additional requirements for cattle, sheep, pigs, goats and horses.

1. **Size and height** – adequate space to stand.

2. **Ventilation** – sufficient space above animals to allow air to circulate.

3. **Inspection** – receptacles to allow inspection. Vehicles provided with openings and footholds.

4. **Roof** – vehicles must have roof to ensure protection against the weather. (Does not apply to sheep on top floor except on international journey (Art 6(3) 1975 Order))

5. **Barriers or straps** provided in vehicles to prevent animal falling out when door not fully closed.

6. **Ramps** to prevent slipping, not too steep, steps not too high, and gaps not too wide.

7. **Tying points** provided if animals normally required to be tied.

8. **Loading** – suitable ramps, bridges, gangways or mechanical lifting gear, slip-proof, side protection to prevent falling (except for horses being led into horse box). May be manually lifted if of a size it can be done by no more than 2 persons, and no injury or unnecessary suffering is likely.

9. **Segregation** – some animals may not be transported in an undivided vehicle with other animals eg, mother with sucklings; bulls over 10 months with other bulls. In all cases injury or unnecessary suffering must be prevented.

10. **Horses** in groups to wear halters and have hind feet unshod.

11. **Journey times** – not to exceed 8 hours except where vehicle meets the following additional requirements:
(a) sufficient bedding; (b) sufficient appropriate food carried; (c) direct access to animals; (d) adequate adjustable ventilation; (e) movable panels to provide separate compartments; (f) connections for water supplies; and (g) for pigs, sufficient drinking liquid.

ANIMALS IN TRANSIT cont

Where advantage is taken of this exception, times are as follows:
(a) unweaned young animals must be given 1 hour rest after 9 hours travelling and may then travel for a further 9 hours; (b) pigs may travel up to 24 hours provided there is continuous access to liquid; (c) horses may travel for up to 24 hours if they are given liquid and fed every 8 hours; and, (d) all other cattle, sheep and goats may travel for 14 hours and then rest for 1 hour, they may then travel for a further 14 hours. If it is in the interests of the animals the above times may be extended by 2 hours.

12. **Route plans** are required (other than for registered horses) where animals are traded between member states or exported to third countries, and the journey time exceeds 8 hours. The route plan must contain information relating to: the transporter; number and species of animals; health certificate numbers; authorisation number; vehicle registration numbers; person in charge; place of loading and destination; date/time of departure and estimated arrival; itinerary for journey; and actual time/date of arrival.
    Route plans must be duly stamped as authorised by the person appointed by the Minister.

13. **Accompaniment by competent person**
    Journey by road lasting 8 hours or more, person accompanying must have either a qualification of specific training, or assessment of practical experience.

14. **Space** available, whether divided by partition or not, must not exceed:
    (a) for sheep, swine & goats – 3.1 m; (b) for horses – 3.7 m; (c) for calves – 2.5 m; and (d) for cattle (not calves) – if space exceeds 3.7m partitions must be fitted so as not to cause injury or unnecessary suffering by animals being thrown about (Art 8(2)-(4) 1975 Order).

15. **Exceptions** for journeys less than 50 km.
    (a) to, from or within agricultural land in a vehicle with an internal length less than 3.7 m, owned by the owner or occupier of the land, exempt from:
    - (i) animal transport certificate
    - (ii) overhead protection
    - (iii) provision of barriers/straps
    - (iv) internal ramps and lifting gear

    (b) exclusively in a single day between the same 2 points, exempt from cleaning and disinfection.

Part 5: Miscellaneous **275**

ANIMALS IN TRANSIT cont
WELFARE OF ANIMALS (TRANSPORT) ORDER 1997

SECTION 3
(SCHED 3 AND ART 8)

Additional requirements for poultry, domestic birds and domestic animals.

1. **Ventilation** to be adequate.

2. **Receptacles** – to allow inspection, sufficient size, prevent protrusion of heads etc of birds, birds not to be carried in a sack or bag.

3. **Segregation** e.g. rabbits from other animals.

4. **Feeding, watering and rest** – suitable food and liquid available at suitable intervals unless journey is less than 12 hours (or less than 24 hours for chicks less than 72 hours old).

SECTION 4
(SCHED 4 AND ART 8)

Additional requirements for domestic dogs and cats.

1. **Ventilation** adequate.

2. **Receptacles** – to allow inspection and proper care.

3. **Size** sufficient space to stand.

4. **Vehicles** with roof to protect from the weather, and tying points if animal normally tied.

5. **Segregation** from other species, females in oestrus from males, and to prevent injury or unnecessary suffering.

6. **Attendant** to look after animals.

7. **Feeding, watering and rest**. Must be fed at least every 24 hours and watered at least every 12 hours. Written instructions to accompany animals.

ANIMALS IN TRANSIT cont
SECTION 5
(SCHED 5 AND ART 8)

Additional requirements for mammals and birds not mentioned above.

1. **Ventilation** adequate.

2. **Size** – adequate space to stand.

3. **Receptacles** to allow inspection.

4. **Roof** – vehicles to have roof to protect from the weather and barriers to prevent animals falling out when door not fully closed.

5. **Ramps** to be slip-proof, not too steep, steps not too high, gaps not too wide.

6. **Tying points** provided if animals normally tied.

7. **Loading** by suitable ramps, bridges, gangways or mechanical lifting gear, floors to prevent slipping, side protection to prevent falling, may be loaded manually if it can be carried by not more than 2 persons without injury or unnecessary suffering.

8. **Segregation** if known to be incompatible.

9. **Attendants** to look after animals.

10. **Notice** to be affixed to transport or receptacle if wild, timid or dangerous.

11. **Sedation** only to be given under supervision of vet. Written details to accompany animal.

12. **Birds** to be kept in semi-darkness.

13. **Feeding and watering** at appropriate intervals and written instructions carried.

SECTION 6
(SCHED 6)

Other vertebrate and cold-blooded animals.
Must be in suitable transport or receptacles and under such conditions as are appropriate for the species.

Part 5: Miscellaneous **277**

REPORTING OF ACCIDENTS
ROAD TRAFFIC ACT 1988, S. 170 AS AMENDED BY S.I.2000/726

IF, OWING TO THE PRESENCE OF A

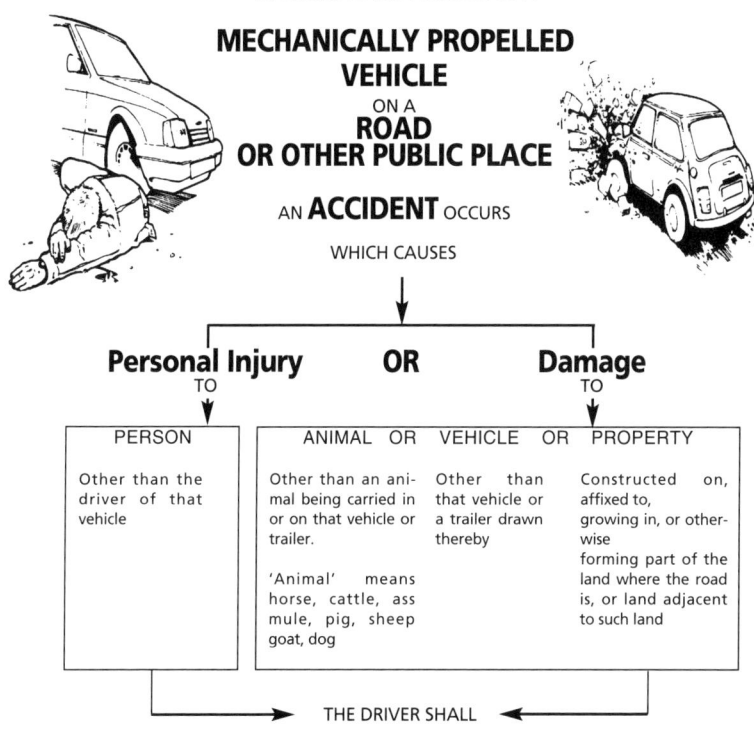

MECHANICALLY PROPELLED VEHICLE
ON A
ROAD
OR OTHER PUBLIC PLACE

AN **ACCIDENT** OCCURS

WHICH CAUSES

Personal Injury OR **Damage**
TO   TO

PERSON	ANIMAL OR	VEHICLE OR	PROPERTY
Other than the driver of that vehicle	Other than an animal being carried in or on that vehicle or trailer. 'Animal' means horse, cattle, ass mule, pig, sheep goat, dog	Other than that vehicle or a trailer drawn thereby	Constructed on, affixed to, growing in, or otherwise forming part of the land where the road is, or land adjacent to such land

THE DRIVER SHALL

STOP

AND IF REQUESTED TO DO SO GIVE HIS NAME AND ADDRESS AND THE NAME AND ADDRESS OF THE OWNER OF THE VEHICLE AND PARTICULARS OF THE VEHICLE TO ANY PERSON HAVING GROUNDS FOR REQUIRING   S 170(2)

IF HE DOESN'T GIVE HIS NAME AND ADDRESS HE MUST
AS SOON AS PRACTICABLE AND IN ANY CASE WITHIN 24 HOURS

report to the police
S 170(3) AND (6)

IF THE ACCIDENT INVOLVES PERSONAL INJURY HE MUST ALSO

produce insurance

AT THE TIME OF THE ACCIDENT OR, IF HE FAILS TO DO SO,
TO THE POLICE AS SOON AS REASONABLY PRACTICABLE AND, IN ANY CASE, WITHIN 24 HOURS (But he will not be guilty of the offence of failing to produce the insurance if he does so within 7 days).   S 170(5) AND (6)

278 The Traffic Officer's Companion

DUTY TO GIVE INFORMATION AS TO DRIVER
S.172 Road Traffic Act, 1988

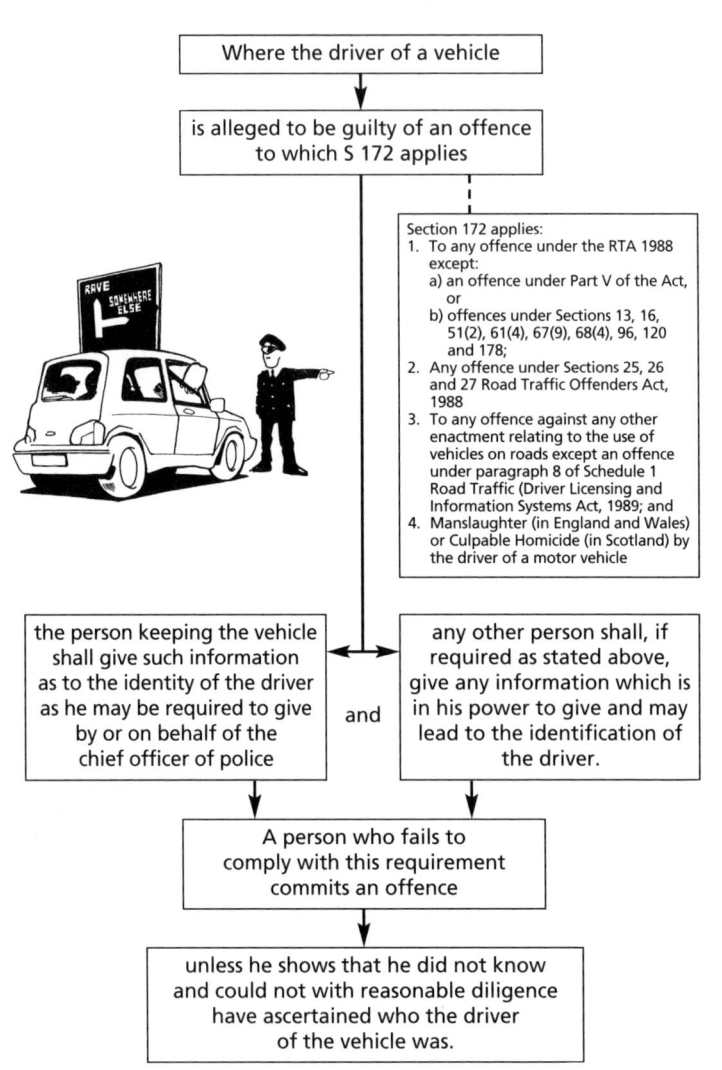

Where the driver of a vehicle

↓

is alleged to be guilty of an offence to which S 172 applies

Section 172 applies:
1. To any offence under the RTA 1988 except:
   a) an offence under Part V of the Act, or
   b) offences under Sections 13, 16, 51(2), 61(4), 67(9), 68(4), 96, 120 and 178;
2. Any offence under Sections 25, 26 and 27 Road Traffic Offenders Act, 1988
3. To any offence against any other enactment relating to the use of vehicles on roads except an offence under paragraph 8 of Schedule 1 Road Traffic (Driver Licensing and Information Systems Act, 1989; and
4. Manslaughter (in England and Wales) or Culpable Homicide (in Scotland) by the driver of a motor vehicle

the person keeping the vehicle shall give such information as to the identity of the driver as he may be required to give by or on behalf of the chief officer of police

and

any other person shall, if required as stated above, give any information which is in his power to give and may lead to the identification of the driver.

↓

A person who fails to comply with this requirement commits an offence

↓

unless he shows that he did not know and could not with reasonable diligence have ascertained who the driver of the vehicle was.

Part 5: Miscellaneous **279**

POWERS OF ARREST WITHOUT WARRANT

POLICE AND CRIMINAL EVIDENCE ACT 1984, S. 24

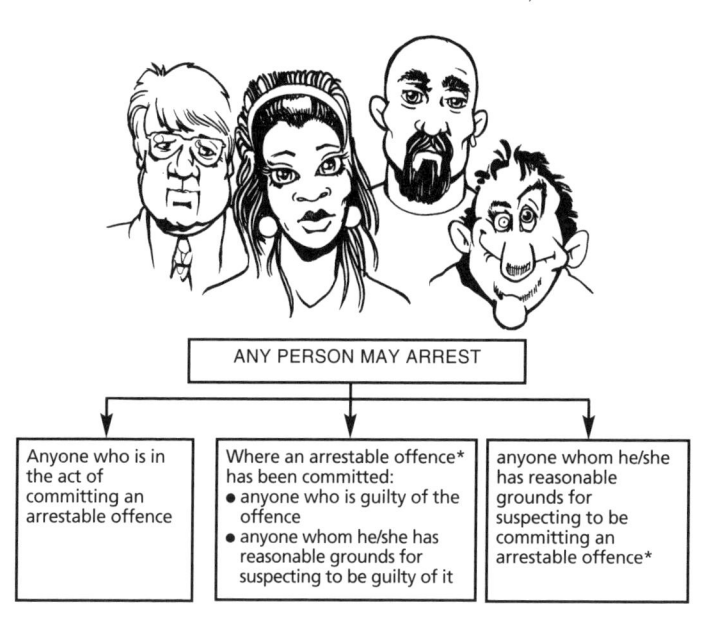

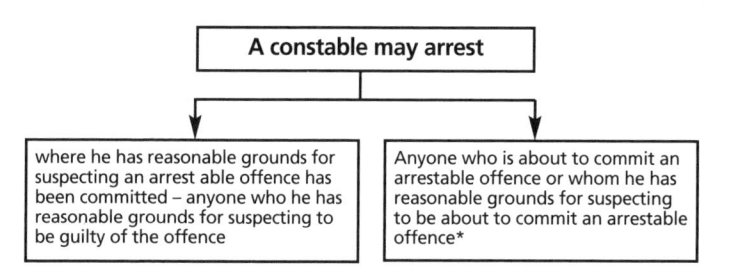

ANY PERSON MAY ARREST

- Anyone who is in the act of committing an arrestable offence

- Where an arrestable offence* has been committed:
  - anyone who is guilty of the offence
  - anyone whom he/she has reasonable grounds for suspecting to be guilty of it

- anyone whom he/she has reasonable grounds for suspecting to be committing an arrestable offence*

A constable may arrest

- where he has reasonable grounds for suspecting an arrest able offence has been committed – anyone who he has reasonable grounds for suspecting to be guilty of the offence

- Anyone who is about to commit an arrestable offence or whom he has reasonable grounds for suspecting to be about to commit an arrestable offence*

Note:
1. **Arrestable offence (see following page).*
2. *Not applicable to Scotland.*

ARRESTABLE OFFENCES
POLICE AND CRIMINAL EVIDENCE ACT 1984, S.24

'Arrestable Offence' means-
1. an offence for which the sentence is fixed by law;
2. an offence for which a person aged 21 years or over (not previously convicted) may be sentenced to imprisonment for 5 years; and
3. any of the following offences-

Customs and Excise Offences	S1(1) Customs and Excise Management Act 1979
Official secrets	Official Secrets Act 1920 and 1989 (except S8(1), (4) or (5))
Causing prostitution of women	S22 Sexual Offences Act 1956
Procuration of girl under 21	S23 Sexual Offences Act 1956
Placing advertisements relating to prostitution	S46 Criminal Justice and Police Act 2001
Taking motor vehicle or other conveyance without authority	S12(1) Theft Act 1968
Going equipped for stealing	S25(1) Theft Act 1968
Making off without payment	S3 Theft Act 1978
Football offences	Football Offences Act 1991
Publication of obscene matter	S2 Obscene Publications Act 1959
Indecent photographs of children	S1 Protection of Children Act 1978
Kerb-crawling	S1 Sexual Offences Act 1985
Failing to stop and report an accident causing personal injury	S170(4) Road Traffic Act 1988
Driving whilst disqualified	S103(1)(b) Road Traffic Act 1988
Sale of football match tickets by unauthorised persons	S166 Criminal Justice and Public Order Act 1994
Publishing material likely to stir up racial hatred	S19 Public Order Act 1986
Touting for hire car services	S167 Criminal Justice and Public Order Act 1994
Carrying offensive weapons	S1(1) Prevention of Crime Act 1953
Having article with blade or point in public place	S139(1) Criminal Justice Act 1988
Having article with blade or point on school premises	S139A Criminal Justice Act 1988
Assaulting a police officer or person assisting	S89(1) Police Act 1996
Harassment	S2 Protection from Harassment Act 1997
Failing to remove disguise	S60AA(7) Criminal Justice and Public Order Act 1994
Racial or religious harassment	S32(1)(a) Crime and Disorder Act 1988
Failing to comply with football banning order	S14J or 21C Football Spectators Act 1989
Alcohol consumption in public place	S12(4) Criminal Justice and Police Act 2001
Taking, etc. wild birds	S1(1) or (2) or (6) Wildlife and Countryside Act 1981
Disturbance of wild birds	S1(5) Wildlife and Countryside Act 1981
Taking, etc. wild animals or plants	S9 or 13(1)(a) or (2) " "
Introduction of new species, etc.	S14 " "
Unauthorised presence in zone or aircraft	S21C(1) or 21D(1) Aviation Security Act 1982
Trespass on aerodrome	S39(1) Civil Aviation Act 1982

Conspiring to commit any of the above offences; inciting, aiding, abetting, counselling or procuring the commission of any of the above offences; and attempting to commit any of the above offences other than summary offences.

Part 5: Miscellaneous **281**

POWERS OF ARREST WITHOUT WARRANT

POLICE AND CRIMINAL EVIDENCE ACT 1984, SS. 24 & 25

Note – not applicable for an arrestable offence

Where **a constable** has reasonable grounds to suspect

↓

that any offence which is not an arrestable offence has been or is being committed or attempted

↓

he may arrest the relevant person *

↓

if it appears to him that service of a summons is impracticable or inappropriate

↓

because any of the general arrest conditions ** is satisfied

Notes

The relevant person

Any person whom the constable has reasonable grounds to suspect of having committed, or having attempted to commit, or of being in the course of committing or attempting to commit the offence.

**General arrest conditions

See following page.

Not applicable to Scotland.

GENERAL ARREST CONDITIONS

POLICE AND CRIMINAL EVIDENCE ACT 1984, S. 25

The general arrest conditions are-

Identity

> That the name of the relevant person is unknown to, and cannot be readily ascertained by, the constable; or that the constable has reasonable grounds for doubting whether a name furnished by the relevant person as his name, is his real name

Address for service

> That the relevant person has failed to furnish a satisfactory address for service; or that the constable has reasonable grounds for doubting whether an address furnished by the relevant person is a satisfactory address for service

>> 'Satisfactory for service' means that the relevant person will be at that address sufficiently long to serve a summons; or that some other specified person will accept service for him.

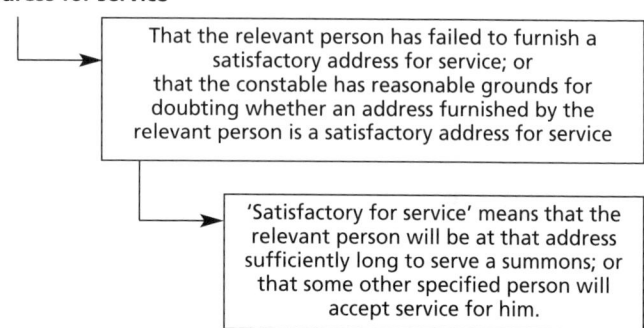

Preventative measures

> That the constable has reasonable grounds for believing that arrest is necessary to prevent the relevant person:
> - causing physical injury to himself or any other person;
> - suffering physical injury;
> - causing loss of, or damage to, property;
> - committing an offence against public decency where members of the public could not be expected to avoid him;
> - causing an unlawful obstruction on the highway.

Protection

> That the constable has reasonable grounds for believing that arrest is necessary to protect a child or other vulnerable person from the relevant person.

Not applicable to Scotland.

MODE OF ARREST

POLICE AND CRIMINAL EVIDENCE ACT 1984, SS 28 AND 30

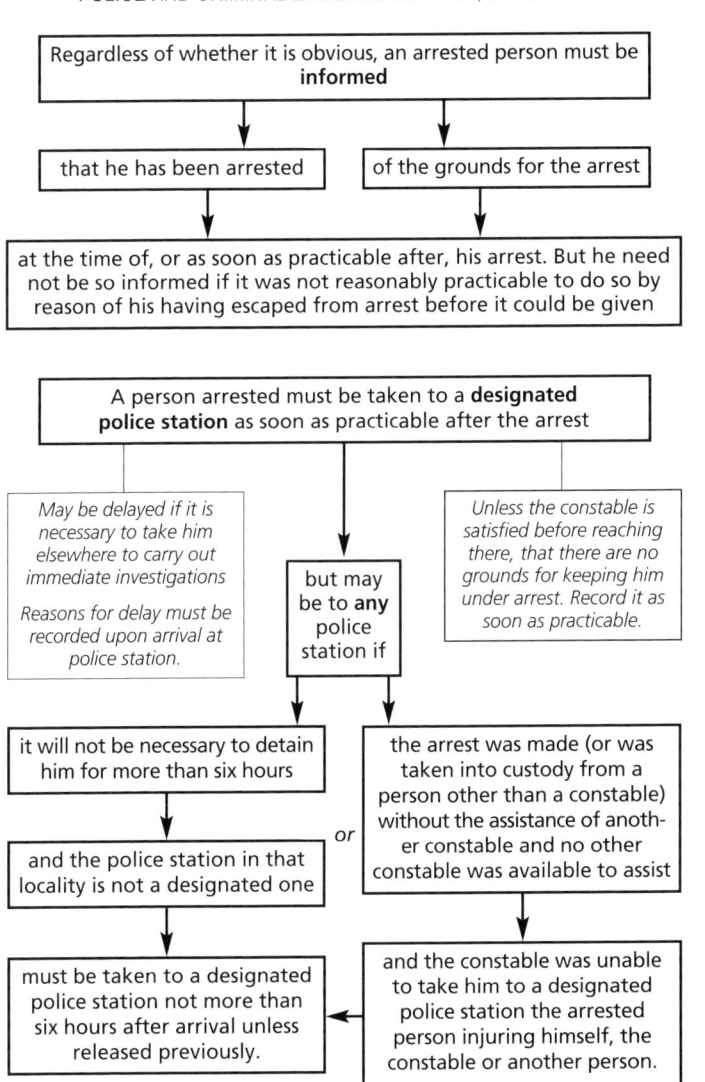

Regardless of whether it is obvious, an arrested person must be **informed**

- that he has been arrested
- of the grounds for the arrest

at the time of, or as soon as practicable after, his arrest. But he need not be so informed if it was not reasonably practicable to do so by reason of his having escaped from arrest before it could be given

---

A person arrested must be taken to a **designated police station** as soon as practicable after the arrest

May be delayed if it is necessary to take him elsewhere to carry out immediate investigations

Reasons for delay must be recorded upon arrival at police station.

but may be to **any** police station if

Unless the constable is satisfied before reaching there, that there are no grounds for keeping him under arrest. Record it as soon as practicable.

- it will not be necessary to detain him for more than six hours

  and the police station in that locality is not a designated one

or

- the arrest was made (or was taken into custody from a person other than a constable) without the assistance of another constable and no other constable was available to assist

  and the constable was unable to take him to a designated police station the arrested person injuring himself, the constable or another person.

must be taken to a designated police station not more than six hours after arrival unless released previously.

Not applicable to Scotland.

ROAD CHECKS

POLICE AND CRIMINAL EVIDENCE ACT 1984, S 4

Under certain circumstances, a police constable needs authority to carry out a road check

What is a road check?

The exercise in a locality of the power conferred by S 163 of the Road Traffic Act 1988, to stop either all vehicles or vehicles selected by any criterion

What type of check needs to be authorised?

Where it is necessary to ascertain whether a vehicle is carrying:

- a person who has committed a serious arrestable offence (other than a traffic or excise offence) and may be in the locality
- a person who is a witness to a serious arrestable offence
- a person who intends to commit a serious arrestable offence and may be in the locality
- a person who is unlawfully at large and may be in the locality

Who can authorise it?

Normally a superintendent must authorise it in writing. But may be authorised by an officer below that rank as a matter of urgency, in which case, as soon as practicable, he must make a written record of the time he gives it and cause a superintendent to be informed

The locality at which the check is to be carried out must be specified

How long may it last?

The superintendent or above (not below) must specify a period, not exceeding seven days, during which it may take place (may be renewed in writing). He may direct whether it shall be continuous or conducted at specified times

Not applicable to Scotland.

STOP AND SEARCH

Serious Violence

Where a superintendent or above (or inspector if incident is imminent) reasonably believes that incidents involving serious violence may take place in his area and it is expedient to prevent their occurrence he may authorise (in writing) stopping and searching of persons and vehicles in that locality for a period not exceeding 24 hours for offensive weapons or dangerous instruments. Constable in uniform may stop any person or vehicle and make any search he thinks fit whether or not he has any grounds for suspecting that weapons or articles of that kind are present.

S 60 CRIMINAL JUSTICE AND PUBLIC ORDER ACT 1994

Prevention of Terrorism

Where it appears to an officer of the rank of commander/assistant chief constable that it is expedient in order to prevent acts of terrorism (connected with Northern Ireland or of any description but not connected solely with the affairs of the UK) he may authorise the stopping and searching of person or vehicles (including ships and aircraft) for up to 28 days in a specified locality. In the exercise of these powers a constable may stop any vehicle or person and make any search he thinks fit whether or not he has any grounds for suspecting that articles of terrorism are being carried.

S 81 CRIMINAL JUSTICE AND PUBLIC ORDER ACT 1994

Raves – stopping persons from attending

If a constable in uniform reasonably believes that a person is on his way to a gathering to which S 63, Criminal Justice and Public Order Act 1994 applies, and in respect of which a direction is in force, he may stop that person and direct him not to proceed in the direction of that gathering. This power may be exercised within five miles of the boundary of the site of the gathering. Failure to comply is an offence and a constable in uniform who reasonably suspects that person is committing the offence may arrest him without warrant

S 65 CRIMINAL JUSTICE AND PUBLIC ORDER ACT 1994

286 The Traffic Officer's Companion

POWER TO STOP VEHICLES
S. 163 ROAD TRAFFIC ACT 1988

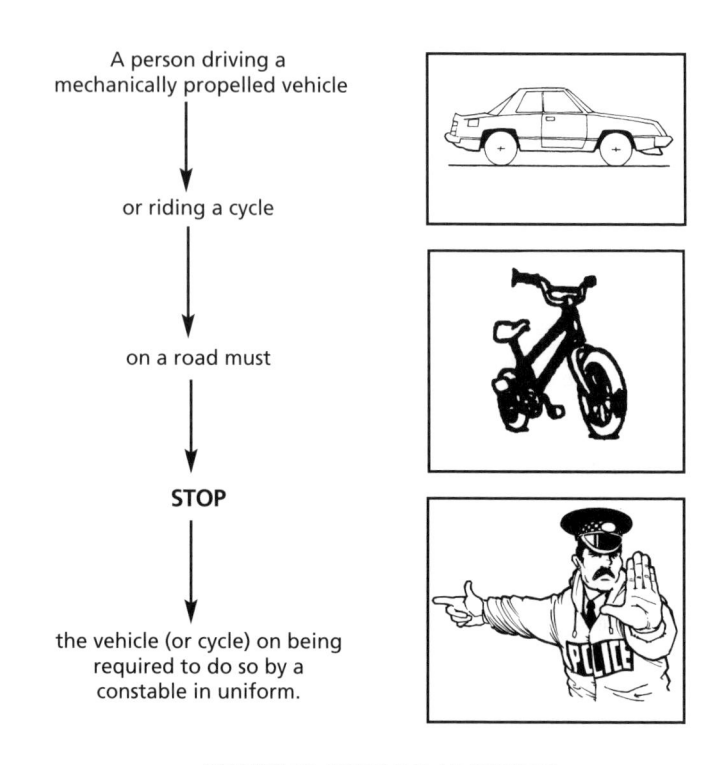

A person driving a mechanically propelled vehicle

↓

or riding a cycle

↓

on a road must

↓

STOP

↓

the vehicle (or cycle) on being required to do so by a constable in uniform.

FAILURE TO COMPLY IS AN OFFENCE.

POWER OF ARREST
(Inserted by the Police Reform Act 2002, s.49(1))

A constable in uniform may arrest a person without warrant if he has reasonable cause to suspect that the person has committed the above offence.

SEIZURE OF VEHICLES
POLICE REFORM ACT 2002, S 59
POLICE (RETENTION AND DISPOSAL OF MOTOR VEHICLES)
REGULATIONS 2002

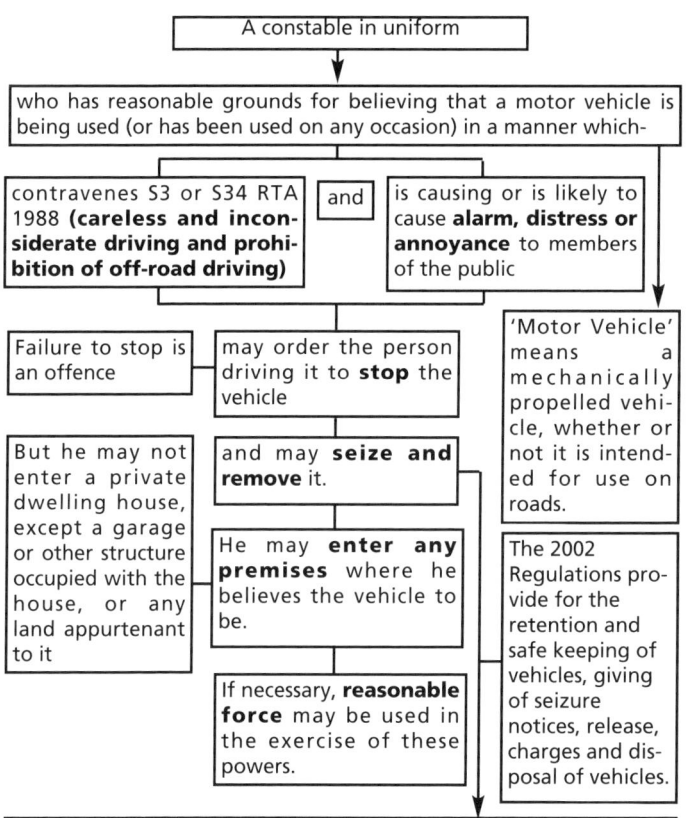

A constable in uniform

who has reasonable grounds for believing that a motor vehicle is being used (or has been used on any occasion) in a manner which—

- contravenes S3 or S34 RTA 1988 **(careless and inconsiderate driving and prohibition of off-road driving)** **and** is causing or is likely to cause **alarm, distress or annoyance** to members of the public

Failure to stop is an offence

may order the person driving it to **stop** the vehicle

But he may not enter a private dwelling house, except a garage or other structure occupied with the house, or any land appurtenant to it

and may **seize and remove** it.

He may **enter any premises** where he believes the vehicle to be.

If necessary, **reasonable force** may be used in the exercise of these powers.

'Motor Vehicle' means a mechanically propelled vehicle, whether or not it is intended for use on roads.

The 2002 Regulations provide for the retention and safe keeping of vehicles, giving of seizure notices, release, charges and disposal of vehicles.

But he must first warn him that he will seize it if such use continues or is repeated; and the use has continued or been repeated after the warning. But a warning need not be given if (a) it is impracticable for him to give the warning; (b) he has already given a warning on that occasion in respect of the use of that vehicle or another vehicle by that or another person; (c) he believes that such a warning has been given on that occasion by someone else; or (d) the person has already been warned by him or someone else within the previous 12 months whether or not it was in respect of the same vehicle or the same or similar use.

TAXI TOUTS

S 167 CRIMINAL JUSTICE AND PUBLIC ORDER ACT 1994

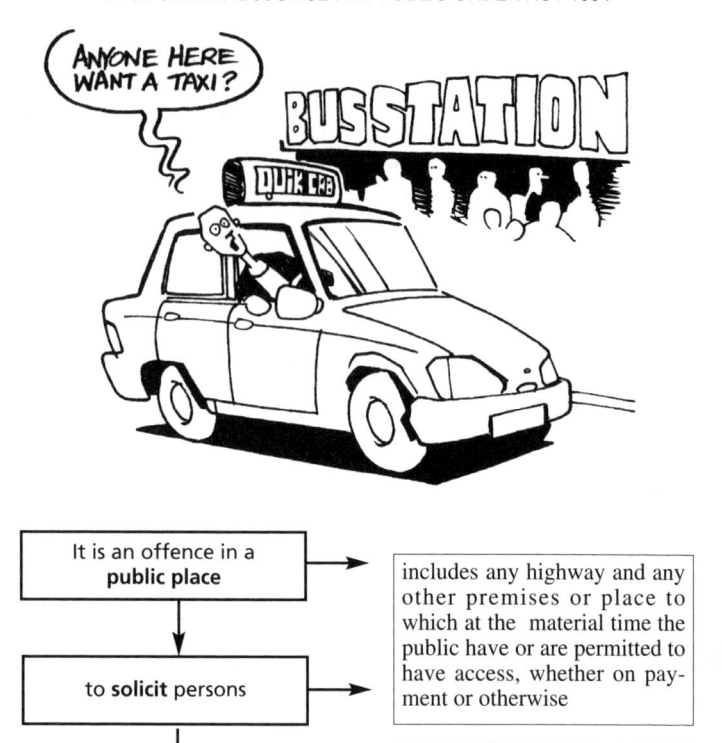

It is an offence in a **public place**	includes any highway and any other premises or place to which at the material time the public have or are permitted to have access, whether on payment or otherwise
to **solicit** persons	
to hire vehicles to carry them as passengers	*mere display of a sign on a vehicle that it is for hire is not soliciting*

Does not include soliciting persons to hire licensed taxis or public service vehicles on behalf of a holder of a PSV operator's licence with his authority.

- **This is an arrestable offence**

Part 5: Miscellaneous **289**

BUILDERS' SKIPS

HIGHWAYS ACT 1980

Offences S 139

- Depositing a skip without the written permission of the highway authority
- Failing to comply with any conditions contained in the authorisation
- Not having skip properly lighted at night
- Not having it removed as soon as reasonably practicable after it has been filled
- Not having name and address or telephone number of owner clearly and indelibly marked on the skip.

'Skip'

A container designed to be carried on a vehicle and deposited on a road for the collection and removal of rubble etc.

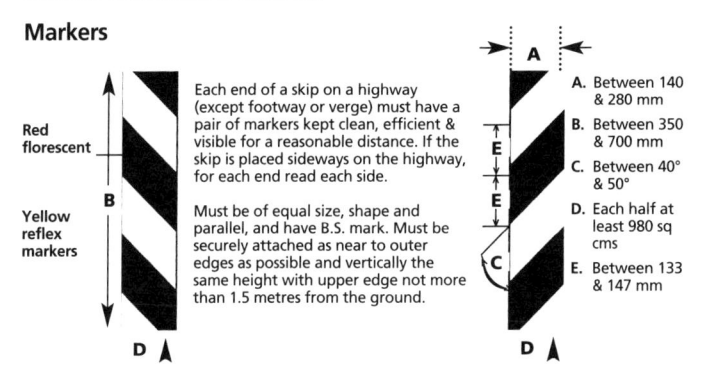

Markers

Red florescent

Yellow reflex markers

Each end of a skip on a highway (except footway or verge) must have a pair of markers kept clean, efficient & visible for a reasonable distance. If the skip is placed sideways on the highway, for each end read each side.

Must be of equal size, shape and parallel, and have B.S. mark. Must be securely attached as near to outer edges as possible and vertically the same height with upper edge not more than 1.5 metres from the ground.

A. Between 140 & 280 mm
B. Between 350 & 700 mm
C. Between 40° & 50°
D. Each half at least 980 sq cms
E. Between 133 & 147 mm

BUILDERS' SKIPS (MARKINGS) REGULATIONS 1984

Proceedings

may be taken against the owner * and/or any person whose act resulted in the offence

* If hired for more than a month or subject of an HP agreement, hirer becomes the owner. An owner hiring out his skip must ensure hirers are aware of their duties.

Defence

That the offence was a result of an act or default of another and reasonable precautions had been taken to avoid any contravention

Police powers

A constable in uniform may require the owner to remove or re-position the skip as soon as possible. The constable has power to remove or re-position it himself and any expenses incurred may be recovered from the owners.   S 140(2)

Not applicable to Scotland – See Scots provisions re Builder's Skips in Roads (Scotland) Act, 1984.

NOTICE OF INTENDED PROSECUTION

ROAD TRAFFIC OFFENDERS ACT 1988, SS. 1 AND 2

In relation to certain offences, a person will not be convicted *unless*:

- **At the time** of the offence he was warned that the question of prosecuting him would be considered
- or within 14 days of the offence a summons was served on him
- or within 14 days of the offence a notice of intended prosecution was sent to the driver or rider (or in the case of motor vehicles, the registered keeper)

By delivering it to him; by addressing it to him and leaving it at his last known address; or by sending it by registered post, recorded delivery service or first class post addressed to him at his last known address

But the above requirement will not apply if, at the time of the offence or immediately thereafter, an accident occurs owing to the presence on a road of a vehicle in respect of which the offence was committed

Offences involved include (SCHED 1)

● Dangerous driving ● Careless and inconsiderate driving ● Leaving a vehicle in a dangerous position ● Dangerous cycling ● Careless and inconsiderate cycling ● Failing to comply with traffic directions ● Failing to comply with traffic signs (see below) ● Exceeding a speed limit or restriction under S14 and S16 (temporary restrictions), S17 (Special Roads), S88 (temporary minimum speed limits) or S89 (speeding generally) of The Road Traffic Regulation Act 1984.

Signs

The offence concerns only the following signs which are contained in Reg 10 of The Traffic Signs Regulations 2002. Contravention of others should be dealt with under the relevant order

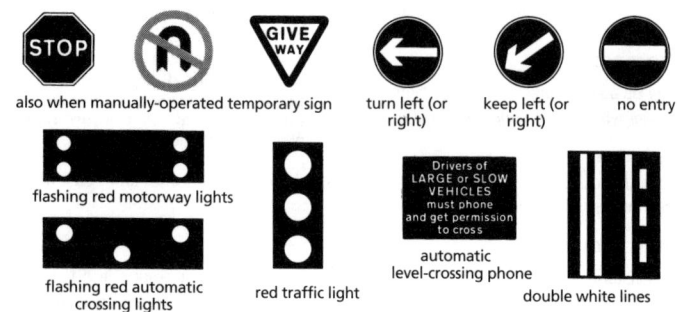

- STOP — also when manually-operated temporary sign
- turn left (or right)
- keep left (or right)
- no entry
- flashing red motorway lights
- flashing red automatic crossing lights
- red traffic light
- automatic level-crossing phone (Drivers of LARGE or SLOW VEHICLES must phone and get permission to cross)
- double white lines

Also: ● weak bridge weight limit contravention ● height limit contravention ● route for use by buses, tram cars, pedal cycles only ● give way to traffic from right at roundabout ● manually operated stop sign at roadworks ● hatch markings on road ● give way at double broken lines ● hatched box at junction or level crossing ● tramcar prohibition sign ● green arrow traffic light

Part 5: Miscellaneous **291**

CRASH HELMETS
S16 TRAFFIC ACT 1988. MOTOR CYCLES (PROTECTIVE HELMETS)
REGULATIONS 1998 AS AMENDED BY S.I. 2000/1488

> **Eye protectors**
> *MOTOR CYCLES (EYE PROTECTORS) REGS 1985*

> If a person driving or riding on a motor cycle uses eye protectors. they must be of a type prescribed (conforming to the relevant British Standard and so marked.)

Protective Headgear

Every person driving or riding on a motor bicycle (otherwise than as a passenger in a sidecar) on a road.

- must wear protective headgear.
- must be securely fastened to the head of the wearer by means of straps or other fastening provided for that purpose.
- must bear a mark indication compliance with the British Standard or be of a type which, by virtue of its shape, material and construction could reasonable be expected to afford protection similar to, or greater than, a helmet which conforms to the British Standard, an accepted EEA Standard or of ECE Regulations.

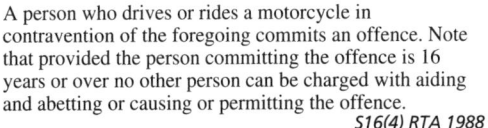

A person who drives or rides a motorcycle in contravention of the foregoing commits an offence. Note that provided the person committing the offence is 16 years or over no other person can be charged with aiding and abetting or causing or permitting the offence.
S16(4) RTA 1988

> The regulations do not apply to
> - mowing machine
> - vehicle being propelled by a person on foot
> - follower of Sikh religion while wearing a turban
> *ROAD TRAFFIC ACT 1988, S 16*

'Motor bicycle'

means a two-wheeled motor cycle with or without a sidecar. If the distance between any two wheels is less than 460mm they shall be regarded as one wheel   *MOTOR CYCLES (PROTECTIVE HELMETS) REGULATIONS 1980*
S 16, ROAD TRAFFIC ACT 1988

MOTOR CYCLE EYE PROTECTORS
ROAD TRAFFIC ACT 1988, S.18
MOTOR CYCLE (EYE PROTECTORS) REGULATIONS 1999

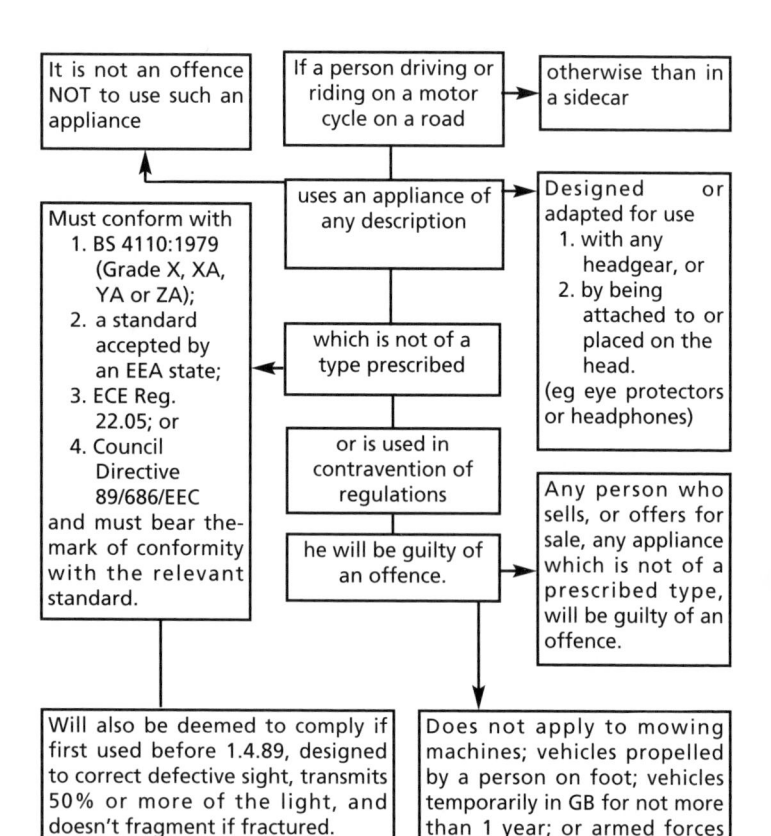

- If a person driving or riding on a motor cycle on a road
- otherwise than in a sidecar
- uses an appliance of any description
- Designed or adapted for use
  1. with any headgear, or
  2. by being attached to or placed on the head.
  (eg eye protectors or headphones)
- which is not of a type prescribed
- Must conform with
  1. BS 4110:1979 (Grade X, XA, YA or ZA);
  2. a standard accepted by an EEA state;
  3. ECE Reg. 22.05; or
  4. Council Directive 89/686/EEC

  and must bear the mark of conformity with the relevant standard.
- or is used in contravention of regulations
- he will be guilty of an offence.
- It is not an offence NOT to use such an appliance
- Any person who sells, or offers for sale, any appliance which is not of a prescribed type, will be guilty of an offence.
- Will also be deemed to comply if first used before 1.4.89, designed to correct defective sight, transmits 50% or more of the light, and doesn't fragment if fractured.
- Does not apply to mowing machines; vehicles propelled by a person on foot; vehicles temporarily in GB for not more than 1 year; or armed forces personnel on duty, wearing service eye protectors.

Part 5: Miscellaneous **293**

MOTORWAYS

MOTORWAYS TRAFFIC (ENGLAND AND WALES) REGULATIONS 1982
(as amended). MOTORWAYS TRAFFIC (SCOTLAND) REGULATIONS 1995.
The following details apply under respective regulations to both sides of the border.
The numbers of the Scottish Regulations are shown in brackets.

Driving
Must not drive on any part of the motorway other than the carriageway. *REG 5 (REG 4)*
Must drive with the central reservation on the right or offside unless directed otherwise. *REG 6 (REG 5)*

Stopping
Must not stop or remain at rest on a carriageway or verge unless broken down (includes mechanical defect, lack of fuel, water or oil), involved in an accident, illness, emergency, to recover or remove an object on the motorway, or to give help to a person in such circumstances.

If stoppage is necessary on the carriageway the vehicle must be moved onto the verge as soon as practicable. If stopped on the verge, must not cause obstruction or danger to vehicles on the carriageway, and shall not remain at rest longer than is necessary in the circumstances. *REG 7 (REG 6)*

Reversing
A vehicle shall not be reversed unless it is necessary to enable it to move forward or to be connected to another vehicle. *REG 8 (REG 7)*

L Drivers
Persons who have not passed a test to drive must not use the motorway. (Does not apply to large goods vehicles or passenger-carrying vehicle (over 16 passengers, or over 8 and for hire or reward)). *REG 11 (REG 10)*

Lanes (three-lane motorways)
The following vehicles may not use the right hand lane of a 3 lane (or more) carriageway: Goods vehicle max laden weight over 7.5 tonnes; passenger vehicle constructed or adapted to carry more than 8 seated passengers in addition to the driver, with maximum laden weight over 7.5 tonnes; motor vehicle drawing a trailer; motor tractor, light locomotive or heavy locomotive; except when necessary to pass an exceptionally wide load.
REG 12 (REG 11)

Pedestrians
Prohibited from using any part of the motorway except when necessary to do so as a result of accident, emergency or vehicle at rest on motorway as a result of circumstances specified in Regulation 7 (above), or with permission of constable to investigate accident, or he is performing his duty as constable, member of fire brigade, or ambulance service, or where necessary to carry out maintenance, repairs cleaning, etc, of motorway or structures on, under, over motorway, or to remove vehicles from motorway, or carry out surveys, inspections, etc, under authority of Secretary of State.
REG 15 (REG 13 – note REG 7 (above) for Scots is REG 6)

Animals
Not to be allowed to leave the vehicle, but if this is necessary, must not be allowed on the carriageway and must be on a lead or kept under proper control
REG 14 (REG 12)

EYESIGHT

S.96 ROAD TRAFFIC ACT 1988
MOTOR VEHICLES (DRIVING LICENCES) REGULATIONS 1999

If a driver's eyesight is such (whether through a defect which cannot be corrected or which is not for the time being corrected) that he cannot comply with the following requirements, he commits an offence:

Category of licence	Size of character	From a distance of
A,B,B+E,F,G,H,K,L,P & the former cat.N. Also C1, C1+E(8.25 tonnes), D1 & D1+E if in force before 1.1.97 or granted on the expiry of such a licence, coming into force not later than 31.12.97	79mm high & 57mm wide	12.3m for cat. K 20.5m in any other case
	79mm high & 50mm wide	12m for cat. K 20m in any other case
Any other category	79.4mm high	20.5m

(S.96 & Regs. 70 & 72)

A constable who suspects that a driver may be guilty of this offence may require him to submit to a test using no other means of correction than he used at the time of driving. It is an offence to refuse to submit to the test. *(Reg. 96)*

PHYSICAL HEALTH

- An applicant for a driving licence must declare whether or not he/she is suffering from or has suffered from a relevant or prospective disability – making a false declaration is an offence. *(S.92)*
- A licence holder who becomes aware that he is suffering from a relevant or prospective disability (which will last for longer than three months) must inform the Secretary of State who may then serve notice on the licence holder, revoking the licence. Failure to notify such disabilities is an offence. *(S.94)*
- The following disabilities are prescribed by Reg 71:
  - epilepsy
  - severe mental handicap
  - liability to sudden attacks of giddiness or fainting for whatever reason, and regardless of whether a heart regulator etc. has been implanted to prevent it
  - persistent use of drugs or alcohol
  - and any other disability likely to cause driving to be a danger to the public.

STOPPING DISTANCES

Highway Code

Speed (mph)	20	30	40	50	60	70
Distance (feet)	40	75	120	175	240	315

Part 5: Miscellaneous **295**

DRIVING INSTRUCTION
ROAD TRAFFIC ACT 1988, Ss 123, 135 & 137
MOTOR CARS (DRIVING INSTRUCTION) REGULATIONS 1989

A driving instructor and his employer, if any, (does not apply to police) will be guilty of an offence if paid instruction in the driving of a motor car is given unless he

is **registered** and he exhibits his certificate on the vehicle

| FRONT OF CERTIFICATE | REAR OF CERTIFICATE |

or has a trainee's licence and he exhibits his licence on the vehicle

| FRONT OF LICENCE | REAR OF LICENCE |

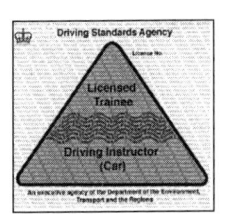

Fitted behind the nearside edge of the windscreen so that the back can be seen from the outside the vehicle and the front can be seen from the nearside seat. Must be produced if required to a police constable or other authorised peson within 7 days or as soon as reasonably practicable.
It is an offence for an unregistered person to —
  a) take or use a prescribed title;
  b) wear or display a prescribed badge or certificate; or
  c) use any title, etc., implying that he is registered.
A badge is issued which resembles the front of the certificate/licence.

296 The Traffic Officer's Companion

PEDESTRIAN CROSSINGS
ZEBRA, PELICAN AND PUFFIN PEDESTRIAN CROSSINGS REGULATIONS AND GENERAL DIRECTIONS 1997 (THE 1997 REGS.)
TRAFFIC SIGNS REGULATIONS 2002 (THE 2002 REGS.)

Zebra, Pelican and Puffin are dealt with by the 1997 Regs., Equestrian, Toucan and Pedestrian Controlled are contained in the 2002 Regs. Light sequences are as follows.

Zebra – Yellow globe mounted to a post at each end of the crossing

Pelican – Light signals in the sequence steady green, steady amber, steady red, flashing amber (the latter indicating that a pedestrian still has precedence otherwise the vehicle may proceed).

Puffin
Equestrian
Toucan } Light signals in the sequence red, red and amber together, green, amber.
Pedestrian-Controlled

Each type has a controlled area indicated by road markings on each side of the crossing.

Offences
(1) Vehicle or any part of it **stopping within the limits of the crossing** unless prevented by circumstances beyond driver's control or to avoid injury or damage. (Zebra, Pelican and Puffin only. Reg. 18 1997 Regs.)
(2) **Pedestrian remaining on crossing** longer than necessary to cross. (Zebra, Pelican and Puffin only. Reg. 19 1997 Regs.)
(3) Vehicle **stopping within a controlled area** (Reg. 20 1997 Regs., Reg. 27 2002 Regs.) except:
   (a) to give precedence to a pedestrian on the crossing
   (b) prevented by circumstances beyond driver's control or to avoid injury or damage
   (c) for police, fire or ambulance purposes
   (d) for purposes of a building operation, demolition or excavation; removal of obstruction; maintenance, etc., of the road; or gas, water, electricity or telecommunications. (But in relation to any of these operations only for so long as is necessary to complete the operation and if the vehicle cannot be stopped elsewhere)
   (e) P.S.V. providing a local service, or carrying passengers at separate fares (but may not stop on the crossing itself)
   (f) vehicle stopping to make a left or right turn
(4) **Contravening red light** at crossing (Reg. 23 1997 Regs., Reg. 36 2002 Regs.)
(5) **Overtaking** within the controlled area on the approach to the crossing (Reg. 24 1997 Regs., Reg. 28 2002 Regs.)
(6) **Failing to give precedence to a pedestrian** on a Zebra crossing (Reg. 25 1997 Regs.)
(7) **Failing to give precedence to a pedestrian** on a Pelican crossing when amber signal is flashing (Reg. 26 1997 Regs.)

MISCELLANEOUS DRIVING OFFENCES

Causing death by dangerous driving (RTA S 1)
A person who causes the death of another person by driving a mechanically propelled vehicle dangerously on a road or other public place is guilty of an offence.

Dangerous driving (RTA S 2)
A person who drives a mechanically propelled vehicle dangerously on a road or other public place is guilty of an offence.

Definition of 'dangerously' (RTA S 2A)
A person drives dangerously if
- the way he drives falls far below what would be expected of a competent driver, and
- it would be obvious to a competent and careful driver that driving in that way would be dangerous.
- it is obvious to a competent and careful driver that driving the vehicle in its current state would be dangerous.

Careless or inconsiderate driving (RTA S 3)
A person who drives a mechanically propelled vehicle on a road or other public place without due care and attention or without reasonable consideration for other persons using the road is guilty of an offence.

Causing death by careless driving having consumed alcohol (RTA S 3A)
A person who causes the death of another person by driving a mechanically propelled vehicle on a road or other public place without due care and attention, or without reasonable consideration for other persons using the road or other public place and
- he is at the time of driving, unfit through drink or drugs, or
- has consumed so much alcohol that the proportion in his breath, blood or urine at that time, exceeds the prescribed limit, or
- he is, within 18 hours after that time, required to provide a specimen in pursuance of S 7 of this Act, but without reasonable excuse fails to provide it, is guilty of an offence.

Dangerous or careless cycling (RTA SS 28 AND 29)
A person who rides a cycle on a road dangerously, without due care and attention or without reasonable consideration for other persons using the road is guilty of an offence.

Causing danger to road users (RTA S 22A)
A person who, intentionally and without lawful authority or reasonable cause,
- causes anything to be on or over a road, or
- interferes with a motor vehicle, trailer or cycle, or
- interferes directly or indirectly with traffic equipment, (traffic signs, barriers, etc)

in such circumstances that it would be obvious to a reasonable person that to do so would be dangerous, is guilty of an offence.

298 The Traffic Officer's Companion

PARKING

ROAD TRAFFIC REGULATION ACT 1984, S 99, REMOVAL AND DISPOSAL OF VEHICLES REGULATIONS 1986

Removal of vehicles illegally, obstructively or dangerously parked or abandoned or broken down

Regulations may be made (see below) to permit the removal of vehicles at rest on a road in contravention of any statutory prohibition or restriction or in such a position or in such condition or in such circumstances as to cause obstruction to persons using the road or as to cause danger to such persons. Reg 4 of the Regulations empowers a constable to remove a vehicle which he could require to be removed or which has been abandoned on a road or on land in the open air.

Emergency removal   ROAD TRAFFIC REGULATION ACT 1984, S 49(4), (4A).

A vehicle left in an authorised parking place may be removed in an emergency where the authority which designated the parking place has so empowered the chief officer of police. A constable acting under the instruction of the chief officer of police may suspend a designated parking place for up to seven days to mitigate congestion or obstruction of traffic or in exceptional circumstances.

Disabled Persons   ROAD TRAFFIC REGULATION ACT 1984 S 117.

DISABLED PERSONS (BADGES FOR MOTOR VEHICLES) (ENGLAND) REGULATIONS 2000 AND LOCAL AUTHORITIES TRAFFICE ORDERS (EXEMPTIONS FOR DISABLED PERSONS)(ENGLAND) REGULATIONS 2000. SIMILAR PROVISIONS HAVE BEEN INTRODUCED FOR WALES AND SCOTLAND)

Restriction of parking orders under Ss 1, 6, 9, 35, 45, or 46 of the Road Traffic Regulation Act 1984 shall provide for an exemption for a disabled person's vehicle displaying in the relevant position a disabled person's badge and, where the period of prohibition is more than 3 hours, an orange parking disk with the time at which parking began marked. Wrongful use of a disabled person's badge is an offence.

PART 6

SUPPLEMENT FOR SCOTLAND

A NOTE TO OFFICERS SERVING IN SCOTTISH POLICE FORCES

The original intention of the *Traffic Officer's Companion* was to provide operational officers serving in English and Welsh police forces with a handy guide book on Road Traffic legislation.

The book has been very successful and has proved itself to be a valuable asset to operational police officers in England and Wales. In discussions with Police Review Publishing I was invited to adapt Gordon Wilson's works in order that officers in Scottish forces could benefit from his skills.

As a result I have prepared the enclosed supplement for officers in the Scottish police forces. This supplement deals not only with Traffic legislation which is only applicable to Scotland but also contains additional legislation common in Scotland.

In keeping with Gordon Wilson's works, the relevant legislation has been subjected to practical interpretation. It should not, therefore be regarded as a definitive work of reference and specific technical details may require further research. On no account should it be used for study purposes by candidates sitting the Police (Scotland) Promotion Examinations.

Unless stated otherwise the text in the main part of this book is applicable to Scotland.

John Pilkington LLB BA
Former Inspector Strathclyde Police

MEANING OF THE TERM 'ROAD':
SECTION 151, ROADS (SCOTLAND) ACT 1984

Definition of 'road'

Any way (other than a waterway) over which there is a public right of passage (by whatever means and whether subject to a toll or not) and includes the road's verge and any bridge (whether permanent or temporary) over which, or tunnel through which, the road passes, and any reference to a road includes a part thereof.

Unless stated otherwise, officers in Scotland should use the above definition of a road as they work through this book.

The term 'public road' as defined for the Vehicle Excise and Registration Act 1994 has the same meaning as is applied by the Roads (Scotland) Act 1984, and means a road which a Roads Authority has a duty to maintain.

302 The Traffic Officer's Companion

CONTROL OF BUILDERS' SKIPS ON ROADS

SECTION 85 ROADS (SCOTLAND) ACT 1984

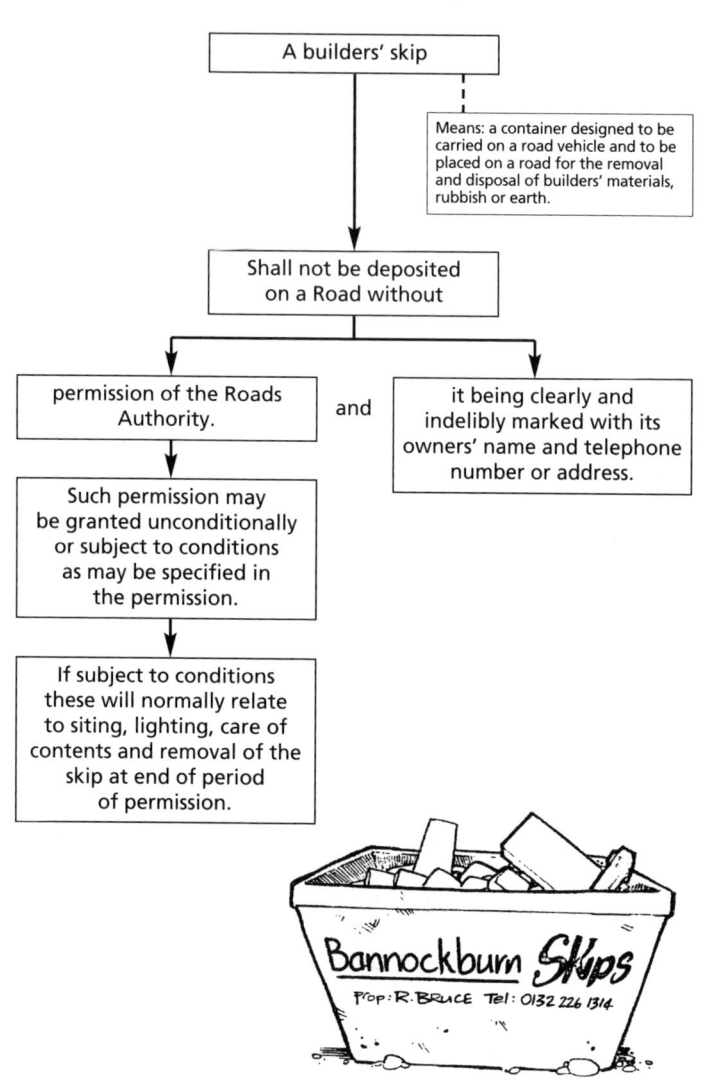

```
A builders' skip
```
Means: a container designed to be carried on a road vehicle and to be placed on a road for the removal and disposal of builders' materials, rubbish or earth.

```
Shall not be deposited on a Road without
```

permission of the Roads Authority. and **it being clearly and indelibly marked with its owners' name and telephone number or address.**

Such permission may be granted unconditionally or subject to conditions as may be specified in the permission.

If subject to conditions these will normally relate to siting, lighting, care of contents and removal of the skip at end of period of permission.

Bannockburn Skips
Prop: R. BRUCE Tel: 0132 226 1314

Part 6: Supplement for Scotland **303**

Offence S 85(3)
For the owner of the skip who uses it, or causes or permits it to be used on a road in contravention of Section 85.

Defence S 85(4)
It is a defence, (except in relation to the offence of not having owner's name etc, on the skip), to prove another person undertook the responsibility of complying with the permission/condition contravened, and that the offence was committed without the consent or connivance of the owner; and that other person may be charged with and convicted of the contravention as if he were the owner.

REMOVAL OF SKIP etc
SECTION 86

```
         A constable in uniform
                  ↓
          who is of the opinion
                  ↓
        that a builders' skip on a road
            ↓              ↓
       is causing   or   is likely to cause
            ↓              ↓
         a danger or obstruction may
            ↓              ↓
    require its removal  or  cause it to be
      or repositioning       removed or repositioned.
                                  ↓
                         Any reasonably incurred
                         expenses may be recovered
                              from the owner.
```

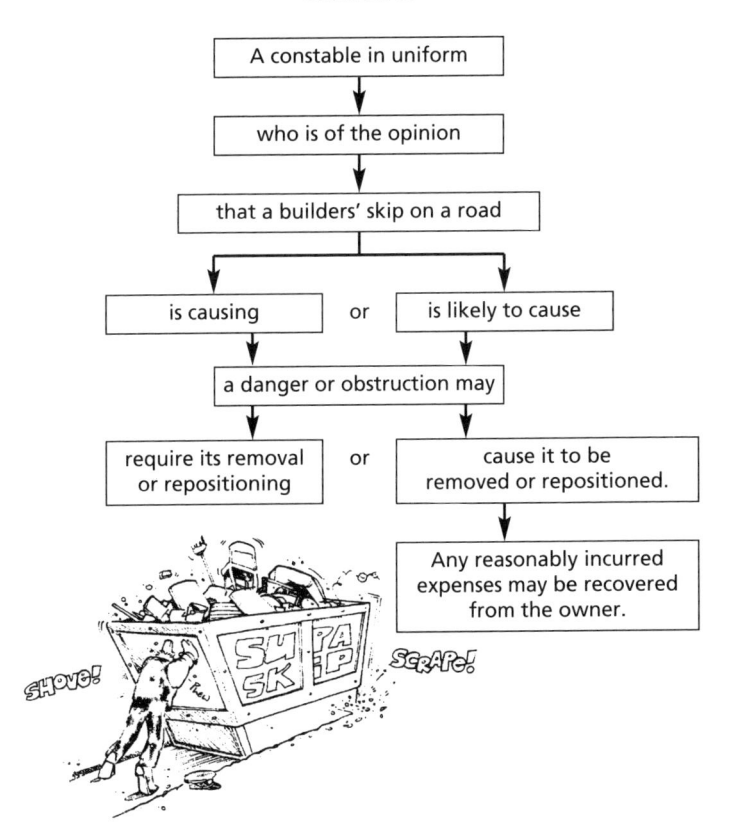

304 The Traffic Officer's Companion

CONTROL OF OBSTRUCTIONS ON ROADS
SECTION 59 ROADS (SCOTLAND) ACT 1984

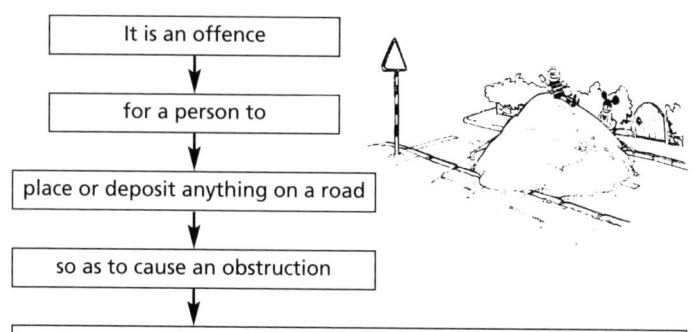

It is an offence

↓

for a person to

↓

place or deposit anything on a road

↓

so as to cause an obstruction

↓

except with the written consent of the Roads Authority and subject to any reasonable conditions attached to the consent.

↓

A person who contravenes Section 59 may be required by the Roads Authority or a constable in uniform to remove the obstruction forthwith.

↓

Failure to comply with this requirement is an offence.

↓

Where:

1. a person does not comply with the above requirement;

2. the person who caused the obstruction cannot be traced; or

3. in a case of emergency, the Roads Authority or a constable may remove the obstruction or cause it to be removed and recover reasonably incurred expenses from the person responsible for the obstruction

---

The provisions of Section 59 do not apply in respect of:

1. the deposit of building materials under provisions of Section 58 of the Act; or

2. deposit of Builders' Skips under Section 85 of the Act;

3. unauthorised abandonment of motor vehicles, etc (which is covered by the provisions of the Refuse Disposal (Amenity) Act 1978; or

4. to works covered by Part IV of the New Roads and Street Works Act 1991.

Part 6: Supplement for Scotland **305**

RESTRICTION ON PLACING BRIDGES, ETC OVER ROADS

SECTION 90 ROADS (SCOTLAND) ACT, 1984

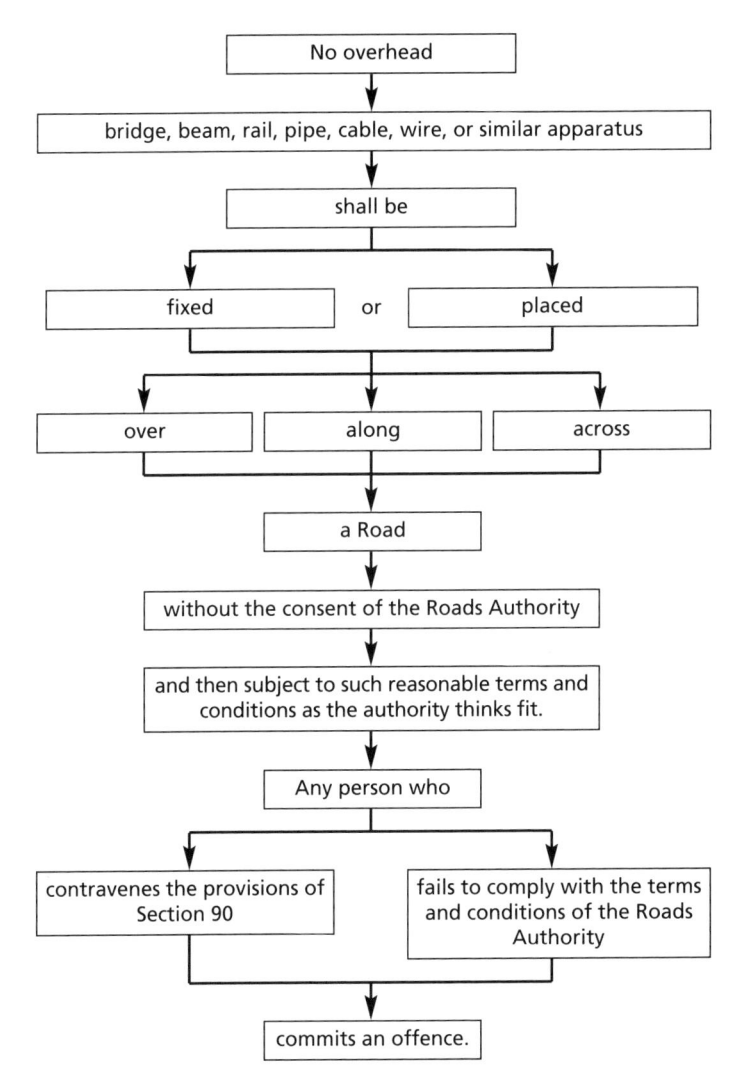

```
No overhead
    ↓
bridge, beam, rail, pipe, cable, wire, or similar apparatus
    ↓
shall be
    ↓
fixed   or   placed
    ↓
over    along    across
    ↓
a Road
    ↓
without the consent of the Roads Authority
    ↓
and then subject to such reasonable terms and
conditions as the authority thinks fit.
    ↓
Any person who
    ↓
contravenes the provisions of Section 90
    |
fails to comply with the terms and conditions of the Roads Authority
    ↓
commits an offence.
```

306 The Traffic Officer's Companion

DEPOSIT OF MUD ETC ON ROAD
SECTION 95 ROADS (SCOTLAND) ACT, 1984

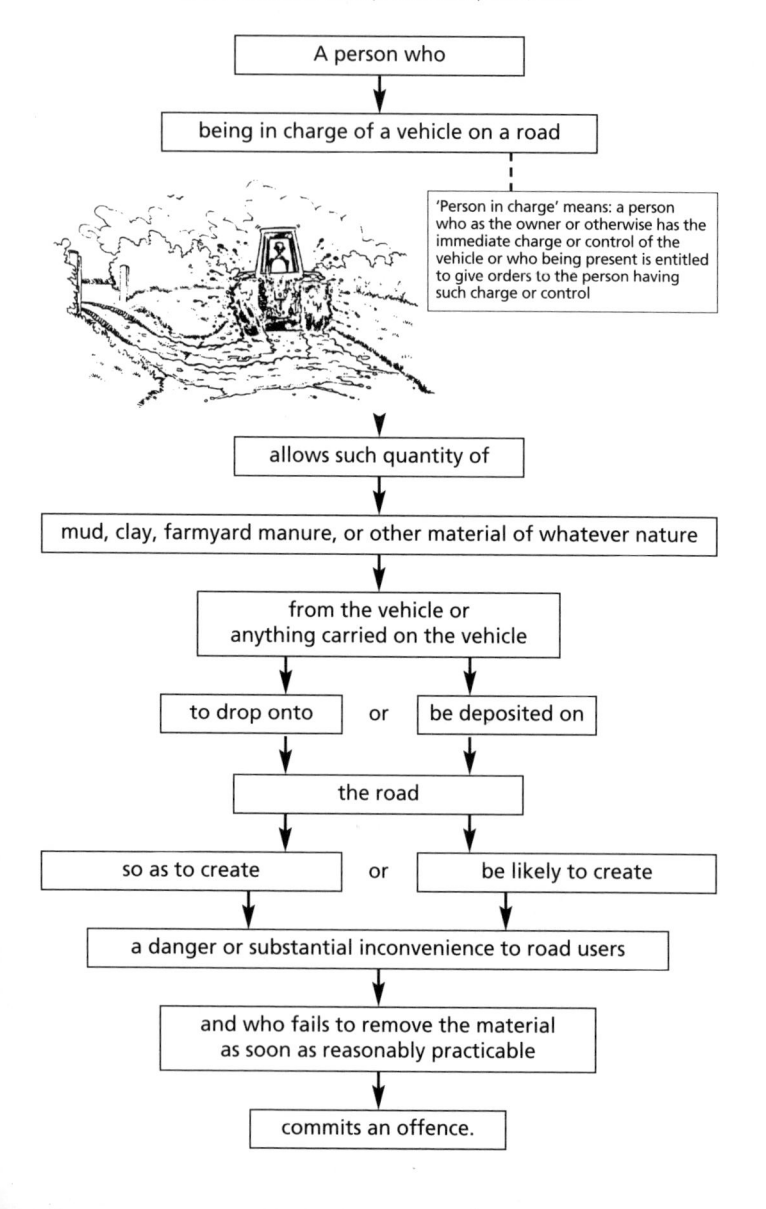

A person who
↓
being in charge of a vehicle on a road

'Person in charge' means: a person who as the owner or otherwise has the immediate charge or control of the vehicle or who being present is entitled to give orders to the person having such charge or control

↓
allows such quantity of
↓
mud, clay, farmyard manure, or other material of whatever nature
↓
from the vehicle or anything carried on the vehicle
↓
to drop onto   or   be deposited on
↓
the road
↓
so as to create   or   be likely to create
↓
a danger or substantial inconvenience to road users
↓
and who fails to remove the material as soon as reasonably practicable
↓
commits an offence.

DAMAGE TO ROADS
SECTION 100 ROADS (SCOTLAND) ACT, 1984

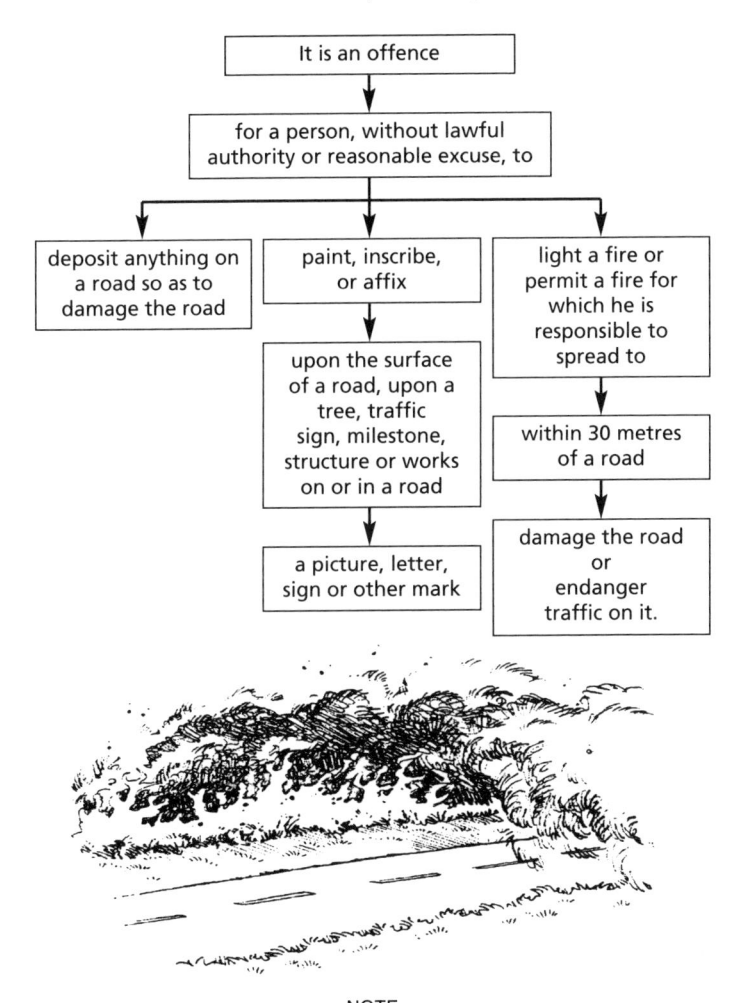

It is an offence ↓ for a person, without lawful authority or reasonable excuse, to

- deposit anything on a road so as to damage the road
- paint, inscribe, or affix → upon the surface of a road, upon a tree, traffic sign, milestone, structure or works on or in a road → a picture, letter, sign or other mark
- light a fire or permit a fire for which he is responsible to spread to → within 30 metres of a road → damage the road or endanger traffic on it.

NOTE
A farmer who culpably and recklessly endangered the public, by neglecting to ensure that no danger was caused to persons on a public road from a fire – he had set to straw in his field, which spread to vegetation at the side of the road and smoke obscured visibility, causing a collision – was found guilty of the common law crime of Culpable and Reckless Fire-Raising.

308 The Traffic Officer's Companion

PLACING ROPES ETC IN ROAD
SECTION 101 ROADS (SCOTLAND) ACT, 1984

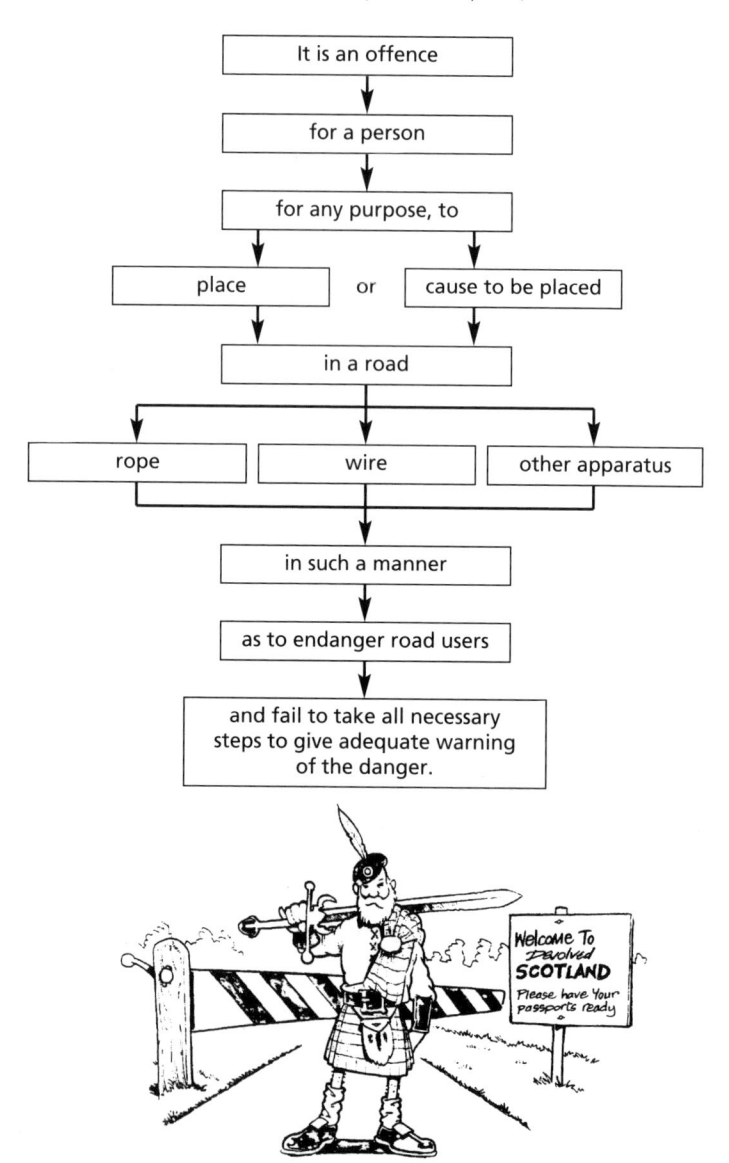

```
            It is an offence
                   ↓
              for a person
                   ↓
           for any purpose, to
              ↓         ↓
         place    or    cause to be placed
                   ↓
               in a road
          ↓        ↓        ↓
        rope     wire    other apparatus
                   ↓
            in such a manner
                   ↓
         as to endanger road users
                   ↓
   and fail to take all necessary
   steps to give adequate warning
            of the danger.
```

AIDING AND ABETTING – ROAD TRAFFIC OFFENCES IN SCOTLAND

In order to charge a person with aiding and abetting the commission of an offence, it is necessary to prove that he knew of the circumstances constituting the offence and helped in its commission.

Section 119 Road Traffic Regulation Act, 1984 contains provisions relating to aiding and abetting certain Traffic offences in Scotland and provides that 'a person who aids, abets, counsels, procures or incites any other person to commit an offence against the provisions of the Road Traffic Regulation Act, 1984 and any regulations made under that Act, shall be guilty of an offence and shall be liable, on conviction, to the same punishment as might be imposed on conviction of the first mentioned offence.

Care has to be taken when dealing with other Traffic offences outwith the scope of the Road Traffic Regulation Act, 1984. Where such offences employ the words **use**, **cause** or **permit**, then an accessory to the offence should be prosecuted for **causing and permitting** the offence rather than **aiding and abetting**. If, however, there is a clear case of a person having aided and abetted a Traffic offence not covered by the Road Traffic Regulation Act 1984, the offender should be charged with a contravention of Section 293 Criminal Procedure (Scotland) Act 1995 and shall be liable to the same penalties as the original offender.

TAKING MOTOR VEHICLES WITHOUT AUTHORITY (STATUTORY CLANDESTINE POSSESSION)
SECTION 178 ROAD TRAFFIC ACT, 1988

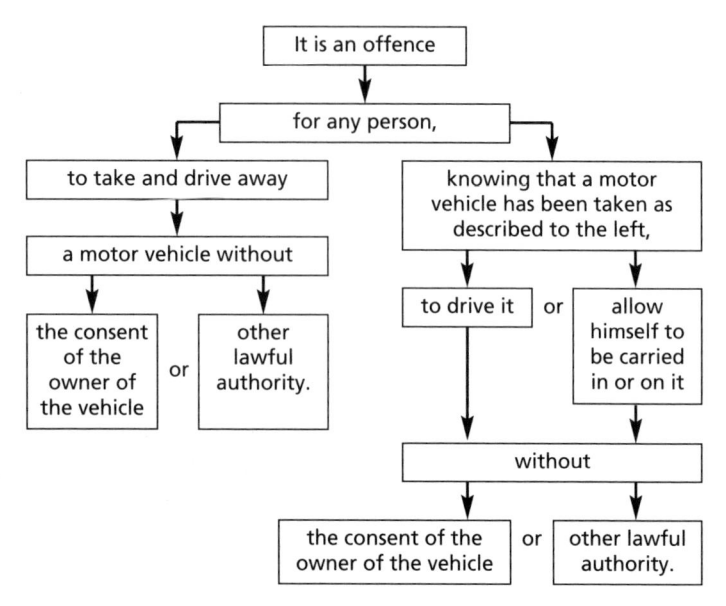

It is an offence for any person,

- to take and drive away a motor vehicle without
  - the consent of the owner of the vehicle, or
  - other lawful authority.
- knowing that a motor vehicle has been taken as described to the left,
  - to drive it, or
  - allow himself to be carried in or on it

without
- the consent of the owner of the vehicle, or
- other lawful authority.

A constable may arrest without warrant any person he reasonably suspects of having committed or having attempted to commit this offence.

An offence under Section 178 may only be committed in respect of motor vehicles (ie, mechanically propelled vehicles intended or adapted for use on the roads). A person who takes and drives away a mechanically propelled vehicle (not intended or adopted for use on the roads) without the consent of owner, etc would commit theft or clandestine possession.

Note 1: An accused who proves he acted in the reasonable belief that he had lawful authority or that the owner of the motor vehicle would, in the circumstances, have given consent if he had been asked for it, shall not be convicted.

Note 2: Section 178 is generally intended to deal with cases where motor vehicles are taken, driven away and then abandoned. If, however, the vehicle were abandoned in a place where it is unlikely to be found, the offender may be held to have committed theft, rather than a contravention of Section 178.

Note 3: Where the police trace the vehicle, while still in the possession of the person(s) who took and drove it away without authority, it is normal to charge the offender(s) with theft, rather than a contravention of Section 178. However, the final decision as to the charge rests with the Procurator Fiscal.

CARELESS DRIVING – CASE LAW re USE OF TELEPHONES IN VEHICLES

As a result of telephones being fitted to vehicles, a body of Scots Case Law has grown up relating to the use of telephones in moving vehicles and the offence of careless driving under Section 3 of the Road Traffic Act, 1988.

There are three main cases to consider:

1. *McPhail v Haddow 1990 S.C.C.R 339*

   In this case, the accused was charged with careless driving for using a portable telephone while driving. The court held that, in the absence of any lack of control over the vehicle or any danger to others, there was no evidence of careless driving.

2. *Rae v Friel 1992 S.C.C.R 688*

   In this case the accused was charged with careless driving for travelling in excess of 70 mph on a motorway while holding a telephone in one hand and overtaking five other vehicles in two overtaking manoeuvres. He had only one hand on the steering wheel during these manoeuvres.

   The court held the important feature was that the accused overtook five vehicles, and that if any of them had happened suddenly to move out into the overtaking lane an emergency would have been created to which the accused would not have been able to react appropriately – as a result the accused was convicted of careless driving.

3. *Stock v Carmichael 1993 S.C.C.R 136*

   In this case, there was no overtaking manoeuvre, but evidence was led that the driver was not aware of a police vehicle alongside him and that the use of the telephone, except in an emergency, was a breach of the Highway Code.

   The court held the driver was guilty of careless driving in this case but stressed that each case depends on its own facts and circumstances.

POWER OF ARREST IN SCOTLAND FOR DANGEROUS OR CARELESS DRIVING OR CYCLING

S 167 ROAD TRAFFIC ACT, 1988

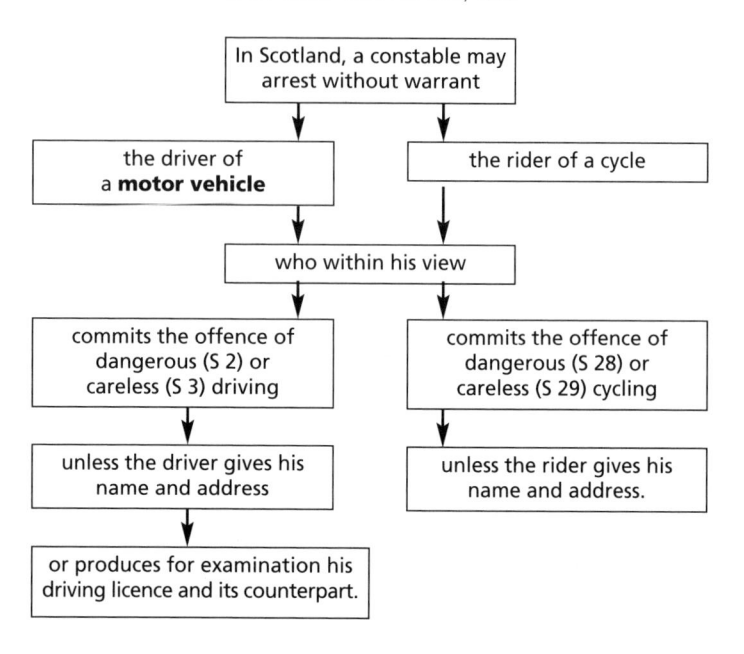

```
                In Scotland, a constable may
                   arrest without warrant
                   ↓                  ↓
      the driver of              the rider of a cycle
      a motor vehicle
              ↓                          ↓
              who within his view
              ↓                          ↓
    commits the offence of      commits the offence of
    dangerous (S 2) or          dangerous (S 28) or
    careless (S 3) driving      careless (S 29) cycling
              ↓                          ↓
    unless the driver gives his  unless the rider gives his
    name and address             name and address.
              ↓
    or produces for examination his
    driving licence and its counterpart.
```

NOTE

Although Section 2 and 3 offences may be committed in any mechanically propelled vehicle, the powers provided under Section 167 in respect of Sections 2 and 3 can only be used against the driver of a **motor vehicle** (ie a mechanically propelled vehicle intended or adapted for use on the roads).

Refusal to provide name and address etc

Section 169 Road Traffic Act 1988 provides that if the driver of a mechanically propelled vehicle, who is alleged to have committed an offence under Section 2 or 3 RTA 1988, or the rider of a cycle who is alleged to have committed an offence under Section 28 or 29 RTA 1988, refuses – on being required by **any person** having reasonable grounds for so requiring – to give his name or address, or gives a false name or address is guilty of an offence.

NOTE: Section 169 applies throughout Great Britain

PEDAL CYCLES

1. Dangerous cycling
S28 ROAD TRAFFIC ACT 1988

It is an offence for a person to ride a cycle dangerously on a road.

A person is to be regarded as riding a cycle dangerously if (and only if):
a) the way he rides falls far below what would be expected of a competent and careful cyclist; and
b) it would be obvious to a competent and careful cyclist that riding in that way would be dangerous.

The term 'dangerous' refers to danger either of injury to any person or of serious damage to property.

2. Careless and inconsiderate cycling
SECTION 29 ROAD TRAFFIC ACT 1988

It is an offence for a person to ride a cycle on a road without due care and attention, or without reasonable consideration for other persons using the road.

314 The Traffic Officer's Companion

PEDAL CYCLES cont

3. Cycling when under the influence of drink or drugs
Section 30 Road Traffic Act, 1988

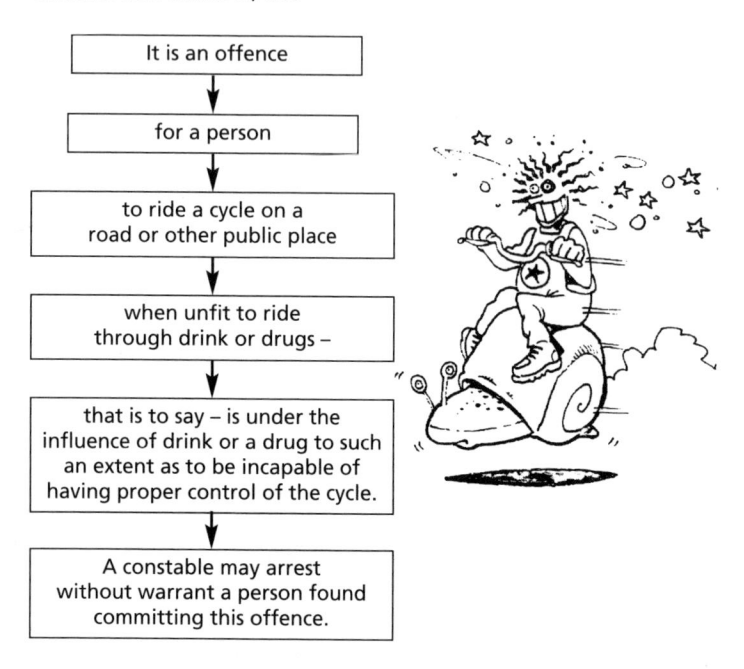

```
It is an offence
       ↓
   for a person
       ↓
to ride a cycle on a
road or other public place
       ↓
when unfit to ride
through drink or drugs –
       ↓
that is to say – is under the
influence of drink or a drug to such
an extent as to be incapable of
having proper control of the cycle.
       ↓
A constable may arrest
without warrant a person found
committing this offence.
```

NOTE

Under the provisions of Section 294 Criminal Procedure (Scotland) Act, 1995 any person who **attempts** to ride a cycle on a road or other public place when unfit to ride through drink or drugs also commits an offence under Section 30 of the Road Traffic Act, 1988.

The police have no power to require a cyclist suspected of contravening Section 30 to provide specimens of breath, blood or urine. However, the cyclist may be requested to provide such specimens and/or undergo a medical examination and tests provided he is informed that he is entitled to refuse and, that if he agrees, the results may be used in evidence.

CONVERSION TABLES

LENGTH

1 Millimetre	= 0.03937 Inch	1 Inch	= 25.4 Millimetres
1 Centimetre	= 0.3937 Inch	1 Inch	= 2.54 Centimetres
1 Metre	= 39.37 Inches	1 Foot	= 0.3048 Metre
1 Metre	= 3.2808 Feet	1 Yard	= 0.9144 Metre
1 Metre	= 1.0936 Yards	1 Mile	= 1.609 Kilometres

WEIGHT

1 Gramme	= 15.432 Grains	1 Ounce	= 28.35 Grammes
1 Gramme	= 0.03527 Ounce	1 Pound	= 453.6 Grammes
1 Kilogramme	= 2.2046 Pounds	1 Ton	= 1.016 Tonnes
1 Tonne	= 0.9842 Ton		

LIQUID MEASURE

½ Litre	= 0.880 Pints	1 Pint	= 20 Fluid Ounces
1 Litre	= 1.760 Pints	1 Pint	= 0.568 Litres
1 Litre	= 0.220 Gallons	1 Quart	= 1.136 Litres
10 Litres	= 2 Galls 1½ Pts (approx)	1 Gallon	= 4.546 Litres

SQUARE MEASURE

1 Sq. Millimetre	= 0.00155 Sq.in.	1 Sq. Kilometre	= 0.3861 Sq. Miles
1 Sq. Centimetre	= 0.155 Sq.inch	1 Sq. Inch	= 6.452 Sq. Cms
1 Sq. Metre	= 10.764 Sq.Feet	1 Sq. Foot	= 0.0929 Sq.Metres
1 Sq. Metre	= 1.196 Sq.Yards	1 Sq. Yard	= 0.836 Sq. Metres
1 Are	= 0.0247 Acres	1 Acre	= 0.4047 Hectare
1 Hectare	= 2.471 Acres	1 Sq.Mile	= 2.5899 Sq. Kms
1 Acre	= 4840 Sq. Yards	1 Sq. Mile	= 640 Acres

VELOCITY

1 M.P.H.	= 0.44704 Metre/Sec.	1 Km./Hr.	= 0.911 Ft./Sec.
1 M.P.H.	= 1.60934 Km./Hr.	1 Km./Hr.	= 0.6214 M.P.H.

INCHES		MILLIMETRES	FEET		METRES
0.039	1	25.4	3.281	1	0.305
0.079	2	50.8	6.562	2	0.610
0.118	3	76.2	9.843	3	0.914
0.157	4	101.6	13.123	4	1.219
0.197	5	127.0	16.404	5	1.524
0.236	6	152.4	19.685	6	1.829
0.276	7	177.8	22.966	7	2.134
0.315	8	203.2	26.247	8	2.438
0.354	9	228.6	29.528	9	2.743
0.394	10	254.0	32.81	10	3.048

YARDS		METRES	SQ. FT.		SQ. METRES
1.094	1	0.914	10.764	1	0.093
2.187	2	1.829	21.528	2	0.186
3.281	3	2.743	32.292	3	0.279
4.375	4	3.658	43.056	4	0.372
5.468	5	4.572	58.819	5	0.456
6.562	6	5.486	64.583	6	0.557
7.655	7	6.401	75.347	7	0.650
8.749	8	7.315	86.111	8	0.743
9.842	9	8.223	96.875	9	0.836
10.936	10	9.114	107.640	10	0.929

OUNCES		GRAMMES	POUNDS		KILOGRAMMES
0.035	1	28.350	2.205	1	0.454
0.071	2	56.699	4.409	2	0.9072
0.106	3	85.049	6.614	3	1.361
0.141	4	113.398	8.819	4	1.814
0.176	5	141.748	11.023	5	2.268
0.212	6	170.097	13.228	6	2.722
0.247	7	198.447	15.432	7	3.175
0.282	8	226.796	17.637	8	3.629
0.317	9	255.146	19.842	9	4.082
0.353	10	283.500	22.046	10	4.536

PINTS		LITRES	GALLONS		LITRES
1.761	1	0.568	0.22	1	4.55
3.521	2	1.136	0.44	2	9.09
5.282	3	1.704	0.66	3	13.64
7.043	4	2.272	0.88	4	18.18
8.804	5	2.840	1.10	5	22.73
10.564	6	3.408	1.32	6	27.28
12.325	7	3.976	1.54	7	31.82
14.086	8	4.544	1.76	8	36.37
15.847	9	5.112	1.98	9	40.91
17.600	10	5.680	2.20	10	45.46

MILES		KILOMETRES	MILES		KILOMETRES
0.31	1/2	0.8	3.42	5 1/2	8.8
0.62	1	1.6	3.73	6	9.7
0.93	1 1/2	2.4	4.04	6 1/2	10.5
1.24	2	3.2	4.35	7	11.3
1.55	2 1/2	4.0	4.66	7 1/2	12.0
1.86	3	4.8	4.97	8	12.9
2.17	3 1/2	5.6	5.28	8 1/2	13.7
2.49	4	6.4	5.59	9	14.5
2.80	4 1/2	7.2	5.90	9 1/2	15.3
3.11	5	8.0	6.21	10	16.1

INDEX

A

Abnormal loads 77 - 80
  Weight 77 - 80
ADR certificate 157
Age, driving for 110, 114
Aggravated vehicle
  taking 239
Agricultural vehicle
  Projections 74
  Wide 73
Anchorage points 54, 55
Animals
  conveyance of 269 - 276
  Loading 272
  Transit 270 - 276
  Transport conditions 273, 276
  Transporter construction 274 -276
Accident
  duty to report 277
Alarms, vehicle 52
Arrest
  general conditions 282
  mode of 283
  powers of 279-283
Arrestable offence
  Definition 280
ATA carnet 157
Articulated vehicle
  Definition 4
  Length 6
  Matching 24
  Weight 23, 24
Axle weights 27-28, 32

B

Beacons, warning 191
Blood specimens 244, 245
Breath specimens 244, 245
Breath tests 242-245
Builders' skips 289
Bus
  Definition 5, 15
  maximum height 15
  maximum weight 18

C

Caravan, passenger 40
Careless
  Cycling 297, 312
  Driving 297, 311
Carriage by road
  Definition 216,251
Categories of
  vehicles 101, 102
Causing death 297
Chemicals
  Conveyance of 251-259
CMR consignment note 157
Closely spaced axle
  Definition 28
Control of vehicle 92
Conversion tables 315, 316
Crash helmets 291

D

Danger to road users 42
Dangerous
  Cycling 297, 312
  Driving 297,312
Dangerous substances
  Conveyance 251- 259
  Hazchem 267
  Hazchem code 267
  hazard warning panels/labels 257-265
  hazard warning signs (diamonds) 260
  Radioactive substances 261-266
  Tremcard 268
Dangerous vehicles 42
Date of birth
  requirement to give 116
Definitions 2-5
Direction indicators 182, 183
Disabled driver
  Parking 298
  speed limits 247
Documentation
  driving licences 100-118
  HGV 112
  producing 116
Doors, opening 93
Drink/driving 241, 244
  breath tests 242, 243
  Causing death 297
  penalties 297
  specimens 244, 245
Driver
  Control 93
  definition 216
  newly qualified 113
Drivers' hours and records
  community rules 212,213
  definitions 216
  domestic rules 214, 215
  general 204
  hours of work 212-215
  police powers 230
  records 217-219
  selector 205, 207
  tachograph 220, 229
Driving
  carelessly 297
  dangerously 297
Driving instruction 295
Driving licences
  foreigners 117,118
  full 103
  groups 105
  HGV classes 112
  HGV types 112
  instructor 295
  LGV/PCV exemptions 104
  LGV licences 112
  minimum ages 114
  motor cycles 110
  newly qualified 113
  ordinary, classes 114
  PCV licences 97
  production 116, 126
  provisional 109, 111
  renewal 115
  signature 115
  trainee 112
Driving under age 115
Dual purpose vehicle
  definition 4
Duty to give information
  as to driver 278

E

Emergency removal of
  vehicle 298
End-outline marker
  lamps 194
Engine stopping 91
Engineering plant 82, 83
Eyesight
  power to test 294
  requirements 294
Excavators 75, 76
Excessive noise
  avoidance 43, 92
Excise duty
  classes 128, 129
Excise licence 127
  classes 128, 129
  exhibition 131
Exhaust system 43
Experimental
  vehicles 72, 85

F

Flashing lights,
  use 182, 183
Fog lamps front 188
  rear 186, 187
Foreign vehicles
  documentation 157,158
  driving licence 117, 118
  excise forms 158
  registration document 158
Forgery etc
  of records 227

G

General arrest
  conditions 282
Glass 66
Goods vehicle
  definition 3, 216
  international
    operation 157, 158
  maximum height 33
  operators' licences 123-126
  plating 138-143
  tests 138-143
Grass cutting
  machines 70
Ground clearance 12

H

Hackney carriages 155
  roof signs 155
Hazard lights 190
Hazard warning
  labels 257-260
  panels 257-260
  Signs (diamonds) 260
Hazchem 267
Hazchem code 267
Headlamps 172-173
  definition 160
Heavy locomotive
  definition 3
Heavy motor car definition 3
Hedge trimmers 70
Height
  maximum 15, 35
  Travelling 33, 40
HGV
  documentation list 96
Horn 52
Hours of darkness
  definition 160
Hours of work 212-215
  definitions 216
  general 204
  selector 205-207
  records 217-219

I

Indicators, direction 182-183
Insecure load 42
Instruction, driving 295
Insurance 122
  European Community
    vehicles 157
  foreign vehicles 157
  International freight
    permit 157
Invalid carriage
  definition 5
  registration mark 132
  speed limits 246-249

L

Lamps, see Lights
Large Goods Vehicles
  definition 5
  licence 104, 112
Length, calculation 9
Light locomotive
  definition 3
Lights
  bicycle 161
  cleanliness 160
  colour 171
  daytime 167
  direction indicators
        182, 183
  end-outline marker 194
  exceptions 166, 167
  flashing 182, 183
  fog, front 188
  fog, rear 186, 187
  front 174, 175
  hazard 190
  headlamps 172, 173
  maintenance 160
  motor cycle 161
  movement 170
  obligatory 160-165
  obligatory
    exemptions 166, 167
  obligatory, use 168, 169
  obstruction of 169
  offences 160
  position 160, 164
  projecting loads 199
  rear 176, 177
  reflectors 178-181
  registration plate 190
  reversing 189
  side marker 192, 193
  stop 184, 185
  using 168, 169
  warning beacons 191
Living van 40
Load
  abnormal 77-80
  insecure 42
  projecting, lights 199

M

Manufacturer's
  plate 16, 141
Marker lamps
  end-outline 194
  side 192, 193
Markers
  projection 200
  reflective, rear 195-198
  side 192, 193
Mascots 91
Medium-sized goods
  vehicle, definition 4
Military vehicles 69
Minibuses, PSV, as 149
Ministry plate 16, 141

Mirrors
  fitting 65
  requirement 64
  use 65
Moped
  definition 5
  plates 144
Motor car, definition 2
Motorcycle
  crash helmets 291
  definition 5
  driving licence 101, 110
  footrests 92
  lamps 161
  noise 92
  plates 144
  registration mark 137
  sidestands 91
  silencer 43
  trailer 38
  training certificate 112
Motor tractor
  definition 3
Motor vehicle
  categories 101, 102
  definition 2
  ground clearance 12
  length 7
Motorways 293
  speed limits 247-249

N

Noise
  excessive 43, 92
Notice of intended
  prosecution 290
Notional gross weight 29

O

Obligatory lights 160-165
  exemptions 166, 167
Obstruction 92
Offences 160
Opening doors 93
Operator's licence 123-126
  exemptions 124, 125
  types 123
Overhang 10

P

Parking
  darkness in 92
  disabled person 298
  emergency removal 298
  lights 161
  obstruction 151
  removal of vehicle 298
Passenger carrying vehicle
  definition 5
  licence 114
Passenger, danger
  - causing 42
Pedal cycles, lamps 161

Index

Pedal cycles
  (Scotland) 313, 314
Pedestrian-controlled
  vehicles 71
Pedestrian crossings 296
Penalties 297
Physical health 294
Plates
  exemptions 143
  goods vehicles 141
  hackney carriages 155
  mopeds 144
  motor cycles 144
  trade 145
  trailer 140
Plating
  goods vehicles 140 - 143
Position lamp
  definition 160
Position lamp, rear 160
Powers of arrest (Scotland)
  careless driving 312
  careless cycling 312, 313
  dangerous cycling 312, 313
  dangerous driving 312
Powers of arrest 279-283
Production of
  documents 277
Projecting load
  lights 199
Projection markers 200
Provisional driving
  licence 109, 111
Public service vehicle
  certificate of fitness 154
  definitions 148
  documentation 150
  local services 149
  minibuses 151 - 154
  operator's disc 150
  test certificate 150

R

Radio - suppression 91
Radioactive
  substances 261-266
Rearguards 89
Records of work 217-219
  books 218-219
  forgery etc 227
  general 204
  selector 205-209
  tachographs 220-229
Reflective markers
  rear 195-198
Reflectors
  front 180
  rear 178, 179,
    195 - 198, 201
  side 181
  trailer 201
Registration marks
  plate light 132

rear plate lamp 190
  requirement 133
  size 132, 135
  trailers 132
Regular passenger
  service definition 216
Removal of vehicles 237, 298
Rest period,
  definition 212-216
Restricted speed
  vehicle 250
Reversing 93
Reversing alarm 52
Reversing lights 189
Road checks 234,
    235, 284
Road friendly
suspension definition 26, 32
Road (Scotland)
  definition 301
  obstruction 304
  restriction on placing
    bridges etc 305
  deposit of mud on 306
  damage to 307
  placing ropes etc 308
Road traffic offences (Scotland)
  aiding and abetting 309
  careless driving (use of
    telephone in vehicles) 311
  taking away motor
    vehicles 310

S

Seat belts
  adults, rear 60
  application 54 - 58
  children 61, 62
  definitions 54, 63
  exemptions 54
  fitting 56, 57
  use 58
Sidecars - fitting 41
Side marker lamps 192, 193
Sideguards 88
Silencers 43
Skips (Scotland)
  control of builders 302
  removal of 303
Small vehicle definition 5
Smoke, excess 67
Special types vehicles
  A-M 68-83
  abnormal loads 77-80
  agricultural 73, 74
  engineering plant 82, 83
  excavators 75, 76
  experimental 72, 85
  general conditions 87
  grass cutting 70
  military, etc 69
  natural gas 84
  propulsion 84

over 4.3 m wide 81
pedestrian controlled road
  maintenance vehicles 71
  straddle carriers 72
  track laying 71
Specified passenger
  seat, definition 54
Specimens
  drink/driving 244, 245
  procedure 245
  venue 244
Speed limiters 250
  plates 250
Speed limits 246-249
  general 246
  road 247-249
  special types 247-249
  vehicles 247-249
Speedometer 53
Spray suppression 90
Stop and search 285
Stop lamps 184, 185
Stopping engine 91
Stopping distances 294
Straddle carriers 72
Suspension road friendly
  definition 26, 32

T

Tachographs 220-229
  chart analysis 221
  defences 228
  description 220
  fitting 222, 223
  irregularities 229
  offences 224-227
  practical points 230, 231
  use of 222, 223
Taking without
  authority 239, 310
Taxis 148
  roof signs 155
  touts 288
Television sets 93
Test
  goods vehicles 140, 143
Testing
  premises on 236
  roads, on 234, 235
'T' forms 157
TIR carnet 157
Towing, see Trailers
Track laying vehicles 71
Trade plates 145, 146
Trailer plates
  triangular 201
Trailers
  description 36, 37
  length 7-8
  living van 6
  motor cycle towing 38
  number, maximum 36
  PSV towing 40

reflectors 195
secondary coupling
vehicle as 41
Travelling height 33
Tremcard 268
Trial vehicles 72, 85
Triangular trailer
plates 201
Turning circles 11
Tyres 46 - 51

U

Unattended vehicle 93
Unlicensed vehicle 130
Urine specimens 244, 245

V

Vehicle
aggravated vehicle
taking 239
alarm 52
categories 208-211
combinations, length 6
definitions 2-5
interference 240
removal of 237
taking without
authority 239
Vision 66

W

Warning beacons 191
Warning instrument 34, 35, 52
Week, definition 216
Weighing, police
powers 17
Weight
additional authorised
weights 30
articulated vehicles 23 - 24
axle 16, 23, 24, 29
bus 15
combined transport
operations 26
locomotive 18
maximum 16-25
maximum laden 16-25
notional gross 29
offences 16
plates 16
power to weigh 17
procedure 17
rigid vehicles 20-22
Trailers 25
Vehicles 30
Vehicle combinations 31
Wide vehicles
over 4.3 m 81
Width
calculations 14
maximum 13
Windscreen

wipers 66
washers 66